D0387029

McElvaine, Robert
S., 1947-
Franklin Delano
Roosevelt

Franklin Delano Roosevelt

Franklin Delano Roosevelt

ROBERT S. McELVAINE
Millsaps College

A Division of Congressional Quarterly Inc.
Washington, D.C.

CQ Press
1255 22nd Street, N.W., Suite 400
Washington, D.C. 20037

202-729-1900; toll-free, 1-866-4CQ-PRESS (1-866-427-7737)

www.cqpress.com

⊚ The paper used in this publication meets the minimum requirements of the American National Standard for Information Sciences—Permanence of Paper for Printed Library Materials, ANSI Z39.48-1992.

Cover illustration by Talia Greenberg
Design by Karen Doody
Composition by Jessica Forman
Editorial development by the Moschovitis Group, Inc.,
    New York, N.Y.

Printed and bound in the United States of America

06 05 04 03 02   5 4 3 2 1

Library of Congress Cataloging-in-Publication Data
McElvaine, Robert S.
    Franklin Delano Roosevelt / Robert S. McElvaine.
        p. cm. — (American presidents reference series)
Includes bibliographical references and index.
    ISBN 1-56802-702-8 (alk. paper)
    1. Roosevelt, Franklin D. (Franklin Delano), 1882-1945. 2. Presidents—United States—Biography. 3. United States—Politics and government—1933-1945. 4. United States—Politics and government—1933-1945—Sources. I. Title. II. Series.
    E807 .M37 2002
    973.917'092—dc21
                                        2002012015

For Edward T. "Ned" Chase
Editor, friend, and Roosevelt man

Contents

Preface

Franklin Delano Roosevelt created the modern American presidency. His successors have been measured, to one degree or another, against his accomplishments and his failings. One need not be a believer in the "great man" concept of history to acknowledge that the United States and the world would have taken a very different course since 1933 had Roosevelt not become president.

FDR was one of the greatest communicators ever to inhabit the White House. His words (and those of his speechwriters) share the pages that follow with mine and with those of many other well-known—and a few virtually unknown—people of the 1930s and 1940s. The combination of original documents and historical analysis will help readers understand the man and his times in a way that a biography alone or a collection of the president's writings and other documents could not do. The documents also allow readers to come to their own conclusions on Roosevelt and his presidency.

The book is arranged in six chapters. The first offers a brief biographical sketch of FDR, concentrating on his life before he became president. The second chapter reports on and analyzes Roosevelt's election campaigns, from his first run for the New York state senate in 1910 to the last of his four presidential races in 1944. Chapter 3 recounts Roosevelt's approaches to domestic policy, the economy, the environment, trade, and foreign policy. The fourth chapter goes into greater depth on the two major crises of the Roosevelt years—the Great Depression and World War II—as well as the somewhat lesser crises and flashpoints that accompanied them. Chapter 5 assesses FDR's relationships with major American institutions, including Congress, the Supreme Court, the military, the media, business, and labor. The sixth chapter assesses Roosevelt's place in history, explaining in detail why he is often ranked as one of the greatest presidents. Two appendixes follow; one presents brief biographical sketches of most of the key figures of the Roosevelt era, the other a timeline of Roosevelt's life.

This project could not have been completed without the outstanding work of my assistant, Janet Bergman Groue. Among her many duties, Janet researched all the material for the brief biographies in the appendix and tracked down numerous primary source documents. Louise Hetrick, my assistant at Millsaps College, provided her usual excellent work in preparing the manuscript and performing other tasks.

I have benefited greatly from conversations over the years with many scholars who have written about Roosevelt and his times, including Anthony Badger, James MacGregor Burns, Frank Freidel, William E. Leuchtenburg, Lawrence W. Levine, Patrick J. Maney, and Arthur M. Schlesinger Jr.

Ned Chase, my longtime editor and friend, to whom this book is dedicated, has frequently discussed Roosevelt with me and provided important insights into the man and his era. My editors for this volume, Valerie A. Tomaselli and Catherine Carter at the Moschovitis Group and Molly Lohman and Christopher Anzalone at CQ Press, have been very helpful in bringing it to completion.

My greatest debt, as always, is to my family. My parents, Edward and Ruth McElvaine, were not supporters of Franklin Roosevelt, but I heard a great deal about him from them as I was growing up. Anne—my wife and my love—lights up my life and inspires my work, as do Kerri, Lauren, Allison, Brett, Scott, and Evan.

Robert S. McElvaine
Millsaps College

FDR and his son James wave to the crowd, December 31, 1934.

Introduction
The Most Important
President of the Twentieth Century

Nearly every professional historian regards Franklin Delano Roosevelt (FDR) as the most important president of the twentieth century. Most historians also see him as the greatest president of that time—and one of the greatest of all time—ranking him alongside Abraham Lincoln and sometimes George Washington.[1] This status was confirmed symbolically with the opening of the Franklin Delano Roosevelt Memorial in Washington, D.C., in 1997, making Roosevelt the only twentieth-century president so honored on the National Mall and only the fourth president in history memorialized in this manner. (And a strong case could be made that two of the others, Washington and Thomas Jefferson, were memorialized more for what they had done earlier in their careers than for their accomplishments as president.)

Franklin Roosevelt was elected to the presidency four times, twice as many as anyone else in American history, and he served as president for just more than twelve years, longer than anyone else. These facts suggest his importance, but longevity in office is no guarantee of greatness.

A TIME FOR GREATNESS

Roosevelt's presidency coincided with the two largest national crises of the twentieth century (and probably the second and third largest crises—

after the Civil War—in U.S history): the Great Depression and World War II. It is difficult to demonstrate greatness if the opportunity does not arise. Theodore Roosevelt, president from 1901 to 1909 and FDR's fifth cousin, lamented that he had not had the good fortune to have a war while he was in office. Without such a stage on which to perform, he remarked, it is almost impossible to be judged a great man. "If there is not a war, you don't get the great general," he said in a 1910 speech in England. "If there is not the great occasion, you don't get the great statesman; if Lincoln had lived in times of peace, no one would have known his name now" (Cooper 1983, 118). A Republican senator, Frank Brandegee of Connecticut, made a similar point just before his party's 1920 convention, where Warren G. Harding would win the presidential nomination. Brandegee said that there were no first-rate candidates in the race for president, but that did not matter because "the times don't require them" (Leuchtenburg 1958, 86). Perhaps he was right, but the times that began a decade later and continued to the end of World War II required a first-rate president—and provided opportunities for that president to prove he was first-rate.

To be presented with crises is not to conquer them, however. William McKinley, president from 1897 to 1901, presided over the end of the Panic of 1893 (the nation's most severe economic collapse until the Great Depression) and over a victorious war with Spain. Also, he was assassinated, which increased the prestige of such presidents as Lincoln and John F. Kennedy. Yet McKinley is never listed among the great presidents.

FDR, like his kinsman Theodore Roosevelt, saw the basic role of the president as providing leadership that could persuade citizens to look beyond narrow self-interest. In this best sense of politics—working in the interest of the *polis*, the community—Franklin D. Roosevelt was a great politician. To most Americans, the word *politician* carries many negative connotations, as it did before FDR's presidency. Although FDR did not fully rehabilitate the term in the minds of most Americans, he did for a time convince most of them that politics could be a noble endeavor that could improve lives. And he did this within a democratic framework. It is true that Roosevelt considerably enhanced the powers of the federal government in general and the executive branch in particular, but, contrary to the claims of some of his most bitter political opponents, he never moved away from democratic principles. The barrage of legislation that made up the Roosevelt program known as the New Deal was indeed democratic: legislation passed by Congress according to prescribed constitutional procedures.

Similarly, Franklin Roosevelt's New Deal programs introduced some reforms into the capitalist system by bringing the free market further under federal regulation. Yet there was no attempt to alter the basic profit motivation or to turn privately run businesses into government-controlled ones. In short, FDR modified American democracy a bit and American capitalism slightly more, but maintained the essence of both.

His admirers credit him with a major role in preserving democracy and capitalism at a time when both were under threat and people around the world had concluded that neither system was workable. When Roosevelt took office, dictatorship—indeed, totalitarianism—was being accepted in several nations as a more efficient mode of government than democracy. Such was the case in Germany, Italy, and the Soviet Union, and the efficacy of capitalism and democracy was in serious question in many other countries. With the hardships of the Great Depression, which had begun in 1929 and continued to worsen in the period before Roosevelt's assumption of the presidency, growing numbers of critics in many nations, including the United States, were arguing that capitalism could not provide for people's basic needs and that democracy was not effective in bringing capitalism under control. Both fascism and communism were gaining popularity as alternatives to capitalism.

Fascism, a concept introduced by Benito Mussolini in Italy in 1919 and later modified by Adolf Hitler in Germany, called for the total regimentation of economic and social life for the purported good of the nation. It demanded unquestioning loyalty to a supreme leader who was not subject to democratic approval or checks on his power. In theory, communism, a dictatorial variant of socialism, turns the ownership of all productive property over to the community, shares work equally, and divides goods among people according to their need. In practice, the supposed workers' paradise of communism in Josef Stalin's Soviet Union was difficult to distinguish from the harsh circumstances of fascist regimes. But both systems held out hope for something better in the midst of the apparent collapse of capitalism and the seemingly ineffective responses of democracy. Mussolini, leader of Italy from 1922 to 1943, and Stalin, leader of the Soviet Union from 1922 to 1953, were solidly entrenched in power when Roosevelt took office, and Hitler had taken charge in Germany only weeks before Roosevelt's inauguration in 1933.[2] As a smiling Roosevelt told the American people that the only thing they had to fear was "fear itself," a scowling Hitler reinforced and exploited all the fears of the German people.

In an important sense, the two great crises of FDR's dozen years in office were actually one immense worldwide crisis that began in international economic collapse and spread into world war. To paraphrase Lincoln at Gettysburg—in the midst of another crisis that tested the nation's mettle—during the 1930s and early 1940s the people of the western world were engaged in a great struggle that tested whether any nation conceived in liberty and dedicated to the propositions that people should govern themselves and that an economy should operate as a free market (albeit with checks and balances) could long endure.

The adhesive that holds together the crises of the Roosevelt years is the Great Depression. It was this event that most emphatically brought the viability of capitalism and democracy into question. Socialists (socialists call for public ownership of the means of production, but are usually distinguished from communists by their adherence to democratic political practices) and fascists had attacked these systems long before 1929, but before the depression neither system seemed in any danger of displacement in the United States. Had there been no depression, there might have been no Franklin Roosevelt presidency. It was the economic collapse that discredited the Republican Party and it was in the depression that Roosevelt's talents and attributes, such as his contagious optimism and flair for experimentation, most appealed to the American electorate. The depression catalyzed Hitler's rise to power and later World War II. It provided Hitler a rationale that persuaded enough Germans to go along with his extremist programs of anti-Semitism, dictatorship, nationalism, and militarism.

On the homefront in the United States, the growth of federal power during World War II, the increased regulation of the economy, the growing role of organized labor, and the redistribution of income through steeply progressive taxation and full employment all mark continuities between the New Deal years and the war years. Many of the objectives of the New Deal that had remained beyond reach during the 1930s, such as full employment, were attained during the war. Although in some ways the nation's problems changed enormously from the 1930s to the 1940s, the underlying issue of whether political and economic freedom would survive remained the same. The prescribed treatment changed as the symptoms shifted from the economic to the military organs of the body politic. But Roosevelt continued the same basic fight. After all, Dr. New Deal and Dr. Win-the-War (language FDR used to describe himself) were the same man, and he was dealing with an extension of the same crisis.

The Right Man in the Right Place

Those who would call Roosevelt the savior of capitalism and democracy surely go too far, but there is no denying that FDR played a critical role in meeting the formidable challenges to economic and political freedom that arose out of the depression and peaked during World War II. His brand of leadership, his ability to provide reassurance through broadcast addresses and radio "fireside chats," his willingness to try new ideas and to renovate economic and political structures to preserve them—all of these qualities made him the right person to be president in the crucial dozen years that he occupied the White House. Outwardly, at least, a cheerful and perpetual optimist who never doubted America's destiny or his own, Roosevelt was capable of telling his fellow citizens—at a moment when at least a quarter of the workforce was unemployed and the nation's banks had closed their doors—that the only thing they had to fear was "fear itself." More remarkable, most Americans believed him. Inwardly, who could tell? He kept his pains, problems, and doubts (if indeed he had any of the latter) to himself. This was appropriate for a time when most people had more than enough of their own troubles.

Another major factor in Roosevelt's fitness for the circumstances of his presidency was his physical disability. Roosevelt had been stricken with polio in 1921 and left without the use of his legs. This misfortune put him in a position to better relate to the different sort of suffering that so many Americans experienced during the depression. His apparent overcoming of his handicap (the degree of his lasting paralysis was hidden from the public) put him in a better position to convince depression victims that they could overcome their hardships.

Franklin Roosevelt was not a systematic thinker, but this, too, may have helped equip him for the times. The systematic thinking of classical economics (the idea of the self-regulating free market, including such dogmas as Say's Law, which held that supply creates its own demand and therefore an economy will always achieve balance without government intervention) that Republican administrations followed religiously in the 1920s seemed to have gotten the economy into the mess it was in; most people were ready for someone willing to experiment until he or she found policies that worked. FDR argued, perhaps even more effectively than his cousin Theodore had during his 1912 "New Nationalism" campaign, that government in a democracy could be the people's instrument, not their enemy.

FDR never accepted the new economics preached by John Maynard Keynes, which held that deficit spending by a government during a time of economic slowdown could stimulate the economy and restore prosperity, but Roosevelt did believe that the government had an obligation to help those in desperate need, even if this required borrowing money. FDR saw government as a means of providing some regulation to an otherwise chaotic economy that too often left workers unemployed. And, because it was clear to many people that the free market had not regulated itself and had helped cause the difficulties they were undergoing, he was able to convince Americans that the government could act in their behalf. The New Deal programs did not end the depression, but they eased some hardships. This was enough to lead a majority of Americans to accept Roosevelt's programs and follow his leadership.

For all these reasons and more, Franklin Roosevelt matched the requirements of his times more closely than all but a few leaders ever have. Those times were, by many measures, the worst of times. But for a leader seeking to unite a people in common goals, these years were also positive and productive. Americans were willing to place their almost congenital individualism in abeyance only when faced with a massive threat. In the Roosevelt years there were two such enormous dangers, the psychological effects of one building on the other.

World War II was "the Good War"—one in which Americans were more unified than in any other war in the nation's history and in which the evil of the enemy was so clearly defined. War always demands sacrifice. In World War II Franklin Roosevelt had the benefit of asking for sacrifice in the face of the manifest deception of Japan and the cruelty of the Nazis. He also found himself in a situation in which sacrifice was much easier to demand because so many Americans were accustomed to depression-induced hardship. Rationing of gasoline and a few other items aside, many Americans sacrificed far less materially in Roosevelt's wartime third term (1941–1945) than they did during his first two terms in peacetime (1933–1941). (Of course, a much greater sacrifice was required in physical terms from those who fought in the war.) So FDR never really had to endanger his standing with the public, as often happens when trying to win support for a war, by trying to persuade citizens to sacrifice beyond the degree to which they had become accustomed.

A FRIEND AT 1600 PENNSYLVANIA AVENUE

Franklin Roosevelt, again like Lincoln, was a polarizing figure—during his presidency and long after his death. Reactions to Roosevelt, both positive and negative, tended to be extreme and heartfelt. In the cases of both these presidents, there were Americans who saw them as anything but great—who saw them even as great evils. Some people in the South still refer to Lincoln as a bloodthirsty tyrant who engaged in a war of aggression against a people exercising their constitutional right of secession. Numerous businessmen and conservatives in the 1930s could not bring themselves to voice Roosevelt's name, referring to him instead as "that man." Many wealthy Americans, including those involved in big business, castigated Roosevelt as a traitor to his class. They despised him for introducing federal regulations that they believed placed unnecessary fetters on economic freedom.

This raises the important question of why he was so loved by so many, especially by those whose socioeconomic background was farthest removed from his privileged upbringing. Part of the reason was his remarkable ability to communicate with masses of people on a seemingly personal level. When Roosevelt's voice was broadcasted into a family's living room, many felt that he was speaking directly to them, that he understood their problems, and that he would find a way to help them. They had a friend at 1600 Pennsylvania Avenue. The bond that so many Americans felt with FDR was much more visceral than rational. Roosevelt received 15,000,000 letters from "ordinary" Americans, and the per capita rate of letter writing was almost four times higher than the next highest rates in American history—to Lincoln during the Civil War and to Woodrow Wilson during World War I.

But if so many people felt close to Roosevelt because of his ability to communicate with them, there was more to his popularity. People liked what he said, but a substantial majority apparently also liked what he did. The transformations in government, economy, and society that Roosevelt oversaw were real and meaningful. They included Social Security, unemployment insurance, minimum wage and maximum hours, regulation of the securities exchange and banks, the income tax hitting the middle class for the first time, a serious attempt at regional planning in the Tennessee Valley Authority, government assurance of a fair playing field for unions seeking to organize workers for collective bargaining, and the first federal patronage of the arts in the United States.

Roosevelt also created a Democratic political coalition by adding to the traditionally Democratic base of southern and urban voters, organized labor, progressives who had been Republicans earlier in the century, and African Americans, who were not singled out for any protections or programs but were included in the benefits of the New Deal to an extent unprecedented since the post–Civil War Reconstruction. This coalition would last for decades after his death. He also helped to cast the Democratic Party's net further by establishing close and lasting ties between the Democrats and the academic community; he turned first to his "brain trust" of advisers from Columbia University and later to other academics for guidance on social and economic policy.

He also improved (to a limited extent) the public's understanding of people with disabilities; his own serious disability, even though kept out of the limelight as much as possible, taught many people a lesson: that a person who once had polio could be president.

NEW DEAL SETS NATION ON A NEW CHART

The most important reason Abraham Lincoln and Franklin Roosevelt are considered two of the greatest presidents is that they each presided over fundamental changes in the basic structure of the nation. Lincoln lived to see the end of his war; Roosevelt died shortly before his came to a successful conclusion, but the outcome was secured before his death. Neither man lived to oversee the reconstruction each had envisioned—in Lincoln's case of the nation or union, in FDR's of the world.

During Lincoln's presidency, the country was transformed from a confederation of states into a nation, albeit one in which the federal government still did not exercise much authority over the states. The plural "these United States" became, at least in theory, the singular "the United

States." Under Roosevelt the move toward the supremacy of the central government that had taken a major step under Lincoln was carried farther. But the changes to the nation during Roosevelt's presidency were in many ways even more dramatic than those during Lincoln's.

The United States after Roosevelt's death was such a different place than it was when he won the presidency that a case might be made to divide American history into periods called BR and AR—Before Roosevelt and After Roosevelt. Before Roosevelt, the United States was potentially the greatest power in the world, but strongly isolationist. After Roosevelt, the United States was far and away the dominant power in the world and was committed to internationalism. Before Roosevelt, the federal government was something that delivered the mail and conscripted men during war. After Roosevelt, the federal government touched numerous aspects of people's everyday lives. Before Roosevelt, the business of America, as Calvin Coolidge had remarked, was business. After Roosevelt, the business of America was more influenced by government. Before Roosevelt, the poor, elderly, infirm, and unemployed were dependent on their own wits and private charity. After Roosevelt, the idea of societal responsibility toward the downtrodden was well established. Before Roosevelt, African Americans voted overwhelmingly for the Republicans, the party of Lincoln. After Roosevelt, African Americans voted overwhelmingly for the Democrats, the party of Roosevelt. Much of the political dialogue of the remainder of the twentieth century was set by the New Deal. Presidents since Roosevelt have all been measured against his standard.

Although Roosevelt could stand only with considerable difficulty and with the support of thick leg braces, he symbolically stood astride his times more completely than has almost any other American leader. Whether he could have so stood in different times or without his own suffering brought on by polio are more difficult questions, to which we shall never have firm answers. Nor is it clear to what extent the huge changes that took place in these years were Roosevelt's doing and to what extent they were the result of greater historical and economic forces, of Roosevelt's fabled luck, or of others in his administration, in Congress, in the academic community, and elsewhere. What is clear is that FDR played such a substantial part in this era that it is most appropriate to refer to the years from 1933 to 1945 as the Roosevelt Years.

NOTES

1. According to the C-SPAN Survey of Presidential Leadership in 2000, fifty-eight professional historians rated FDR the number one twentieth-century president and second overall to Abraham Lincoln. The survey was based on ten factors, including public persuasion, moral authority, relations with Congress, crisis leadership, and vision/setting agenda. For more on the survey see www.americanpresidents.org/survey. For more on Abraham Lincoln, see Matthew Pinsker, *Abraham Lincoln* (Washington, D.C.: CQ Press, 2002).

2. Roosevelt's time as a national leader coincided almost precisely with Hitler's. The Nazi dictator's death came less than a month after Roosevelt's. Occupying the world stage simultaneously, these two men dramatically embodied the contrast between positive democratic leadership and negative totalitarian control.

BIBLIOGRAPHY

Two works were cited in this chapter: John Milton Cooper Jr., *The Warrior and the Priest: Woodrow Wilson and Theodore Roosevelt* (Cambridge: Belknap Press of Harvard University Press, 1983); and William E. Leuchtenburg, *The Perils of Prosperity, 1914–32* (Chicago: University of Chicago Press, 1958).

FDR, Eleanor Roosevelt, and Eleanor's mother, Sara, pose with the Roosevelt children, Washington, D.C., June 12, 1919.

CHAPTER ONE

From Child of Privilege to Champion of World Democracy

Biographical Sketch

F ranklin Delano Roosevelt's background was similar in important respects to those of the first six presidents of the United States, but very different from those of later presidents.[1] The early presidents were men of privilege, either Virginia planters or Massachusetts Adamses. After the revolt of the "common man" resulted in Andrew Jackson's election in 1828, the route to the presidency changed dramatically. Thereafter, presidential aspirants were expected to be "self-made men," preferably of log cabin birth. Accused of having been born privileged, a candidate could expect a swift end to his campaign. The principal exceptions to this tradition were Theodore Roosevelt and his fifth cousin, Franklin.

Franklin D. Roosevelt was born on January 30, 1882, into the closest approximation of a landed aristocracy that remained in the United States after the Civil War. With an estate overlooking the Hudson River just south of the village of Hyde Park and eighty miles north of New York City, the Roosevelts were unquestionably of the highest social class, although by no means of the highest wealth. They were "Old Money" in an age when fortunes that dwarfed theirs were being accumulated by the *nouveau riche* in such fields as industry and transportation. The Roosevelts measured their wealth in hundreds of thousands of dollars, whereas some of the newly rich counted theirs in tens of millions. But what did it matter? The Roosevelt family's high social status was firmly established and its wealth more than sufficient to assure a lifestyle to match. The young Roosevelt was taught at home by governesses and tutors, traveled abroad frequently, and had ponies, a yacht, and a summer home on Campobello Island in New Brunswick, Canada.

Franklin Roosevelt's mother, Sara Delano Roosevelt, was the second wife of his father, James Roosevelt, and was twenty-six years younger than her husband, who had fathered one child (Franklin's half-brother, James Roosevelt Roosevelt, nicknamed "Rosy") with his first wife. Franklin was his mother's only child and, his half-brother being thirty years his senior, was in effect almost an only child to his father, as well.

This background played a major role in shaping the future president. Both his unstinting optimism and his self-confidence grew out of his youthful experiences as the only child in a home of privilege. (A hint of that confidence was already evident in a brief note he wrote to his mother shortly before his sixth birthday; see Document 1.1.) Young men of Roosevelt's class and generation were taught the principles of *noblesse oblige*—the obligations of people of nobility. His parents were firm believers in civic responsibility and passed this on to their son. From an early age FDR was taught that those who enjoy privilege must be willing to give back to the community, and that people of wealth, especially large landholders, should practice stewardship—conserve the land and other resources for future generations and help improve conditions for the poorer residents in their area.

Such expectations provided some balance in the young Roosevelt's life, keeping him from being just a spoiled rich boy. His mother certainly indulged him, and he came to expect to get whatever he wanted—a likely source of his great confidence as an adult that things would go as he wished. But he was by all accounts a cheerful boy and one who took responsibility seriously.

The concept of the responsibilities of the upper class was further instilled in young Franklin Roosevelt when, at the age of fourteen he took his first steps beyond his sheltered world to enroll at Groton, an exclusive private school in Massachusetts. Groton was another sheltered world, but one in which well-born boys were exposed to the problems of the larger world. Under the tutelage of headmaster Endicott Peabody, Roosevelt and his schoolmates were groomed to be leaders, encouraged to be active, and taught that their duty was to work to rectify social ills. Young Roosevelt joined competitions both physical and academic, but did not distinguish himself in either (see Documents 1.2 and 1.3).

A ROLE MODEL IN THE FAMILY

Peabody's influence on Roosevelt was exceeded by that of another upper-class man cut from a similar mold: Theodore Roosevelt. Franklin was so taken by his cousin's personality and his much-publicized exploits in the Spanish-American War that the younger man began adopting language and affectations of the elder. By 1900 FDR had even taken to wearing pince-nez (eyeglasses that clip onto the nose), as Teddy did. But this was just the beginning. Franklin would go on to borrow the entire script for his career from cousin Ted.

When Theodore Roosevelt became president after President William McKinley's assassination, his admiring cousin was attending Harvard University. There FDR did not distinguish himself academically, and his failure to win a place in the exclusive Porcellian social club—to which both his father and his idolized cousin had belonged—was a severe and lasting disappointment. Yet FDR's ingrained optimism, self-assurance, and sense of personal destiny were so strong that they could (and would) survive this and far more serious blows. He became the editor of the college newspaper, the *Crimson,* in his last year at Harvard. Some of the outlook that would guide his policies as president can be seen in his editorials, which tended to emphasize the strenuous life advocated by Peabody and Theodore Roosevelt. "Be always active," FDR admonished incoming freshmen in 1903. echoing the advice of Theodore: "Get action, do things; be sane!" (Roosevelt 1947, 1:502–504). Indeed, FDR's editorial advising freshmen on what was expected of them at Harvard is an excellent reflection of how young FDR saw himself and his role in society (see Document 1.4). While at Harvard, Roosevelt appears to have been influenced by a watered-down version of the new philosophy of pragmatism, which judged principles and actions by their results. This meshed with his personal outlook and became the basis of the experimental approach to social and economic problems that he would employ as president.

But the most significant developments of Roosevelt's undergraduate years involved his family rather than his college. Cousin Theodore's ascension to the presidency of the United States in 1901 was the first of these notable occurrences. This event capped the political career that FDR hoped to emulate. Then, during FDR's senior year at Harvard, he became engaged to the president's niece and his own fifth cousin once removed, Anna Eleanor Roosevelt.

Despite their close family links (so close that Eleanor's father was FDR's godfather), Eleanor and Franklin Roosevelt had strikingly different personalities. He was gregarious, she reserved. He loved joking, telling stories, and drinking; she preferred to be alone with a book and disapproved of alcohol, which had played a major role in the death of her beloved father. The pair loved each other deeply in the years preceding and immediately following their marriage (see Document 1.5). The differences in their personal tastes presumably played some role in FDR's later infidelity, which would almost end their marriage in 1918. But in some important ways Eleanor's vastly different outlook would become a source of influence and strength as the two formed a political partnership in the 1920s that would last until FDR's death in 1945. Eleanor's commitment to social justice became a continuing reinforcement of the concepts of stewardship, responsibility, and public service that FDR had acquired from his parents and headmaster Peabody. During their courtship, for example, Eleanor had FDR meet her at several different tenements on New York's lower east side where she was volunteering work, showing him living conditions of which he had been unaware.

Sara Delano Roosevelt was not pleased with her son's engagement, but she could only postpone, not prevent, the wedding. Sara Roosevelt thought Eleanor too plain and not a good "catch" for her son, and, in any case, she preferred to keep him for herself, hoping he wouldn't marry until he was older (see Document 1.6). Franklin and Eleanor were married on St. Patrick's Day, 1905, in New York City, with president Theodore stealing most of the attention. Sara's wedding present was a New York townhouse that connected with her own and which she furnished without consulting Eleanor. This affront was an early example of the continuing irritation that Sara would provide to her daughter-in-law.

Although Eleanor chafed under Sara's dominance—grandmother insisted on choosing the nurses for her grandchildren and often acted as if they were her own children—she played the traditional role of submissive wife and mother in the early years of her marriage. She bore six children between 1906 and 1916 (Anna; James; Franklin Jr., who died in his second year; Elliot; a second Franklin Jr.; and John). While Eleanor was thus occupied, Franklin Roosevelt was plotting out and then beginning to follow his plan for a political career. After two years of undistinguished study at Columbia University Law School, he passed the bar examination and began to clerk with a Wall Street firm in 1907. This plainly was not his calling, as he was willing to tell his fellow clerks. One day at work he outlined his career plan: he would win a seat in the New York State Assembly, later become assistant secretary of the navy, then governor of New York. "Once you're elected Governor of New York," he declared, "if you do well enough in that job, you have a good show to be President" (Davis 1972, 214). This forecast of his own future was an almost exact replica of the path that Theodore Roosevelt had taken to the White House.

Franklin Roosevelt came of age politically during the Progressive Era of the early twentieth century. He was influenced not only by the era's ideals—increasing democracy (through such innovations as primary elections and the initiative, referendum, and recall), regulating business, fighting political corruption, and uplifting the working class—but by his association with and admiration for the period's two leading political figures, Theodore Roosevelt and Woodrow Wilson. Theodore was FDR's hero and role model, and Wilson became the man under whom he served and the one he most admired in the Democratic Party. Progressivism was a natural fit for FDR. Like him, it was optimistic and believed that government action could improve people's lives. Particularly under Theodore Roosevelt, progressivism emphasized energetic leadership.

When FDR began his political career he had to depart slightly from Theodore's blueprint. He had hoped to be elected to the state assembly, but in 1910 he agreed to take on the tougher assignment of winning a state senate seat in a district that had been carried by a Democrat only once since the 1850s. FDR benefited from the intervention in New York politics of his cousin, who angered the leadership of the Republican Party by securing the gubernatorial nomination for progressive Henry L. Stimson. FDR also profited from the surname he shared with the highly popular former president. FDR ran a strenuous campaign in a red Maxwell touring car that was sure to attract a crowd. But the automobile tended to confirm his distance from working-class Democrats, which was also evident in his fancy style of dress and speech. Still, although he said little more than that he was in favor of honesty and efficiency in government, Roosevelt won with 52 percent of the vote.

As a state senator Roosevelt quickly gained publicity by leading the fight against Tammany Hall, the New York City Democratic machine, which was trying to choose "Blue-Eyed Billy" Sheehan as a U.S. senator. (New York, like many other states, still selected its U.S. senators through the state legislature.) Roosevelt gained additional attention by advocating the direct election of senators by the voters. Although Roosevelt and his good-government colleagues eventually succeeded in blocking Sheehan, they were obliged to accept a candidate with even stronger ties to Tammany Hall, James A. O'Gorman. Pretending that this defeat was a victory, Roosevelt moved on, but his hostile relationship with Tammany Hall, which did not take kindly to reformers and especially not to New York Democrats who opposed the machine, would cause problems for him for years. Roosevelt's self-righteousness angered not only Tammany, but many other New York political insiders. One, senate clerk Patrick "Packy" McCabe, summed up the general view of the young FDR when he denounced him as one of "the snobs in our party . . . political accidents . . . fops and cads who come as near being political leaders as a green pea does a circus tent" (Miller 1983, 86).

During Roosevelt's brief tenure in the state senate he continued to denounce corruption, but he also began to move more broadly in the progressive direction that his later career would take. Following the lead of his famous kinsman, he advocated conservation. He also endorsed an array of social reforms, including women's suffrage, though without much enthusiasm. In one 1912 speech Roosevelt clearly foreshadowed the basic viewpoint he would hold as president: community interest must come before individual interest (see Document 2.1).

During his bid for reelection that year, Roosevelt fell ill and was unable to campaign personally. He turned for help to a highly skilled but cynical newspaper man, Louis McHenry Howe, and so began an association that would last through Roosevelt's election to the presidency. With Howe providing the publicity, Roosevelt easily won reelection. (For details on this and other early Roosevelt campaigns, see Chapter 2.)

THE WILSON ADMINISTRATION AND WARS FOREIGN AND DOMESTIC

The election of Woodrow Wilson over the divided Republicans in 1912 gave Roosevelt a chance to leave his fights with Tammany behind—at least for a time—and join the administration in Washington. As an early supporter of Wilson, FDR got the political appointment he most desired: assistant secretary of the navy. His avid interest in sailing and ships inclined him in this direction, but, more importantly, this was the same position that Theodore Roosevelt held before winning his governorship and then the presidency. FDR was ecstatic.

Roosevelt quickly showed his belief in the sort of approach termed "the white man's burden," or in Wilson's case, missionary diplomacy. He supported the exercise of American power abroad for humanitarian and commercial purposes, making it clear that Latin Americans needed their northern neighbors to deliver the blessings of civilization.

In 1914 Roosevelt demonstrated his political immaturity by deciding to seek election to the U.S. Senate from New York. Still campaigning against Tammany—hardly a promising route to a Democratic nomination in his home state—Roosevelt was defeated in the primary by a mortifying margin of almost three to one.

In his position in the Navy Department, Roosevelt showed no loyalty to or respect for his immediate superior, Secretary of the Navy Josephus Daniels. When war broke out in Europe in August 1914, Roosevelt assumed a bellicose tone more in keeping with his cousin's positions than that of the president and administration. In 1917 when the United States finally did enter the war on the Allied side, as FDR had hoped all along, he attempted once more to follow in Theodore's footsteps by trying to resign from the Navy Department and enter active military service (as, indeed, his cousin was pressing him to do). Daniels and Wilson refused to let him leave, maintaining that he was needed in Washington. Roosevelt performed well for the Navy Department for the remainder of the war. He paid an official visit to Europe in the summer of 1918 and got close enough to the front that he would be able to say truthfully in his 1936 campaign, "I have seen war" (Rosenman 1969, 5:289).

Upon his return Roosevelt was determined to resign so he could enter active military service. Before he got back to the United States, however, he developed pneumonia. And then he found himself involved in a household war. While organizing some of FDR's correspondence, Eleanor found love letters to her husband from her social secretary, Lucy Mercer. Eleanor had suspected the affair the previous summer, when she delayed her departure for Campobello because she thought her husband wanted to get rid of her. After she left, FDR wrote to reassure her that he wanted to be with her all summer (see Document 1.7). Eleanor was devastated and demanded that her husband stop seeing Lucy or agree to a divorce. A divorce would have ended his political career in an era not yet accepting of failed marriages. According to some accounts, FDR was willing to pay this price and perhaps even give up the family fortune to marry Mercer, but she informed him that as a Catholic she could not marry a divorced man. (These accounts also say his mother threatened to disinherit him if he went through with a divorce; Maney 1992, 22). In any case, Roosevelt agreed to terminate his extramarital relationship (an agreement to which he did not live up in the long run) and he and Eleanor agreed to act as husband and wife in public, but not in private.

The Roosevelts' marital crisis took place wholly outside the public view but had great consequences for FDR's public life. The crisis was the beginning of a new partnership between Franklin and Eleanor Roosevelt, one that would be of enormous significance to Roosevelt's career and especially to his success as president.

CAMPAIGNS AGAINST REPUBLICANS AND DISEASE, 1920–1928

Franklin Roosevelt became the Democratic nominee for vice president in 1920. Joining a ticket headed by James Cox of Ohio that was almost certain to be defeated in the backlash against Wilsonian idealism and internationalism may not have seemed a wise career move. But Roosevelt emerged from the defeat with a good chance for a presidential nomination in an election year more propitious for a Democrat.

As he waited for such an opportunity, FDR confronted a personal challenge that tested him and his sense of optimism as no other had. While vacationing at the family home on Campobello Island in August 1921, Roosevelt became unusually tired and began to feel numbness in one of his legs. Soon he was unable to walk. Although it took some time before the doctors realized it, Roosevelt had been stricken with infantile paralysis (polio; see Document 1.8). Although he continued for years to believe that he would eventually recover fully, Roosevelt would never again walk without assistance.

His mother saw his illness as an undeniable end to FDR's political life and urged him to retire to Hyde Park. He would have none of it. In a remarkable display of self-confidence and determination, Roosevelt was soon planning his political future along with his physical recovery (see Document 1.9). He did not let his paralysis deter him from a continued and ultimately successful quest to fulfill what he saw as his personal destiny. Roosevelt's response to his physical misfortune made it clearer than ever that his high ambition was backed by an extraordinary resolve. With the strong support of his wife and of his newspaper friend Louis Howe, FDR released statements indicating that he was recovering and would soon be politically active. Eleanor and Howe worked over the years to keep Roosevelt's name before the public and to maintain contacts with key Democrats around the nation.

For his part, FDR maintained correspondences with political figures but concentrated on his recovery. He underwent treatments at Warm Springs, Georgia, a health spa in which he invested not only his hopes but much of his family fortune. Although a physical miracle never occurred, Roosevelt's work with the Warm Springs Foundation and the National Foundation for Infantile Paralysis helped other people deal with their affliction. His example was an inspiration to other victims of the disease and greatly increased public understanding that people with handicaps could still offer much to society (see Document 1.10).

Many historians have emphasized the importance of Roosevelt's disability in shaping him into the man he would be as president. This influence operated in a variety of ways. Most obvious, his disability gave him an experience with hardship and deprivation that someone from his background would otherwise be unlikely to encounter. This helped link him to people suffering economic hardship during the Great Depression. And that link worked in both directions. Not only was Roosevelt able to empathize with victims of the depression, but these victims knew that he had experienced—and seemingly overcome—great adversity. Roosevelt's illness may have changed his outlook and temperament. He appears to have become more serious and at least somewhat less superficial. If he was going to reach his destiny, he would now have to work much harder.

Less obvious, but perhaps even more important, Roosevelt's struggle with polio kept him on the political sidelines during the Republican ascendancy in the mid-1920s. Had he run for office then he probably would have lost—and probably would have been eliminated from presidential consideration. Even if he had won high office during that period, it might have derailed his quest by pushing him into a Democratic presidential nomination at the height of Republican prosperity, when he almost certainly would have been defeated.

Finally, as historian Patrick Maney has put it, Roosevelt's "triumph over adversity gave a heroic dimension to his life that had been missing before. In a way, polio did for Franklin Roosevelt what the Spanish-

American War had done for Theodore Roosevelt" (Maney 1992, 27). Polio was an ill wind that blew Franklin Roosevelt considerable good.

Another positive outcome of Roosevelt's handicap was that he came to depend much more on his wife in political matters. Eleanor Roosevelt served as her husband's proxy at political gatherings and, in the process, developed a self-confidence that would make her a major force on the national and world stages. With Louis Howe working tirelessly to keep FDR's name before the public and Eleanor maintaining and expanding personal contacts, Roosevelt remained a political player in the 1920s. He made a triumphant appearance at the 1924 Democratic National Convention to give a nominating speech for New York governor Alfred E. Smith. Four years later, Smith as the Democratic presidential nominee persuaded Roosevelt to run for governor. FDR's victory put him in position for a presidential run in 1932. (For details on the 1928 gubernatorial campaign, see Chapter 2.)

PROGRESSIVE GOVERNOR AND PRESIDENTIAL ASPIRANT, 1929–1932

Franklin Roosevelt's first task as governor was to prove he could handle the position. Smith had expected Roosevelt to defer to him and to be an inactive governor. He was disappointed on both counts. Not only did Roosevelt decline Smith's advice, but he appointed his own people to top jobs and kept Smith's appointees in just a few posts. Roosevelt was demonstrating that he was up to the job physically and that he was his own man. "I've *got* to be Governor of the State of New York and I have got to be it MYSELF," he had told Frances Perkins, his incoming state industrial commissioner, a few days before he took the office" (Miller 1983, 226).

Roosevelt wasted no time in establishing himself as a progressive. A firm believer in the general upward trajectory of history, Roosevelt had a faith in the national and human future that was as sanguine as the personal future he confidently predicted. He pushed a wide array of reforms, from conservation to education to old age insurance and utility regulation.

For some time Roosevelt failed to perceive the extraordinary nature of the national economic collapse that occurred in his first year as governor and the opportunity it afforded him to reach the White House.

But he eventually took the lead among governors in offering responses. He pressured the legislature for banking reforms and, most notably, created in 1931 the nation's first state agency to provide unemployment relief, the Temporary Emergency Relief Administration (TERA). Under the direction of Harry Hopkins, this state agency created jobs and provided monetary relief, thus establishing a model for similar federal programs that Roosevelt would initiate and Hopkins would administer beginning in 1933.

Although Roosevelt appeared to many political observers to have no particular vision, on several occasions during his governorship he articulated a social philosophy that emphasized interdependence, mutual obligations, and the importance of government as an instrument to help people meet their obligations to one another and regulate the excesses of a free market economy (see Document 1.11).

After a landslide reelection as governor in 1930, FDR became the heavy favorite for the Democratic presidential nomination in 1932. When he won that nomination, his election over President Herbert Hoover, who had been totally discredited by the Great Depression, was a foregone conclusion. (For full details on FDR's presidential campaigns, see Chapter 2.)

The economic crisis deepened during the four months between Roosevelt's election and his taking office on March 4, 1933. No such period between an election and inauguration had been as critical since that in 1860–1861 before Abraham Lincoln's first term. By this time Americans saw the crisis facing the United States as the worst since the Civil War. And they didn't have much confidence that the incoming president could turn the situation around. Though it appeared to many observers in these months that Roosevelt was playing the role of Nero and "fiddling while Rome burned," he was in fact laying the groundwork for his attempt to reverse the nation's downward spiral. The defeated president Hoover repeatedly asked Roosevelt to join him in statements of policy that would have amounted to a Roosevelt endorsement of Hoover's approach to the crisis. This would hardly have helped restore confidence. If the economy hit rock bottom just before Roosevelt took office, moreover, he would be in a better position to rally the nation behind his programs.

As the nation's banking system neared total collapse in February 1933, Roosevelt joined several wealthy friends, including New York real estate magnate Vincent Astor, on an eleven-day yacht cruise to the Bahamas, giving the impression, as one columnist noted, that he had forgotten the "forgotten man" about whom he had spoken during the campaign (Maney 1992, 44–45). Upon Roosevelt's return from the ill-advised trip, a would-be assassin opened fire with a pistol on Roosevelt while he was sitting in his car in Miami talking with Chicago's mayor, Anton Cermak. Roosevelt was unhurt, but five other people were wounded, Cermak fatally. Roosevelt responded to the attack with complete calm. As Secret Service agents began to rush him away, he saw the fallen Cermak and insisted that they go back to help him, although the agents warned that there might be other gunmen lying in wait. The president-elect comforted the wounded mayor as the car rushed him to a hospital. Later that night FDR appeared completely unshaken by the life-threatening incident.

Roosevelt's courageous reaction to the attempt on his life enhanced the public's impression of the nation's new leader in much the same way as did President Ronald Reagan's joking, unflappable response to his near-fatal shooting in March 1981. In fact, the men's similarities go beyond that public response. Both Roosevelt and Reagan seem to have had a sense of destiny, viewing the failed assassination attempts as signs that God had intervened to ensure the men would complete God's plan. For FDR this was apparently the second instance of divine intervention (the first being his survival of polio). This notion of God intervening to bolster a president and cure the nation's ills was reflected in a strange movie that enjoyed a brief period of popularity around the time of Roosevelt's inauguration. *Gabriel over the White House* depicts a president who lies at death's door after an automobile accident. The intervention of an angel from God restores him to life and transforms him into an active champion of the people, a champion who pursues a program that eerily foreshadows the New Deal (combined with a heaping of fascism). Many who had known or observed Roosevelt in earlier days thought he had experienced something like divine intervention. "That fellow in there," said Norman Davis, who had worked with Roosevelt in the Wilson Administration, pointing to the White House, "is not the fellow we used to know. There's been a miracle here" (Schlesinger 1958, 21; for full details on the crisis of 1932–1933 and Roosevelt's reaction to it, see Chapter 4).

THE FIRST NEW DEAL, 1933–1934

Taking office in the midst of the worst crisis the nation had experienced since the Civil War, Franklin Roosevelt's first task as president was to restore some hope to the people. He proved to be wonderfully suited to this role, as first evidenced in his uplifting inaugural address (see Document 3.1). The rapid-fire legislation of FDR's first hundred days as president was a mixture that generally did little to bring about economic recovery, but did provide people with a sense that their president and government cared about their suffering and were trying to help.

Roosevelt was much more an inspirational leader—someone who understood the presidency as a "bully pulpit," a term his cousin Theodore had coined—than an architect of legislation. The importance of his inspirational role cannot be denied, and it is highly unlikely that much of the legislation of the early New Deal would have been enacted had Roosevelt not been playing that role. Yet it must also be realized that of the fifteen major laws passed in FDR's first hundred days, Roosevelt himself initiated only two of them; and one of those, the Economy Act, was economically counterproductive. Roosevelt's other personally designed project was the Civilian Conservation Corps (CCC), a program that placed young men in conservation work in parks and forests. The rest of what soon came to be known as the "alphabet soup" of federal programs, ranging from the Agricultural Adjustment Act (AAA) through the Tennessee Valley Authority (TVA) and the Federal Emergency Relief Administration (FERA) to the National Industrial Recovery Act (NIRA), were the results of the pooled efforts of many people, often including the president, but also his advisers and members of Congress. (For details on the measures of the first New Deal, see Chapter 4.)

THE SECOND NEW DEAL AND A SECOND TERM, 1935–1938

By late 1934, while Roosevelt remained very popular, discontent with the New Deal was growing. On the right, some segments of the business community, which had been largely stilled in its criticism of Roosevelt during the early days of the New Deal because of the depth of the crisis, began to voice their bitter opposition openly. The formation of the American Liberty League in 1934 brought together Roosevelt's business opponents with political conservatives, including FDR's former ally, Alfred E. Smith. Roosevelt resented this opposition because he had been attempting to build a consensus and because he truly believed, as he had said at least as early as 1912, that there was no basic dividing line between capital and labor and that he could bring them together. During his first two years as president he had seen himself as president of all the people. But it now seemed that business leaders would not allow him to continue in this role. As FDR saw it, he had saved the necks of the rich and preserved capitalism, but they turned on him anyway.

From the other side of the political spectrum, a rising crescendo called "thunder on the left" was demanding attention. Strikes were growing in number. Popular political movements were cropping up and calling for radical change. Numerous people, including Sen. Huey Long, D-La.; Father Charles Coughlin; and Dr. Francis Townsend, were peddling panaceas. The signs were everywhere that the president needed new initiatives to catch up with his putative followers. The result was the "second New Deal" of 1935, which yielded, among other things, Social Security, the National Labor Relations Act, and a massive work relief program (the Works Progress Administration). (For details on the challenges from the left and the second New Deal, see Chapters 3 and 4.)

The second New Deal solidified Roosevelt's credentials as a champion of the people, and he was able to crush Republican Alf Landon in 1936 in the largest landslide victory in a contested presidential election up to that time (see Chapter 2). Taking his huge victory as a mandate, Roosevelt foolishly launched an effort to change the composition of the Supreme Court—which had been invalidating New Deal laws—by enlarging the size of the Court with an additional appointee for each member over the age of seventy. This apparent attempt to upset the constitutional balance among the branches of government provided Roosevelt's opponents with an issue around which they could rally support for their cause. When this blow to FDR's prestige was combined with a new downturn in the economy in 1937, Roosevelt's domestic program slowed considerably in his second term (see Chapter 4).

ATTENTION SHIFTS TO A DIFFERENT KIND OF WAR, 1938–1941

In the late 1930s Roosevelt's domestic program was adrift and he was uncertain which way to redirect it. So when foreign problems moved onto center stage at this time, Roosevelt likely saw it as a welcome development. Always an internationalist at heart, FDR viewed the growth of Nazism and Japanese militarism with concern and believed that the United States would have to respond to the rising threats of aggression.

But most Americans in the mid- and late 1930s adamantly opposed involvement in any new war. A major part of Roosevelt's skill as a democratic politician was in avoiding attempts to lead the people where they were not ready to go.

As the crises in Europe and the Pacific deepened, Roosevelt tried to nudge the country toward a bolder, more active foreign policy. When war broke out in Europe in September 1939, Roosevelt made no pretense of complete neutrality. He, along with the bulk of Americans, saw this struggle as one in which right was clearly on the side fighting against Hitler. But although most Americans hoped the Allies would win, they were not ready to get directly involved. Roosevelt's leadership success during this time was in slowly gaining public acceptance for the provision of direct material assistance to Britain. In the fall of 1940 he arranged an exchange with British Prime Minister Winston Churchill wherein the United States sent fifty naval destroyers to Great Britain in return for ninety-nine–year leases on naval bases in several British possessions in the Western Hemisphere. (For details on Roosevelt's actions during the onset of World War II, see Chapter 4.)

By the time the destroyers-for-bases deal was finalized, the 1940 presidential campaign was nearing an end. Roosevelt broke the precedent set by George Washington by accepting a nomination for a third term. He argued that the nation needed his experience as it faced the worldwide crisis of war. Although some people feared the implications of a third term, Roosevelt easily defeated the novice Republican candidate Wendell Willkie. (For full details on FDR's 1940 campaign, see Chapter 2.)

WARTIME LEADER, 1941–1945

Although by the end of the 1940 campaign Roosevelt was promising voters that "Your boys are not going to be sent into any foreign wars," he knew that American entry into the war was likely (Rosenman 1969, 9:514). It came, of course, with the Japanese attack on Pearl Harbor on December 7, 1941. With this new crisis Roosevelt proved to be as capable a leader in war as he had been during the Great Depression. Once again he reassured a fearful populace.

Roosevelt found his new role as wartime leader invigorating after the many disappointing confrontations with Congress in his second term. He jumped with zeal into the jobs of devising strategy, building morale, and mobilizing resources. His meetings and extensive correspondence with Churchill, both of which had started well before the United States entered the war, took on new significance now that their countries were formal wartime allies. There were considerable, albeit generally friendly, struggles between the two men over a variety of strategic issues. Although Roosevelt followed Churchill's lead on some matters, he often found himself in the middle between Churchill and his own military advisers.

The two leaders agreed on the most basic strategic question: defeating Germany had to be the priority, with only limited resources going to the Pacific theater until after the war against Germany was brought to a successful conclusion. Roosevelt was eager to engage the enemy as quickly as possible, but Churchill persuaded him that it would be premature to launch an Allied invasion of Europe as early as 1942. Over the objections of the U.S. military, FDR agreed to a late 1942 campaign in North Africa. Meeting with Churchill at Casablanca at the beginning of 1943, FDR again allowed himself to be persuaded to postpone an attack across the English Channel; U.S. and British forces instead concentrated on a campaign in Italy that year.

Late in 1943 Roosevelt met for the first time with Soviet dictator Josef Stalin, as well as Churchill, at Teheran. There the "Big Three" agreed that the invasion of Europe across the English Channel would finally be launched in the spring of 1944.

The long-awaited opening of the campaign to liberate Europe began with the D day invasion in Normandy on June 6, 1944. Although the success of the beachhead was in question for a time, once British, U.S., and other troops were on the continent the demise of the Third Reich was only a matter of time. That end would come, however, only after Roosevelt's death. (For more on the war, see Chapter 4.)

Having broken the tradition of serving only two terms, Roosevelt does not appear to have seriously questioned running for a fourth term in 1944. The war was reaching its climax and he was the leader of the forces ridding the world of fascism. Roosevelt was finding out more and more of the atrocities being committed by the Nazis, and he informed the American public of some of the horrors in an address in March 1944 (see Document 1.12). Stepping down at a time like that would have been unthinkable for Roosevelt. Yet his health was in serious decline and his appearance was noticeably older. But the American voters were not about to change leaders at this point, and Roosevelt defeated New York governor Thomas E. Dewey handily, albeit by the smallest margin of any of his four presidential victories. (For details on the Election of 1944, see Chapter 2.)

With the war in Europe nearing an end, Roosevelt spent what turned out to be the last months of his life working on questions concerning the shape of the postwar world. More practical than Woodrow Wilson but more idealistic than Theodore Roosevelt, FDR sought to create a more effective successor to the League of Nations, but one which would place the primary responsibility for maintaining international security in the hands of the major powers. Although he did not live to see the formal creation of the United Nations, FDR did represent the United States at the Big Three meeting at Yalta in the Soviet Union in February 1945, at which time the final disagreements over the structure of the new organization were resolved. Many more specific issues were left undecided, however, and had to be addressed by Roosevelt's successor, Harry S. Truman.

The war against Japan, although given a lower priority than the war in Europe, had seen steady advances by American forces along two separate routes across the Pacific. The troops were closing in on Japan when Roosevelt, his health deteriorating by the day, decided in late March of 1945 to go to Warm Springs, Georgia, to try to recuperate. Two weeks into his stay the president looked better and seemed to be regaining some of his strength. But on the afternoon of April 12, as he was sitting for a portrait, Roosevelt complained of a terrible headache and then slumped in his chair. He had suffered a cerebral hemorrhage and was pronounced dead at 3:35 p.m. Adolf Hitler, who had taken power in Germany a few weeks before Roosevelt's first inauguration, outlived his American adversary by only eight weeks. FDR missed seeing the end of the war against Japan by four months. His legacy in numerous areas of American life and, indeed, in the world, would last far longer. (For Roosevelt's legacy, see Chapter 6.)

NOTE

1. The first six presidents were George Washington, John Adams, Thomas Jefferson, James Madison, James Monroe, and John Quincy Adams.

BIBLIOGRAPHY

Biographies of Franklin D. Roosevelt come in all shapes and sizes. Even Abraham Lincoln has not been the subject of as many books and articles. There is space here to mention only some of the more important works in different categories.

Among the one-volume biographies, one of the best short and highly analytical books is Patrick J. Maney, *The Roosevelt Presence: A Biography of Franklin D. Roosevelt* (New York: Twayne, 1992). Maney is much less reverential toward his subject than have been many FDR biographers. The result of this approach is a very revealing and generally accurate view of FDR's strengths and weaknesses. General readers will find worthwhile two single-volume biographies aimed at popular audiences: Nathan Miller, *FDR: An Intimate History* (Garden City, N.Y.: Doubleday, 1983); and Ted Morgan, *FDR: A Biography* (New York: Simon and Schuster, 1985).

Among the many books written by people who knew or worked with Roosevelt, two stand out as important biographies rather than just memoirs: Rexford G. Tugwell, *The Democratic Roosevelt: A Biography of Franklin D. Roosevelt* (Garden City, N.Y.: Doubleday, 1957); and Joseph Alsop, *FDR, 1882–1945: A Centenary Remembrance* (New York: Viking, 1982). Blanche Wiesen Cook, *Eleanor Roosevelt, Volume 1, 1884–1933* (New York: Viking, 1992); and *Eleanor Roosevelt, Volume 2, 1933–1938* (New York: Viking, 1999) are superb on Eleanor Roosevelt, but also shed light on Franklin.

The best of the multivolume biographies remains James MacGregor Burns's two-volume study, *Roosevelt: The Lion and the Fox* (New York: Harcourt Brace, 1956); and *Roosevelt: The Soldier of Freedom* (New York: Harcourt Brace Jovanovich, 1970). Burns is favorable to Roosevelt on the whole, but also offers excellent critical analysis and does not hesitate to fault his subject when it seems warranted. Also cited in this chapter is Samuel I. Rosenman, ed., *The Public Papers and Addresses of Franklin D. Roosevelt*, 13 vols. (1938–1950; reprint, New York: Russell and Russell, 1969).

Frank Freidel's unfinished multivolume biography, *Franklin D. Roosevelt: The Apprenticeship; The Ordeal; The Triumph;* and *Launching the New Deal* (Boston: Little, Brown, 1952–1973) is the essential starting point for an in-depth exploration of Roosevelt's life. Arthur M. Schlesinger Jr.'s unfinished life and times of Roosevelt, *The Age of Roosevelt: The Crisis of the Old Order; The Coming of the New Deal;* and *The Politics of*

Upheaval (Boston: Houghton Mifflin, 1957–1960) is overly laudatory but highly readable and brimming with wonderful anecdotes. The most detailed account of Roosevelt's life is in Kenneth S. Davis's favorable multivolume biography, *F.D.R.: The Beckoning of Destiny, 1882–1928* (New York: Putnam, 1972); *F.D.R.: The New York Years, 1928–1933* (New York: Random House, 1985); *F.D.R.: The New Deal Years, 1933–1937* (New York: Random House, 1986); *F.D.R.: Into the Storm, 1937–1940* (New York: Random House, 1993); and *F.D.R.: The War President, 1940–1943* (New York: Random House, 2000).

Anyone interested in understanding Roosevelt and his role cannot afford to miss Richard Hofstadter's outstanding essay, "Franklin D. Roosevelt: The Patrician as Opportunist," in *The American Political Tradition—And the Men Who Made It* (New York: Knopf, 1948).

On key segments of Roosevelt's life, see Geoffrey C. Ward, *Before the Trumpet: Young Franklin D. Roosevelt, 1882–1905* (New York: Harper and Row, 1985) on his youth and Ward's *A First Class Temperament: The Emergence of Franklin D. Roosevelt* (New York: Harper and Row, 1989) on his early career. Richard Thayer Goldberg examines the impact of Roosevelt's struggle with infantile paralysis in shaping him into the man he was as president in *The Making of Franklin D. Roosevelt: Triumph over Disability* (Cambridge, Mass.: Abt Books, 1981). Hugh Gregory Gallagher, *FDR's Splendid Deception* (New York: Dodd, Mead, 1985) focuses on the continuing impact of Roosevelt's disability. Doris Kearns Goodwin explores the lives of the president and first lady during the war in *No Ordinary Time: Franklin and Eleanor Roosevelt: The Home Front in World War II* (New York: Simon and Schuster, 1994). Robert H. Ferrell, *The Dying President: FDR, 1944–1945* (Columbia: University of Missouri Press, 1998) details Roosevelt's last year.

Elliot Roosevelt compiled his father's personal letters in *F.D.R.: His Personal Letters* (New York: Duell, Sloan, and Pearce, 1947)

Document 1.1   Note to His Mother, January 1888

This brief note to his mother is the second known letter written by Franklin D. Roosevelt, shortly before his sixth birthday. On the back of the penciled note is a notation by his mother saying that the boy knew his letters but was told how to spell the words.

my dear mama,

we coasted! Yesterday nothing dangerous yet, look out for tomorrow!!

Your boy.

F

Source: Elliot Roosevelt, ed., *F.D.R.: His Personal Letters* (New York: Duell, Sloan, and Pearce, 1947), 1:6.

Document 1.2   Letter to His Parents after He Enrolled at the Groton School, September 18, 1896

In his first letter home after he arrived at the Groton School, young FDR assured his parents that he was "getting on finely both mentally and physically."

Dear Mommerr & Popperr

I am getting on finely both mentally and physically. I sit next to a boy named A. Gracie King at meals, he is from Garrisons and knows the Pells and Morgans. Do you know him?

I am still in the third A & I think I am about half way up. I am all right in Latin, Greek, Science and French; a little rusty in Algebra but not more so than the others. I played football today on the 4th twenty-two (7th eleven) & tackled Taddy [his half nephew James Roosevelt Roosevelt Jr.] twice successfully. I play right halfback or fullback on Saturday—

Just got your letter and also one from Mr. Dumper. He is in Mt. Vernon & well. It rained this morning, but it has stopped now

We have just had Latin and Algebra, and we study French tonight. We went to Mrs. Peabody's Parlor last night for half an hour and played games. [Fanny Peabody, the headmaster's wife, entertained the boys at tea and helped them get over their homesickness.]

I got the shoes last night with the tooth-powder; the shoes are just right.

We are off to dinner now so I cannot write more but I will write you on Sunday.

With lots of love to Pa and yourself

F.D.R.

Source: Elliot Roosevelt, ed., *F.D.R.: His Personal Letters* (New York: Duell, Sloan, and Pearce, 1947), 1:35.

Document 1.3   Letter to His Parents from Groton, March 6, 1898

This letter to FDR's parents from Groton illustrates the interests and concerns of a young man from a privileged background.

My dear Mama and Papa,

The winter Sports meeting began yesterday morning with the ten yards dash. I came in second in my heat, and so lose all chance for the cup. In the afternoon we began with Potato Race which is always very amusing. I got on very well until one of my potatoes fell out of the bucket, and in my haste to put it in I fell down, and my potato rolled away!

After the Potato Race we had Featherweight Boxing, several good matches between kids. After that came Light-weight Boxing in which I had two three minute rounds with Fuller Potter. We both came out with bloody noses and cut lips, but the match was decided in his favor. I did not much expect to win as this is the third year he has boxed and even then we were quite close.

It is too lovely to think that I am coming home in two weeks, even though a week of exams comes first. I think I shall pass nearly all, but I may fail one or two as I am so very busy now, and am not going to grub much for them. . . .

I can hardly realize that you sail next month and I think that in some ways it would be nicer if we could all go together later, but in that case we should have to give up Campobello.

I have not yet received the plans for my boat but expect them every day, and shall send them to you when they come. Please don't forget to bring up something to take my ulster [a long, loose overcoat] and extra clothes home in when you come on the 16th. . . .

Ever with dear love to you both
F.D.R.

Source: Elliot Roosevelt, ed., *F.D.R.: His Personal Letters* (New York: Duell, Sloan, and Pearce, 1947), 1:183–184.

Document 1.4   FDR's Editorial in the Harvard *Crimson*, September 30, 1903

Roosevelt's first editorial in the Harvard Crimson *emphasizes the sort of values pushed by Theodore Roosevelt and Groton headmaster Endicott Peabody: responsibility, philanthropic work, and a strenuous life.*

Even as the oldest institution of learning on this continent is growing greater and better every year, so we hope that the class which enters Harvard today will prove the largest and the best which ever came here. Many hundreds of young men are today assuming for the first time much of the responsibility which they will have to face in after life, and it is here that the first, and in many cases the final, judgment will be made of the work of every individual. In the four years of undergraduate life not only can individual careers be made much as they are in the outside world, but the class as a whole will be judged favorably or the reverse, directly according to the success of its separate members.

It is this idea of responsibility which every Freshman should keep constantly before him—responsibility to the University, to his class and to himself; and the only way to fulfill this is to be always active. The opportunities are almost unlimited: There are athletics—dozens of kinds—and athletic management, literary work on the University publications and the outside press, philanthropic and religious work, and many other interests that are bound to exist. Surely the average Freshman can choose at least one of these and go into it with all his energy. Every man should have a wholesome horror of that happy go-lucky state of doing nothing but enough classroom work to keep off probation. It is not so much brilliance as effort that is appreciated here—determination to accomplish something.

Thus only can the class of 1907 come to be known as a "good class." The University is confident that every one of its members will realize his obligations at the outset and that resulting success will attend the class throughout its future.

Source: Elliot Roosevelt, ed., *F.D.R.: His Personal Letters* (New York: Duell, Sloan, and Pearce, 1947), 1:502–504.

Document 1.5   Eleanor Roosevelt's Letter to FDR a Month after Their Engagement, Christmas Eve, 1903

Eleanor's letter conveys the great happiness that the couple found in their love for each other in the early years of their relationship.

Darling,

I am sending this in the hope that you may get it on Christmas day as I want you to have a line from me. You know dearest all that I wish you and I only hope that your Christmas will be very, very happy dearest & that the New Year will bring you more joy than you have ever known before. I could never tell you how much happiness you have brought to me my dearest boy, but I can never remember feeling half so happy before. I haven't opened your package yet, as I wanted to have something from you in the morning, so I can't thank you really now but I will on Saturday!

I must stop now but Merry Xmas again dear, think of me often tomorrow & miss me as much as I shall miss you, then you will really be glad to see me on Saturday—

Ever your loving
"Little Nell"

Source: Joseph P. Lash, *Love, Eleanor: Eleanor Roosevelt and Her Friends* (Garden City, N.Y.: Doubleday, 1982), 47.

Document 1.6   Letter from Eleanor Roosevelt to Sara Delano Roosevelt, December 2, 1903

Eleanor Roosevelt wrote this letter just after FDR told his mother he intended to marry Eleanor. In it, Eleanor seeks the approval of her future mother-in-law, but foreshadows the problems Sara would cause for her.

Dearest Cousin Sally,

I must write you & thank you for being so good to me yesterday. I know just how you feel & how hard it must be, but I do so want you to learn to love me a little. You must know that I will always try to do what you wish for I have grown to love you very dearly during the past summer.

It is impossible for me to tell you how I feel toward Franklin, I can only say that my one great wish is always to prove worthy of him.

I am counting the days until the 12th when I hope Franklin & you will both be here again & if there is anything which I can do for you you will write me, won't you?

With much love dear Cousin Sally,
Always devotedly

ELEANOR

Source: Elliot Roosevelt, ed., *F.D.R.: His Personal Letters* (New York: Duell, Sloan, and Pearce, 1947), 1:517.

Document 1.7   FDR's Letter to Eleanor Roosevelt, July 16, 1917
In this letter FDR tries to reassure his wife that he did not want her to leave for the summer so he could engage in an affair. Eleanor's suspicions were, in fact, well grounded.

Dearest Babs,

I had a vile day after you left, stayed home, coughed, dozed, tried to read and work and failed even to play Miss Millikin [a game of solitaire]! But today I am practically all right and have been here at office as usual, except for lunch with the Blanpre's and am going to dine with Warren and Irene alone. I really can't stand that house all alone without you, and you were a goosy girl to think or even pretend to think that I don't want you here *all* the summer, because you know I do! But honestly *you* ought to have six weeks straight at Campo, just as *I* ought to, only you can and I can't! I *know* what a whole summer here does to people's nerves and at the end of this summer I will be like a bear with a sore head until I get a change or some cold weather—in fact as you know I am unreasonable and touchy now—but I shall try to improve. . . .

Kiss the chicks for me all round and many many for you.

Your devoted
F

Source: Elliot Roosevelt, ed., *F.D.R.: His Personal Letters* (New York: Duell, Sloan, and Pearce, 1948), 2:347.

Document 1.8   Eleanor Roosevelt's Letter to James Roosevelt on FDR's Illness, August 23, 1921

In this letter Eleanor Roosevelt informs FDR's half-brother, James Roosevelt "Rosy" Roosevelt that the cause of her husband's illness may be infantile paralysis ("I.P.").

Dear Rosy,

Many thanks for your telegram and both letters. Uncle Fred is meeting Mama on the 31st and Aunt Kassie seems to be going down also. I will get Uncle Fred to make reservations for her on the 1st as she could not leave the day she landed and there is no hurry for no change can occur here. The doctors agree that there is no doubt but that F. is suffering from the after effects of a congestion of the lower part of the spinal cord which was of unusually short duration so far as the acute symptoms. (His temp. has been a little subnormal the past few days but is up to 98 to-day.) It is too early yet to say positively if all this came from his chill and exposure which brought to a focus an irritation that had existed some time, or from an attack of Infantile Paralysis. The symptoms so far would be much the same. On Uncle Fred's urgent advice, which I feel I must follow on Mama's account, I have asked Dr. Keen to try to get Dr. Lovett here for a consultation to determine if it is I.P. or not. Dr. Keen thinks *not* but the treatment at this stage differs in one particular and no matter what it costs I feel and I am sure Mama would feel we must leave no stone unturned to accomplish the best results.

Franklin cannot be moved before Sept. 15th and then by boat to N.Y. to avoid jar and he must stay in N.Y. first, because it is only there that he can have all the after treatments necessary and second, if, as he hopes he can carry on his various business activities it can only be done there.

I will wire you after consultation which I hope will be Thursday. Love to Betty and Helen and to you. Franklin was much cheered by your letters.

Devotedly
E. R.

Source: Elliot Roosevelt, ed., *F.D.R.: His Personal Letters* (New York: Duell, Sloan, and Pearce, 1948), 2:526.

Document 1.9   Letter to His Mother on Progress in Regaining the Use of His Legs, February 22, 1924

Franklin Roosevelt's extraordinary optimism allowed him to believe he would regain the use of his legs and that he was making more progress than he actually was.

Dearest Mama,

At last we are in Miami after many adventures with sand banks, etc. There is a good deal to be done to the boat so we shall stay here till Monday. For the past week the weather has been really heavenly and Maunsell [Maunsell S. Crosby was FDR's neighbor from Rhinebeck, N.Y.] and I have sat around in our bathing suits, though it has been too cold to swim in the inside waters. From now on however the waters of the Gulf Stream are close at hand. Today Maunsell and I took the motor boat to an inlet, fished, got out on the sandy beach, picnicked and swam and lay in the sun for hours. I know it is doing the legs good, and though I have worn the braces hardly at all, I get lots of exercise crawling around, and I know the muscles are better than ever before. Maunsell has been a delightful companion and we have any number of tastes in common from birds and forestry to collecting stamps! For the happy thought of asking him you are responsible! . . .

I am in *fine* health and spend my time painting chairs, making boats and writing a history of the United States!

A great deal of love and give my love too to the Aunts and to Uncle Fred when you see them.

Your affectionate son,
FDR

Source: Elliot Roosevelt, ed., *F.D.R.: His Personal Letters* (New York: Duell, Sloan, and Pearce, 1948), 2:543–544.

Document 1.10   Letter to His Aunt, Anna Roosevelt Sheffield, on His Work at Warm Springs, June 29, 1927
FDR took a great interest in developing Warm Springs, Georgia, as a place for treating and rehabilitating people stricken with polio.

Dear Auntie Bye:

I have been very remiss in answering your note, but I know what the taking of Rosy [FDR's half brother had died on May 7, 1927] has meant to you as well as to me. It is very hard to realize when I am at Hyde Park that he is no longer there and in so many more ways than I had realized, I depended on his companionship and on his judgment.

I am sending you some of our folders about Warm Springs. The work of starting a combined resort and therapeutic center has been most fascinating for it is something which, so far as I know, has never been done in this country before.

We have already 30 patients there this summer and our total capacity for this coming year will be only 50, a figure I think we shall reach in a few weeks.

Most of the patients are suffering from infantile paralysis though we have two arthritis cases at the present time and expect several others, and also hope to have a good many people come there next winter for a few weeks of after cure succeeding operations or serious illness. It ought to be a success as the doctors are most enthusiastic and, at the same time, the climate is a delightful one all the year round. The elevation of 1000 feet makes it cool enough even in summer and it is far enough south to make it dry and bracing, and yet warm enough during the winter.

Aside from the therapeutic value, we have so many natural resources for the families or patients that the swimming, golf, riding and quail shooting ought to appeal to those in perfect health. The whole property I have put under the Georgia Warm Springs Foundation and am now busily engaged in trying to raise two or three hundred thousand dollars to carry out the improvements and pay the mortgage on the property.

Oh, I do wish that you could be wafted down there and placed gently in a chair and slide gracefully down a ramp into the water. You would love the informality and truly languid southern atmosphere of the place! My one fear is that this gentle charm will appeal to some of our rich friends who are suffering from nervous prosperity and that they will come down there and ruin our atmosphere. Cousin Susy Parish talks of a visit there, but I am not certain that she could endure our southern cooking.

Do send me some nice souls this coming winter, but not the kind who would insist on full dress for dinner every evening.

Always affectionately yours,
[F.D.R.]

Source: Elliot Roosevelt, ed., *F.D.R.: His Personal Letters* (New York: Duell, Sloan, and Pearce, 1948), 2:623–624.

Document 1.11   First Inaugural Address as Governor of New York, January 1, 1929

In his first inaugural address Franklin Roosevelt praised his predecessor, Alfred E. Smith, but made a stand as his own man by addressing issues that had not been prominent in Smith's administration. The speech's theme of interdependence was one FDR had favored in the past and one that would become central to his appeal during the Great Depression.

Governor and Mrs. Smith, Mr. Secretary of State, my friends:—

This day is notable not so much for the inauguration of a new Governor as that it marks the close of the term of a Governor who has been our Chief Executive for eight years.

I am certain that no Governor in the long history of the State has accomplished more than he in definite improvement of the structure of our State Government, in the wise, efficient and honorable administration of its affairs, and finally in his possession of that vibrant understanding heart attuned to the needs and hopes of the men, the women and the children who form the sovereignty known as "the People of the State of New York."

To Alfred E. Smith, a public servant of true greatness, I extend on behalf of our citizens our affectionate greetings, our wishes for his good health and happiness and our prayer that God will watch over him and his in the years to come.

It is a proud thing to be a citizen of the State of New York, not because of our great population and our natural resources, not on account of our industries, our trade, or our agricultural development, but because the citizens of this State more than any other State in the Union, have grown to realize the interdependence on each other which modern civilization has created.

Under the leadership of the great Governor whose place you have selected me to fill has come a willingness on our part to give as well as to receive, to aid, through the agency of the State, the well-being of the men and women who, by their toil, have made our material prosperity possible.

I object to having this spirit of personal civil responsibility to the State and to the individual which has placed New York in the lead as a progressive commonwealth, described as "humanitarian." It is far more than that. It is the recognition that our civilization cannot endure unless we, as individuals, realize our personal responsibility to and dependence on the rest of the world. For it is literally true that the "self-supporting" man or woman has become as extinct as the man of the stone age. Without the help of thousands of others, any one of us would die, naked and starved. Consider the bread upon our table, the clothes upon our backs, the luxuries that make life pleasant; how many men worked in sunlit fields, in dark mines, in the fierce heat of molten metal, and among the looms and wheels of countless factories, in order to create them for our use and enjoyment.

I am proud that we of this State have grown to realize this dependence, and, what is more important, have also come to know that we, as individuals, in our turn must give our time and our intelligence to help those who have helped us. To secure more of life's pleasures for the farmer; to guard the toilers in the factories and to insure them a fair wage and protection from the dangers of their trades; to compensate them by adequate insurance for injuries received while working for us; to open the doors of knowledge to their children more widely; to aid those who are crippled and ill;

to pursue with strict justice, all evil persons who prey upon their fellow men; and at the same time, by intelligent and helpful sympathy, to lead wrongdoers into right paths—all of these great aims of life are more fully realized here than in any other State in the Union. We have but started on the road, and we have far to go; but during the last six years in particular, the people of this State have shown their impatience of those who seek to make such things a football of politics or by blind, unintelligent obstruction, attempt to bar the road to Progress.

Most gratifying of all, perhaps, is the practical way in which we have set about to take the first step toward this higher civilization, for, first of all, has been the need to set our machinery of government in order. If we are to reach these aims efficiently without needless waste of time or money we must continue the efforts to simplify and modernize. You cannot build a modern dynamo with the ancient forge and bellows of the medieval blacksmith. The modernization of our administrative procedure, not alone that of the State, but also of those other vital units of counties, of cities, of towns and of villages, must be accomplished; and while in the unit of the State we have almost reached our goal, I want to emphasize that in other units we have a long road to travel.

Each one of us must realize the necessity of our personal interest, not only toward our fellow citizens, but in the Government itself. You must watch, as a public duty, what is done and what is not done at Albany. You must understand the issues that arise in the Legislature, and the recommendations made by your Governor, and judge for yourselves if they are right or wrong. If you find them right it is your duty as citizens on next election day to repudiate those who oppose, and to support by your vote those who strive for their accomplishment. . . .

Source: Samuel I. Rosenman, ed., *The Public Papers and Addresses of Franklin D. Roosevelt* (1938; reprint, New York: Russell and Russell, 1969), 1:75–80.

Document 1.12   Presidential Statement Condemning German and Japanese War Crimes, March 24, 1944

The failure of the Roosevelt administration to take action against the Nazi death camps is one of the worst blots on FDR's record. He did, however, inform the American people of some of the war crimes being committed.

The United Nations are fighting to make a world in which tyranny and aggression cannot exist; a world based upon freedom, equality, and justice; a world in which all persons regardless of race, color, or creed may live in peace, honor, and dignity.

In the meantime in most of Europe and in parts of Asia the systematic torture and murder of civilians—men, women, and children—by the Nazis and the Japanese continue unabated. In areas subjugated by the aggressors, innocent Poles, Czechs, Norwegians, Dutch, Danes, French, Greeks, Russians, Chinese, Filipinos—and many others—are being starved or frozen to death or murdered in cold blood in a campaign of savagery.

The slaughters of Warsaw, Lidice, Kharkov, and Nanking—the brutal torture and murder by the Japanese, not only of civilians but of our own gallant American soldiers and fliers—these are startling examples of what goes on day by day, year in and year out, wherever the Nazis and the Japs are in Military control—free to follow their barbaric purpose.

In one of the blackest crimes of all history—begun by the Nazis in the day of peace and multiplied by them a hundred times in time of war—the wholesale systematic murder of the Jews of Europe goes on unabated every hour. As a result of the events of the last few days hundreds of thousands of Jews, who while living under persecution have at least found a haven from death in Hungary and the Balkans, are now threatened with annihilation as Hitler's forces descend more heavily upon these lands. That these innocent people, who have already survived a decade of Hitler's fury, should perish on the very eve of triumph over the barbarism which their persecution symbolizes would be a major tragedy.

It is therefore fitting that we should again proclaim our determination that none who participate in these acts of savagery shall go unpunished. The United Nations have made it clear that they will pursue the guilty and deliver them up in order that justice be done. That warning applies not only to the leaders but also to their functionaries and subordinates in Germany and in the satellite countries. All who knowingly take part in the deportation of Jews to their death in Poland or Norwegians and French to their death in Germany are equally guilty with the executioner. All who share the guilt shall share the punishment.

Hitler is committing these crimes against humanity in the name of the German people. I ask every German and every man everywhere under Nazi domination to show the world by his action that in his heart he does not share these insane criminal desires. Let him hide these pursued victims, help them to get over their borders, and do what he can to save them from the Nazi hangman. I ask him also to keep watch, and to record the evidence that will one day be used to convict the guilty.

In the meantime, and until the victory that is now assured is won, the United States will persevere in its efforts to rescue the victims of brutality of the Nazis and the Japs. Insofar as the necessity of military operations permit, this government will use all means at its command to aid the escape of all intended victims of the Nazi and Jap executioner—regardless of race or religion or color. We call upon the free peoples of Europe and Asia temporarily to open their frontiers to all victims of oppression. We shall find havens of refuge for them, and we shall find the means for their maintenance and support until the tyrant is driven from their homelands and they may return.

In the name of justice and humanity let all freedom-loving people rally to this righteous undertaking.

Source: Samuel I. Rosenman, ed., *The Public Papers and Addresses of Franklin D. Roosevelt* (1950; reprint, New York: Russell and Russell, 1969), 13:103–105.

Roosevelt delivers his acceptance speech for the vice presidential nomination, Hyde Park, N.Y., August 9, 1920.

CHAPTER TWO

Campaigns and Elections

F ranklin D. Roosevelt began to develop a strategy to be elected president of the United States before he entered politics at any level. His admiration for his cousin, Theodore Roosevelt, who was elected governor of New York in 1898 and vice president of the United States in 1900, and assumed the presidency after William McKinley was assassinated in 1901, led FDR to imagine himself following a similar path. Not only politics, but presidential politics, seemed to him the extended-family business that he should inherit.

1910 STATE SENATE CAMPAIGN

FDR showed in his first political campaign in 1910, for the New York state senate, that he was daring and supremely confident—perhaps even arrogant. Dutchess County Democratic leaders approached FDR about a run for a state assembly seat they expected to be vacated by a retiring Democratic incumbent. The seat was what young FDR had been hoping for—it had been the first stop on the trail blazed by TR and was looking like an easy Democratic win. When the incumbent assemblyman surprised the party by deciding to run again, Roosevelt was offered the nomination for a state senate seat, one that appeared unattainable for a Democrat. The Republican incumbent senator, John Schlesser, was seeking reelection and had won the previous election by a huge margin. In fact, the senate district had gone Democratic only once since before the Civil War (and then only because of a three-way race). Although somewhat apprehensive, Roosevelt decided to go for it. The decision was a reflection of his extraordinary self-confidence at the outset of his political career. It would not be the last time that Roosevelt's sense of destiny would lead him into campaigns that seemed, at best, long shots for advancing his career.

To many Democratic insiders, Franklin Roosevelt in 1910 was a dandy and an intellectual lightweight. But his campaign that fall was innovative and well designed. Against the advice of political operatives, FDR traveled around the district in an automobile. This had never before been done in the area, and it drew crowds on whom Roosevelt turned his charm (which was not nearly as polished as it would be later in his career). His speaking ability was not yet well developed, but Roosevelt identified himself with the cause of reform and its popular leader, Cousin Ted. Theodore Roosevelt had, in fact, split the New York Republican Party in 1910 in much the same way he would the national Republican party two years later, opening the way in both cases for Democratic victories. Yet Franklin Roosevelt also won many votes on his own, running in his district well ahead of Democrats seeking other offices. In his first and second terms he articulated a progressive vision of cooperation supplementing pure self-interest and governmental responsibility to intervene for the public good (see Document 2.1). When the votes were counted, the young squire of Hyde Park had defeated the supposedly invincible incumbent 15,708 to 14,568.

1912 STATE SENATE CAMPAIGN

When FDR sought reelection to his state senate seat in 1912, he already had an eye on the next rung of the political ladder. Having supported the successful candidacy of Woodrow Wilson for the 1912 Democratic presidential nomination, FDR hoped that Wilson's almost certain triumph over the divided Republicans would yield a post for FDR in the new administration in Washington, D.C. (President William Howard Taft was the Republican nominee and Theodore Roosevelt was running under the banner of the newly created Progressive Party. FDR's commitment to the Democratic Party and his own future in it outweighed his family ties.)

Shortly after winning a renomination—not an easy feat when the New York Democratic Party had split between reformers and Tammany Hall regulars—Roosevelt fell ill, probably with typhoid fever. He had planned to reprise his automobile tour of the district, but his illness prevented active campaigning. To avert a defeat that could have ended his political career, Roosevelt called in Louis McHenry Howe, a newspaperman whom FDR had hired to help with Wilson's preconvention campaign in New York. Howe had ingratiated himself with Roosevelt by sending him a letter of congratulations after Wilson won the presidential nomination; the letter began, "Beloved and Revered Future President" (Freidel 1990, 22).

Howe was very ambitious, but his physical appearance precluded any realistic hope for election. He claimed to be "one of the four ugliest men, if what is left of me can be dignified by the name of man, in New York" (Miller 1983, 97). So he had decided to use his talents to promote someone else—someone who had the physical attractiveness and leadership ability that Howe lacked. Howe saw Roosevelt as the potentially great man he was looking for, and Howe linked his own hopes to FDR's destiny. Howe's role would be that of "the man behind the man." He began by saving Roosevelt's campaign in 1912. Roosevelt gave Howe almost complete control over the campaign, and Howe devised a superb one. Howe's greatest innovation was a "personal" letter from Roosevelt to his constituents addressing farm and labor issues and explaining that he wanted to discuss these issues in person but could not because of his illness. The letters were mass produced but appeared individually typed. A stamped envelope addressed to FDR was enclosed and people were asked to send him their thoughts on his proposals. Howe then created several more "personal" letters directed at specific segments of the senator's constituency. It was a stroke of genius and the first step in a technique that Roosevelt would hone, with Howe's assistance, in later campaigns and in the presidency. The strategy of establishing a feeling of personal contact between the voters and the candidate or officeholder was a winner.

Despite an eleventh hour Republican charge that he was biased against Catholics, Roosevelt won reelection by a larger margin than he had in 1910—15,590 to 13,889—with the Progressive Party candidate getting 2,628. Defeat would have been disastrous when both Wilson and the Democratic candidate for governor, William Sulzer, were carrying FDR's district. Louis Howe was already playing a major role as the man behind the man, and he would continue to do so all the way to the White House.

1914 U.S. SENATE CAMPAIGN

After bitter struggles with Tammany Hall (the Democratic political machine that dominated the party in New York City and had clout in party affairs statewide) and its head, Boss Charles Murphy, during his first two years in the state senate, Roosevelt had established himself as a leader of Democratic progressives in New York. Although happy in his position as assistant secretary of the navy in the Wilson administration—a job to which he was appointed after supporting Wilson's successful campaign—Roosevelt foolishly let himself be talked into running for the Democratic nomination for the U.S. Senate from New York in 1914. This would be the first time the party in New York chose its candidate through a primary, a reform Roosevelt had pushed for. Howe was vacationing when Roosevelt agreed to run, and in his absence Roosevelt made a serious mistake.

Although Howe threw himself into the race with all his talents and used a strategy and tactics similar to those he had employed in the state senate race two years earlier, the campaign was doomed. Roosevelt told voters that he had the implicit support of President Wilson. But when Tammany finally found a candidate, it was James W. Gerard, Wilson's ambassador to Germany. Because World War I had just begun in Europe, Gerard would not return from Berlin to campaign. This meant that Roosevelt had no opponent to campaign against, and he could not plausibly claim that Wilson favored him over the ambassador in the most critical post in the world. Roosevelt, moreover, stayed at the family's summer home on Campobello Island into early September, losing weeks that could and should have been spent campaigning. The primary was a humiliating defeat for Roosevelt. Gerard won 210,765 votes to Roosevelt's paltry 76,888. But Franklin Roosevelt was not easily cowed. He rebounded to campaign for the Wilson administration—and Gerard and the whole Democratic ticket. He had also learned a valuable political lesson: twisting the tail of the Tammany tiger might be good for getting headlines and winning votes in the Hudson River valley, but a Democrat who hoped to win statewide could not afford the hostility of the New York City machine. By the time he again sought elective office, FDR would have mended some fences with Tammany.

1920 VICE PRESIDENTIAL CAMPAIGN

Franklin Roosevelt became the Democratic nominee for vice president in 1920. Why he was offered the position, when he had held no elective office beyond a two-year term in the state senate and had lost badly in his only bid for a higher office, seems clear: his name was Roosevelt. Democrats hoped he could help the presidential candidate, James M. Cox of Ohio, woo some of the progressive Republicans who had left their party to support Theodore Roosevelt in 1912. Why FDR accepted the nomination is a more interesting question. Given Americans' obvious desire to return to "normalcy"—a term coined by the Republican presidential nominee, Warren G. Harding, that meant a turn inward, away from progressive social reform and Wilsonian internationalism—it was all but certain that the Democratic ticket would be defeated. The vice presidency, even if won, was traditionally a stepping-stone to political oblivion unless the president died in office. (Between Martin Van Buren in 1836 and George Bush in 1988, no vice president was elected president without first having reached the office through the death of the president under whom he served.) The political futures of defeated vice presidential candidates were nonexistent. In light of this history, Roosevelt's willingness to sign on as second mate on a sinking ship was either foolhardy or daring. Actually, it was probably more a reflection of his high self-confidence. The fact that no one had ever gone from a losing vice presidential campaign to a successful presidential one was no reason to think he couldn't do it.

The 1920 election gave Roosevelt a chance to campaign across the nation and become widely known. He made a few serious mistakes, including a boast (apparently in an attempt to emulate TR's bravado) that he had written Haiti's constitution, but FDR emerged from his crushing defeat on the Cox ticket as a man with a real chance to be at the top of a Democratic national ticket. Democrats knew that FDR was not to blame for their ticket's crushing defeat.

1928 GUBERNATORIAL CAMPAIGN

Roosevelt's battle with polio (see Chapter 1) kept him mostly on the political sidelines throughout the presidencies of Harding and Coolidge, which was almost certainly a good thing for his long-term prospects—

the Republican Party had complete dominance in that decade of prosperity.

In 1924 New York governor Alfred E. Smith asked Roosevelt to make his first public appearance since contracting polio—to deliver a speech nominating Smith for the presidency at the Democratic National Convention in Madison Square Garden. It was a disastrous convention in which the Democratic Party, deeply and almost equally divided between rural and urban factions, nearly disintegrated. It took sixteen days and 103 ballots before they were able to choose a compromise candidate. The only person to emerge from this debacle with a rising star was Roosevelt. He moved onto the speakers' platform on crutches, showing great courage and taking the enormous risk of falling in front of the entire convention. When he reached the podium he put aside his crutches and smiled triumphantly, and the divided delegates cheered wildly. In his nominating speech, Roosevelt referred to Smith as "the Happy Warrior," a name that a speechwriter had taken from William Wordsworth (Davis 1972, 753). The nickname stuck with Smith, but it clearly applied even more to Roosevelt.

In an attempt to improve his own national prospects, Al Smith had given Roosevelt's career a major boost in 1924. He repeated the unintended favor four years later when he was the Democratic presidential nominee. Concerned that he might have difficulty carrying New York in the 1928 presidential election, Smith asked Roosevelt to run for governor. In some respects it was a situation similar to FDR's vice presidential nomination in 1920. Smith's motive was clear. As an Irish Catholic from New York City, he was suspect among upstate voters. Roosevelt was likely to add to Democratic vote totals upstate and so help Smith win New York's essential electoral votes. Smith did not take Roosevelt seriously as a potential rival for Democratic leadership in the state or nation, both because he still perceived FDR to be a lightweight and because of Roosevelt's disability.

Roosevelt almost turned Smith down. FDR still hoped that continued treatments at Warm Springs, Georgia, would bring back use of his legs. More important, prosperity reigned in 1928 and it appeared likely that Roosevelt would lose the race. Another loss would almost certainly have ended his political career. Even a victory might be disadvantageous, because it would propel him toward the 1932 presidential nomination, and if prosperity continued, as most observers expected it would, Herbert Hoover would likely win reelection. Both Roosevelt and Howe agreed that it made sense to defer a gubernatorial race until 1932. Although FDR repeatedly declined overtures from Smith and intentionally made himself nearly unreachable in Warm Springs, his belief in the unfolding of a divine plan led him to accept the possibility that the seemingly foolish step might turn out to be the right one. He relented— a decision that proved decisive in positioning him to achieve the destiny he had long believed was his.

If a victory in the 1928 governor's race could lead to a premature presidential nomination, a defeat could mean he would never get nominated at all. This fact would have been sufficient reason for Roosevelt to run a vigorous campaign. He had the additional incentive of having something to prove: that his disability would not prevent him from campaigning and governing effectively. He had, in short, to meet the health issue head-on. He was, in any case, a Roosevelt, and given the precedent set by Cousin Ted, that meant a strenuous effort in any such undertaking. It was during this 1928 campaign that Roosevelt brought together many of the aides and advisers who would serve him when he became president. Among them were Edward J. Flynn, Frances Perkins, James A. Farley, Raymond Moley, Henry Morganthau Jr., Samuel I. Rosenman, and William H. Woodin. Running a dynamic campaign that often left his team and the press corps exhausted, FDR won in November by a tiny margin (25,564 votes, a plurality of 0.6 percent), while Smith was losing New York and Hoover was achieving a national landslide.

1930 Gubernatorial Campaign

Franklin Roosevelt's victory made him a leading contender for the 1932 Democratic presidential nomination. As governor, FDR quickly mastered the relatively new medium of radio and became arguably the most effective politician ever to communicate over it. Similarly, Roosevelt built friendly relationships with most of the reporters who covered him. Both of these techniques would serve him well in Washington.

The term of New York governors at the time was two years, so Roosevelt had an opportunity to go before the state's voters again in 1930 and demonstrate their approval of his leadership. As the depression worsened, Roosevelt slowly came to see it as the major issue on the state and national agendas. He continued to emphasize the duty of the government to intervene in the free-market system to protect citizens (see Document 2.2).

His resounding victory, in which he increased his 25,000 vote margin of 1928 to a whopping 725,000, was heard in political circles around the nation. "The Democrats," humorist Will Rogers wrote the day after the election, "nominated their President yesterday, Franklin D. Roosevelt" (Davis 1985, 190n).

1932 PRESIDENTIAL CAMPAIGN

His huge victory in the state with the most electoral votes made Franklin D. Roosevelt the clear front-runner for the 1932 Democratic presidential nomination—a nomination that had become very much worth having after the Jazz Age and its prosperity had, in the words of F. Scott Fitzgerald, "leaped to a spectacular death in October, 1929" (Fitzgerald 1931). The day after Roosevelt's landslide reelection as governor, New York Democratic chairman Jim Farley issued a statement that made headlines around the United States. "I do not see how Mr. Roosevelt can escape becoming the next presidential candidate of his party, even if no one should raise a finger to bring this about" (Davis 1985, 198). From this point onward, even more than had already been the case, Roosevelt's actions in Albany were fully intertwined with his presidential campaign. As the depression deepened, FDR knew that his reaction to the crisis in New York would likely determine whether he would be chosen as the Democratic presidential nominee in 1932. Although he was as conventional as Hoover when it came to believing in the necessity of a balanced budget, Roosevelt's pragmatic approach made him more open to new ideas. In his speech to the legislature that year calling for the establishment of the Temporary Emergency Relief Administration (TERA), the governor proclaimed that the government ought to be seen as the servant of the people and that assistance to the unemployed must be provided by the government "not as a matter of charity, but as a matter of *social duty*" (Rosenman 1969, 1:459).

Taking a more active approach than most other governors to the economic crisis and assistance for the unemployed solidified Roosevelt's position as the front-runner for the presidential nomination. One of his more innovative moves was to bring in academics, mostly from Columbia University, as advisers. This group, initially headed by Raymond Moley of the Columbia Law School and including Rexford G. Tugwell and Adolf A. Berle, was dubbed the "brain trust." They helped Roosevelt develop policy ideas and craft campaign speeches.

A major consideration for a front-runner like Roosevelt was the party requirement that a candidate secure the support of two-thirds of delegates, not just a simple majority. This provision, which the Democrats had adopted in 1836 and which had been used to reassure southern Democrats that they could veto any potential nominee, necessitated the building of a truly nationwide following. But sharp regional divisions within the party made reaching such a supermajority difficult. Roosevelt would concentrate first on the South and West and then try to add the urban Northeast.

The Democratic nomination, almost worthless at the height of Republican prosperity four years before, had become tantamount to election. But it was not a prize that Roosevelt would be given without a fight. Al Smith, the man with the useless presidential nomination in 1928, had said he would not run again. But by 1932, with the economy as his ally rather than his enemy, he dearly wanted another chance. Though it was unlikely that Smith, carrying the political albatross of his Roman Catholic faith, could command majority support, there was a danger that he could gather enough support to keep his fellow New Yorker from reaching the two thirds threshold.

The other more or less serious contender was John Nance Garner, D-Texas, the Speaker of the House, who had the important backing of newspaper magnate William Randolph Hearst. Several other contenders and favorite-son candidates would lock up delegates on early ballots and make it more difficult for Roosevelt to attain the required supermajority.

Roosevelt's basic strategy for winning the nomination was to take advantage of the continuing antipathy between the followers of William Gibbs McAdoo and Al Smith, who had been bitter rivals through 103 ballots at the party's 1924 convention. Roosevelt needed to keep them from uniting against his candidacy, to keep himself acceptable to both factions, and to convince both that blocking his nomination would produce another suicidal split in the party, thus squandering the golden opportunity that the depression offered Democrats. Roosevelt also intended to remind members of each faction that stopping him might lead to the nomination of someone from the other wing of the party.

It was a sound strategy, but to implement it, Roosevelt had to overcome two obstacles. The first was the perception that his health was not adequate for campaigning and performing the duties of office. McAdoo shared this concern with a fellow Democrat when he whispered, "We don't want a dead man on the ticket" (Schlesinger 1957, 286). But Roosevelt's greatest handicap may not have been his physical disability. Rather, it was probably the concern that financier and powerful Democratic insider Bernard Baruch voiced when he said Roosevelt was wishy-washy. Influential columnist Walter Lippmann gave the public a similar assessment of Roosevelt early in 1932: "Franklin D. Roosevelt is no crusader. He is no tribune of the people. He is no enemy of entrenched privilege. He is a pleasant man who, without any important qualifications for the office, would very much like to be President" (Nevins 1932; see Document 2.3).

It is hard not to appear wishy-washy when trying to appeal to two widely divergent factions within your own party. The New York governor added fuel to the fire when, to appease Hearst and the isolationists, he announced in February 1932 that he no longer supported American entry into the League of Nations. In making himself acceptable to Hearst, Roosevelt was confirming the impression that he was, in Lippmann's words, "too eager to please," and that "the Roosevelt bandwagon would seem to be moving in two opposite directions" (Nevins 1932). In June, the Scripps-Howard newspaper chain editorialized on this issue in the most derogatory terms: "In Franklin Roosevelt, we have another Hoover" (Schlesinger 1957, 291).

Yet, for all the disappointment that FDR's defection on the League of Nations brought to many of his internationalist supporters (Bertie Hamlin, a friend since FDR was ten years old, complained, "I am devoted to Franklin but he ought to be spanked" [Freidel 1990, 69], the decision was politically astute. Had he not removed this obstacle to winning Hearst's support as the 1932 convention progressed, Roosevelt probably would have lost the nomination.

When Roosevelt staked out a strongly progressive position in an April radio address, calling for an economic cure that went "to the killing of the bacteria in the system rather than to the treatment of external symptoms" and for assistance to "the forgotten man at the bottom of the economic pyramid" (Rosenman 1969, 1:624–627; see Document 2.4), he cheered party liberals but drew public jeers from Smith and business interests within the party. Smith's response was particularly angry. "I will take off my coat and vest," he proclaimed at the Democratic National Committee's Jefferson Day dinner in April, "and fight to the end against any candidate who persists in any demagogic appeal to the masses of working people of this country to destroy themselves by setting class against class and rich against poor!" (Maney 1992, 37).

With the fight against what he termed "class prejudice" as his mission, Smith, who had declared his candidacy in February, now saw himself on a crusade. Roosevelt fell into a trap when he foolishly entered the late April primary in Massachusetts. In this heavily Catholic state—one of only two states outside the historically Democratic South that Smith had carried in his 1928 presidential campaign—Roosevelt had little hope of winning. Smith routed FDR by a three-to-one margin. Smith also beat Roosevelt in other New England states and made a strong showing in Pennsylvania. From the other side of the country came more bad news for FDR when Garner defeated him in the California primary. Once again, as in his disastrous 1914 Senate race, Roosevelt was finding that the primary elections he had championed could not be depended on to return the favor. Suddenly his nomination was in jeopardy.

With Smith challenging him from the right, Roosevelt steered left, although always in vague terms. In a commencement address at Oglethorpe University in Georgia on May 22, Roosevelt expressed ideas heavily influenced by a philosophic and policy memorandum Moley had prepared for him. "The country needs and, unless I mistake its temper, the country demands bold, persistent experimentation," the candidate declared. "It is common sense to take a method and try it: If it fails, admit it and try another. But above all try something." Perhaps more important, Roosevelt spoke of dire consequences if the stand-pat approach of Hoover (and, by implication, Smith) was not reversed. "The millions who are in want," Roosevelt warned, "will not stand silently by forever while the things to satisfy their needs are within easy reach" (Rosenman 1969, 1:639–647). Reading between the lines, he was suggesting that Democratic delegates and the nation's voters had a simple choice: Roosevelt or revolution.

Louis Howe was among those who thought this move to the left was bad politics, and he told Roosevelt so. But the depression had changed the political landscape and with it what was foolish and what wise. In fact, Moley and Roosevelt were moving in the direction of the new center of political gravity in 1932.

The 1932 Democratic convention in Chicago began with Roosevelt holding a substantial lead, but well short of the requisite two-thirds. The desire to stop Roosevelt gave birth to a strange and inherently unstable alliance between Smith and McAdoo. For Roosevelt to be nominated, he would have to split one side off that alliance. Given the hostility Smith now exhibited toward Roosevelt, the McAdoo side was the logical target. When the front-runner does not have enough votes to win on the first ballot, he has to keep some of his support in reserve so that he can gain on each subsequent ballot. Even a small drop in the vote total for the leader from one ballot to the next is likely to be taken as a sign that he cannot win and so to begin a rapid defection. Roosevelt gained on the second ballot, but almost lost it all on the third. The Mississippi delegation, which had gone for FDR on the first two ballots, was about to desert him. Then Louisiana senator Huey P. Long, a demagogue who did not like Roosevelt but may have appreciated his rhetoric about the "forgotten man," talked the Mississippi delegation into sticking with FDR for another ballot. Roosevelt was then able to win over the California and Texas delegations with help from Hearst, McAdoo, and Garner; the prospect that the convention would turn to Newton D. Baker, Wilson's secretary of war, was unpalatable to Hearst (because of Baker's association with Wilsonian internationalism) and to McAdoo (because of Baker's closeness to business interests). Roosevelt won the nomination and Garner, with some reluctance, agreed to take the vice presidential slot on the ticket.

By deciding to travel to the convention in Chicago to accept the nomination in person (thus going against the tradition of waiting to be informed of a nomination at a later date), FDR demonstrated both his physical capability and his willingness to break the mold and try new things. In his acceptance speech, Roosevelt said that the Democrats "will break foolish traditions and leave it to the Republican leadership, far more skilled in that art, to break promises" (Rosenman 1969, 1:647–659). The barb at Republican *leadership* was designed to separate average Republican voters from Republican leaders. In this speech FDR also called for a "new deal" for the American people (see Document 2.5).

The campaign against President Hoover in the fall of 1932 was little more than a formality. Hoover had been in charge when the economy collapsed and most Americans did not think that his responses to the crisis were adequate. It was time for a change, and people would vote against Hoover almost without regard to who his opponent was. Nonetheless, Roosevelt ran a vigorous campaign. He was, after all, a Roosevelt, and he still felt the need to reassure the public that he was physically up to the presidency.

In the general election campaign, Roosevelt continued to bounce back and forth on some key issues, which did little to reassure voters. In Columbus, Ohio, FDR criticized Hoover for overregulation, while in Portland, Oregon, he declared that he wanted to use the government "to protect the welfare of the people against selfish greed" (Rosenman 1969, 1:727–742). He did, however, provide an outline of a progressive program that foreshadowed much of the New Deal in one campaign speech, at the Commonwealth Club in San Francisco in September. Declaring that the nation and its economy were in a new age that required a different governmental approach, Roosevelt said the tasks were "of meeting the problem of underconsumption, of adjusting production to consumption, of distributing wealth and products more equitably, of adapting existing economic organizations to the service of the people" (Rosenman 1969, 1:742–756). Yet in a speech less than a month later in Pittsburgh, FDR lashed the Hoover administration for "extravagant government spending" and pledged "absolute loyalty" to a plank in the Democratic platform promising a cut in federal spending of "not less than 25 percent." To top it off, Roosevelt accused Hoover of trying "to center control of everything in Washington as rapidly as possible" (Rosenman 1969, 1:795–811). This may have been reassuring to some fiscally conservative Americans, including the Al Smith wing of the Democratic Party, but it hardly fit with the vision that FDR had outlined in San Francisco a month before—or with what he would do as a president a few months later.

Roosevelt's two greatest allies in the 1932 campaign were the depression and President Herbert Hoover. If Roosevelt seemed unclear about where he stood in the ideological spectrum, Hoover had no doubt. He told the voters that Roosevelt wanted "to change our form of government and our social and our economic system." Roosevelt, Hoover said, "would destroy the very foundations of the American system of life"

(*Public Papers* 1977, 750–751). With a majority of voters apparently thinking that those foundations had already been destroyed under Hoover, the suggestion that Roosevelt would change the current system could only help the Democrat. Hoover, in short, was providing the definition of Roosevelt that the Democrat's own campaign was blurring.

When the ballots were counted, Roosevelt had defeated the incumbent by the huge margin of 57.4 percent to 39.7 percent and won the electoral vote 472 to 59, an even larger margin than Hoover had captured against Smith four years before.

1936 PRESIDENTIAL CAMPAIGN

By 1935 most of the business community had turned bitterly against Roosevelt. And there was a growing "thunder on the left" from such demagogues as Sen. Huey Long and Father Charles Coughlin, the followers of Dr. Francis Townsend's plan for lavish old-age pensions, several state political movements to the left of the New Deal, and a resurgent organized labor movement. Midterm election results in 1934 showed a marked turn to the left by a large segment of the electorate. (For more on the rise of the left and the subsequent second New Deal, see Chapter 4.)

The combination of the push from the right and the pull to the left gave FDR little choice but to respond. The defection of business meant that governing by consensus was no longer an option. The apparent shift of the electorate to the left made it clear where a majority of the votes were. If the economic crisis (and the Roosevelt administration's response to it) had underscored a class division in the United States and made the key political question the one asked in an early 1930s labor song, "Which Side Are You On?," Roosevelt would have to throw in his lot with the larger side, that of the workers. If it is true that a wise and successful leader must not get too far ahead of his followers, it is even more true that he must not allow his followers to get too far ahead of him— or to veer in another direction. Suffice it to say that Roosevelt was a wise and successful leader.

The president began the election year of 1936 with a dramatic evening appearance before Congress to deliver his State of the Union message, which was broadcast to the nation at the time when the largest number of people were listening to their radios. A president had made such an appearance before Congress only once before, when Wilson had asked for a declaration of war against Germany in 1917. Roosevelt was using that precedent to suggest a similar crisis: the need for "unceasing warfare" against an "economic autocracy" that wanted "enslavement of the public" (Rosenman 1969, 5:8–18). Less than a week later, Roosevelt used a radio hookup to tell Democrats at 3,000 Jackson Day dinners around the country that he, like Andrew Jackson, would lead the struggle against "the forces of greed and privilege" (Rosenman 1969, 5:38–44).

FDR spent the next several months engaged in "nonpolitical" activities, including trips to inspect New Deal projects. The trips' real purpose was evident when Roosevelt said to Democratic National Chairman Jim Farley with a laugh and a wink, "Of course, there won't be anything political about . . . inspection trips" (Freidel 1990, 198). For the first time since 1912, Roosevelt was facing an election without the counsel of Louis Howe, who was ill and would die in April 1936. Howe might have tried to restrain Roosevelt's increasingly class-oriented rhetoric in the campaign, but it seems unlikely that Roosevelt would have paid much heed. In any case, Howe's death spurred the president to turn more than ever to his wife, Eleanor, to give advice and carry out political tasks. Her advice usually encouraged a further tilt to the left, and the political realities of 1935–1936 led FDR to listen to such advice more in that period than he did at other times.

Given the nation's shift to the left, the Republicans could not afford to be too critical of the New Deal in 1936. They chose as their nominee a moderate governor from west of the Mississippi River, a vast region that Roosevelt had swept in 1932. Alfred M. Landon of Kansas avoided a frontal assault on the New Deal, contending instead that he and the Republicans could do a better job of achieving many of the same things that Roosevelt wanted. But Roosevelt was too savvy to let Landon escape from the taint of his party's association with archconservatives, big business, and greed. Ignoring Landon's moderate positions, Roosevelt ran against Hoover, the Liberty League, and assorted other members of what the public thought should be the FBI's Ten Most Wanted list.

It was at the official beginning of the 1936 campaign, in his acceptance speech at the Democratic National Convention in late June, that Roosevelt gave perhaps his best summary of his basic ideals as recast to reflect the class division theme. The speech was, though, a typical Rooseveltian "weaving together" of opposites. He had commissioned two different drafts, one more conciliatory toward business and one "fighting speech," and then combined the two (Freidel 1990, 202). Denouncing "economic royalists," whom he linked with the royalists at the time of the American Revolution and so with un-American sentiments, Roosevelt contrasted "a Government that lives in a spirit of charity" with one that is "frozen in the ice of its own indifference" (Rosenman 1969, 5:230–236; see Document 2.6).

There was virtually no chance that Landon could defeat Roosevelt in a two-man race, but there was some concern in the president's camp that a third party candidacy encompassing the followings of the demagogues of the left might drain enough votes from Roosevelt to allow Landon to win. The Union Party (which advocated radical economic measures, such as restrictions on wealth and guaranteed income for workers), nominated Rep. William Lemke of North Dakota, but he attracted scant support. Still, this threat from the left gave Roosevelt added incentive to identify more strongly with that side of the political spectrum.

By the end of the campaign Roosevelt was attacking what he described as his enemies and the people's enemies: "business and financial monopoly, speculation, reckless banking. . . ." "Never before in all our history," he proudly declared, "have these forces been so united against one candidate as they stand today. They are unanimous in their hate for me—and I welcome their hatred" (Rosenman 1969, 5:566–573).

Roosevelt's journey from "President of All the People" in 1934 to "Leader of the Masses' War against the Plutocrats" in 1936 might be summarized by turning around a familiar adage: If you can't join them, beat them.

And beat them he did, by an extraordinary margin. Roosevelt won 27,751,597 votes to Landon's 16,679,583 and Lemke's 882,479 (only a few hundred more votes than Socialist Norman Thomas had received in 1932). The incumbent carried the electoral college by the astounding margin of 523 to 8, losing only Maine and Vermont. The 60.8 percent of the popular vote Roosevelt won in 1936 was the largest percentage anyone had ever won up until that time; it has since been exceeded only once, by Lyndon Johnson in 1964. And the 98.4 percent of the electoral votes FDR captured is the highest percentage any candidate has ever won in a contested presidential election in the United States, exceeded only by George Washington's unanimous elections in 1789 and 1792.

One major reason for Roosevelt's extraordinary landslide was a huge increase in the number of people who voted in 1936. Nearly six million more Americans voted in 1936 than had in 1932, an increase of almost 15 percent of the electorate. Why? In a word: Roosevelt. FDR won more than 84 percent of the six million new votes. He did not, however, win over very many of those who had voted for Hoover in 1932. The new voters probably did not think in 1932 that a president made much difference in their lives. By 1936, Roosevelt had convinced them otherwise.

1940 PRESIDENTIAL CAMPAIGN

Since George Washington had declined a third term in 1796, no incumbent president had ever run for a third term. FDR's cousin Theodore had come closest to breaking the unwritten rule when he served from 1901 to 1908 and then, having promised not to run again in 1908, ran for a third term in 1912. As the 1940 election approached the major political question was whether Roosevelt would treat the two-term limit as another of the "foolish traditions" he had promised in 1932 to break. To do so openly would be a dangerous move that would remind people of his Court-packing plan (a plan to break another "foolish tradition" by increasing the number of Supreme Court justices; see Chapter 5) and fuel right-wing charges that Roosevelt sought to become something close to a dictator.

Remembering that Cousin Ted had regretted his pledge not to seek reelection, FDR declined in 1936 to say that he would not run again. Thereafter, he continued to decline to say one way or the other what his plans for 1940 were. The combination of Roosevelt's commanding presence, which hindered other Democrats' efforts to establish reputations, and the president's refusal to say whether he would accept a nomination for a third term made it difficult for serious alternative candidates to emerge. It appears that Roosevelt had genuinely not made a final decision at the beginning of 1940. Retirement had its attractions, but he loved the presidency and, like many Americans by this time, probably found it hard to imagine anyone else as president. The outbreak of war in Europe the previous September had made the decision that much more important. Roosevelt felt that he was best able to guide the nation through such perilous times. And, beyond the war, there were his domestic policies to preserve. Surely Roosevelt would put up a fight if his party appeared likely to nominate an opponent of the New Deal.

So the president continued to keep his own counsel. He offered encouragement to several possible Democratic candidates, especially Harry Hopkins, the former federal relief administrator and head of the Works Progress Administration who was moving steadily closer to the role he would hold during World War II as Roosevelt's closest adviser. But Hopkins's health declined seriously in 1939 and it became clear that he would not be able to run. By encouraging several different candidates, the president was making it difficult for any one of them to gain support. One person that Roosevelt did not encourage was Vice President John Nance Garner, with whom he had increasingly parted ways. (In truth, they had never been close and the friction only grew in the second term.) Other potential candidates included Secretary of State Cordell Hull and Democratic National Chairman James Farley.

There was no question that Roosevelt could have the nomination if he sought it, but he could not openly seek it without serious risk that the voters would see him as power hungry. What the president needed was to be drafted by the convention. That way he could answer the call of duty in the face of national crisis.

The turn of the war in Europe in the spring, culminating in the fall of France in June, meant that Roosevelt had a perfectly valid reason for concentrating on his presidential responsibilities and not discussing his or his party's political future, even as the Democratic convention in Chicago drew near. The deepening crisis also took precedence over public concern about the implications of a third term.

When the convention opened, Roosevelt remained noncommittal, saying neither that he wanted the nomination nor that he would refuse it if offered to him. God would provide a candidate, he told his aides. Finally, Roosevelt had Sen. Alben Barkley, D-Kent., relay to the convention the president's message that he had no desire to continue in the presidency and that he wished "in all earnestness to make it clear that all the delegates to this Convention are free to vote for any candidate" (Burns 1956, 427).

For a few moments there was silence as delegates tried to understand whether this meant that the president was withdrawing himself from consideration. But the answer came quickly, as loudspeakers in the convention hall began to resonate with shouts of "We want Roosevelt." Soon the convention floor was in pandemonium, with delegates shouting Roosevelt's name and waving placards. Roosevelt's statement of not wanting the presidency launched the draft that he needed. The voting the next day produced an overwhelming renomination of the president, with 946 votes, over a smattering of double- and single-digit totals for Farley, Garner, Hull, and Millard Tydings of Maryland.

But the matter was not yet over. Roosevelt had up to this point given no indication of whom he wanted as a running mate. Now he sent word that he wanted Secretary of Agriculture Henry A. Wallace. Roosevelt felt that the New Deal would be in friendly hands should Wallace succeed to the presidency, but many leading Democrats saw Wallace as too liberal and impractical, and a rebellion brewed on the convention floor. As it appeared possible that the delegates would defy the president and nominate Speaker of the House William B. Bankhead, D-Ala., the president drafted a statement declining the nomination. All indications are that he was serious about doing this if the convention forced Bankhead on him (Burns 1956, 429). In the end, Wallace won the nomination by a narrow margin. Instead of sending his message of withdrawal, Roosevelt addressed the convention via radio from the White House. He told the delegates that he had mixed feelings about accepting the nomination, but classified his service as akin to that which young people were being called upon to perform in the military. This commander in chief would not shirk his duty. It was the best face that could be put on the end of the tradition set by George Washington (see Document 2.7).

Roosevelt was not entering this general election campaign in as strong a position as he had in the two previous elections. What appeared to have been an orchestration of his own "draft," followed by insistence on Wallace's nomination as vice president, reinforced the perception that Roosevelt was devious and too desirous of staying in power. These were views that he would have to combat along with the Republicans.

The Republicans had, in a great surprise, chosen a largely unknown utility executive and former Democrat, Wendell Willkie. Events in France had undermined the two leading GOP candidates: New York district attorney Thomas E. Dewey, who was considered too young to be a wartime leader, and Robert Taft, whose isolationism seemed less marketable in light of the rapid Nazi advances. Willkie had voted for Roosevelt in 1932, supported Landon as a Democrat in 1936, and switched to the Republican Party only in 1938. He had also vigorously fought the

Tennessee Valley Authority, and now portrayed himself as a leading business victim of New Deal excesses. But he had endorsed many of Roosevelt's programs and would be difficult to portray as another Hoover.

Yet with the growing realization that the war in Europe posed a major menace to the United States, the chances that American voters would replace the experienced Roosevelt with an untested novice politician were slim. Through most of the campaign, Roosevelt gave the public the impression that he was ignoring Willkie and the election to concentrate on the more important business of building up the defenses of the United States against possible attack. The point (and the strategy) was clear: the commander in chief had more important things to do than make political speeches and appearances. Roosevelt had already laid the groundwork for the idea that he was the national leader, not a party politician, with the startling announcement shortly before the Republican convention that he was naming two very prominent Republicans to key defense positions in his cabinet. Hoover's secretary of state, Henry Stimson, would become Roosevelt's secretary of war, and Frank Knox, the 1936 Republican vice presidential candidate, would be secretary of the navy. Roosevelt was defining the race for the voters as one of a national-unity government versus partisan Republicans.

But there was also an unusual unity—or at least an odd coalition—on the other side. Joining together behind the Republican candidate were the usual big business interests, but also all the disparate enemies Roosevelt had made, especially during his second term: Al Smith and other conservative Democrats, isolationists such as William Randolph Hearst, and Congress of Industrial Organizations president John L. Lewis. Lewis had been a staunch Roosevelt supporter four years earlier but now bitterly opposed the president he believed had turned on him during the "Little Steel" strike of 1937 (see Chapter 4); Lewis said he would resign his position if FDR were reelected. The only thing these elements had in common was their antipathy toward Franklin Roosevelt.

In the weeks before election day, Willkie seemed to be scoring points by saying that Roosevelt was a warmonger. Indeed, Roosevelt had just taken a huge political risk by announcing on September 3, 1940, that he had agreed to send the British fifty old American destroyers in exchange for leases on ports in British territories in the Western Hemisphere (see Chapter 4). After Willkie's criticism, Roosevelt came out swinging. In Philadelphia, he ridiculed the idea that Republicans now cared about working people. He pointed out that recovery (stimulated by military spending) was now evident (see Document 2.8). Then, in Boston a few days later, the president responded directly to the issue on which Willkie appeared to have a chance of defeating him. "Your boys," the president pledged to Americans, "are not going to be sent into any foreign wars" (Rosenman 1969, 9:514–524; see Document 2.9). It was a promise FDR had to know he couldn't keep. But telling people what they wanted to hear served its purpose at the time. It was not, however, that pledge that produced another overwhelming victory for Roosevelt. Rather, a substantial majority of Americans still loved him.

When the votes were counted, Willkie had done better against FDR than had either Hoover or Landon, but Roosevelt had won another decisive victory. Willkie's 22,305,198 votes were, in fact, the most popular votes a Republican had ever received, and his 45 percent of the popular vote was a substantial improvement over the 39.9 percent and 36.8 percent won by his two GOP predecessors. But Roosevelt's total of 27,244,160 was down only marginally from what he had received at the height of his popularity in 1936, and winning 55 percent of the popular vote constituted another landslide for him. Willkie also did better than Hoover or Landon against Roosevelt in the electoral college, where he added eight additional states to Landon's Maine-Vermont base from 1936 and won 82 electoral votes to Roosevelt's 449. But that was still only 15.4 percent of the electoral vote, and Republicans could find little in the returns to cheer about.

1944 PRESIDENTIAL CAMPAIGN

In the minds of some, particularly those who distrusted Franklin Roosevelt the most, the first question about the 1944 election was whether there would be one. Rumors circulated among right-wingers that the president would use the war emergency to postpone the election and simply remain in power until the war ended. Although Winston Churchill had deferred a British election for the duration, Roosevelt seems never to have considered such a move. He told reporters in February 1944 that the Constitution was clear on when elections were to be held. The other major question—" Will he run again?"—was never in serious doubt. Roosevelt would not voluntarily leave his post in the midst of the largest war in history.

Although conventional wisdom is that voters do not want to "change horses in midstream" during a war that is going well, as World War II was for the Allies following the D day invasion in June 1944 (see Chapter 4), opinion polls indicated that the public mood was shifting to the right and there was little support for further domestic reform after the war. This could spell trouble for the incumbent. On the other hand, FDR was considered by many to be something approaching the "indispensable man," not only to complete the victory over the Axis nations but to deal with Stalin and Churchill in shaping the postwar world. A Roper poll taken late in 1943 showed that Roosevelt's conduct of the war and foreign policy had the approval of 70 percent of Americans. It was not surprising, then, that the president announced at the end of 1943 that "Dr. New Deal" had been replaced by "Dr. Win-the-War" (Rosenman 1969, 12:569–575). It was in the latter role that he wanted to face voters at the polls the following November (see Document 2.10).

Although Wendell Willkie had wanted another crack at Roosevelt, he had alienated party regulars by openly criticizing them. Some Republicans hoped to nominate Gen. Douglas MacArthur, but he backed away after an embarrassing letter he had written became public; the letter was written to a Republican congressman and was highly critical of the commander in chief. That left Thomas Dewey, now forty-two years old and the governor of New York. Dewey easily won the nomination on the first ballot at the Republican National Convention in Chicago.

Roosevelt removed any suspense in July when he gave reporters copies of a letter to the Democratic national chairman saying that he would like to retire, but if the convention nominated him and the people, to whom he referred as "the Commander in Chief of us all," told him that it was his duty, he would be a "good soldier" and serve again (Rosenman 1969, 13:197–198).

But who would serve with him? The ultraliberal incumbent Henry Wallace was strongly opposed by many elements within the party. The fear was that Roosevelt might not complete a fourth term and that whomever was chosen would become president. Democratic conservatives wanted to be sure it would not be Wallace. Roosevelt discussed many possibilities with aides and kept indicating that he favored one or another on a list that included Wallace, former South Carolina senator and Supreme Court Justice James F. Byrnes, who was now director of the Office of War Mobilization, Supreme Court Justice William O. Douglas, and Missouri senator Harry S. Truman. In the end, Truman was the choice, but relations were strained with the others who felt that FDR had misled them. In Roosevelt's acceptance, given by radio from San Diego to the convention in Chicago, he said he would not campaign in the usual sense, because it would not be fitting in such tragic times (see Document 2.11).

A major issue only slightly beneath the surface in the 1944 campaign was Roosevelt's health. The demands of the presidency and his long struggle with the effects of polio were taking their toll, and rumors spread around the nation that the president was seriously ill. Roosevelt countered the rumors by being president—and a fairly active one at that. In June he signed into law the G.I. Bill of Rights, which effectively combined New Deal social legislation with a popular military measure by making available to veterans college educations and low interest loans for homes (see Chapter 3). The same month he welcomed delegates from several nations to a meeting at Bretton Woods, New Hampshire, on creating a stable world economic system for the postwar era. Such developments reminded voters of what Roosevelt had accomplished and was continuing to accomplish.

Roosevelt laid the health issue largely to rest with a first-rate, humorous, and pointed performance at a Teamsters Union dinner in late September. Saying that the Republicans had gone beyond attacking him and his family and were now attacking his little dog, Fala, the president intoned, "I don't resent attacks, and my family doesn't resent attacks, but—Fala *does* resent them" (Rosenman 1969, 13:284–292; see Document 2.12). A performance like this was probably all that many voters needed to be reassured of FDR's competence.

But in case it wasn't enough, on October 21, 1944, he traveled in an open car in a downpour through the streets of New York City on a four-hour, fifty-mile trip that passed upwards of two million cheering citizens. It worked well for the short-run objective of showing that the president had the health and stamina to continue in office, but the ordeal probably took a toll on that health and stamina.

In Chicago at the end of October, Roosevelt gave one of his more memorable speeches, in which he assured the American people, "We are not going to turn the clock back" (Rosenman 1969, 13:369–378). An increasingly desperate Dewey lashed out at Roosevelt as a tool of the Communists. Roosevelt, genuinely angry, struck back hard, saying that he could not remember a campaign filled with such falsehood as Dewey's. The bitterness toward Dewey was heartfelt. On election night, with another Roosevelt victory clearly secured, Dewey waited until 3:00 a.m. to concede. Roosevelt privately remarked of his opponent shortly after the concession: "I still think he's a son of a bitch" (Burns 1970, 530).

Roosevelt's totals in the popular vote (25,602,504, 53.8 percent) and electoral vote (432, 81.4 percent) were down a bit from 1940. So the slow upward trajectory for support of the Republican opponent continued in 1944. Dewey's ninety-nine electoral votes constituted 18.6 percent of the total, up slightly from Willkie's 15.4 percent in 1940. And Dewey's 22,006,285 votes amounted to 46.2 percent of the popular vote, up from Willkie's 45 percent. But any Republican optimism might be tempered by the fact that at this rate of increase, their candidate would not pull even with Roosevelt in the popular vote until 1960.

BIBLIOGRAPHY

Succinct but reliable essays on all four of FDR's presidential elections can be found in Arthur M. Schlesinger Jr. and Fred L. Israel, eds., *History of American Presidential Elections, 1798–1968* (New York: Chelsea House, 1971). The major speeches of the four presidential campaigns are contained in Samuel I. Rosenman, ed., *The Public Papers and Addresses of Franklin D. Roosevelt*, 13 vols. (1938–1950; reprint, New York: Russell and Russell, 1969). Among the single-volume biographies of Roosevelt, the best in general and in their explanations of his political strategies are Patrick J. Maney, *The Roosevelt Presence: A Biography of Franklin D. Roosevelt* (New York: Twayne, 1992); and Frank Freidel, *Franklin D. Roosevelt: A Rendezvous with Destiny* (Boston: Little, Brown, 1990).

David M. Kennedy, *Freedom from Fear: The American People in Depression and War, 1929–1945* (New York: Oxford University Press, 1999) offers analyses of all four elections incorporating recent scholarship. William E. Leuchtenburg's classic *Franklin D. Roosevelt and the New Deal, 1932–1940* (New York: Harper and Row, 1963), provides brief but solid and interesting accounts of FDR's first three elections. Also strong on the first three elections is James MacGregor Burns, *Roosevelt: The Lion and the Fox* (New York: Harcourt Brace, 1956). Burns's second volume, *Roosevelt: Soldier of Freedom* (New York: Harcourt Brace

Jovanovich, 1970), contains a good chapter on the wartime election of 1944.

Among the most complete discussions of Franklin D. Roosevelt's 1932 campaign is contained in Kenneth S. Davis, *FDR: The New York Years, 1928–1933* (New York: Random House, 1985). Roosevelt's road to the presidency and his 1932 campaign are also covered in considerable detail in the third volume of Frank Freidel's biography, *Franklin D. Roosevelt: The Triumph* (Boston: Little, Brown, 1956).

Elliot A. Rosen, *Hoover, Roosevelt, and the Brains Trust: From Depression to New Deal* (New York: Columbia University Press, 1977) emphasizes FDR's personal political skills in the struggle for the 1932 nomination.

Herbert S. Parmet and Marie B. Hecht, *Never Again: A President Runs for a Third Term* (New York: Macmillan, 1968); and Bernard F. Donahue, *Private Plans and Public Dangers: The Story of FDR's Third Nomination* (South Bend, Ind.: University of Notre Dame Press, 1965) give the most detailed accounts of the 1940 nomination and campaign. Doris Kearns Goodwin discusses in some detail both the 1940 and 1944 elections from the Roosevelts' personal perspective in *No Ordinary Time: Franklin and Eleanor Roosevelt: The Home Front in World War II* (New York: Simon and Schuster, 1994). The 1944 presidential campaign can be viewed from the Republican side in Richard Norton Smith, *Thomas E. Dewey and His Times* (New York: Simon and Schuster, 1982).

Additional works cited in this chapter include Kenneth S. Davis, *FDR: The Beckoning of Destiny, 1882–1928* (New York: Putnam, 1972); F. Scott Fitzgerald, "Echoes of the Jazz Age," *Scribners's*, November 1931, http://www.ru.ac.za/academic/departments/history/jazz_echoes.htm; Nathan Miller, *F.D.R.: An Intimate History* (Garden City, N.Y.: Doubleday, 1983); Allan Nevins, ed., *Walter Lippmann's Interpretations, 1931–1932* (New York: Simon and Schuster, 1932); *Public Papers of the Presidents of the United States: Herbert Hoover, 1932–33* (Washington, D.C.: U.S. Government Printing Office, 1977); and Arthur M. Schlesinger Jr., *The Crisis of the Old Order, 1919–1933* (Boston: Houghton Mifflin, 1957).

Document 2.1   Speech at the People's Forum, Troy, New York, March 3, 1912

Roosevelt gave this speech while he was a member of the New York state senate in 1912. The speech provides insight into his early views that government needed a wider role and his political approach that sought to bring together competing interests.

. . . Competition has been shown to be useful up to a certain point and no further, but cooperation, which is the thing we must strive for today, begins where competition leaves off. . . .

The right of any one individual to work or not as he sees fit, to live to a great extent where and how he sees fit is not sufficient. . . .

[Because of the denuding of the land by unregulated cutting of trees, the German people had] passed beyond the liberty of the individual to do as he pleased with his property and found it necessary to check this liberty for the benefit of the whole people. . . .

We are beginning to see that it is necessary for our health and happiness of the whole people of the state that individuals and lumber companies should not go into our wooded areas like the Adirondacks and the Catskills and cut them off root and branch for the benefit of their own pocket. . . .

As it is with the conservation of natural resources so also it is bound to become with the production of food supply. The two go hand in hand, so much so that if we can prophesy today, that the state (in other words the people as a whole) will shortly tell a man how many trees he must cut, then why can we not, without being called radical, predict that the state will compel every farmer to till his land or raise beef or horses. After all, if I own a farm of a hundred acres and let it lie waste and overgrown, I am just as much a destroyer of the liberty of the community—and by liberty we mean happiness and prosperity—as the strong man who stands idle on the corner, refusing to work, a destroyer of his neighbor's happiness, prosperity and liberty. . . .

Neither can capital exist without the cooperation of labor, nor labor without the cooperation of capital. Therefore, I say there is no struggle between the two, not even a dividing line.

Source: Nathan Miller, *FDR: An Intimate History* (Garden City, N.Y.: Doubleday, 1983), 89–90.

Document 2.2   Address to the State Charities Aid Association, New York, January 17, 1930

Roosevelt made this speech as he prepared to seek reelection during his second year as governor of New York. His sights were set beyond that statewide race, however, to the presidential election two years later. FDR gave this speech less than three months after the 1929 stock market crash and before the magnitude of the depression was fully apparent. Yet he made clear his belief that a modern government's first duty is to promote the welfare of its citizens. This would be a major theme of his presidential campaign.

The most striking and important difference between the civilization of today and the civilization of yesterday is the universal recognition that the first duty of a State, and by that I mean a Government, is to promote the welfare of the citizens of that State. It is no longer sufficient to protect them from invasion, from lawless and criminal acts, from injustice and persecution, but the State must protect them, so far as lies in its power, from disease, from ignorance, from physical injury, and from old-age want.

It is difficult for us who live in the present day to realize what a tremendous change this is from the time, comparatively recent in the world's history, when the State was the instrument of despots for their own aggrandizement and the great body of its citizens were mere serfs, chattels, or cannon fodder at the service of their overlords.

We speak lightly of this being the era of Democracy without realizing what a tremendous change has been brought about, or how it has revolutionized the everyday existence of every one of us. In this building up of a theory of a government "by the people, for the people" our country has been the leader of the civilized nations of the world, and I think I can proudly add that our State has been the leader of our country. . . .

Then there is another very important matter, and that is our public health. It is becoming increasingly apparent that illness is a thing which can be prevented as well as cured. There is much sound common sense in the traditional Chinese method of paying the doctor for the days you are well instead of for the days that you are sick. Here your society has been and can be particularly helpful because there are limits beyond which, under our theory of home rule, the State cannot go. Much must be done by the counties themselves, and I hope that a centralized system of county health units will become a recognized and necessary part of every county government.

I have left to the last the most pressing and important matter of all—what we now call "mental hygiene." Under that head comes the entire tremendous problem of the insane and the mentally defective, a problem already heavy which, I am sorry to say, is increasing under the stress of our swiftly moving modern civilization. Here, as in the case of our criminals, society too long has been content to concern itself with self-protection. It was not so very long ago that the imprisonment of the criminal and the virtual imprisonment of the insane were considered in much the same light. We have progressed a little more rapidly from that unenlightened viewpoint in the case of the mentally diseased than in the case of the criminal, because here there is obviously no confusing question of moral delinquency involved. We now realize that we must endeavor to cure instead of merely to incarcerate in both instances. But even in the matter of the mentally diseased or defective our facilities for cure are still woefully inadequate. No small part of the large expenditure required by the State this year is made necessary by our past neglect to enlarge these facilities as they must be enlarged from year to year.

The further step, which is something that must be undertaken in each case, is the prevention of both insanity and crime. This has just begun. Money spent for prevention represents many times that amount saved by the State in the future. As a State we have done practically nothing toward the prevention of crime and insanity. It is something I hope we will seriously take up immediately. . . .

Source: Samuel I. Rosenman, ed., *The Public Papers and Addresses of Franklin D. Roosevelt* (1938; reprint, New York: Russell and Russell, 1969), 1:330–333.

Document 2.3   Walter Lippmann, "Governor Roosevelt's Candidacy," New York *Herald-Tribune*, January 8, 1932

This column by Walter Lippmann is perhaps the most famous example of the skeptical and largely negative view of Roosevelt's capacities as he embarked on his quest for the presidency in 1932.

It is now plain that sooner or later some of Governor Roosevelt's supporters are going to feel badly let down. For it is impossible that he can continue to be such different things to such different men. He is, at the moment, the highly preferred candidate of left-wing progressives like Senator Wheeler of Montana, and of Bryan's former secretary, Representative Howard of Nebraska. He is, at the same time, receiving the enthusiastic support of the New York *Times*.

Senator Wheeler, who would like to cure the depression by debasing the currency, is Mr. Roosevelt's most conspicuous supporter in the West, and Representative Howard has this week hailed the Governor as "the most courageous enemy of the evil influences" emanating from the international bankers. The New York *Times,* on the other hand, assures its readers that "no upsetting plans, no Socialistic proposals, however mild and winning in form," could appeal to the Governor.

The Roosevelt bandwagon would seem to be moving in two opposite directions.

There are two questions raised by this curious situation. The first is why Senator Wheeler and the *Times* should have such contradictory impressions of their common candidate. The second, which is also the more important question, is which has guessed rightly.

The art of carrying water on both shoulders is highly developed in American politics, and Mr. Roosevelt has learned it. His message to the Legislature, or at least that part of it devoted to his Presidential candidacy, is an almost perfect specimen of the balanced antithesis. . . .

The message is so constructed that a left-wing progressive can read it and find just enough of his own phrases in it to satisfy himself that Franklin D. Roosevelt's heart is in the right place. . . . On the other hand, there are all necessary assurances to the conservatives. "We should not seek in any way to destroy or to tear down"; our system is "everlasting"; we must insist "on the permanence of our fundamental institutions."

That this is a studied attempt to straddle the whole country I have no doubt whatever. Every newspaper man knows the whole bag of tricks by heart. He knows too that the practical politician supplements these two-faced platitudes by what are called private assurances, in which he tells his different supporters what he knows they would like to hear. Then, when they read the balanced antithesis, each believes the half that he has been reassured about privately and dismisses the rest as not significant. . . .

In the case of Mr. Roosevelt, it is not easy to say with certainty whether his left-wing or his right-wing supporters are the most deceived. The reason is that Franklin D. Roosevelt is a highly impressionable person, without a firm grasp of public affairs and without very strong convictions.

He might plump for something which would shock the conservatives. There is no telling. Yet when Representative Howard of Nebraska says that he is "the most dangerous enemy of evil influences," New Yorkers who know the Governor know that Mr. Howard does not know the Governor. For Franklin D. Roosevelt is an amiable man with many philanthropic impulses, but he is not the dangerous enemy of anything. He is too eager to please. The notion, which seems to prevail in the West and South, that Wall Street fears him, is preposterous. Wall Street thinks he is too dry, not that he is too radical. Wall Street does not like some of his supporters. Wall Street does not like his vagueness, and the uncertainty as to what he does think, but if any Western Progressive thinks that the Governor has challenged directly or indirectly the wealth concentrated in New York City, he is mightily mistaken.

Mr. Roosevelt is, as a matter of fact, an excessively cautious politician. He has been Governor for three years, and I doubt whether anyone can point to a single act of his which involved any political risk. . . .

. . . For Franklin D. Roosevelt is no crusader. He is no tribune of the people. He is no enemy of entrenched privilege. He is a pleasant man who, without any important qualifications for the office, would very much like to be President. . . .

Source: Allan Nevins, ed., *Walter Lippmann's Interpretations, 1931–1932* (New York: Simon and Schuster, 1932).

Document 2.4   "Forgotten Man" Radio Address, April 7, 1932

In this radio address during his quest for the 1932 Democratic presidential nomination, FDR identified himself with the victims of the Great Depression. The talk went over well with much of the public, but it led 1928 Democratic presidential nominee Al Smith to lash out at Roosevelt for appealing to class antagonism.

Although I understand that I am talking under the auspices of the Democratic National Committee, I do not want to limit myself to politics. I do not want to feel that I am addressing an audience of Democrats or that I speak merely as a Democrat myself. The present condition of our national affairs is too serious to be viewed through partisan eyes for partisan purposes.

. . . The generalship of that moment [World War I] conceived of a whole Nation mobilized for war, economic, industrial, social and military resources gathered into a vast unit capable of and actually in the process of throwing into the scales ten million men equipped with physical needs and sustained by the realization that behind them were the united efforts of 110,000,000 human beings. It was a great plan because it was built from bottom to top and not from top to bottom.

In my calm judgment, the Nation faces today a more grave emergency than in 1917.

It is said that Napoleon lost the battle of Waterloo because he forgot his infantry—he staked too much on the more spectacular but less substantial cavalry. The present administration in Washington provides a close parallel. It has either forgotten or it does not want to remember the infantry of our economic army.

These unhappy times call for the building of plans that rest upon the forgotten, the unorganized but the indispensable units of economic power, for plans like those of 1917 that build from the bottom up and not from the top down, that put their faith once more in the forgotten man at the bottom of the economic pyramid. . . .

. . . A real economic cure must go to the killing of the bacteria in the system rather than to the treatment of external symptoms. . . .

Such objectives as these three, restoring farmers' buying power, relief to the small banks and home-owners and a reconstructed tariff policy, are only a part of ten or a dozen vital factors. But they seem to be beyond the concern of a national administration which can think in terms only of the top of the social and economic structure. It has sought temporary relief from the top down rather than permanent relief from the bottom up. It has totally failed to plan ahead in a comprehensive way. It has waited until something has cracked and then at the last moment has sought to prevent total collapse.

It is high time to get back to fundamentals. It is high time to admit with courage that we are in the midst of an emergency at least equal to that of war. Let us mobilize to meet it.

Source: Samuel I. Rosenman, ed., *The Public Papers and Addresses of Franklin D. Roosevelt* (1938; reprint, New York: Russell and Russell, 1969), 1:624–627.

Document 2.5   Acceptance Speech at the Democratic
National Convention, Chicago, July 2, 1932

Roosevelt's speech accepting the Democratic nomination in 1932 was a dramatic event. No previous presidential nominee had given an address in person at the convention. FDR's appearance was especially significant, because he flew from Albany to Chicago to demonstrate that he was not incapacitated by his disability and that he was willing to break with what he termed "absurd traditions." In the speech, FDR pledged to give the American people a "new deal."

Chairman Walsh, my friends of the Democratic National Convention of 1932:

I APPRECIATE your willingness after these six arduous days to remain here, for I know well the sleepless hours which you and I have had. I regret that I am late, but I have no control over the winds of Heaven and could only be thankful for my Navy training.

The appearance before a National Convention of its nominee for President, to be formally notified of his selection, is unprecedented and unusual, but these are unprecedented and unusual times. I have started out on the tasks that lie ahead by breaking the absurd traditions that the candidate should remain in professed ignorance of what has happened for weeks until he is formally notified of that event many weeks later.

My friends, may this be the symbol of my intention to be honest and to avoid all hypocrisy or sham, to avoid all silly shutting of the eyes to the truth in this campaign. You have nominated me and I know it, and I am here to thank you for the honor.

Let it also be symbolic that in so doing I broke traditions. Let it be from now on the task of our Party to break foolish traditions. We will break foolish traditions and leave it to the Republican leadership, far more skilled in that art, to break promises.

Let us now and here highly resolve to resume the country's interrupted march along the path of real progress, of real justice, of real equality for all of our citizens, great and small. . . .

As we enter this new battle, let us keep always present with us some of the ideals of the Party: The fact that the Democratic Party by tradition and by the continuing logic of history, past and present, is the bearer of liberalism and of progress and at the same time of safety to our institutions. And if this appeal fails, remember well, my friends, that a resentment against the failure of Republican leadership—and note well that in this campaign I shall not use the word "Republican Party," but I shall use, day in and day out, the words, "Republican leadership"—the failure of Republican leaders to solve our troubles may degenerate into unreasoning radicalism.

The great social phenomenon of this depression, unlike others before it, is that it has produced but a few of the disorderly manifestations that too often attend upon such times.

Wild radicalism has made few converts, and the greatest tribute that I can pay to my countrymen is that in these days of crushing want there persists an orderly and hopeful spirit on the part of the millions of our people who have suffered so much. To fail to offer them a new chance is not only to betray their hopes but to misunderstand their patience.

To meet by reaction that danger of radicalism is to invite disaster. Reaction is no barrier to the radical. It is a challenge, a provocation. The way to meet that danger is to offer a workable program of reconstruction, and the party to offer it is the party with clean hands.

This, and this only, is a proper protection against blind reaction on the one hand and an improvised, hit-or-miss, irresponsible opportunism on the other.

There are two ways of viewing the Government's duty in matters affecting economic and social life. The first sees to it that a favored few are helped and hopes that some of their prosperity will leak through, sift through, to labor, to the farmer, to the small business man. That theory belongs to the party of Toryism, and I had hoped that most of the Tories left this country in 1776.

But it is not and never will be the theory of the Democratic Party. This is no time for fear, for reaction or for timidity. Here and now I invite those nominal Republicans who find that their conscience cannot be squared with the groping and the failure of their party leaders to join hands with us; here and now, in equal measure, I warn those nominal Democrats who squint at the future with their faces turned toward the past, and who feel no responsibility to the demands of the new time, that they are out of step with their Party.

Yes, the people of this country want a genuine choice this year, not a choice between two names for the same reactionary doctrine. Ours must be a party of liberal thought, of planned action, of enlightened international outlook, and of the greatest good to the greatest number of our citizens.

Now it is inevitable—and the choice is that of the times—it is inevitable that the main issue of this campaign should revolve about the clear fact of our economic condition, a depression so deep that it is without precedent in modern history. It will not do merely to state, as do Republican leaders to explain their broken promises of continued inaction, that the depression is worldwide. That was not their explanation of the apparent prosperity of 1928. The people will not forget the claim made by them then that prosperity was only a domestic product manufactured by a Republican President and a Republican Congress. If they claim paternity for the one they cannot deny paternity for the other.

I cannot take up all the problems today. I want to touch on a few that are vital. Let us look a little at the recent history and the simple economics, the kind of economics that you and I and the average man and woman talk.

In the years before 1929 we know that this country had completed a vast cycle of building and inflation; for ten years we expanded on the theory of repairing the wastes of the War, but actually expanding far beyond that, and also beyond our natural and normal growth. Now it is worth remembering, and the cold figures of finance prove it, that during that time there was little or no drop in the prices that the consumer had to pay, although those same figures proved that the cost of production fell very greatly; corporate profit resulting from this period was enormous; at the same time little of that profit was devoted to the reduction of prices. The consumer was forgotten. Very little of it went into increased wages; the worker was forgotten, and by no means an adequate proportion was even paid out in dividends—the stockholder was forgotten.

And, incidentally, very little of it was taken by taxation to the beneficent Government of those years.

What was the result? Enormous corporate surpluses piled up—the most stupendous in history. Where, under the spell of delirious speculation, did those surpluses go? Let us talk economics that the figures prove and that we can understand. Why, they went chiefly in two directions: first, into new and unnecessary plants which now stand stark and idle; and second, into the call-money market of Wall Street, either directly by the corporations, or indirectly through the banks. Those are the facts. Why blink at them?

Then came the crash. You know the story. Surpluses invested in unnecessary plants became idle. Men lost their jobs; purchasing power dried up; banks became frightened and started calling loans. Those who had money were afraid to part with it. Credit contracted. Industry stopped. Commerce declined, and unemployment mounted.

And there we are today.

Translate that into human terms. See how the events of the past three years have come home to specific groups of people: first, the group dependent on industry; second, the group dependent on agriculture; third, and made up in large part of members of the first two groups, the people who are called "small investors and depositors." In fact, the strongest possible tie between the first two groups, agriculture and industry, is the fact that the savings and to a degree the security of both are tied together in that third group—the credit structure of the Nation.

Never in history have the interests of all the people been so united in a single economic problem. Picture to yourself, for instance, the great groups of property owned by millions of our citizens, represented by credits issued in the form of bonds and mortgages—Government bonds of all kinds, Federal, State, county, municipal; bonds of industrial companies, of utility companies; mortgages on real estate in farms and cities, and finally the vast investments of the Nation in the railroads. What is the measure of the security of each of those groups? We know well that in our complicated, interrelated credit structure if any one of these credit groups collapses they may all collapse. Danger to one is danger to all.

How, I ask, has the present Administration in Washington treated the interrelationship of these credit groups? The answer is clear: It has not recognized that interrelationship existed at all. Why, the Nation asks, has Washington failed to understand that all of these groups, each and every one, the top of the pyramid and the bottom of the pyramid, must be considered together, that each and every one of them is dependent on every other; each and every one of them affecting the whole financial fabric?

Statesmanship and vision, my friends, require relief to all at the same time. . . .

One more word about the farmer, and I know that every delegate in this hall who lives in the city knows why I lay emphasis on the farmer. It is because one-half of our population, over 50,000,000 people, are dependent on agriculture; and, my friends, if those 50,000,000 people have no money, no cash, to buy what is produced in the city, the city suffers to an equal or greater extent.

That is why we are going to make the voters understand this year that this Nation is not merely a Nation of independence, but it is, if we are to survive, bound to be a Nation of interdependence—town and city, and North and South, East and West. That is our goal, and that goal will be understood by the people of this country no matter where they live.

Yes, the purchasing power of that half of our population dependent on agriculture is gone. Farm mortgages reach nearly ten billions of dollars today and interest charges on that alone are $560,000,000 a year. But that is not all. The tax burden caused by extravagant and inefficient local government is an additional factor. Our most immediate concern should be to reduce the interest burden on these mortgages.

Rediscounting of farm mortgages under salutary restrictions must be expanded and should, in the future, be conditioned on the reduction of interest rates. Amortization payments, maturities should likewise in this crisis be extended before rediscount is permitted where the mortgagor is sorely pressed. That, my friends, is another example of practical, immediate relief: Action.

I aim to do the same thing, and it can be done, for the small home-owner in our cities and villages. We can lighten his burden and develop his purchasing power. Take away, my friends, that spectre of too high an interest rate. Take away that spectre of the due date just a short time away. Save homes; save homes for thousands of self-respecting families, and drive out that spectre of insecurity from our midst. . . .

My program, of which I can only touch on these points, is based upon this simple moral principle: the welfare and the soundness of a Nation depend first upon what the great mass of the people wish and need; and second, whether or not they are getting it.

What do the people of America want more than anything else? To my mind, they want two things: work, with all the moral and spiritual values that go with it; and with work, a reasonable measure of security—security for themselves and for their wives and children. Work and security—these are more than words. They are more than facts. They are the spiritual values, the true goal toward which our efforts of reconstruction should lead. These are the values that this program is intended to gain; these are the values we have failed to achieve by the leadership we now have.

Our Republican leaders tell us economic laws—sacred, inviolable, unchangeable—cause panics which no one could prevent. But while they prate of economic laws, men and women are starving. We must lay hold of the fact that economic laws are not made by nature. They are made by human beings.

Yes, when—not if—when we get the chance, the Federal Government will assume bold leadership in distress relief. For years Washington has alternated between putting its head in the sand and saying there is no large number of destitute people in our midst who need food and clothing, and then saying the States should take care of them, if there are. Instead of planning two and a half years ago to do what they are now trying to do, they kept putting it off from day to day, week to week, and month to month, until the conscience of America demanded action.

I say that while primary responsibility for relief rests with localities now, as ever, yet the Federal Government has always had and still has a continuing responsibility for the broader public welfare. It will soon fulfill that responsibility.

And now, just a few words about our plans for the next four months. By coming here instead of waiting for a formal notification, I have made it clear that I believe we should eliminate expensive ceremonies and that we should set in motion at once, tonight, my friends, the necessary machinery for an adequate presentation of the issues to the electorate of the Nation.

I myself have important duties as Governor of a great State, duties which in these times are more arduous and more grave than at any previous period. Yet I feel confident that I shall be able to make a number of short visits to several parts of the Nation. My trips will have as their first objective the study at first hand, from the lips of men and women of all parties and all occupations, of the actual conditions and needs of every part of an interdependent country.

One word more: Out of every crisis, every tribulation, every disaster, mankind rises with some share of greater knowledge, of higher decency, of purer purpose. Today we shall have come through a period of loose thinking, descending morals, an era of selfishness, among individual men and women and among Nations. Blame not Governments alone for this. Blame ourselves in equal share. Let us be frank in acknowledgment of the truth that many amongst us have made obeisance to Mammon, that the profits of speculation, the easy road without toil, have lured us from the old barricades. To return to higher standards we must abandon the false prophets and seek new leaders of our own choosing.

Never before in modern history have the essential differences between the two major American parties stood out in such striking contrast as they do today. Republican leaders not only have failed in material things, they have failed in national vision, because in disaster they have held out no hope, they have pointed out no path for the people below to climb back to places of security and of safety in our American life.

Throughout the Nation, men and women, forgotten in the political philosophy of the Government of the last years look to us here for guidance and for more equitable opportunity to share in the distribution of national wealth.

On the farms, in the large metropolitan areas, in the smaller cities and in the villages, millions of our citizens cherish the hope that their old standards of living and of thought have not gone forever. Those millions cannot and shall not hope in vain.

I pledge you, I pledge myself, to a new deal for the American people. Let us all here assembled constitute ourselves prophets of a new order of competence and of courage. This is more than a political campaign; it is a call to arms. Give me your help, not to win votes alone, but to win in this crusade to restore America to its own people.

Source: Samuel I. Rosenman, ed., *The Public Papers and Addresses of Franklin D. Roosevelt* (1938; reprint, New York: Russell and Russell, 1969), 1:647–659.

Document 2.6   Speech Accepting a Second Presidential Nomination, Philadelphia, June 27, 1936

When Roosevelt campaigned for reelection in 1936, political allegiances were drawn along class lines. In his acceptance address, Roosevelt acknowledged this political reality and aligned himself with the middle and lower classes, calling the rich "economic royalists."

. . . America will not forget these recent years, will not forget that the rescue was not a mere party task. It was the concern of all of us. In our strength we rose together, rallied our energies together, applied the old rules of common sense, and together survived.

In those days we feared fear. That was why we fought fear. And today, my friends, we have won against the most dangerous of our foes. We have conquered fear.

But I cannot, with candor, tell you that all is well with the world. Clouds of suspicion, tides of ill-will and intolerance gather darkly in many places. In our own land we enjoy indeed a fullness of life greater than that of most Nations. But the rush of modern civilization itself has raised for us new difficulties, new problems which must be solved if we are to preserve to the United States the political and economic freedom for which Washington and Jefferson planned and fought. . . .

Throughout the Nation, opportunity was limited by monopoly. Individual initiative was crushed in the cogs of a great machine. The field open for free business was more and more restricted. Private enterprise, indeed, became too private. It became privileged enterprise, not free enterprise.

An old English judge once said: "Necessitous men are not free men." Liberty requires opportunity to make a living—a living decent according to the standard of the time, a living which gives man not only enough to live by, but something to live for.

For too many of us the political equality we once had won was meaningless in the face of economic inequality. A small group had concentrated into their own hands an almost complete control over other people's property, other people's money, other people's labor—other people's lives. For too many of us life was no longer free; liberty no longer real; men could no longer follow the pursuit of happiness.

Against economic tyranny such as this, the American citizen could appeal only to the organized power of Government. The collapse of 1929 showed up the despotism for what it was. The election of 1932 was the people's mandate to end it. Under that mandate it is being ended.

The royalists of the economic order have conceded that political freedom was the business of the Government, but they have maintained that economic slavery was nobody's business. They granted that the Government could protect the citizen in his right to vote, but they denied that the Government could do anything to protect the citizen in his right to work and his right to live.

Today we stand committed to the proposition that freedom is no half-and-half affair. If the average citizen is guaranteed equal opportunity in the polling place, he must have equal opportunity in the market place.

These economic royalists complain that we seek to overthrow the institutions of America. What they really complain of is that we seek to take away their power. Our allegiance to American institutions requires the overthrow of this kind of power. In vain they seek to hide behind the Flag and the Constitution. In their blindness they forget what the Flag and the Constitution stand for. Now, as always, they stand for democracy, not tyranny; for freedom, not subjection; and against a dictatorship by mob rule and the overprivileged alike. . . .

We seek not merely to make Government a mechanical implement, but to give it the vibrant personal character that is the very embodiment of human charity. . . .

Governments can err, Presidents do make mistakes, but the immortal Dante tells us that divine justice weighs the sins of the cold-blooded and the sins of the warm-hearted in different scales.

Better the occasional faults of a Government that lives in a spirit of charity than the consistent omissions of a Government frozen in the ice of its own indifference.

There is a mysterious cycle in human events. To some generations much is given. Of other generations much is expected. This generation of Americans has a rendezvous with destiny. . . .

Source: Samuel I. Rosenman, ed., *The Public Papers and Addresses of Franklin D. Roosevelt* (1938; reprint, New York: Russell and Russell, 1969), 5:230–236.

Document 2.7   Speech Accepting a Third Presidential Nomination, 1940

Roosevelt had said he did not want a third term, but had left his party with no realistic alternative to nominating him again. He accepted the unprecedented nomination in a radio address to the convention from the White House.

Members of the Convention—my friends:

It is very late; but I have felt that you would rather that I speak to you now than wait until tomorrow.

It is with a very full heart that I speak tonight. I must confess that I do so with mixed feelings—because I find myself, as almost everyone does sooner or later in his lifetime, in a conflict between deep personal desire for retirement on the one hand, and that quiet, invisible thing called "conscience" on the other.

Because there are self-appointed commentators and interpreters who will seek to misinterpret or question motives, I speak in a somewhat personal vein; and I must trust to the good faith and common sense of the American people to accept my own good faith—and to do their own interpreting.

When, in 1936, I was chosen by the voters for a second time as President, it was my firm intention to turn over the responsibilities of Government to other hands at the end of my term.

That conviction remained with me. Eight years in the Presidency, following a period of bleak depression, and covering one world crisis after another, would normally entitle any man to the relaxation that comes from honorable retirement.

During the spring of 1939, world events made it clear to all but the blind or the partisan that a great war in Europe had become not merely a possibility but a probability, and that such a war would of necessity deeply affect the future of this nation.

When the conflict first broke out last September, it was still my intention to announce clearly and simply, at an early date, that under no conditions would I accept reelection. This fact was well known to my friends, and I think was understood by many citizens.

It soon became evident, however, that such a public statement on my part would be unwise from the point of view of sheer public duty. As President of the United States, it was my clear duty, with the aid of the Congress, to preserve our neutrality, to shape our program of defense, to meet rapid changes, to keep our domestic affairs adjusted to shifting world conditions, and to sustain the policy of the Good Neighbor.

It was also my obvious duty to maintain to the utmost the influence of this mighty nation in our effort to prevent the spread of war, and to sustain by all legal means those governments threatened by other governments which had rejected the principles of democracy.

Swiftly moving foreign events made necessary swift action at home and beyond the seas. Plans for national defense had to be expanded and adjusted to meet new forms of warfare. American citizens and their welfare had to be safeguarded in many foreign zones of danger. National unity in the United States became a crying essential in the face of the development of unbelievable types of espionage and international treachery.

Every day that passed called for the postponement of personal plans and partisan debate until the latest possible moment. The normal conditions under which I would have made public declaration of my personal desires were wholly gone.

And so, thinking solely of the national good and of the international scene, I came to the reluctant conclusion that such declaration should not be made before the national Convention.

It was accordingly made to you within an hour after the permanent organization of this Convention.

Like any other man, I am complimented by the honor you have done me. But I know you will understand the spirit in which I say that no call of Party alone would prevail upon me to accept reelection to the Presidency.

The real decision to be made in these circumstances is not the acceptance of a nomination, but rather an ultimate willingness to serve if chosen by the electorate of the United States. Many considerations enter into this decision.

During the past few months, with due Congressional approval, we in the United States have been taking steps to implement the total defense of America. I cannot forget that in carrying out this program I have drafted into the service of the nation many men and women, taking them away from important private affairs, calling them suddenly from their homes and their businesses. I have asked them to leave their own work, and to contribute their skill and experience to the cause of their nation.

I, as the head of their Government, have asked them to do this. Regardless of party, regardless of personal convenience, they came—they answered the call. Every single one of them, with one exception, has come to the nation's Capital to serve the nation.

These people, who have placed patriotism above all else, represent those who have made their way to what might be called the top of their professions or industries through their proven skill and experience.

But they alone could not be enough to meet the needs of the times.

Just as a system of national defense based on man power alone, without the mechanized equipment of modern warfare, is totally insufficient for adequate national defense, so also planes and guns and tanks are wholly insufficient unless they are implemented by the power of men trained to use them.

Such man power consists not only of pilots and gunners and infantry and those who operate tanks. For every individual in actual combat service, it is necessary for adequate defense that we have ready at hand at least four or five other trained individuals organized for non-combat services.

Because of the millions of citizens involved in the conduct of defense, most right thinking persons are agreed that some form of selection by draft is as necessary and fair today as it was in 1917 and 1918.

Nearly every American is willing to do his share or her share to defend the United States. It is neither just nor efficient to permit that task to fall upon any one section or any one group. For every section and every group depend for their existence upon the survival of the nation as a whole.

Lying awake, as I have, on many nights, I have asked myself whether I have the right, as Commander-in-Chief of the Army and Navy, to call on men and women to serve their country or to train themselves to serve and, at the same time, decline to serve my country in my own personal capacity, if I am called upon to do so by the people of my country.

In times like these—in times of great tension, of great crisis the compass of the world narrows to a single fact. The fact which dominates our world is the fact of armed aggression, the fact of successful armed aggression, aimed at the form of Government, the kind of society that we in the United States have chosen and established for ourselves. It is a fact which no one longer doubts—which no one is longer able to ignore.

It is not an ordinary war. It is a revolution imposed by force of arms, which threatens all men everywhere. It is a revolution which proposes not to set men free but to reduce them to slavery—to reduce them to slavery in the interest of a dictatorship which has already shown the nature and the extent of the advantage which it hopes to obtain.

That is the fact which dominates our world and which dominates the lives of all of us, each and every one of us. In the face of the danger which confronts our time, no individual retains or can hope to retain, the right of personal choice which free men enjoy in times of peace. He has a first obligation to serve in the defense of our institutions of freedom—a first obligation to serve his country in whatever capacity his country finds him useful.

Like most men of my age, I had made plans for myself, plans for a private life of my own choice and for my own satisfaction, a life of that kind to begin in January, 1941. These plans, like so many other plans, had been made in a world which now seems as distant as another planet. Today all private plans, all private lives, have been in a sense repealed by an overriding public danger. In the face of that public danger all those who can be of service to the Republic have no choice but to offer themselves for service in those capacities for which they may be fitted.

Those, my friends, are the reasons why I have had to admit to myself, and now to state to you, that my conscience will not let me turn my back upon a call to service.

The right to make that call rests with the people through the American method of a free election. Only the people themselves can draft a President. If such a draft should be made upon me, I say to you, in the utmost simplicity, I will, with God's help, continue to serve with the best of my ability and with the fullness of my strength.

To you, the delegates of this Convention, I express my gratitude for the selection of Henry Wallace for the high office of Vice President of the United States. His first-hand knowledge of the problems of Government in every sphere of life and in every single part of the nation—and indeed of the whole world qualifies him without reservation. His practical idealism will be of great service to me individually and to the nation as a whole. . . .

In some respects, as I think my good wife suggested an hour or so ago—the next few months will be different from the usual national campaigns of recent years.

Most of you know how important it is that the President of the United States in these days remain close to the seat of Government. Since last Summer I have been compelled to abandon proposed journeys to inspect many of our great national projects from the Alleghenies to the Pacific Coast.

Events move so fast in other parts of the world that it has become my duty to remain either in the White House itself or at some near-by point where I can reach Washington and even Europe and Asia by direct telephone—where, if need be, I can be back at my desk in the space of a very few hours. And in addition, the splendid work of the new defense machinery will require me to spend vastly more time in conference with the responsible administration heads under me. Finally, the added task which the present crisis has imposed also upon the Congress, compelling them to forego their usual adjournment, calls for constant cooperation between the Executive and Legislative branches, to the efficiency of which I am glad indeed now to pay tribute.

I do expect, of course, during the coming months to make my usual periodic reports to the country through the medium of press conferences and radio talks. I shall not have the time or the inclination to engage in purely political debate. But I shall never be loath to call the attention of the nation to deliberate or unwitting falsifications of fact, which are sometimes made by political candidates.

I have spoken to you in a very informal and personal way. The exigencies of the day require, however, that I also talk with you about things which transcend any personality and go very deeply to the roots of American civilization.

Our lives have been based on those fundamental freedoms and liberties which we Americans have cherished for a century and a half. The establishment of them and the preservation of them in each succeeding generation have been accomplished through the processes of free elective Government—the democratic-republican form, based on the representative system and the coordination of the executive, the legislative and the judicial branches.

The task of safeguarding our institutions seems to me to be twofold. One must be accomplished, if it becomes necessary, by the armed defense forces of the nation. The other, by the united effort of the men and women of the country to make our Federal and State and local Governments responsive to the growing requirements of modern democracy.

There have been occasions, as we remember, when reactions in the march of democracy have set in, and forward looking progress has seemed to stop.

But such periods have been followed by liberal and progressive times which have enabled the nation to catch up with new developments in fulfilling new human needs. Such a time has been the past seven years. Because we had seemed to lag in previous years, we have had to develop, speedily and efficiently, the answers to aspirations which had come from every State and every family in the land.

We have sometimes called it social legislation; we have sometimes called it legislation to end the abuses of the past; we have sometimes called it legislation for human security; and we have sometimes called it legislation to better the condition of life of the many millions of our fellow citizens, who could not have the essentials of life or hope for an American standard of living.

Some of us have labeled it a wider and more equitable distribution of wealth in our land. It has included among its aims, to liberalize and broaden the control of vast industries—lodged today in the hands of a relatively small group of individuals of very great financial power.

But all of these definitions and labels are essentially the expression of one consistent thought. They represent a constantly growing sense of human decency, human decency throughout our nation.

This sense of human decency is happily confined to no group or class. You find it in the humblest home. You find it among those who toil, and among the shopkeepers and the farmers of the nation. You find it, to a growing degree, even among those who are listed in that top group which has so much control over the industrial and financial structure of the nation. Therefore, this urge of humanity can by no means be labeled a war of class against class. It is rather a war against poverty and suffering and ill-health and insecurity, a war in which all classes are joining in the interest of a sound and enduring democracy.

I do not believe for a moment, and I know that you do not believe either, that we have fully answered all the needs of human security. But we have covered much of the road. I need not catalogue the milestones of seven years. For every individual and every family in the whole land know that the average of their personal lives has been made safer and sounder and happier than it has ever been before. I do not think they want the gains in these directions to be repealed or even to be placed in the charge of those who would give them mere lip-service with no heart service.

Yes, very much more remains to be done, and I think the voters want the task entrusted to those who believe that the words "human betterment" apply to poor and rich alike.

And I have a sneaking suspicion too, that voters will smile at charges of inefficiency against a Government which has boldly met the enormous problems of banking, and finance and industry which the great efficient bankers and industrialists of the Republican Party left in such hopeless chaos in the famous year 1933.

But we all know that our progress at home and in the other American nations toward this realization of a better human decency—progress along free lines—is gravely endangered by what is happening on other continents. In Europe, many nations, through dictatorships or invasions, have been compelled to abandon normal democratic processes. They have been compelled to adopt forms of government which some call "new and efficient.". . .

Whatever its new trappings and new slogans, tyranny is the oldest and most discredited rule known to history. And whenever tyranny has replaced a more human form of Government it has been due more to internal causes than external. Democracy can thrive only when it enlists the devotion of those whom Lincoln called the common people. Democracy can hold that devotion only when it adequately respects their dignity by so ordering society as to assure to the masses of men and women reasonable security and hope for themselves and for their children.

We in our democracy, and those who live in still unconquered democracies, will never willingly descend to any form of this so called security of efficiency which calls for the abandonment of other securities more vital to the dignity of man. It is our credo unshakable to the end—that we must live under the liberties that were first heralded by Magna Carta and placed into glorious operation through the Declaration of Independence, the Constitution of the United States and the Bill of Rights. . . .

All that I have done to maintain the peace of this country and to prepare it morally, as well as physically, for whatever contingencies may be in store, I submit to the judgment of my countrymen.

> We face one of the great choices of history.
> It is not alone a choice of Government by the people versus dictatorship.
> It is not alone a choice of freedom versus slavery.
> It is not alone a choice between moving forward or falling back.
> It is all of these rolled into one.

It is the continuance of civilization as we know it versus the ultimate destruction of all that we have held dear—religion against godlessness; the ideal of justice against the practice of force; moral decency versus the firing squad; courage to speak out, and to act, versus the false lullaby of appeasement.

But it has been well said that a selfish and greedy people can not be free.

The American people must decide whether these things are worth making sacrifices of money, of energy, and of self. They will not decide by listening to mere words or by reading mere pledges, interpretations and claims. They will decide on the record—the record as it has been made—the record of things as they are.

The American people will sustain the progress of a representative democracy, asking the Divine Blessing as they face the future with courage and with faith.

Source: Samuel I. Rosenman, ed., *The Public Papers and Addresses of Franklin D. Roosevelt* (1941; reprint, New York: Russell and Russell, 1969), 9:293–303.

Document 2.8   Campaign Speech, Philadelphia, October 23, 1940

In his first official speech of the 1940 campaign, FDR reminded voters of the nation's condition when Republicans had been in power and all that the New Deal had accomplished for the American people.

Mr. Chairman, my friends of Philadelphia:

LAST JULY I stated a plain obvious fact, a fact which I told the national convention of my party that the pressure of national defense work and the conduct of national affairs would not allow me to conduct any campaign in the accepted definition of that term.

Since July, hardly a day or a night has passed when some crisis, or some possibility of crisis in world affairs, has not called for my personal conference with our great Secretary of State and with other officials of your Government.

With every passing day has come some urgent problem in connection with our swift production for defense, and our mustering of the resources of the nation.

Therefore, it is essential—I have found it very essential in the national interest—to adhere to the rule never to be more than twelve hours distant from our National Capital.

But last July I also said this to the Chicago Convention: "I shall never be loath to call the attention of the nation to deliberate or unwitting falsifications of fact," which are sometimes made by political candidates.

The time has come for me to do just that.

This night and four other nights, I am taking time to point out to the American people what the more fantastic misstatements of this campaign have been. I emphasize the words "more fantastic," because it would take three hundred and sixty-five nights to discuss all of them.

All these misstatements cannot possibly be what I called last July, "unwitting falsifications" of fact; many of them must be and are "deliberate falsifications" of fact.

The young people who are attending dinners in every State of the Union tonight know that they are already a part of the whole economic and social life of the nation. I am particularly glad to discuss with them—and with you—these misstatements and the facts which refute them.

Truthful campaign discussion of public issues is essential to the American form of Government; but wilful misrepresentation of fact has no place either during election time or at any other time. For example, there can be no objection to any party or any candidate urging that the undeveloped water power of this nation should be harnessed by private utility companies rather than by the Government itself; or that the social security law should be repealed, or that the truth-in-securities act should be abrogated.

But it is an entirely different thing for any party or any candidate to state, for example, that the President of the United States telephoned to Mussolini and Hitler to sell Czechoslovakia down the river; or to state that the unfortunate unemployed of the nation are going to be driven into concentration camps; or that the social security funds of the Government of the United States will not be in existence when the workers of today become old enough to apply for them; or that the election of the present Government means the end of American democracy within four years. I think they know, and I know we know that all those statements are false.

Certain techniques of propaganda, created and developed in dictator countries, have been imported into this campaign. It is the very simple technique of repeating and repeating and repeating falsehoods, with the idea that by constant repetition and reiteration, with no contradiction, the misstatements will finally come to be believed.

Dictators have had great success in using this technique; but only because they were able to control the press and the radio, and to stifle all opposition. That is why I cannot bring myself to believe that in a democracy like ours, where the radio and a part of the press—I repeat, where the radio and a *part* of the press—remain open to both sides, repetition of deliberate misstatements will ever prevail.

I make the charge now that those falsifications are being spread for the purpose of filling the minds and the hearts of the American people with fear. They are used to create fear by instilling in the minds of our people doubt of each other, doubt of their Government, and doubt of the purposes of their democracy.

This type of campaign has a familiar ring. It reminds us of the scarecrow of four years ago, that the social security funds were going to be diverted from the pockets of the American working man.

It reminds us of the famous old scarecrow of 1932, "Grass will grow in the streets of a hundred cities; a thousand towns; the weeds will overrun the fields of millions of farms."

The American people will not be stampeded into panic. The effort failed before and it will fail again. The overwhelming majority of Americans will not be scared by this blitzkrieg of verbal incendiary bombs. They are now calmly aware that, once more, "The only thing we have to fear is fear itself."

I consider it a public duty to answer falsifications with facts. I will not pretend that I find this an unpleasant duty. I am an old campaigner, and I love a good fight.

My friends, the Presidency is not a prize to be won by mere glittering promises. It is not a commodity to be sold by high-pressure salesmanship and national advertising. The Presidency is a most sacred trust and it ought not to be dealt with on any level other than an appeal to reason and humanity.

The worst bombshell of fear which the Republican leaders have let loose on this people is the accusation that this Government of ours, a Government of Republicans and Democrats alike, without the knowledge of the Congress or of the people, has secretly entered into agreements with foreign nations. They even intimate that such commitments have endangered the security of the United States, or are about to endanger it, or have pledged in some way the participation of the United States in some foreign war. It seems almost unnecessary to deny such a charge. But so long as the fantastic misstatement has been made, I must brand it for what it is.

I give to you and to the people of this country this most solemn assurance: There is no secret treaty, no secret obligation, no secret commitment, no secret understanding in any shape or form, direct or indirect, with any other Government, or any other nation in any part of the world, to involve this nation in any war or for any other purpose.

The desperation of partisans who can invent secret treaties drives them to try to deceive our people in other ways. Consider, for example, the false charge they make that our whole industrial system is prostrate—that business is stifled and can make no profits.

The American people have not forgotten the condition of the United States in 1932. We all remember the failures of the banks, the bread line of starving men and women, the youth of the country riding around in freight cars, the farm foreclosures, the home foreclosures, the bankruptcy and the panic.

At the very hour of complete collapse, the American people called for new leadership. That leadership, this Administration and a Democratic Congress supplied.

Government, no longer callous to suffering, moved swiftly to end distress, to halt depression, to secure more social and economic justice for all.

The very same men who must bear the responsibility for the inaction of those days are the ones who now dare falsely to state that we are all still in the depth of the depression into which they plunged us; that we have prevented the country from recovering, and that it is headed for the chaos of bankruptcy. They have even gone to the extent of stating that this Administration has not made one man a job.

I say that those statements are false. I say that the figures of employment, of production, of earnings, of general business activity—all prove that they are false.

The tears, the crocodile tears, for the laboring man and laboring woman now being shed in this campaign come from those same Republican leaders who had their chance to prove their love for labor in 1932—and missed it.

Back in 1932, those leaders, were willing to let the workers starve if they could not get a job.

Back in 1932, they were not willing to guarantee collective bargaining.

Back in 1932, they met the demands of unemployed veterans with troops and tanks.

Back in 1932, they raised their hands in horror at the thought of fixing a minimum wage or maximum hours for labor; they never gave one thought to such things as pensions for old age or insurance for the unemployed.

In 1940, eight years later, what a different tune is played by them! It is a tune played against a sounding board of election day. It is a tune with overtones which whisper: "Votes, votes, votes."

These same Republican leaders are all for the new progressive measures now; they believe in them. They believe in them so much that they will never be happy until they can clasp them to their own chests and put their own brand upon them. If they could only get control of them, they plead, they would take so much better care of them, honest-to-goodness they would. . . .

Let us call the roll of some of the specific improvements in the lot of the working men and women that have come about during the past eight years.

More than forty-two million American employees are now members of the old-age pension system. An additional two million men and women, over sixty-five years of age, are now receiving cash grants each month.

Twenty-nine million American employees have been brought under the protection of unemployment insurance.

Collective bargaining has been guaranteed.

A minimum wage has been established.

A maximum work week of forty hours has been fixed, with provision for time-and-a-half for overtime.

Child labor has been outlawed.

The average hourly earnings of factory workers were fifty-six cents in the boom year of 1929. By February, 1933—before I went to Washington—they had dropped to forty-five cents an hour. They are now sixty-seven cents an hour—not only higher than in 1933, but, mark you, nearly eleven cents an hour higher than in 1929 itself.

Factory pay envelopes—most of you get them—had fallen to five billion dollars a year by 1932. By 1940, factory payrolls are running at the rate of ten billion dollars.

And, something else, we must not forget that the cost of living today is twenty-two per cent lower than it was in 1929. That means something to the average American family.

An equally unpardonable falsification about our economy is made when Republican leaders talk about American business—how it cannot make a profit, how little confidence it has in this Administration, and how this Administration hates business.

We know, if we but look at the record, that American business, big and small business, is way up above the level of 1932, and on a much sounder footing than it was even in the twenties. . . .

If it is true that the New Deal is the enemy of business, and that the Republican leaders, who brought business to the brink of ruin in 1932, are the friends of business—then I can only say that American business should continue to be saved from its friends. . . .

For the American people as a whole—the great body of its citizens—the standard of living has increased well above that of 1929.

We do not advertise "a chicken in every pot" or even "two cars in every garage." We know that it is more important that the American people this year are building more homes, are buying more pairs of shoes, more washing machines, more electric refrigerators, more electric current, more textile products than in the boom year of 1929.

This year there is being placed on the tables of America more butter, more cheese, more meat, more canned goods—more food in general than in that luxurious year of 1929. . . .

Every single man, woman and child has a vital interest in this recovery. But if it can be said to affect any single group more than any other, that group would be the young men and women of America.

It may be hard for some of you younger people to remember the dismal kind of world which the youth of America faced in 1932.

The tragedy of those days has passed. There is today in the youth of the nation a new spirit, a new energy, a new conviction that a sounder and more stable economy is being built for them.

In 1940, this generation of American youth can truly feel that they have a real stake in the United States.

Through many Government agencies these millions of youth have benefited by training, by education, and by jobs. . . .

Tonight there is one more false charge—one outrageously false charge—that has been made to strike terror into the hearts of our citizens. It is a charge that offends every political and religious conviction that I hold dear. It is the charge that this Administration wishes to lead this country into war.

That charge is contrary to every fact, every purpose of the past eight years. Throughout these years my every act and thought have been directed to the end of preserving the peace of the world, and more particularly, the peace of the United States—the peace of the Western Hemisphere.

As I saw the war coming, I used every ounce of the prestige of the office of the President of the United States to prevent its onset.

When war came, I used every ounce of the prestige of the office to prevent its spread to other nations. When the effort failed, I called upon the Congress, and I called upon the nation, to build the strong defenses that would be our best guarantee of peace and security in the American Hemisphere.

To Republicans and Democrats, to every man, woman and child in the nation I say this: Your President and your Secretary of State are following the road to peace.

We are arming ourselves not for any foreign war.

We are arming ourselves not for any purpose of conquest or intervention in foreign disputes. I repeat again that I stand on the Platform of our Party: "We will not participate in foreign wars and we will not send our army, naval or air forces to fight in foreign lands outside of the Americas except in case of attack."

It is for peace that I have labored; and it is for peace that I shall labor all the days of my life.

Source: Samuel I. Rosenman, ed., *The Public Papers and Addresses of Franklin D. Roosevelt* (1941; reprint, New York: Russell and Russell, 1969), 9:485–495.

Document 2.9   Campaign Speech, Boston, October 28, 1940

Responding to Republican charges that he was moving the nation toward war, Roosevelt stated in this campaign address that "Your boys are not going to be sent into any foreign wars."

Mr. Mayor, my friends of New England:

I've had a glorious day here in New England. And I do not need to tell you that I have been glad to come back to my old stamping ground in Boston. There's one thing about this trip that I regret. I have to return to Washington tonight, without getting a chance to go into my two favorite States of Maine and Vermont.

In New York City two nights ago, I showed by the cold print of the Congressional Record how Republican leaders, with their votes and in their speeches, have been playing, and still are playing politics with national defense.

Even during the past three years, when the dangers to all forms of democracy throughout the world have been obvious, the Republican team in the Congress has been acting only as a Party team.

Time after time, Republican leadership refused to see that what this country needs is an all-American team.

Those side-line critics are now saying that we are not doing enough for our national defense. I say to you that we are going full speed ahead! . . .

And within the past two months your Government has acquired new naval and air bases in British territory in the Atlantic Ocean; extending all the way from Newfoundland in the north to that part of South America where the Atlantic Ocean begins to get narrow, with Africa not far away.

I repeat: Our objective is to keep any potential attacker as far from our continental shores as we possibly can. . . .

Campaign orators seek to tear down the morale of the American people when they make false statements about the Army's equipment. I say to you that we are supplying our Army with the best fighting equipment in all the world.

Yes, the Army and the Defense Commission are getting things done with speed and efficiency. More than eight billion dollars of contracts for defense have been let in the past few months.

I am afraid that those campaign orators will pretty soon be under the painful necessity of coming down to Washington later on and eating their words. . . .

And while I am talking to you mothers and fathers, I give you one more assurance.

I have said this before, but I shall say it again and again and again:

Your boys are not going to be sent into any foreign wars.

They are going into training to form a force so strong that, by its very existence, it will keep the threat of war far away from our shores.

The purpose of our defense is defense. . . .

In ten months this Nation has increased our engine output for planes 240 per cent; and I am proud of it.

Remember, too, that we are scattering them allover the country. We are building brand new plants for airplanes and airplane engines in places besides the Pacific Coast and this coast.

We are also building them in centers in the Middle West.

Last spring and last winter this great production capacity program was stepped up by orders from overseas. In taking these orders for planes from overseas, we are following and were following hard-headed self-interest.

Building on the foundation provided by these orders, the British on the other side of the ocean are receiving a steady stream of airplanes. After three months of blitzkrieg in the air over there, the strength of the Royal Air Force is actually greater now than when the attack began. And they know and we know that that increase in strength despite battle losses is due in part to the purchases made from American airplane industries. . . .

The productive capacity of the United States which has made it the greatest industrial country in the world, is not failing now. It will make us the strongest air power in the world. And that is not just a campaign promise!

I have been glad in the past two or three days to welcome back to the shores of America that Boston boy, beloved by all of Boston and a lot of other places, my Ambassador to the Court of St. James, Joe Kennedy.

Actually on the scene where planes were fighting and bombs were dropping day and night for many months, he has been telling me just what you and I have visualized from afar—that all the smaller independent nations of Europe—Sweden, Switzerland, Greece, Ireland and the others—have lived in terror of the destruction of their independence by Nazi military might.

And so, my friends, we are building up our armed defenses to their highest peak of efficiency for a very good reason, the reason of the possibility of real national danger to us; but these defenses will be inadequate unless we support them with a strong national morale, a sound economy, a sense of solidarity and economic and social justice.

When this Administration first came to office, the foundation of that national morale was crumbling. In the panic and misery of those days no democracy could have built up an adequate armed defense.

What we have done since 1933 has been written in terms of improvement in the daily life and work of the common man. . . .

I would not single him out except that he is of national interest now, because at the time of his appointment as Republican National Chairman this handsome verbal bouquet, this expensive orchid, was pinned upon him: "In public life for many years Joe Martin has represented all that is finest in American public life."

Considering the source of that orchid, Martin must be slated for some Cabinet post. So let's look for a minute at the voting record of this representative of what they call, "all that is finest in American public life." Martin voted against the Public Utility Holding Company Act, the Tennessee Valley Authority Act, the National Securities Exchange Act, and the extension of the Civilian Conservation Corps Act. He voted against practically all relief and work relief measures, and against the appropriation for rural electrification.

Martin voted against the Civil Service Extension Act and against the United States Housing Act.

What I particularly want to say on the radio to the farmers of the Nation, and to you here in this hall, is that Republican National Chairman Martin voted against every single one of the farm measures that were recommended by this Administration. Perhaps Brother Martin will be rewarded for this loyal service to the principles of his party by being appointed Secretary of Agriculture.

He is one of that great historic trio which has voted consistently against every measure for the relief of agriculture—Martin, Barton and Fish. [Bruce Barton and Hamilton Fish were conservative Republican congressmen.]

I have to let you in on a secret. It will come as a great surprise to you. And it's this:

I'm enjoying this campaign. I'm really having a fine time.

I think you know that the office of President has not been an easy one during the past years.

The tragedies of this distracted world have weighed heavily on all of us.

But—there is revival for everyone of us in the sight of our own national community.

In our own American community we have sought to submerge all the old hatreds, all the old fears, of the old world.

We are Anglo-Saxon and Latin, we are Irish and Teuton and Jewish and Scandinavian and Slav—we are American. We belong to many races and colors and creeds—we are American.

And it seems to me that we are most completely, most loudly, most proudly American around Election Day.

Because it is then that we can assert ourselves—voters and candidates alike. We can assert the most glorious, the most encouraging fact in all the world today—the fact that democracy is alive—and going strong.

We are telling the world that we are free—and we intend to remain free and at peace.

We are free to live and love and laugh.

We face the future with confidence and courage. We are American.

Source: Samuel I. Rosenman, ed., *The Public Papers and Addresses of Franklin D. Roosevelt* (1941; reprint, New York: Russell and Russell, 1969), 9:514–524.

Document 2.10   News Conference, December 28, 1943

In this news conference at the end of 1943, Roosevelt foreshadowed his fourth presidential campaign by saying that Dr. Win-the-War had replaced Dr. New Deal. But he also said he was looking forward to new programs after the war.

. . . *Q.* Mr. President, after our last meeting with you, it appears that someone stayed behind and received word that you no longer like the term "New Deal." Would you care to express any opinion to the rest of us?

THE PRESIDENT: Oh, I supposed somebody would ask that. I will have to be terribly careful in the future how I talk to people after these press conferences. However, what he reported was accurate reporting, and—well, I hesitated for a bit as to whether I would say anything. It all comes down, really, to a rather puerile and political side of things. I think that the two go very well together—puerile and political.

However, of course lots of people have to be told how to spell "cat," even people with a normally good education. And so I got thinking the thing over, and I jotted down some things that a lot of people who can't spell "cat" had forgotten entirely.

And of course, the net of it is this—how did the New Deal come into existence? It was because there was an awfully sick patient called the United States of America, and it was suffering from a grave internal disorder—awfully sick—all kinds of things had happened to this patient, all internal things. And they sent for the doctor. And it was a long, long process—took several years before those ills, in that particular illness of ten years ago, were remedied. But after a while they were remedied. And on all those ills of 1933, things had to be done to cure the patient internally. And it was done; it took a number of years.

And there were certain specific remedies that the old doctor gave the patient, and I jotted down a few of those remedies. The people who are peddling all this talk about "New Deal" today, they are not telling about why the patient had to have remedies. I am inclined to think that the country ought to have it brought back to their memories, and I think the country ought to be asked too, as to whether all these rather inexperienced critics shouldn't be asked directly just which of the remedies should be taken away from the patient, if you should come down with a similar illness in the future. It's all right now— it's all right internally now—if they just leave him alone.

But since then, two years ago, the patient had a very bad accident—not an internal trouble. Two years ago, on the seventh of December, he was in a pretty bad smashup—broke his hip, broke his leg in two or three places, broke a wrist and an arm, and some ribs; and they didn't think he would live, for a while. And then he began to "come to"; and he has been in charge of a partner of the old doctor. Old Dr. New Deal didn't know "nothing" about legs and arms. He knew a great deal about internal medicine, but nothing about surgery. So he got his partner, who was an orthopedic surgeon, Dr. Win-the-War, to take care of this fellow who had been in this bad accident. And the result is that the patient is back on his feet. He has given up his crutches. He isn't wholly well yet, and he won't be until he wins the war .

And I think that is almost as simple, that little allegory, as learning again how to spell "cat."

The remedies that the old Dr. New Deal used were for internal troubles. He saved the banks of the United States and set up a sound banking system. We don't need to change the law now, although obviously there are some people who don't like saving the banks who would like to change the whole system, so that banks would have the great privilege under American freedom of going "bust" any time they wanted to again.

Well, at the same time, one of the old remedies was Federal deposit insurance, to guarantee bank deposits; and yet I suppose there must be some people, because they make so much smoke, who would like to go back to the old system and let any bank, at will, go and lose all its depositors' money with no redress.

In those days, another remedy was saving homes from foreclosure, through the H.O.L.C. [Home Owners' Loan Corporation]; saving farms from foreclosure by the Farm Credit Administration. I suppose some people today would like to repeal all that and go back to the conditions of 1932, when the people out West mobbed a Federal Judge because he was trying to carry out the existing law of the land in foreclosing a farm; rescuing agriculture from disaster—which it was pretty close to—by the Triple A [Agricultural Adjustment Administration] and Soil Conservation; establishing truth in the sale of securities and protecting stock investors through the S.E.C. [Securities and Exchange Commission] And yet I happen to know that there is an undercover drive going on in this country today to repeal the S.E.C., and "let's sell blue-sky securities to the widows and orphans and everybody else in this country." A lot of people would like to do that, take off all the rules and let old Mr. Skin skin the public again.

Well, we have got slum clearance—decent housing; and there hasn't been enough done on slum clearance. I don't think that people who go into slums in this country would advocate stopping that, or curtailing the program, although of course a small percentage of real-estate men would like to have slums back again, because they pay money.

Reduction of farm tenancy.

Well, your old doctor, in the old clays, old Doctor New Deal, he put in old-age insurance, he put in unemployment insurance. I don't think the country would want to give up old-age insurance or unemployment insurance, although there are a lot of people in the country who would like to keep us from having it.

We are taking care of a great many crippled and blind people, giving a great deal of maternity help, through the Federal aid system. Well, some people want to abolish it all.

And the public works Program, to provide work, to build thousands of permanent improvements—incidentally, giving work to the unemployed, both the P.W.A. [Public Works Administration] and W.P.A. [Works Progress Administration]

Federal funds, through F.E.R.A. [Federal Emergency Relief Administration], to starving people.

The principle of a minimum wage and maximum hours.

Civilian Conservation Corps.

Reforestation.

The N.Y.A. [National Youth Administration], for thousands of literally underprivileged young people.

Abolishing child labor. It was not thought to be constitutional in the old days, but it turned out to be.

Reciprocal trade agreements, which of course do have a tremendous effect on internal diseases.

Stimulation of private home building through the F.H.A. [Federal Housing Administration].

The protection of consumers from extortionate rates by utilities. The breaking up of utility monopolies, through Sam Rayburn's [Rayburn was a Democratic congressman from Texas] law.

The resettlement of farmers from marginal lands that ought not to be cultivated; regional physical developments, such as T.V.A. [Tennessee

Valley Authority]; getting electricity out to the farmers through the R.E.A. [Rural Electrification Administration]; flood control; and water conservation; drought control—remember the years we went through that!—and drought relief; crop insurance, and the ever normal granary; and assistance to farm cooperatives. Well, conservation of natural resources.

Well, my list just totaled up to thirty, and I probably left out half of them. But at the present time, obviously, the principal emphasis, the overwhelming first emphasis should be on winning the war. In other words, we are suffering from that bad accident, not from an internal disease.

And when victory comes, the program of the past, of course, has got to be carried on, in my judgment, with what is going on in other countries—postwar program—because it will pay. We can't go into an economic isolationism, any more than it would pay to go into a military isolationism.

This is not just a question of dollars and cents, although some people think it is. It is a question of the long range, which ties in human beings with dollars, to the benefit of the dollars and the benefit of the human beings as apart of this postwar program, which of course hasn't been settled on at all, except in generalities.

But, as I said about the meeting in Teheran and the meeting in Cairo, we are still in the generality stage, not in the detail stage, because we are talking about principles. Later on we will come down to the detail stage, and we can take up anything at all and discuss it then. We don't want to confuse people by talking about it now.

But it seems pretty clear that we must plan for, and help to bring about, an expanded economy which will result in more security, in more employment, in more recreation, in more education, in more health, in better housing for all of our citizens, so that the conditions of 1932 and the beginning of 1933 won't come back again.

Now, have those words been sufficiently simple and understood for you to write a story about?

Q. Does that all add up to a fourth-term declaration? (Laughter)

THE PRESIDENT: Oh, now, we are not talking about things like that now. You are getting picayune. That's a grand word to use—another word beginning with a *p*—picayune. I know you won't mind my saying that, but I have to say something like that.

Q. *I* don't mean to be picayune, but I am not clear about this parable. The New Deal, I thought, was dynamic, and I don't know whether you mean that you had to leave off to win the war and then will take up again the social program, or whether you think the patient is cured?

THE PRESIDENT: I will explain it this way. I will ask you a question.

In 1865, after the Civil War, there was a definite program arranged for and carried through under the leadership of the Congressman from Pennsylvania, Thaddeus Stevens, who was the leader of the Republican Party at that time. That was the policy. It lasted for nearly ten years, a policy of repression and punishment of the whole of the South. That was the policy of the United States. Well, they didn't like it at all—the country didn't. And finally, after ten years, they threw it out.

Now, do you think that twenty-five years later, in 1890, that we should have gone back to the same old policy? I don't. The country didn't go back to it.

You have a program to meet the needs of the country. The 1933 program that started to go into effect that year took a great many years. If you remember what I said, it was a program to meet the problems of 1933. Now, in time, there will have to be a new program, whoever runs the Government.

We are not talking in terms of 1933's program. We have done nearly all of that, but that doesn't avoid or make impossible or unneedful another program, when the time comes. When the time comes.

Source: Samuel I. Rosenman, ed., *The Public Papers and Addresses of Franklin D. Roosevelt* (1950; reprint, New York: Russell and Russell, 1969), 12:569–575.

Document 2.11   Speech Accepting a Fourth Presidential Nomination, San Diego, July 20, 1944

FDR accepted the 1944 Democratic presidential nomination by radio from a naval base in San Diego. He indicated that in the midst of the war he would not campaign in the usual sense.

I HAVE already indicated to you why I accept the nomination that you have offered me—in spite of my desire to retire to the quiet of private life.

You in this Convention are aware of what I have sought to gain for the Nation, and you have asked me to continue.

It seems wholly likely that within the next four years our armed forces, and those of our allies, will have gained a complete victory over Germany and Japan, sooner or later, and that the whole world once more will be at peace—under a system, we hope that will prevent a new world war. In any event, whenever that time comes, new hands will then have full opportunity to realize the ideals which we seek.

In the last three elections the people of the United States have transcended party affiliation. Not only Democrats but also forward-looking Republicans and millions of independent voters have turned to progressive leadership—a leadership which has sought consistently—and with fair success—to advance the lot of the average American citizen who had been so forgotten during the period after the last war. I am confident that they will continue to look to that same kind of liberalism to build our safer economy for the future.

I am sure that you will understand me when I say that my decision, expressed to you formally tonight, is based solely on a sense of obligation to serve if called upon to do so by the people of the United States.

I shall not campaign, in the usual sense, for the office. In these days of tragic sorrow, I do not consider it fitting. And besides, in these days of global warfare, I shall not be able to find the time. I shall, however, feel free to report to the people the facts about matters of concern to them and especially to correct any misrepresentations.

During the past few days I have been coming across the whole width of the continent, to a naval base where I am speaking to you now from the train.

As I was crossing the fertile lands and the wide plains and the Great Divide, I could not fail to think of the new relationship between the people of our farms and cities and villages and the people of the rest of the world overseas—on the islands of the Pacific, in the Far East, and in the other Americas, in Britain and Normandy and Germany and Poland and Russia itself.

For Oklahoma and California, for example, are becoming a part of all these distant spots as greatly as Massachusetts and Virginia were a part of the European picture in 1778. Today, Oklahoma and California are being defended in Normandy and on Saipan; and they must be defended there—for what happens in Normandy and Saipan vitally affects the security and well-being of every human being in Oklahoma and California.

Mankind changes the scope and the breadth of its thought and vision slowly indeed. In the days of the Roman Empire eyes were focused on Europe and the Mediterranean area. The civilization in the Far East was barely known. The American continents were unheard of.

And even after the people of Europe began to spill over to other continents, the people of North America in Colonial days knew only their Atlantic seaboard and a tiny portion of the other Americas, and they turned mostly for trade and international relationship to Europe. Africa, at that time, was considered only as the provider of human chattels. Asia was essentially unknown to our ancestors.

During the nineteenth century, during that era of development and expansion on this continent, we felt a natural isolation—geographic, economic, and political—an isolation from the vast world which lay overseas.

Not until this generation—roughly this century—have people here and elsewhere been compelled more and more to widen the orbit of their vision to include every part of the world. Yes, it has been a wrench perhaps—but a very necessary one.

It is good that we are all getting that broader vision. For we shall need it after the war. The isolationists and the ostriches who plagued our thinking before Pearl Harbor are becoming slowly extinct. The American people now know that all Nations of the world—large and small—will have to play their appropriate part in keeping the peace by force, and in deciding peacefully the disputes which might lead to war.

We all know how truly the world has become one—that if Germany and Japan, for example, were to come through this war with their philosophies established and their armies intact, our own grandchildren would again have to be fighting in their day for their liberties and their lives.

Some day soon we shall all be able to fly to any other part of the world within twenty-four hours. Oceans will no longer figure as greatly in our physical defense as they have in the past. For our own safety and for our own economic good, therefore if for no other reason—we must take a leading part in the maintenance of peace and in the increase of trade among all the Nations of the world.

And that is why your Government for many, many months has been laying plans, and studying the problems of the near future—preparing itself to act so that the people of the United States may not suffer hardships after the war, may continue constantly to improve their standards, and may join with other Nations in doing the same. There are even now working toward that end, the best staff in all our history—men and women of all parties and from every part of the Nation. I realize that planning is a word which in some places brings forth sneers. But, for example, before our entry into the war it was planning which made possible the magnificent organization and equipment of the Army and Navy of the United States which are fighting for us and for our civilization today.

Improvement through planning is the order of the day. Even in military affairs, things do not stand still. An army or a navy trained and equipped and fighting according to a 1932 model would not have been a safe reliance in 1944. And if we are to progress in our civilization, improvement is necessary in other fields—in the physical things that are a part of our daily lives, and also in the concepts of social justice at home and abroad.

I am now at this naval base in the performance of my duties under the Constitution. The war waits for no elections. Decisions must be made—plans must be laid—strategy must be carried out. They do not concern merely a party or a group. They will affect the daily lives of Americans for generations to come.

What is the job before us in 1944? First, to win the war—to win the war fast, to win it overpoweringly. Second, to form worldwide international organizations, and to arrange to use the armed forces of the sovereign Nations of the world to make another war impossible within the foreseeable future. And third, to build an economy for our returning veterans and for all Americans—which will provide employment and provide decent standards of living.

The people of the United States will decide this fall whether they wish to turn over this 1944 job—this worldwide job—to inexperienced or immature hands, to those who opposed lend-lease and international cooperation against the forces of aggression and tyranny, until they could read the polls of popular sentiment; or whether they wish to leave it to those who saw the danger from abroad, who met it head-on, and who now have seized the offensive and carried the war to its present stages of success—to those who, by international conferences and united actions have begun to build that kind of common understanding and cooperative experience which will be so necessary in the world to come.

They will also decide, these people of ours, whether they will entrust the task of postwar reconversion to those who offered the veterans of the last war breadlines and apple-selling and who finally led the American people down to the abyss of 1932; or whether they will leave it to those who rescued American business, agriculture, industry, finance, and labor in 1933, and who have already planned and put through much legislation to help our veterans resume their normal occupations in a well-ordered reconversion process.

They will not decide these questions by reading glowing words or plat-form pledges—the mouthings of those who are willing to promise any-thing and everything—contradictions, inconsistencies, impossibilities—anything which might snare a few votes here and a few votes there.

They will decide on the record—the record written on the seas, on the land, and in the skies.

They will decide on the record of our domestic accomplishments in recovery and reform since March 4, 1933.

And they will decide on the record of our war production and food pro-duction—unparalleled in all history, in spite of the doubts and sneers of those in high places who said it cannot be done.

They will decide on the record of the International Food Conference, of U.N.R.R.A. [United Nations Relief and Rehabilitation Administration], of the International Labor Conference, of the International Education Conference, of the International Monetary Conference.

And they will decide on the record written in the Atlantic Charter, at Casablanca, at Cairo, at Moscow, and at Teheran.

We have made mistakes. Who has not?

Things will not always be perfect. Are they ever perfect, in human affairs?

But the objective at home and abroad has always been clear before us. Constantly, we have made steady, sure progress toward that objective. The record is plain and unmistakable as to that—a record for everyone to read.

The greatest wartime President in our history, after a wartime election which he called the "most reliable indication of public purpose in this country," set the goal for the United States, a goal in terms as applicable today as they were in 1865 terms which the human mind cannot improve:

". . . with firmness in the right, as God gives us to see the right, let us strive on to finish the work we are in; to bind up the Nation's wounds; to care for him who shall have borne the battle, and for his widow, and his orphan—to do all which may achieve and cherish a just and lasting peace among ourselves, and with all Nations."

Source: Samuel I. Rosenman, ed., *The Public Papers and Addresses of Franklin D. Roosevelt* (1950; reprint, New York: Russell and Russell, 1969), 13:201–206.

Document 2.12   Speech at Teamsters Dinner, Washington, D.C., September 23, 1944

The only major question that voters had about FDR in 1944 concerned his health. His aides and family were worried about what sort of performance he would give in his speech to the Teamsters union in September. It turned out to be a triumph for Roosevelt. This speech is best remembered for his humorous defense of his dog against alleged Republican attacks.

WELL, here we are together again—after four years—and what years they have been! You know, I am actually four years older, which is a fact that seems to annoy some people. In fact, in the mathematical field there are millions of Americans who are more than eleven years older than when we started in to clear up the mess that was dumped in our laps in 1933.

We all know that certain people who make it a practice to depreciate the accomplishments of labor—who even attack labor as unpatriotic—they keep this up usually for three years and six months in a row. But then, for some strange reason they change their tune—every four years   just before election day. When votes are at stake, they suddenly discover that they really love labor and that they are anxious to protect labor from its old friends.

I got quite a laugh, for example—and I am sure that you did—when I read this plank in the Republican platform adopted at their National Convention in Chicago last July:

"The Republican Party accepts the purposes of the National Labor Relations Act, the Wage and Hour Act, the Social Security Act and all other Federal statutes designed to promote and protect the welfare of American working men and women, and we promise a fair and just administration of these laws."

You know, many of the Republican leaders and Congressmen and candidates, who shouted enthusiastic approval of that plank in that Convention Hall would not even recognize these progressive laws if they met them in broad daylight. Indeed, they have personally spent years of effort and energy—and much money—in fighting everyone of those laws in the Congress, and in the press, and in the courts, ever since this Administration began to advocate them and enact them into legislation. That is a fair example of their insincerity and of their inconsistency.

The whole purpose of Republican oratory these days seems to be to switch labels. The object is to persuade the American people that the Democratic Party was responsible for the 1929 crash and the depression, and that the Republican Party was responsible for all social progress under the New Deal.

Now, imitation may be the sincerest form of flattery—but I am afraid that in this case it is the most obvious common or garden variety of fraud.

Of course, it is perfectly true that there are enlightened, liberal elements in the Republican Party, and they have fought hard and honorably to bring the Party up to date and to get it in step with the forward march of American progress. But these liberal elements were not able to drive the Old Guard Republicans from their Republican positions.

Can the Old Guard pass itself off as the New Deal?

I think not.

We have all seen many marvelous stunts in the circus but no performing elephant could turn a hand-spring without falling flat on his back.

I need not recount to you the centuries of history which have been crowded into these four years since I saw you last.

There were some—in the Congress and out—who raised their voices against our preparations for defense—before and after 1939—objected to them, raised their voices against them as hysterical war mongering, who cried out against our help to the Allies as provocative and dangerous. We remember the voices. They would like to have us forget them now. But in 1940 and 1941—my, it seems a long time ago—they were loud voices. Happily they were a minority and—fortunately for ourselves, and for the world—they could not stop America.

There are some politicians who kept their heads buried deep in the sand while the storms of Europe and Asia were headed our way, who said that the lend-lease bill "would bring an end to free government in the United States," and who said, "only hysteria entertains the idea that Germany, Italy, or Japan contemplates war on us." These very men are now asking the American people to intrust to them the conduct of our foreign policy and our military policy.

What the Republican leaders are now saying in effect is this:

"Oh, just forget what we used to say, we have changed our minds now—we have been reading the public opinion polls about these things and now we know what the American people want." And they say: "Don't leave the task of making the peace to those old men who first urged it and who have already laid the foundations for it, and who have had to fight all of us inch by inch during the last five years to do it. Why, just turn it all over to us. We'll do it so skillfully—that we won't lose a single isolationist vote or a single isolationist campaign contribution."

I think there is one thing that you know: I am too old for that.

I cannot talk out of both sides of my mouth at the same time. . . .

And while I am on the subject of voting, let me urge every American citizen—man and woman—to use your sacred privilege of voting, no matter which candidate you expect to support. Our millions of soldiers and sailors and merchant seamen have been handicapped or prevented from voting by those politicians and candidates who think that they stand to lose by such votes. You here at home have the freedom of the ballot. Irrespective of party, you should register and vote this November. I think that is a matter of plain good citizenship.

Words come easily, but they do not change the record. You are, most of you, old enough to remember what things were like for labor in 1932.

You remember the closed banks and the breadlines and the starvation wages; the foreclosures of homes and farms, and the bankruptcies of business; the "Hoovervilles," and the young men and women of the Nation facing a hopeless, jobless future; the closed factories and mines and mills; the ruined and abandoned farms; the stalled railroads and the empty docks; the blank despair of a whole Nation—and the utter impotence of the Federal Government.

You remember the long, hard road, with its gains and its setbacks, which we have traveled together ever since those days.

Now there are some politicians who do not remember that far back, and there are some who remember but find it convenient to forget. No, the record is not to be washed away that easily.

The opposition in this year has already imported into this campaign a very interesting thing, because it is foreign. They have imported the propaganda technique invented by the dictators abroad. Remember, a number of years ago, there was a book, *Mein Kampf*, written by Hitler himself. The technique was all set out in Hitler's book—and it was copied by the aggressors of Italy and Japan. According to that technique, you should never use a small falsehood; always a big one, for its very fantastic nature would make it more credible—if only you keep repeating it over and over and over again.

Well, let us take some simple illustrations that come to mind. For example, although I rubbed my eyes when I read it, we have been told that it was not a Republican depression, but a Democratic depression from which

this Nation was saved in 1933 that this Administration—this one—today—
is responsible for all the suffering and misery that the history books and
the American people have always thought had been brought about during
the twelve ill-fated years when the Republican party was in power.

Now, there is an old and somewhat lugubrious adage which says:
"Never speak of rope in the house of a man who has been hanged." In the
same way, if I were a Republican leader speaking to a mixed audience, the
last word in the whole dictionary that I think I would use is that word
"depression." . . .

But perhaps the most ridiculous of these campaign falsifications is the
one that this Administration failed to prepare for the war that was coming.
I doubt whether even Goebbels [Joseph Goebbels was the Nazi's propaganda and culture minister] would have tried that one. For even he would
never have dared hope that the voters of America had already forgotten that
many of the Republican leaders in the Congress and outside the Congress
tried to thwart and block nearly every attempt that this Administration made
to warn our people and to arm our Nation. Some of them called our 50,000
airplane program fantastic. Many of those very same leaders who fought
every defense measure that we proposed are still in control of the Republican party—look at their names—were in control of its National Convention in Chicago, and would be in control of the machinery of the Congress
and of the Republican party, in the event of a Republican victory this fall.

These Republican leaders have not been content with attacks on me, or
my wife, or on my sons. No, not content with that, they now include my
little dog, Fala. Well, of course, I don't resent attacks, and my family does-
n't resent attacks, but Fala *does* resent them. You know, Fala is Scotch, and
being a Scottie, as soon as he learned that the Republican fiction writers in
Congress and out had concocted a story that I had left him behind on the
Aleutian Islands and had sent a destroyer back to find him—at a cost to
the taxpayers of two or three, or eight or twenty million dollars—his Scotch
soul was furious. He has not been the same dog since. I am accustomed to
hearing malicious falsehoods about myself—such as that old, worm-eaten
chestnut that I have represented myself as indispensable. But I think I have
a right to resent, to object to libelous statements about my dog.

Well, I think we all recognize the old technique. The people of this
country know the past too well to be deceived into forgetting. Too much
is at stake to forget. There are tasks ahead of us which we must now complete with the same will and the same skill and intelligence and devotion
that have already led us so far along the road to victory.

There is the task of finishing victoriously this most terrible of all wars as speedily as possible and with the least cost in lives.

There is the task of setting up international machinery to assure that the peace, once established, will not again be broken.

And there is the task that we face here at home—the task of reconverting our economy from the purposes of war to the purposes of peace.

These peace-building tasks were faced once before, nearly a generation ago. They were botched by a Republican administration. That must not happen this time. We will not let it happen this time.

Fortunately, we do not begin from scratch. Much has been done. Much more is under way. The fruits of victory this time will not be apples sold on street corners. . . .

This is not the time in which men can be forgotten as they were in the Republican catastrophe that we inherited. The returning soldiers, the workers by their machines, the farmers in the field, the miners, the men and women in offices and shops, do not intend to be forgotten.

No, they know that they are not surplus. Because they know that they are America.

We must set targets and objectives for the future which will seem impossible—like the airplanes—to those who live in and are weighted down by the dead past.

We are even now organizing the logistics of the peace, just as Marshall and King and Arnold, MacArthur, Eisenhower, and Nimitz are organizing the logistics of this war.

I think that the victory of the American people and their allies in this war will be far more than a victory against Fascism and reaction and the dead hand of despotism of the past. The victory of the American people and their allies in this war will be a victory for democracy. It will constitute such an affirmation of the strength and power and vitality of government by the people as history has never before witnessed.

And so, my friends, we have had affirmation of the vitality of democratic government behind us, that demonstration of its resilience and its capacity for decision and for action—we have that knowledge of our own strength and power—we move forward with God's help to the greatest epoch of free achievement by free men that the world has ever known.

Source: Samuel I. Rosenman, ed., *The Public Papers and Addresses of Franklin D. Roosevelt* (1950; reprint, New York: Russell and Russell, 1969), 13:284–292.

Roosevelt holds a "fireside chat" on New Deal work relief programs, Washington, D.C., April 28, 1935.

CHAPTER THREE

Administration Policies

The three plus administrations of Franklin D. Roosevelt developed significant initiatives in all the major policy categories. The Great Depression's toll on society and the economy demanded responses in domestic, economic, and trade policy. The massive drought that transformed large portions of the Great Plains into the dust bowl required new environmental policies. And the rise of fascism and Japanese militarism, followed by World War II, required momentous foreign policy decisions.

DOMESTIC POLICY

Franklin Roosevelt's domestic policy was more substantial and far-reaching than any president before him. Largely a response to the second greatest domestic crisis (after the Civil War) in American history, the Great Depression, the policies are generally placed under the collective label, "the New Deal," but that singular name obscures a variety of sometimes conflicting approaches.

Unlike his predecessor, Herbert Hoover, FDR was not wedded to any particular ideology. Rather, as he had famously said during the 1932 presidential campaign, he believed in an experimental approach: "It is common sense to take a method and try it: If it fails, admit it frankly and try another. But above all, try something" (Rosenman 1969, 1:646). FDR

121

tried many "somethings," some of which worked well, others less well, and some not at all. But the sheer magnitude of the domestic proposals and legislation was without precedent.

Historians have long debated whether the first New Deal (1933) differed in approach from the second New Deal (1935), and some historians have identified a third New Deal (after 1937), which they say adopted yet another general approach. Others argue that there was not enough consistency in the varied proposals in any of these periods to define changes in direction.

In Roosevelt's first inaugural address he said that, if circumstances warranted it, he would ask Congress for "broad Executive power to wage a war against the emergency, as great as the power that would be given to me if we were in fact invaded by a foreign foe" (Rosenman 1969, 2:11–16; see Document 3.1). The foe in 1933 was primarily domestic, and the first maneuvers in Roosevelt's war—the banking bill (which sought to restore confidence in the nation's banking system without fundamentally reforming it) and the Economy Act (which sought to reduce government spending)—looked more like collaboration with the enemy than an attack against it. That course would soon change somewhat, as Roosevelt was fond of feinting in one direction and then taking another. If a war it was, Roosevelt was undeniably the commander in chief, and his role in the remarkable barrage of governmental action fired at the enemy was very large, but its nature is often misunderstood. Although FDR lacked ideological consistency and had no clear plan of exactly what he wanted to do, he did clearly believe in certain basic principles, such as social interdependence and the need for active government. He sought a society, as he put it in his first inaugural address, based on "social values more noble than mere monetary profit" (Rosenman 1969, 2:12). FDR's vision of an ideal society was akin to that of a Progressive Era mayor of Toledo, Ohio, Samuel "Golden Rule" Jones: get everyone to treat others as they would want to be treated themselves. A nice idea, but one difficult to reconcile with an economic system based on the pursuit of self-interest. And an amorphous goal at best, for Roosevelt was unclear about the specifics of how to achieve it. Rather, he favored an experimental approach and the blending even of seemingly incompatible ideas.

For all his inconsistencies, however, Roosevelt's domestic policies were tied together by the principles of social interdependence and active government. He believed that excessive competition could be detrimental to the public interest, that government had a responsibility to assist those most in need, and that a system based on the free market must be maintained but regulated to curb the more serious problems that competition could produce. Thus the New Deal's basic domestic objective was to reform capitalism, but certainly not to abolish it.

The nation's domestic problems were so overwhelming and diverse when Roosevelt took office that any serious attempt to address them required a multitude of proposals. The first New Deal was based largely on the progressive tradition and particularly on Theodore Roosevelt's postpresidential "New Nationalism" concept of using big government to regulate big business for the public good. This was especially evident in the National Recovery Administration, which brought together competing businesses in each industry to draw up a code of acceptable practices, including minimum wages and maximum hours, to which all participants were to adhere. (For details on the measures of the first and second New Deals, see Chapter 5.)

Though Roosevelt's leadership skills were crucial in providing the momentum that produced the flood of legislation in the spring of 1933, he initiated only two of the fifteen major laws passed in the first hundred days, the Economy Act and the Civilian Conservation Corps (CCC). The president helped create several of the other measures of the early New Deal, but they were at least as much the products of his advisers and members of Congress as they were Roosevelt's offspring.

Relief, Recovery, and Reform

One way to categorize the domestic policies in the New Deal is to divide them into the three areas that Roosevelt advocated: relief, recovery, and reform. Providing relief to those suffering the most from unemployment was the first priority. And the first line of attack was the Federal Emergency Relief Administration (FERA), which provided direct monetary and food relief to people in dire need. Like Hoover, Roosevelt was convinced that giving people "handouts" would undermine their self-respect, initiative, and self-reliance. Unlike Hoover, however, FDR understood that starvation was worse. Both Roosevelt and his chief relief administrator, Harry Hopkins, saw work relief (the provision of a government-sponsored job in exchange for relief payments) as preferable to a dole (direct relief payments with no work requirement), but they understood that the need for quick action required at least a temporary program of direct relief. With Hopkins's prodding, Roosevelt pushed a huge work relief program to help the unemployed get through the first winter of his administration, in 1933–1934. The Civil Works Administration (CWA) demonstrated the efficacy of work relief in lifting people's spirits and at least temporarily reviving their self-respect. Although Roosevelt closed down the CWA early in 1934, it served as a model for the much larger Works Progress Administration (WPA) that was launched a year later.

Roosevelt's initial quest for economic recovery involved an attempt, carried out through the Agricultural Adjustment Administration (AAA), to restore farmers' purchasing power and a more direct attempt to stimulate the economy through the National Industrial Recovery Act (NIRA). These will be discussed in the "Economy" section of this chapter.

If the short-term goals of Roosevelt's domestic policy were relief and recovery, the long-term goal was lasting reforms. These included reforms to prevent another economic collapse and reforms that would further progressives' long-held objectives. Because some of the long-range reforms might help instigate recovery and because the crisis atmosphere and Roosevelt's extraordinary popularity in the early months of his administration made the time ripe for reform, the president began offering reform measures during his first months in office without awaiting the achievement of relief and recovery.

One of the largest reforms was simply to increase the role of the federal government in the economic and social life of the United States. This expanded role shone through in all of the relief and recovery measures. The AAA sought to establish a lasting reform of American agriculture as well as an immediate revival of the economy through increased purchasing power for farm families. The NIRA included a provision—section 7(a)—that protected labor unions. Although employers subverted this section by setting up company-dominated unions, it set the precedent for the National Labor Relations Act (Wagner Act) of 1935, one of the most important long-term reforms of the New Deal. It made it possible for workers in mass production industries to form and join labor unions, through which they were able to raise themselves into a middle-class standard of living. The federally facilitated unionization of mass production workers also helped to prevent future economic collapses by assuring that large numbers of Americans would have greater purchasing power.

The creation of the Tennessee Valley Authority (TVA), an experiment in regional planning and development, was one of Roosevelt's major efforts at reform. The TVA will be discussed in the "Environment" section of this chapter.

Another reform of the first hundred days of the New Deal (and also a relief measure) was the Home Owners' Loan Act, which created the Home Owners' Loan Corporation (HOLC), through which the federal government took over the mortgages of home buyers who were unable to meet the payments. Although this legislation was of greater benefit to banks and other lenders than to home owners, it did assist many of the latter to keep houses that they would otherwise have lost in foreclosures.

Surely the most important reform of the New Deal was the establishment of old-age and unemployment insurance through the Social Security Act of 1935 (see Document 3.2). This long-sought-after objective brought the United States more in line with other industrial nations in the area of social protections, but pressure from conservatives and interest groups forced the system to be scaled back from the plan originally envisioned. Health insurance, for example, was not included because of the powerful opposition of the American Medical Association.

Similarly, the Fair Labor Standards Act of 1938 was a significant but watered-down achievement. This legislation achieved one of the major goals espoused by progressives earlier in the century: placing a federally mandated floor under wages and an upper limit on the hours a person could work in a week. But political pressures, particularly from southern Democrats, kept some occupations most in need of these protections, such as agriculture and domestic labor, out of the bill's coverage. (For more on the Social Security Act, the Fair Labor Standards Act, and other legislation mentioned in this chapter, see Chapter 4.)

The half-a-loaf tactic used in the Social Security Act and the wages and hours legislation is a prime example of Franklin Roosevelt's belief that politics is the art of the possible. Despite frequent lobbying by his wife, Eleanor, and Secretary of the Interior Harold Ickes, FDR did not attempt to obtain legislation that would directly benefit racial minorities. He refused, most notably, to put his prestige behind a move to make lynching a federal crime. Roosevelt felt that such a bill would only meet with a filibuster in the Senate, and that his open support for it would alienate southern Democrats, whose favor he needed to pass other social legislation. Instead, FDR tried to secure programs that would help the poorest Americans, who were often blacks and other minorities. This was successful enough that a large majority of blacks shifted from the Republican to the Democratic Party during Roosevelt's first term.

The one notable exception to Roosevelt's hands-off policy on race came in 1941, when a movement led by A. Philip Randolph, president of the Brotherhood of Sleeping Car Porters, called for a massive march on Washington to demand equal opportunity in defense industries and desegregation of the armed forces. Concerned that the march might give the country a bad image, especially if whites attacked the marchers, the president sent his wife, Eleanor, a noted champion of civil rights, to try to talk Randolph and other march organizers out of proceeding. When this failed, Roosevelt issued an executive order (8802) that established a Fair Employment Practices Commission (FEPC) to look into allegations of bias in industries with government contracts for military equipment (see Document 3.3).

Domestic Policy in Wartime

American entry into World War II did not spell the end of Roosevelt's concern with domestic policy. Indeed, those who had complained about the growth of federal power and regulation of the economy during the New Deal saw a much greater expansion of controls after the war began. For the most part, business was somewhat more amenable to controls in wartime, and the new "alphabet soup" of wartime agencies, including the War Production Board (WPB), the Office of War Mobilization (OWM), the Office of Production Management (OPM), and the Office of Price Administration and Civilian Supply (OPA) were generally successful in directing production to assist the war effort, rationing scarce consumer items, and checking inflation. Business participated partly because Roosevelt was more willing to have the government enter into cooperative arrangements with business than he had been in preceding years, thus making government intervention more of a help than a hindrance to business interests.

But Roosevelt was not through with reform in the New Deal spirit. Indeed, some progressive measures that had stalled in Congress before the war passed through easily during wartime. In the fall of 1942 Roosevelt appointed a committee of educators to devise a plan to provide postwar education for veterans. Enacted in 1944, the G.I. Bill of Rights helped hundreds of thousands of veterans receive a college or technical education and helped many veterans buy homes with low-interest, government-backed mortgages (see Document 3.4). The G.I. Bill and the earlier Wagner Act opened the American dream of home ownership and a middle class lifestyle to millions of Americans who never had the opportunity before FDR's presidency.

ECONOMIC POLICY

The economy was, of course, the dominant concern of Roosevelt's first term and much of his second term. The new president believed that restoring the purchasing power of the one-quarter of Americans who depended on agriculture for their income was the key to reviving the economy. Therefore he concentrated on developing farm legislation and had no intention of proposing an industrial recovery program.

The Black Bill soon prompted FDR into action on industrial recovery. Authored by Sen. Hugo L. Black, D-Ala., and introduced in December 1932, the bill would limit workers who manufactured products sold in interstate commerce to thirty hours of work per week. The intent of the Black Bill was to spread work among more people and, it was hoped, increase purchasing power by putting wages in more hands. The president did not favor this approach, but when the Senate passed it in April 1933 he felt that he could not afford to veto the bill, so he decided to head it off by offering an alternate program for industrial recovery. The result was the 1933 National Industrial Recovery Act, which created the National Recovery Administration (NRA) and the Public Works Administration (PWA; see Document 3.5).

The first part of this dual approach to industrial recovery was to restore confidence and improve buying power by setting minimum wages, working conditions, and the like to reduce competition among businesses. This was, as historian William Leuchtenburg neatly put it, an attempt to "civilize competition" (Leuchtenburg 1963, 69). The second part was the creation of a massive public construction program that would employ workers on the projects and also stimulate other industries by increasing demand for the materials needed in building roads, dams, bridges, and other structures. The NRA was not particularly successful, and the Supreme Court pronounced it unconstitutional in the 1935 case of *Schechter Poultry Corp. v. United States* (see Chapter 5). The

PWA was more successful, but moved much too slowly to stimulate economic recovery.

Another major development in economic policy in the early months of the New Deal was Roosevelt's decision to take the United States off the gold standard, thus enabling the U.S. government to control the domestic supply of money. Sen. Elmer Thomas, D-Okla., had added to the agriculture bill an amendment that would prescribe steps to bring about price inflation. When Senate leaders told FDR that the Thomas Amendment could not be blocked, he decided to accept it as long as the president had a variety of inflationary methods from which to choose. FDR's budget director, Lewis Douglas, pronounced the president's agreement to pursue inflation to be "the end of Western civilization" (Leuchtenburg 1963, 50). But Roosevelt's decision on April 19, 1933, to take the nation off the gold standard was a key move that stemmed deflation and made it possible to take other economic measures toward recovery without international factors getting in the way.

Among the many sectors of the economy that clearly needed reform in 1933 was the stock market, whose unchecked excesses had helped produce the 1929 crash. The reform had two major parts: the Truth-in-Securities Act, signed into law in May 1933, which required full disclosure in the issuance of all new securities, and the Securities Exchange Act of 1934, which created the Securities and Exchange Commission (SEC) to oversee the stock market.

The Roosevelt administration moved to stabilize and restore confidence in the nation's banking system by supporting the provisions in the Glass-Steagall bill separating investment from commercial banking and creating the Federal Deposit Insurance Corporation (FDIC) to insure small bank deposits. Roosevelt was skeptical of the FDIC, but, as he usually did, tried to make a virtue of necessity by accepting what he could not prevent.

FDR made effective use of the Reconstruction Finance Corporation (RFC), which had been started under President Herbert Hoover. Under the direction of Jesse Jones, the RFC was transformed from a lender propping up banks into the nation's largest single source of investment in economic expansion.

The important economic measures of the second New Deal of 1935, in addition to the Wagner Act and the Social Security Act, were the immense Emergency Relief Appropriation (which pumped into the economy an unprecedented $4.8 billion of stimulus, the lion's share of which went to the new Works Progress Administration), the Public Utilities Holding Company Act (also called the Wheeler-Rayburn Act), and the "Wealth Tax Act." The utilities bill took a different approach from such earlier New Deal initiatives as the NRA by seeking to break up large (in this instance, utility) corporations rather than use big government to regulate big business. The bill that finally became law under the misnomer of the Wealth Tax Act of 1935 did little to increase taxes on the wealthy or redistribute income or wealth. It was the result of a message that Roosevelt sent to Congress in June 1935 calling for higher personal income tax rates for the top brackets, a graduated corporate income tax, and federal inheritance and gift taxes (see Document 5.4.) The message was effective politically, but the final version that became law did no more than impose token estate and corporate taxes.

Although FDR engaged in low levels of deficit spending as a matter of social, economic, and political necessity, he refused to accept the teachings of British economist John Maynard Keynes, which called for the intentional creation of large deficits to stimulate the depressed economy. Thus when Roosevelt's reelection was secured in 1936, a president fearful of incurring too much debt for the nation ordered substantial cuts in spending, especially for WPA work relief programs. This action, combined with other factors, led to a new and sharp downturn in the economy in 1937–1938. Roosevelt had no choice but to increase spending again on work relief to try to stem this "recession." In April 1938 the president, who blamed his enemies in big business for the new downturn, called for an investigation of the concentration of economic power. The Temporary National Economic Committee (TNEC), chaired by Sen. Joseph O'Mahoney, D-Wyo., postponed any real action while it held hearings and worked on a report for nearly three years. In fact, as former aide Raymond Moley said, the president's call for the TNEC study was "the final expression of Roosevelt's personal indecision about what policy his administration ought to follow in its relation with business" (Moley 1939, 376).

The coming of World War II created an economic policy for Roosevelt. That policy was unintentional Keynesianism. Preparation for the war and then participation in it forced massive deficit spending and finally brought about recovery through the method prescribed by Keynes and by American economists William Trufant Foster and Waddill Catchings as early as 1930.

The war also brought other substantial changes in Roosevelt's economic policy.

Both taxation and regulation increased during World War II. Such agencies as the Office of Price Administration, Office of Production Management, War Production Board, and War Labor Board regulated the economy to a degree unprecedented in American history. Tax rates on the highest incomes and on excess war profits reached above 90 percent. The sort of soaking of the rich to which Roosevelt had given lip service in 1935 had come to pass by the time of his death a decade later. This tax policy and, more important, the full employment produced by the war, lessened the maldistribution of income that had been a major cause of the economic collapse.

ENVIRONMENTAL POLICY

Like his kinsman Theodore Roosevelt, FDR was a committed conservationist. He also had a sense of stewardship from his aristocratic upbringing. Roosevelt put these values into practice as governor of New York and continued as president to pursue projects that protected resources and the environment. In his first three years in the White House, Roosevelt more than tripled the amount of land in the national forest system. Long a champion of public power, particularly at the federally built dam at Muscle Shoals, Alabama, Roosevelt moved dramatically as president to combine soil conservation, human development, and public power in the establishment of the Tennessee Valley Authority.

The Civilian Conservation Corps (CCC), which sent young men into wilderness areas to do conservation work, was probably the program dearest to FDR's heart. Although criticized in some quarters for its quasi military organization, the CCC accomplished a great deal of worthwhile conservation work in national parks and forests and elsewhere. It even did a good amount of human conservation by providing useful employment in healthy surroundings for 2.5 million poor youths, many of them from the congested and polluted cities. The CCC was particularly important in reforestation work.

Workers on the Civil Works Administration and WPA also engaged in many conservation activities, and the Agricultural Adjustment Administration worked on soil conservation. Through the shelterbelt project Roosevelt introduced the federal government into the effort to overcome the environmental catastrophe of the dust bowl, the vast region on the plains of Texas, Oklahoma, Colorado, New Mexico, and Kansas that was hit by severe drought and resulting massive dust storms in the mid 1930s. The administration made other efforts through the Soil Conservation Service and the Taylor Grazing Act, which regulated grazing on public lands. FDR's administration was, in fact, the first to see soil conservation as an important objective. *Fortune* magazine suggested in 1935 that in the distant future saving the nation's soil resources might be seen as the decade's most lasting accomplishment.

TRADE POLICY

Roosevelt was unsure about where he should stand on trade policy. During the 1932 campaign, when he was given two opposing drafts of a speech on trade policy, one advocating protectionism and the other free trade, FDR asked a dumbstruck Raymond Moley to combine them. Wavering at the outset of his presidency between a desire to increase trade and a need to seal the American economy off from foreign influence to try to revive it, Roosevelt at first strongly pushed the idea that the World Economic Conference (to be held in London in June 1933) might be able to lift the planet out of depression. Then he did an abrupt about-face and sent what was called a "bombshell message" to the conference, stating that the United States would refuse to go along with any stabilization of the value of the dollar in relation to other currencies, thus dooming the conference (see Document 3.6).

Although Roosevelt followed the advice of such economic nationalists as Raymond Moley and Rexford Tugwell and decided to pursue a go-it-alone strategy for bringing about economic recovery in the United States, he did endorse reciprocal trade agreements. This concept, favored by Secretary of State Cordell Hull, avoided the political thicket of attempting general tariff reduction by giving the president the authority to negotiate mutually beneficial trade agreements with other nations. The Trade Agreements Act of 1934 gave Roosevelt the power to work out reciprocal agreements to reduce tariffs by up to 50 percent.

The 1944 wartime economic conference at Bretton Woods, New Hampshire, pointed toward a more interrelated world economy in the postwar period by laying the groundwork for the International Monetary Fund and the World Bank. Although Roosevelt did not play a direct role in this effort, he was very much in favor of creating such institutions and helped to initiate the discussions.

FOREIGN POLICY

The unprecedented economic crisis the nation confronted at the beginning of Franklin Roosevelt's presidency obliged him to concentrate his policy efforts on domestic issues. Foreign policy necessarily took a back seat, especially after Roosevelt decided to pursue recovery at home rather than through international effort. FDR was, however, always interested in foreign affairs, and he turned his attention increasingly in that direction as his long presidency evolved.

An Internationalist President
Leads an Isolationist Country

FDR's service in the Woodrow Wilson administration and his admiration for Theodore Roosevelt had inspired FDR to make a mark in world affairs. But as a committed Wilsonian internationalist he found himself presiding over a nation that was solidly isolationist throughout the 1930s. In domestic policy FDR followed the principle that politics was the art of the possible. Similarly, he moved cautiously in foreign policy, trying to be sure that he did not get too far in front of his constituents. He demonstrated this modus operandi even before he won the Democratic nomination in 1932, when he reversed himself and said he opposed U.S. entry into the League of Nations. This reversal, though a disappointment to some, won over William Randolph Hearst and other isolationists in the party.

Roosevelt's first significant foray into foreign policy, the fiasco of the World Economic Conference in 1933, was not auspicious. Through the mid-1930s Roosevelt was certainly much more internationalist than the increasingly isolationist American populace. His support for a Good Neighbor policy toward Latin America, though composed more of rhetoric than substance, indicated a growth from his immature boasting in 1920 about having written Haiti's constitution. Perhaps more important, it was a break with the long tradition of almost automatic United States intervention in any Latin American nation facing a crisis. FDR was, in short, taking at least short steps away from the Latin American policies of Theodore Roosevelt and Wilson. The Good Neighbor policy was an implicit modification of the (Theodore) Roosevelt Corollary to the Monroe Doctrine and of Wilson's policies toward Mexico and the Caribbean, both of which had involved unilateral United States intervention whenever the U.S. government thought it warranted.

In reaction to the major international crises of the middle years of the decade—German rearmament, Italy's invasion of Ethiopia, the Spanish Civil War, and Japan's invasion of China—Roosevelt felt constrained by public opinion from acting as forcefully as he would have liked. The president believed that the world was headed toward war and that the growing belligerence of Nazi Germany was a threat not only to Europe but to the United States as well. But the popular view in the United States, fueled by revisionist historians and a 1934 Senate investigation headed by Gerald P. Nye, R-N.D., of the role of the armaments industry and other economic interests in bringing the United States into World War I, was that the nation had been led into war in 1917 by special interests. With this in mind Congress passed the Neutrality Act of 1935, which placed a mandatory embargo on American shipments of implements of war to any belligerent in a war. Roosevelt reluctantly signed the bill into law. When Congress passed the more sweeping Neutrality Act of 1937, which extended the arms embargo to civil wars, thus blocking any aid to the Spanish Republic in its fight against fascist rebels, Roosevelt raised no public objection.

Roosevelt did, however, test the possibilities of getting public support for a bolder foreign policy when he declared in an October 1937 speech in Chicago that if aggressor nations succeeded in other parts of the world, the United States would be in danger. He proposed a "quarantine" to keep the disease of war contained within those nations (Rosenman 1969, 6:411; see Document 3.7). The reaction from isolationists was bitter, with several members of Congress calling for Roosevelt's impeachment. "It's a terrible thing to look over your shoulder when you're trying to lead," the president lamented, "and to find no one there" (Burns 1956, 318–319). Just how reluctant Americans were to consider going to war was made clear ten weeks after the Quarantine Speech when Japanese planes bombed an American gunboat, the *Panay*, in the Yangtze River in China. It was unquestionably a deliberate act and it killed two Americans and wounded several others. Yet instead of clamoring for war, as Americans had done in 1898 after the (likely accidental) sinking of the *Maine*, which led to war with Spain, the public insisted that the nation avoid war. Given the public mood and FDR's declining popularity, there was little he could do but watch as Adolf Hitler incorporated Austria into the German Reich in early 1938 and the British and French sought to appease him by agreeing at Munich in October to allow him to take over a portion of Czechoslovakia.

The crisis in Europe grew quickly in the weeks after the Munich conference. When the Nazis unleashed a brutal nationwide attack on Jews in November (*Kristallnacht,* the Night of Broken Glass), FDR recalled the American ambassador to Berlin and declared at a press conference, "I myself could scarcely believe that such things could occur in a twentieth century civilization" (Freidel 1990, 314).

Roosevelt shared his true feelings on the ominous situation in Europe in early 1939 when he told a group of senators that German expansion threatened the entire world. He was misquoted in the press as having said that America's frontier was on the Rhine. Though this brought cheer to many in France and Britain, it produced another storm of outrage from isolationists in the United States. When Hitler abandoned his pledge to respect the independence of the remainder of Czechoslovakia by taking over the country in March and then demanding that Germany be ceded the Free City of Danzig and a route across the Polish Corridor that separated East Prussia from the rest of Germany, Roosevelt became less restrained in his public statements. He called on Hitler and Mussolini to pledge not to attack a list of thirty-one countries. The two dictators responded with sarcasm and contempt. Lacking public support, the president could do no more.

Escalation Brings Intervention

When Germany, following the signing of a nonaggression pact with the Soviet Union, invaded Poland on September 1, 1939, the new European war Roosevelt had long anticipated was underway. The president could not avoid issuing a proclamation of American neutrality, as was required by the 1937 Neutrality Act. But he made it clear that he was not impartial in this war. In a "fireside chat" on September 3, FDR told the people directly that he would not repeat Woodrow Wilson's call of 1914 for impartial thinking. "Even a neutral," he said, "cannot be asked to close his mind or his conscience." Roosevelt did promise, though, to keep the United States out of the war "as long as it remains within my power" (Rosenman 1969, 8:463–464).

The German army quickly overran much of Poland, with the Soviets occupying eastern portions of the country. Then came the "phony war." German troops did not move on other fronts through the winter of 1939–1940. Spring, however, brought a rapid succession of campaigns by the highly mobile German forces—*blitzkrieg*, "lightning war," it was called—that conquered Denmark, Norway, the Netherlands, Belgium, Luxembourg, and moved into France. Roosevelt called for a rapid buildup of American military capacity to defend the nation and the Western Hemisphere. By putting the issue in these terms, the president outflanked isolationists and won support for his program. After France fell to the Germans in June 1940, Roosevelt had to choose between trying to help the British survive and forsaking them to devote all American military production to U.S. forces. The new British prime minister, Winston Churchill, worked feverishly to persuade Roosevelt to help Britain. Roosevelt's first impression of Churchill's fitness for the job did not strengthen the British case. When FDR first heard of Churchill's elevation to the head of government, he told members of his cabinet that Churchill might be the best man the British had, even though he was drunk half the time.

Nonetheless, Roosevelt took steps to help the British withstand the German onslaught. The first significant move was an agreement in the fall of 1940 to exchange fifty old naval destroyers for long-term American leases on bases at ports in several British possessions in the western Atlantic (see Document 3.8).

Soon after Roosevelt's reelection that year, he moved more decisively to aid the beleaguered British. First, he proposed a way to continue to send military equipment to the British when they could no longer pay cash for it. The so-called Lend-Lease program allowed Britain to "borrow" ships and other military goods with the understanding that they would either be returned after the war or that Britain would pay for them at that time. In a fireside chat at the end of 1940, Roosevelt told the American people that the United States must become "the great arsenal for democracy" (Rosenman 1969, 9:643). In his annual message to Congress in January 1941, Roosevelt set forth his vision for the future of the world in what amounted to a statement of war aims by the leader of a nation that was not in the war. The Four Freedoms that he enunciated at that time—freedom of speech and religion and freedom from want and fear—would become the basis of U.S. objectives when it entered the war (see Document 3.9).

As 1941 went on, Roosevelt moved more completely into full cooperation with the British. American naval vessels began protecting British
convoys across much of the Atlantic. Following Hitler's sudden attack
on the Soviet Union in July, the United States extended Lend-Lease aid
to the Soviets. Then in August Roosevelt met with Churchill at Argen-
tia Harbor, Newfoundland. There they agreed to a joint declaration that
came to be known as the Atlantic Charter. Once again, and now in concert with one of the belligerents, Roosevelt was setting forth war aims
for a war in which his country was not an official belligerent (see Document 3.10).

That status was to be changed less than four months after the Atlantic
Charter by events in the Pacific. The United States had been increasing pressure on the Japanese to cease their brutal war in China. Economic sanctions cut off high-grade scrap metal and aviation gasoline
shipments from the United States to Japan in July of 1940, stopped all
scrap metal shipments three months later, and then froze Japanese
assets in the United States and placed an embargo on all oil sales in July
1941. But pressure and sanctions were achieving no better results in Asia
than appeasement had in Europe. The more bellicose elements in the
Japanese military gained the upper hand in the government and with
Emperor Hirohito by arguing that the United States could never be
counted upon to treat Japan fairly or to be a reliable supplier of raw
materials. These militants set the Japan on a course of war with the
United States, beginning with a surprise attack on the U.S. naval instal-
lation at Pearl Harbor in December 1941. (For details on American
entry into World War II, see Chapter 4.)

Axis and Allies

After Pearl Harbor, Roosevelt's true internationalist sentiments could
come to the fore. He became the leader of the struggle against fascism.
He quickly developed a partnership with Churchill that would prove crucial to Roosevelt's role as wartime leader. Delighted that the Japanese
had finally brought the United States into the war (and that Hitler had
then foolishly declared war on the United States, removing the possibility that an enraged American public and Congress would declare war
only on Japan and leave the British and Soviets to deal with Hitler),
Churchill wasted no time in traveling to Washington to meet with Roosevelt and make joint war plans.

There was no disagreement between the now formal allies that the war strategy must be based on the principle of "Europe first." Although Japan had attacked the United States, Roosevelt firmly believed that Germany was the more formidable foe and that the major war effort must be aimed at Europe. Churchill was able quickly to convince FDR that the first step should be an attack on German forces in North Africa. Now that he was in the war at last, the American president was eager for what he had called for almost nine years earlier in the context of the depression: "action, and action now" (Rosenman 1969, 2:12). Indeed, although the campaign in North Africa was somewhat questionable (several U.S. military leaders saw it as Churchill's attempt to use U.S. troops to protect the British Empire rather than defeat Germany quickly), Roosevelt believed it necessary to involve U.S. troops in combat as soon as was practicable so that Americans would see themselves as truly engaged in war. The resulting Operation Torch did not start until November 1942, but the foundation had been laid in Washington, D.C., in December 1941 and January 1942. On New Year's Day, 1942, Roosevelt, Churchill, and representatives of the Soviet Union and China signed a document creating what Roosevelt had decided to call the United Nations, pledging themselves to carry on the war to victory and to pursue the ideals that had been set forth in the Atlantic Charter.

Meanwhile, as Soviet dictator Josef Stalin continued to demand the opening of a western front on the continent of Europe so that the Germans would have to move troops away from the Russian front, Roosevelt journeyed to Casablanca, Morocco, in January 1943 to meet again with Churchill and discuss the next phase of the war and the war's ultimate goals. Roosevelt was delighted with all the precedents he was breaking with the trip. He became the first president to fly, the first to leave the United States during wartime, and the first since Lincoln to visit a war zone. The Casablanca conference had two major outcomes. One was Roosevelt's announcement that the Allies would accept nothing less than the unconditional surrender of Germany and Japan. Why? The Allied leaders wanted to avoid a repeat of the situation at the end of World War I, when Germany had not been invaded at the time of the armistice. This had made it possible for Hitler to convince many Germans that they had not really lost the war, but rather, that the German military, which Hitler claimed could still have won the war, had been stabbed in the back by the new republic set up at the end of the war. On the whole the unconditional surrender doctrine worked well, as the successful reconstruction of Germany and Japan after the war attests. There is, however, some question about whether the policy hindered efforts to obtain Japanese surrender before the dropping of atomic bombs.

The other outcome of Casablanca was much more dubious. Churchill again persuaded Roosevelt that it was not time to invade Europe across the English Channel. Instead, the British leader argued for a strike at what he termed the "soft underbelly" of the continent—to move from North Africa to Sicily and then the Italian mainland. The resulting Italian campaign in 1943 accomplished little of strategic importance and proved to be a harsh trek up the mountainous peninsula in which U.S. and British forces suffered heavy casualties.

Stalin finally joined the other two major Allied leaders in person for the first time at Teheran, Iran, in late 1943. Following a meeting with Churchill and Chinese generalissimo Chiang Kai-shek in Cairo, Roosevelt flew to Teheran for his first meeting with the Soviet dictator. The actions of the western Allies in Africa and Italy had provided little relief for the embattled Soviet troops on the Russian front and had fueled Stalin's suspicions that Churchill and Roosevelt were conspiring to ensure that the Soviet Red Army would suffer the bulk of the casualties in the fight against Germany. The three major Allies differed in their visions for the postwar world. Stalin was adamant about a Soviet sphere of influence in Eastern Europe to serve as a buffer against yet another German invasion. Churchill was not opposed to spheres of influence as long as that included the maintenance of the British Empire. Roosevelt, the old Wilsonian, wanted to place supervision of postwar world security in the hands of a world body (the United Nations), but with dependence on four major powers—the United States, Britain, the Soviet Union, and China—to act as "four policemen" with special responsibilities for security (Freidel 1990, 486–487). FDR, like most Americans, had little interest in preserving Britain's hold on its colonies. The major Allies did not reach an agreement on any of this at Teheran, but they did set a date for an invasion of France across the English Channel, Operation Overlord, in the spring of 1944.

That summer, delegates of the United States, Britain, and the Soviet Union met at a residence called Dumbarton Oaks in the Georgetown section of Washington, D.C. Their mission was dear to Roosevelt's heart: create an international organization to replace the League of Nations that could achieve Woodrow Wilson's dream of lasting world peace. The Dumbarton Oaks meeting ended with agreement on the outlines of such an organization, but with serious differences on such issues as major power veto of action by the United Nations and the number of votes that the Soviet Union would have.

As the war in Europe neared its end, no clear agreement had yet been reached among the Allies on the shape of the postwar world. To address this question once more, Roosevelt and Churchill journeyed in February 1945 to the resort town of Yalta on the Crimean Peninsula in the Soviet Union to meet with Stalin. This, Roosevelt's final "Big Three" conference, settled nothing in Europe. His health in serious decline and exhausted from the long trip, FDR tried to get Soviet agreement for a democratic government in Poland, but with the Red Army occupying the country that had three times in a century and a half served as a route of terrible invasion into Russia (Napoleon and the two world wars), Stalin would not be budged from his demand for a Soviet-friendly government in Poland. Given the hostility between Poland and the Soviets, no democratic government could meet that criterion. Roosevelt returned home with little accomplished, but he put a good face on it when he reported to Congress on the Yalta conference in March (see Document 3.11).

When Franklin Roosevelt died on April 12, 1945, he missed by two weeks the beginning of the meeting in San Francisco that would complete one of his major foreign policy objectives, the creation of the United Nations. He missed by less than a month the final victory over Germany and by four months the defeat of Japan. Nonetheless, by the time of his death it was clear that all of these key elements of FDR's foreign policy would be achieved. Roosevelt's legacy in world affairs would be as lasting as his legacy in domestic politics and in the American society and economy.

BIBLIOGRAPHY

Roosevelt's policies in all areas of his presidency are discussed thoroughly in David M. Kennedy, *Freedom from Fear: The American People in Depression and War, 1929–1945* (New York: Oxford University Press, 1999).

FDR's domestic policy is examined in the major studies of the New Deal, including Anthony J. Badger, *The New Deal* (New York: Farrar, Straus, and Giroux, 1989); Paul Conkin, *The New Deal*, 3d ed. (Arlington

Heights, Ill.: Harlan-Davidson, 1992); Robert S. McElvaine, *The Great Depression: America, 1929–1941* (New York: Times Books, 1993); and Roger Biles, *A New Deal for the American People* (DeKalb: Northern Illinois University Press, 1991).

Economic policy is explored in William J. Barber, *Designs within Disorder: Franklin D. Roosevelt, the Economists, and the Shaping of American Economic Policy* (New York: Cambridge University Press, 1996); Theodore Rosenof, *Economics in the Long Run: New Deal Theorists and Their Legacies* (Chapel Hill: University of North Carolina Press, 1997); Ellis W. Hawley, *The New Deal and the Problem of Monopoly* (1966; reprint, New York: Fordham University Press, 1995); and Albert U. Romasco, *The Politics of Recovery* (New York: Oxford University Press, 1983). David E. Hamilton, *From New Day to New Deal: American Farm Policy from Hoover to Roosevelt* (Chapel Hill: University of North Carolina Press, 1991) examines the Roosevelt administration's agricultural policies. Bernard Bellush, *The Failure of the NRA* (New York: Norton, 1975) provides an account of the administration's first attempt to bring about economic recovery.

Donald Worster, *Dust Bowl: The Southern Plains in the 1930s* (New York: Oxford University Press, 1979) is the starting point for studying the environment in the 1930s. Catherine McNicol Stock, *Main Street in Crisis: The Great Depression and the Old Middle Class on the Northern Plains* (Chapel Hill: University of North Carolina Press, 1992) is excellent on the human effects of the environmental disaster stemming from the drought of the decade. Thomas K. McGraw, *TVA and the Power Fight* (Philadelphia: Lippincott, 1971) examines the New Deal agency that had one of the most important impacts on the environment.

Some aspects of trade policy can be studied through Cordell Hull, *Memoirs* (New York: Macmillan, 1948) and Lloyd C. Gardner, *Economic Aspects of New Deal Diplomacy* (Madison: University of Wisconsin Press, 1964).

Robert Dallek, *Franklin D. Roosevelt and American Foreign Policy, 1933–1945* (New York: Oxford University Press, 1979) is the place to begin a deeper exploration of Roosevelt's foreign policies. Warren F. Kimball, *The Juggler: Franklin Roosevelt as Wartime Statesman* (Princeton: Princeton University Press, 1991) sees FDR's wartime foreign policy as pursuing consistent objectives. Frederick W. Marks III, *Wind over Sand: The Diplomacy of Franklin D. Roosevelt* (Athens: University of Georgia Press, 1988) takes a much more critical view of Roosevelt's diplomatic policies. Henry L. Stimson and McGeorge Bundy, *On Active Service in Peace and War* (New York: Harper, 1948) criticizes some aspects of FDR's foreign policy for not being sufficiently interventionist. Waldo Heinrichs, *Threshold of War: Franklin D. Roosevelt and American Entry into World War II* (New York: Oxford University Press, 1988) is more sympathetic to the obstacles Roosevelt faced in bringing the country into a more interventionist position. Russell D. Buhite, *Decisions at Yalta: An Appraisal of Summit Diplomacy* (Wilmington, Del.: Scholarly Resources, 1986) provides a good introduction to Roosevelt's controversial last Big Three meeting.

Additional works cited in this chapter are James MacGregor Burns, *Roosevelt: The Lion and the Fox* (New York: Harcourt, Brace, and World, 1956); Frank Freidel, *Franklin D. Roosevelt: A Rendezvous with Destiny* (Boston: Little, Brown, 1990); William E. Leuchtenburg, *Franklin D. Roosevelt and the New Deal* (New York: Harper and Row, 1963); Raymond Moley, *After Seven Years: A Political Analysis of the New Deal* (New York: Harper and Brothers, 1939); and Samuel I. Rosenman, ed., *The Public Papers and Addresses of Franklin D. Roosevelt*, 13 vols. (1938–1950; reprint, New York: Russell and Russell, 1969).

Document 3.1   First Presidential Inaugural Address, March 4, 1933

Roosevelt's first inaugural address is one of the most famous speeches in U.S. history. By reassuring the American people that "the only thing [they had] to fear [was] fear itself," the new president lifted spirits in a way that outgoing president Herbert Hoover had never been able to do. In addition, Roosevelt spoke of themes that were among his most basic beliefs: interdependence and the need to use government to advance the public interest.

I AM CERTAIN that my fellow Americans expect that on my induction into the Presidency I will address them with a candor and a decision which the present situation of our Nation impels. This is preeminently the time to speak the truth, the whole truth, frankly and boldly. . . . So, first of all, let me assert my firm belief that the only thing we have to fear is fear itself—nameless, unreasoning, unjustified terror which paralyzes needed efforts to convert retreat into advance. In every dark hour of our national life a leadership of frankness and vigor has met with that understanding and support of the people themselves which is essential to victory. I am convinced that you will again give that support to leadership in these critical days.

In such a spirit on my part and on yours we face our common difficulties. They concern, thank God, only material things. Values have shrunken to fantastic levels; taxes have risen; our ability to pay has fallen; government of all kinds is faced by serious curtailment of income; the means of exchange are frozen in the currents of trade; the withered leaves of industrial enterprise lie on every side; farmers find no markets for their produce; the savings of many years in thousands of families are gone.

More important, a host of unemployed citizens face the grim problem of existence, and an equally great number toil with little return. Only a foolish optimist can deny the dark realities of the moment.

Yet our distress comes from no failure of substance. . . . Plenty is at our doorstep, but a generous use of it languishes in the very sight of the supply. Primarily this is because rulers of the exchange of mankind's goods have failed through their own stubbornness and their own incompetence, have admitted their failure, and have abdicated. Practices of the unscrupulous money changers stand indicted in the court of public opinion, rejected by the hearts and minds of men.

True they have tried, but their efforts have been cast in the pattern of an outworn tradition. Faced by failure of credit they have proposed only the lending of more money. Stripped of the lure of profit by which to induce our people to follow their false leadership, they have resorted to exhortations, pleading tearfully for restored confidence. They know only the rules of a generation of self-seekers. They have no vision, and when there is no vision the people perish.

The money changers have fled from their high seats in the temple of our civilization. We may now restore that temple to the ancient truths. The measure of the restoration lies in the extent to which we apply social values more noble than mere monetary profit.

. . . The joy and moral stimulation of work no longer must be forgotten in the mad chase of evanescent profits. These dark days will be worth all they cost us if they teach us that our true destiny is not to be ministered unto but to minister to ourselves and to our fellow men.

Recognition of the falsity of material wealth as the standard of success goes hand in hand with the abandonment of the false belief that public office and high political position are to be valued only by the standards of pride of place and personal profit; and there must be an end to a conduct in banking and business which too often has given to a sacred trust the likeness of callous and selfish wrongdoing. Small wonder that confidence languishes, for it thrives only on honesty, on honor, the sacredness of obligations, on faithful protection, on unselfish performance; without them it cannot live.

Restoration calls, however, not for changes in ethics alone. This nation asks for action, and action now. . . .

If I read the temper of our people correctly, we now realize as we have never realized before our interdependence on each other; that we cannot merely take but we must give as well; that if we are to go forward, we must move as a trained and loyal army willing to sacrifice for the good of a common discipline, because without such discipline no progress is made, no leadership becomes effective. We are, I know, ready and willing to submit our lives and property to such discipline, because it makes possible a lead ership which aims at a larger good. This I propose to offer, pledging that the larger purposes will bind upon us all as a sacred obligation with a unity of duty hitherto evoked only in time of armed strife.

With this pledge taken, I assume unhesitatingly the leadership of this great army of our people dedicated to a disciplined attack upon our common problems. . . .

I am prepared under my constitutional duty to recommend measures that a stricken Nation in the midst of a stricken world may require. These measures, or such other measures as the Congress may build out of its experience and wisdom, I shall seek in my constitutional authority, to bring to speedy adoption.

But in the event that the Congress shall fail to take one of these two courses, and in the event that the national emergency is still critical, I shall not evade the clear course of duty that will then confront me. I shall ask the Congress for the one remaining instrument to meet the crisis—broad Executive power to wage a war against the emergency, as great as the power that would be given to me if we were in fact invaded by a foreign foe. . . .

We do not distrust the future of essential democracy. The people of the United States have not failed. In their need they have registered a mandate that they want direct, vigorous action. They have asked for discipline and direction under leadership. They have made me the present instrument of their wishes. In the spirit of the gift I take it. . . .

Source: Samuel I. Rosenman, ed., *The Public Papers and Addresses of Franklin D. Roosevelt* (1938; reprint, New York: Russell and Russell, 1969), 2:11–16.

––––––––––

Document 3.2   The Social Security Act, August 14, 1935

The Social Security Act, a major feature of the "second New Deal" of 1935, was probably the most important reform of the Roosevelt presidency. It provided for federal old-age pensions, survivors' benefits, and an unemployment insurance system. Some observers criticized the plan because it was funded by a regressive payroll tax; it left out some of the poorest workers, including farm laborers and domestic servants; and it did not include health insurance.

AN ACT

To provide for the general welfare by establishing a system of Federal old-age benefits, and by enabling the several States to make more adequate provision for aged persons, blind persons, dependent and crippled children, maternal and child welfare, public health, and the administration of their unemployment compensation laws; to establish a Social Security Board; to raise revenue; and for other purposes.

Be it enacted by the Senate and House of Representatives of the United States of America in Congress assembled . . .

TITLE II—FEDERAL OLD-AGE BENEFITS
OLD AGE RESERVE ACCOUNT

SECTION 201. (a) There is hereby created an account in the Treasury of the United States to be known as the "Old-Age Reserve Account" hereinafter in this title called the "Account." There is hereby authorized to be appropriated to the Account for each fiscal year, beginning with the fiscal year ending June 30, 1937, an amount sufficient as an annual premium to provide for the payments required under this title, such amount to be determined on a reserve basis in accordance with accepted actuarial principles, and based upon such tables of mortality as the Secretary of the Treasury shall from time to time adopt, and upon an interest rate of 3 per centum per annum compounded annually. The Secretary of the Treasury shall submit annually to the Bureau of the Budget an estimate of the appropriations to be made to the Account.

(b) It shall be the duty of the Secretary of the Treasury to invest such portion of the amounts credited to the Account as is not, in his judgment, required to meet current withdrawals. Such investment may be made only in interest-bearing obligations of the United States or in obligations guaranteed as to both principal and interest by the United States. For such purpose such obligations may be acquired (1) on original issue at par, or (2) by purchase of outstanding obligations at the market price. The purposes for which obligations of the United States may be issued under the Second Liberty Bond Act, as amended, are hereby extended to authorize the issuance at par of special obligations exclusively to the Account. Such special obligations shall bear interest at the rate of 3 per centum per annum. Obligations other than such special obligations may be acquired for the Account only on such terms as to provide an investment yield of not less than 3 per centum per annum.

(c) Any obligations acquired by the Account (except special obligations issued exclusively to the Account) may be sold at the market price, and such special obligations may be redeemed at par plus accrued interest.

(d) The interest on, and the proceeds from the sale or redemption of, any obligations held in the Account shall be credited to and form a part of the Account.

(e) All amounts credited to the Account shall be available for making payments required under this title.

(f) The Secretary of the Treasury shall include in his annual report the actuarial status of the Account.

OLD AGE BENEFIT PAYMENTS
SEC. 202. (a) Every qualified individual (as defined in section 210) shall be entitled to receive, with respect to the period beginning on the date he attains the age of sixty-five, or on January 1, 1942, whichever is the later, and ending on the date of his death, an old-age benefit (payable as nearly as practicable in equal monthly installments) as follows:

(1) If the total wages (as defined in section 210) determined by the Board to have been paid to him, with respect to employment (as defined in section 210) after December 31, 1936, and before he attained the age of sixty-five, were not more than $3,000, the old-age benefit shall be at a monthly rate of one-half of 1 per centum of such total wages;

(2) If such total wages were more than $3,000, the old-age benefit shall be at a monthly rate equal to the sum of the following:
    (A) One-half of 1 per centum of $3,000; plus

    (B) One-twelfth of 1 per centum of the amount by which such total wages exceeded $3,000 and did not exceed $45,000; plus

    (C) One-twenty-fourth of 1 per centum of the amount by which such total wages exceeded $45,000.

  (b) In no case shall the monthly rate computed under subsection (a) exceed $85.

  (c) If the Board finds at any time that more or less than the correct amount has theretofore been paid to any individual under this section, then, under regulations made by the Board, proper adjustments shall be made in connection with subsequent payments under this section to the same individual.

  (d) Whenever the Board finds that any qualified individual has received wages with respect to regular employment after he attained the age of sixty-five, the old-age benefit payable to such individual shall be reduced, for each calendar month in any part of which such regular employment occurred, by an amount equal to one months benefit. Such reduction shall be made, under regulations prescribed by the Board, by deductions from one or more payments of old-age benefit to such individual.

PAYMENTS UPON DEATH

SEC. 203. (a) If any individual dies before attaining the age of sixty-five, there shall be paid to his estate an amount equal to 3½ per centum of the total wages determined by the Board to have been paid to him, with respect to employment after December 31, 1936.

  (b) If the Board finds that the correct amount of the old-age benefit payable to a qualified individual during his life under section 202 was less than 3½ per centum of the total wages by which such old-age benefit was measurable, then there shall be paid to his estate a sum equal to the amount, if any, by which such 3½ per centum exceeds the amount (whether more or less than the correct amount) paid to him during his life as old-age benefit.

  (c) If the Board finds that the total amount paid to a qualified individual under an old-age benefit during his life was less than the correct amount to which he was entitled under section 202, and that the correct amount of such old-age benefit was 3½ per centum or more of the total wages by which such old-age benefit was measurable, then there shall be paid to his estate a sum equal to the amount, if any, by which the correct amount of the old-age benefit exceeds the amount which was so paid to him during his life. . . .

DEFINITIONS

SEC. 210. When used in this title—

(a) The term "wages" means all remuneration for employment, including the cash value of all remuneration paid in any medium other than cash; except that such term shall not include that part of the remuneration which, after remuneration equal to $3,000 has been paid to an individual by an employer with respect to employment during any calendar year, is paid to such employer with respect to employment during such calendar year.

(b) The term "employment" means any service, of whatever nature, performed within the United States by an employee for his employer, except—

(1) Agricultural labor;

(2) Domestic service in a private home;

(3) Casual labor not in the course of the employer's trade or business;

(4) Service performed as an officer or member of the crew of a vessel documented under the laws of the United States or of any foreign country;

(5) Service performed in the employ of the United States Government or of an instrumentality of the United States;

(6) Service performed in the employ of a State, a political subdivision thereof, or an instrumentality of one or more States or political subdivisions;

(7) Service performed in the employ of a corporation, community chest, fund, or foundation, organized and operated exclusively for religious, charitable, scientific, literary, or educational purposes, or for the prevention of cruelty to children or animals, no part of the net earnings of which inures to the benefit of any private shareholder or individual.

(c) The term "qualified individual" means any individual with respect to whom it appears to the satisfaction of the Board that—

(1) He is at least sixty-five years of age; and

(2) The total amount of wages paid to him, with respect to employment after December 31, 1936, and before he attained the age of sixty-five, was not less than $2,000; and

(3) Wages were paid to him, with respect to employment on some five days after December 31, 1936, and before he attained the age of sixty-five, each day being in a different calendar year.

TITLE III—GRANTS TO STATES FOR UNEMPLOYMENT COMPENSATION ADMINISTRATION
APPROPRIATION

SECTION 301. For the purpose of assisting the States in the administration of their unemployment compensation laws, there is hereby authorized to be appropriated, for the fiscal year ending June 30, 1936, the sum of $4,000,000, and for each fiscal year thereafter. . . .

TITLE IV—GRANTS TO STATES FOR AID TO DEPENDENT CHILDREN
APPROPRIATION

SECTION 401. For the purpose of enabling each State to furnish financial assistance, as far as practicable under the conditions in such State, to needy dependent children, there is hereby authorized to be appropriated for the fiscal year ending June 30, 1936, the sum of $24,750,000, and there is hereby authorized to be appropriated for each fiscal year thereafter a sum sufficient to carry out the purposes of this title. The sums made available under this section shall be used for making payments to States which have submitted, and had approved by the Board, State plans for aid to dependent children. . . .

TITLE V—GRANTS TO STATES FOR MATERNAL AND CHILD WELFARE
PART 1—MATERNAL AND CHILD HEALTH SERVICES
APPROPRIATION

SECTION 501. For the purpose of enabling each State to extend and improve, as far as practicable under the conditions in such State, services for promoting the health of mothers and children, especially in rural areas and in areas suffering from severe economic distress, there is hereby authorized to be appropriated for each fiscal year, beginning with the fiscal year ending June 30, 1936, the sum of $3,800,000. The sums made available under this section shall be used for making payments to States which have submitted, and had approved by the Chief of the Children's Bureau, State plans for such services. . . .

PART 2—SERVICES FOR CRIPPLED CHILDREN

APPROPRIATION

SECTION 511. For the purpose of enabling each State to extend and improve (especially in rural areas and in areas suffering from severe economic distress), as far as practicable under the conditions in such State, services for locating crippled children and for providing medical, surgical, corrective, and other services and care, and facilities for diagnosis, hospitalization, and aftercare, for children who are crippled or who are suffering from conditions which lead to crippling, there is hereby authorized to be appropriated for each fiscal year beginning with the fiscal year ending June 30, 1936, the sum of $2,850,000. The sums made available under this section shall be used for making payments to States which have submitted, and had approved by the Chief of the Children's Bureau, State plans for such services. . . .

PART 3—CHILD WELFARE SERVICES

SEC. 521. (a) For the purpose of enabling the United States, through the Children's Bureau, to cooperate with State public-welfare agencies establishing, extending, and strengthening, especially in predominantly rural areas, public-welfare services (hereinafter in this section referred to as "child-welfare services") for the protection and care of homeless, dependent, and neglected children, and children in danger of becoming delinquent, there is hereby authorized to be appropriated for each fiscal year, beginning with the year ending June 30, 1936, the sum of $1,500,000. Such amount shall be allotted by the Secretary of Labor for use by cooperating State public-welfare agencies on the basis of plans developed jointly by the State agency and the Children's Bureau, to each State, $10,000, and the remainder to each State on the basis of such plans, not to exceed such part of the remainder as the rural population of such State bears to the total rural population of the United States. The amount so allotted shall be expended for payment of part of the cost of district, county or other local child-welfare services in areas predominantly rural, and for developing State services for the encouragement and assistance of adequate methods of community child-welfare organization in areas predominantly rural and other areas of special need. The amount of any allotment to a State under this section for any fiscal year remaining unpaid to such State at the end of such fiscal year shall be available for payment to such State under this section until the end of the second succeeding fiscal year. No payment to a State under this section shall be made out of its allotment for any fiscal year until its allotment for the preceding fiscal year has been exhausted or has ceased to be available. . . .

TITLE VIII—TAXES WITH RESPECT TO EMPLOYMENT
INCOME TAX ON EMPLOYEES

SECTION 801. In addition to other taxes, there shall be levied, collected, and paid upon the income of every individual a tax equal to the following percentages of the wages (as defined in section 811) received by him after December 31, 1936, with respect to employment (as defined in section 811) after such date:

> (1) With respect to employment during the calendar years 1937, 1938, and 1939, the rate shall be 1 per centum.
>
> (2) With respect to employment during the calendar years 1940, 1941, and 1942, the rate shall 1½ per centum.
>
> (3) With respect to employment during the calendar years 1943, 1944, and 1945, the rate shall be 2 per centum.
>
> (4) With respect to employment during the calendar years 1946, 1947, and 1948, the rate shall be 2½ per centum.
>
> (5) With respect to employment after December 31, 1948, the rate shall be 3 per centum.

DEDUCTION ON TAXES FROM WAGES

SEC. 802. (a) The tax imposed by section 801 shall be collected by the employer of the taxpayer by deducting the amount of the tax from the wages as and when paid. Every employer required so to deduct the tax is hereby made liable for the payment of such tax, and is hereby indemnified against the claims and demands of any person for the amount of any such payment made by such employer. . . .

EXCISE TAX ON EMPLOYERS

SEC. 804. In addition to other taxes, every employer shall pay an excise tax, with respect to having individuals in his employ, equal to the following percentages of the wages (as defined in section 811) paid by him after December 31, 1936, with respect to employment (as defined in section 811) after such date:

> (1) With respect to employment during the calendar years 1937, 1938, and 1939, the rate shall be 1 per centum.

(2) With respect to employment during the calendar years 1940, 1941, and 1942, the rate shall be 1½ per centum.

(3) with respect to employment during the calendar years 1943, 1944, and 1945, the rate shall be 2 per centum.

(4) with respect to employment during the calendar years 1946, 1947, and 1948, the rate shall be 2½ per centum.

(5) with respect to employment after December 31, 1948, the rate shall be 3 per centum. . . .

SHORT TITLE

SEC. 1105. This Act may be cited as the "Social Security Act."

Approved, August 14, 1935.

Source: 49 Stat. 620

Document 3.3   Executive Order 8802, June 25, 1941

Roosevelt issued Executive Order 8802 to head off a march on Washington, D.C., by African Americans and their supporters. The march, planned by A. Philip Randolph, president of the Brotherhood of Sleeping Car Porters, was to advocate for equal opportunity in defense industries. The executive order indicated that nondiscrimination in defense industries was the policy of the United States, and it created the Committee on Fair Employment Practice to back that policy.

WHEREAS it is the policy of the United States to encourage full participation in the national defense program by all citizens of the United States, regardless of race, creed, color, or national origin, in the firm belief that the democratic way of life within the Nation can be defended successfully only with the help and support of all groups within its borders; and

WHEREAS there is evidence that available and needed workers have been barred from employment in industries engaged in defense production solely because of considerations of race, creed, color, or national origin, to the detriment of workers' morale and of national unity:

NOW, THEREFORE, by virtue of the authority vested in me by the Constitution and the statutes, and as a prerequisite to the successful conduct of our national defense production effort, I do hereby reaffirm the policy of the United States that there shall be no discrimination in the employment of workers in defense industries or government because of race, creed, color, or national origin, and I do hereby declare that it is the duty of employers and of labor organizations, in furtherance of said policy and of this order, to provide for the full and equitable participation of all workers in defense industries, without discrimination because of race, creed, color, or national origin;

And it is hereby ordered as follows:

1. All departments and agencies of the Government of the United States concerned with vocational and training programs for defense production shall take special measures appropriate to assure that such programs are administered without discrimination because of race, creed, color, or national origin;

2. All contracting agencies of the Government of the United States shall include in all defense contracts hereafter negotiated by them a provision obligating the contractor not to discriminate against any worker because of race, creed, color, or national origin;

3. There is established in the Office of Production Management a Committee on Fair Employment Practice, which shall consist of a chairman and four other members to be appointed by the President. The Chairman and members of the Committee shall serve as such without compensation but shall be entitled to actual and necessary transportation, subsistence and other expenses incidental to performance of their duties. The Committee shall receive and investigate complaints of discrimination in violation of the provisions of this order and shall take appropriate steps to redress grievances which it finds to be valid. The Committee shall also recommend to the several departments and agencies of the Government of the United States and to the President all measures which may be deemed by it necessary or proper to effectuate the provisions of this order.

Franklin D. Roosevelt
The White House,
June 25, 1941.

Source: Samuel I. Rosenman, ed., *The Public Papers and Addresses of Franklin D. Roosevelt* (1950; reprint, New York: Russell and Russell, 1969), 10:233–235.

Document 3.4   Statement on the Signing of the
G.I. Bill of Rights, June 22, 1944

The G.I. Bill of Rights of 1944 was one of the most important social programs of the Roosevelt administration. Although there was by this point considerable opposition in Congress to New Deal–style social programs, benefits targeted at veterans were another matter.

This bill, which I have signed today, substantially carries out most of the recommendations made by me in a speech on July 28, 1943, and more specifically in messages to the Congress dated October 27, 1943, and November 23, 1943.

1. It gives servicemen and -women the opportunity of resuming their education or technical training after discharge, or of taking a refresher or retainer course, not only without tuition charge up to five hundred dollars per school year, but with the right to receive a monthly living allowance while pursuing their studies.
2. It makes provision for the guarantee by the federal government of not to exceed 50 percent of certain loans made to veterans for the purchase or construction of homes, farms, and business properties.
3. It provides for reasonable unemployment allowances payable each week up to a maximum period of one year, to those veterans who are unable to find a job.
4. It establishes improved machinery for effective job counseling for veterans and for finding jobs for returning soldiers and sailors.
5. It authorizes the construction of all necessary additional hospital facilities.
6. It strengthens the authority of the Veterans Administration to enable it to discharge its existing and added responsibilities with promptness and efficiency.

With the signing of this bill a well-rounded program of special veterans' benefits is nearly completed. It gives emphatic notice to the men and women in our armed forces that the American people do not intend to let them down.

By prior legislation, the federal government has already provided for the armed forces of this war: adequate dependency allowances; mustering-out pay; generous hospitalization, medical care, and vocational rehabilitation and training; liberal pensions in case of death or disability in military service; substantial war-risk life insurance, and guarantee of premiums on commercial policies during service; protection of civil rights and suspension of enforcement of certain civil liabilities during service; emergency maternal care for wives of enlisted men; and reemployment rights for returning veterans.

This bill therefore and the former legislation provide the special benefits which are due to the members of our armed forces—for they "have been compelled to make greater economic sacrifice and every other kind of sacrifice than the rest of us, and are entitled to definite action to help take care of their special problems." While further study and experience may suggest some changes and improvements, the Congress is to be congratulated on the prompt action it has taken.

There still remains one recommendation which I made on November 23, 1943, which I trust that the Congress will soon adopt—the extension of social security credits under the Federal Old-Age and Survivors' Insurance Law to all servicemen and women for the period of their service.

I trust that the Congress will also soon provide similar opportunities for postwar education and unemployment insurance to the members of the merchant marine, who have risked their lives time and again during this war for the welfare of their country.

But apart from these special benefits which fulfill the special needs of veterans, there is still much to be done.

As I stated in my message to the Congress of November 23, 1943:

> What our servicemen and women want, more than anything else, is the assurance of satisfactory employment upon their return to civil life. The first task after the war is to provide employment for them and for our demobilized workers. . . . The goal after the war should be the maximum utilization of our human and material resources.

As a related problem the Congress has had under consideration the serious problem of economic reconversion and readjustment after the war, so that private industry will be able to provide jobs for the largest possible number. This time we have wisely begun to make plans in advance of the day of peace, in full confidence that our war workers will remain at their essential war jobs as long as necessary until the fighting is over.

The executive branch of the government has taken, and is taking, whatever steps it can, until legislation is enacted. I am glad to learn that the Congress has agreed on a bill to facilitate the prompt settlement of terminated contracts. I hope that the Congress will also take prompt action, when it reconvenes, on necessary legislation which is now pending to facilitate the development of unified programs for the demobilization of civilian war workers, for their reemployment in peacetime pursuits, and for provision, in cooperation with the states, of appropriate unemployment benefits during the transition from war to peace. I hope also that the Congress, upon its return, will take prompt action on the pending legislation to facilitate the orderly disposition of surplus property.

A sound postwar economy is a major present responsibility.

Source: Samuel I. Rosenman, ed., *The Public Papers and Addresses of Franklin D. Roosevelt* (1950; reprint, New York: Russell and Russell, 1969), 13:180–182.

Document 3.5   National Industrial Recovery Act, June 16, 1933

The National Industrial Recovery Act (NIRA) was a catch-all piece of legislation that Roosevelt created as an alternative to the bill introduced by Sen. Hugo L. Black, D-Ala. To incite economic recovery, Black's bill banned from interstate commerce any products made by people working more than thirty hours per week. The NIRA included two main provisions. Title I sought to allow companies in each industry to draw up rules for fair competition, with the hope that this would result in higher wages and more purchasing power for worker-consumers. Title II created the Public Works Administration (PWA) to provide jobs through government construction projects.

AN ACT

To encourage national industrial recovery, to foster fair competition, and to provide for the construction of certain useful public works, and for other purposes.

Be it enacted by the Senate and House of Representatives of the United States of America in Congress assembled,

TITLE I—INDUSTRIAL RECOVERY
DECLARATION OF POLICY

SECTION 1. A national emergency productive of widespread unemployment and disorganization of industry, which burdens interstate and foreign commerce, affects the public welfare, and undermines the standards of living of the American people, is hereby declared to exist. It is hereby declared to be the policy of Congress to remove obstructions to the free flow of interstate and foreign commerce which tend to diminish the amount thereof; and to provide for the general welfare by promoting the organization of industry for the purpose of cooperative action among trade groups, to induce and maintain united action of labor and management under adequate governmental sanctions and supervision, to eliminate unfair competitive practices, to promote the fullest possible utilization of the present productive capacity of industries, to avoid undue restriction of production (except as may be temporarily required), to increase the consumption of industrial and agricultural products by increasing purchasing power, to reduce and relieve unemployment, to improve standards of labor, and otherwise to rehabilitate industry and to conserve natural resources.

ADMINISTRATIVE AGENCIES

SEC. 2. (a) To effectuate the policy of this title, the President is hereby authorized to establish such agencies, to accept and utilize such voluntary and uncompensated services, to appoint, without regard to the provisions of the civil service laws, such officers and employees, and to utilize such Federal officers and employees, and, with the consent of the State, such State and local officers and employees, as he may find necessary, to prescribe their authorities, duties, responsibilities, and tenure, and, without regard to the Classification Act of 1923, as amended, to fix the compensation of any officers and employees so appointed.

(b) The President may delegate any of his functions and powers under this title to such officers, agents, and employees as he may designate or appoint, and may establish an industrial planning and research agency to aid in carrying out his functions under this title.

(c) This title shall cease to be in effect and any agencies established hereunder shall cease to exist at the expiration of two years after the date of enactment of this Act, or sooner if the President shall by proclamation or the Congress shall by joint resolution declare that the emergency recognized by section 1 has ended.

CODES OF FAIR COMPETITION

SEC. 3. (a) Upon the application to the President by one or more trade or industrial associations or groups, the President may approve a code or codes of fair competition for the trade or industry or subdivision thereof, represented by the applicant or applicants, if the President finds (1) that such associations or groups impose no inequitable restrictions on admission to membership therein and are truly representative of such trades or industries or subdivisions thereof, and (2) that such code or codes are not designed to promote monopolies or to eliminate or oppress small enterprises and will not operate to discriminate against them, and will tend to effectuate the policy of this title: *Provided,* That such code or codes shall not permit monopolies or monopolistic practices: *Provided further,* That where such code or codes affect the services and welfare of persons engaged in other steps of the economic process, nothing in this section shall deprive such persons of the right to be heard prior to approval by the President of such code or codes. The President may, as a condition of his approval of any such code, impose such conditions (including requirements for the making of reports and the keeping of accounts) for the protection of consumers, competitors, employees, and others, and in furtherance of the public interest, and may provide such exceptions to and exemptions from the provisions of such code, as the President in his discretion deems necessary to effectuate the policy herein declared.

(b) After the President shall have approved any such code, the provisions of such code shall be the standards of fair competition for such trade or industry or subdivision thereof. Any violation of such standards in any transaction in or affecting interstate or foreign commerce shall be deemed an unfair method of competition in commerce within the meaning of the Federal Trade Commission Act, as amended; but nothing in this title shall be construed to impair the powers of the Federal Trade Commission under such Act, as amended.

(c) The several district courts of the United States are hereby invested with jurisdiction to prevent and restrain violations of any code of fair competition approved under this title; and it shall be the duty of the several district attorneys of the United States, in their respective districts, under the direction of the Attorney General, to institute proceedings in equity to prevent and restrain such violations.

(d) Upon his own motion, or if complaint is made to the President that abuses inimical to the public interest and contrary to the policy herein declared are prevalent in any trade or industry or subdivision thereof, and if no code of fair competition therefor has theretofore been approved by the President, the President, after such public notice and hearing as he shall specify, may prescribe and approve a code of fair competition for such trade or industry or subdivision thereof, which shall have the same effect as a code of fair competition approved by the President under subsection (a) of this section.

(e) On his own motion, or if any labor organization, or any trade or industrial organization, association, or group, which has complied with the provisions of this title, shall make complaint to the President that any article or articles are being imported into the United States in substantial quantities or increasing ratio to domestic production of any competitive article or articles and on such terms or under such conditions as to render ineffective or seriously to endanger the maintenance of any code or agreement under this title, the President may cause an immediate investigation to be made by the United States Tariff Commission, which shall give precedence to investigations under this subsection, and if, after such investigation and such public notice and hearing as he shall specify, the President shall find the existence of such facts, he shall, in order to effectuate the policy of this title, direct that the article or articles concerned shall be permitted entry into the United States only upon such terms and conditions and subject to the payment of such fees and to such limitations in the total quantity which may be imported (in the course of any specified period or periods) as he shall find it necessary to prescribe in order that the entry thereof shall not render or tend to render ineffective any code or agreement made under this title. In order to enforce any limitations imposed on the total quantity of imports, in any specified period or periods of any article or articles under this subsection, the President may forbid the importation of such article or articles unless the importer shall have first obtained from the Secretary of the Treasury a license pursuant to such regulations as the President may prescribe. Upon information of any action by the President under this subsection the Secretary of the Treasury shall, through the proper officers, permit entry of the article or articles specified only upon such terms and conditions and subject to such fees, to such limitations in the quantity which may be imported, and to such requirements of license, as the President shall have directed. The decision of the President as to facts shall be conclusive. Any condition or limitation of entry under this subsection shall continue in effect until the President shall find and inform the Secretary of the Treasury that the conditions which led to the imposition of such condition or limitation upon entry no longer exists.

(f) When a code of fair competition has been approved or prescribed by the President under this title, any violation of any provision thereof in any transaction in or affecting interstate or foreign commerce shall be a misdemeanor and upon conviction thereof an offender shall be fined not more than $500 for each offense, and each day such violation continues shall be deemed a separate offense.

AGREEMENTS AND LICENSES

SEC. 4. (a) The President is authorized to enter into agreements with, and to approve voluntary agreements between and among, persons engaged in a trade or industry, labor organizations, and trade or industrial organizations, associations, or groups, relating to any trade or industry, if in his judgment such agreements will aid in effectuating the policy of this title with respect to transactions in or affecting interstate or foreign commerce, and will be consistent with the requirements of clause (2) of subsection (a) of section 3 for a code of fair competition.

(b) Whenever the President shall find that destructive wage or price cutting or other activities contrary to the policy of this title are being practiced in any trade or industry or any subdivision thereof, and, after such public notice and hearing as he shall specify, shall find it essential to license business enterprises in order to make effective a code of fair competition or an agreement under this title or otherwise to effectuate the policy of this title, and shall publicly so announce, no person shall, after a date fixed in such announcement, engage in or carry on any business, in or affecting interstate or foreign commerce, specified in such announcement, unless he shall have first obtained a license issued pursuant to such regulations as the President shall prescribe. The President may suspend or revoke any such license, after due notice and opportunity for hearing, for violations of the terms or conditions thereof. Any order of the President suspending or revoking any such license shall be final if in accordance with law. Any person who, without such a license or in violation of any condition thereof, carries on any such business for which a license is so required, shall, upon conviction thereof, be fined not more than $500, or imprisoned not more than six months, or both, and each day such violation continues shall be deemed a separate offense. Notwithstanding the provisions of section 2 (c), this subsection shall cease to be in effect at the expiration of one year after the date of enactment of this Act or sooner if the President shall by proclamation or the Congress shall by joint resolution declare that the emergency recognized by section 1 has ended. . . .

SEC. 7. (a) Every code of fair competition, agreement, and license approved, prescribed, or issued under this title shall contain the following conditions: (1) That employees shall have the right to organize and bargain collectively through representatives of their own choosing, and shall be free from the interference, restraint, or coercion of employers of labor, or their agents, in the designation of such representatives or in self-organization or in other concerted activities for the purpose of collective bargaining or other mutual aid or protection; (2) that no employee and no one seeking employment shall be required as a condition of employment to join any company union or to refrain from joining, organizing, or assisting a labor organization of his own choosing; and (3) that employers shall comply with the maximum hours of labor, minimum rates of pay, and other conditions of employment, approved or prescribed by the President.

(b) The President shall, so far as practicable, afford every opportunity to employers and employees in any trade or industry or subdivision thereof with respect to which the conditions referred to in clauses (1) and (2) of subsection (a) prevail, to establish by mutual agreement, the standards as to the maximum hours of labor, minimum rates of pay, and such other conditions of employment as may be necessary in such trade or industry or subdivision thereof to effectuate the policy of this title; and the standards established in such agreements, when approved by the President, shall have the same effect as a code of fair competition, approved by the President under subsection (a) of section 3.

(c) Where no such mutual agreement has been approved by the President he may investigate the labor practices, policies, wages, hours of labor, and conditions of employment in such trade or industry or subdivision thereof; and upon the basis of such investigations, and after such hearings as the President finds advisable, he is authorized to prescribe a limited code of fair competition fixing such maximum hours of labor, minimum rates of pay, and other conditions of employment in the trade or industry or subdivision thereof investigated as he finds to be necessary to effectuate the policy of this title, which shall have the same effect as a code of fair competition approved by the President under subsection (a) of section 3. The President may differentiate according to experience and skill of the employees affected and according to the locality of employment; but no attempt shall be made to introduce any classification according to the nature of the work involved which might tend to set a maximum as well as a minimum wage. . . .

TITLE II—PUBLIC WORKS AND CONSTRUCTION PROJECTS
FEDERAL EMERGENCY ADMINISTRATION OF PUBLIC WORKS

SECTION 201. (a) To effectuate the purposes of this title, the President is hereby authorized to create a Federal Emergency Administration of Public Works, all the powers of which shall be exercised by a Federal Emergency Administrator of Public Works (hereafter referred to as the "Administrator"), and to establish such agencies, to accept and utilize such voluntary and uncompensated services, to appoint, without regard to the civil service laws, such officers and employees, and to utilize such Federal officers and employees, and, with the consent of the State, such State and local officers and employees as he may find necessary, to prescribe their authorities, duties, responsibilities, and tenure, and, without regard to the Classification Act of 1923, as amended, to fix the compensation of any officers and employees so appointed. The President may delegate any of his functions and powers under this title to such officers, agents, and employees as he may designate or appoint. . . .

SEC. 202. The Administrator, under the direction of the President, shall prepare a comprehensive program of public works, which shall include among other things, the following: (a) Construction repair, and improvement of public highways and park ways, public buildings, and any publicly owned instrumentalities and facilities; (b) conservation and development of natural resources, including control, utilization, and purification of waters, prevention of soil or coastal erosion, development of water power, transmission of electrical energy, and construction of river and harbor improvements and flood control and also the construction of any river or drainage improvement required to perform or satisfy any obligation incurred by the United States through a treaty with a foreign Government heretofore ratified and to restore or develop for the use of any State or its citizens water taken from or denied to them by performance on the part of the United States of treaty obligations heretofore assumed: *Provided,* That no river or harbor improvements shall be carried out unless they shall have heretofore or hereafter been adopted by the Congress or are recommended by the Chief of Engineers of the United States Army; (c) any projects of the character heretofore constructed or carried on either directly by public authority or with public aid to serve the interests of the general public; (d) construction, reconstruction, alteration, or repair under public regulation or control of low-cost housing and slum-clearance projects; (e) any project (other than those included in the foregoing classes) of any character heretofore eligible for loans under subsection (a) of section 201 of the Emergency Relief and Construction Act of 1932, as amended, and paragraph (3) of such subsection (a) shall for such purposes be held to include loans for the construction or completion of hospitals the operation of which is partly financed from public funds, and of reservoirs and pumping plants and for the construction of dry docks; and if in the opinion of the President it seems desirable, the construction of naval vessels within the terms and/or limits established by the London Naval Treaty of 1930 and of aircraft required therefor and construction of heavier-than-air aircraft and technical construction for the Army Air Corps and such Army housing projects as the President may approve, and provision of original equipment for the mechanization or motorization of such Army tactical units as he may designate: *Provided, however,* That in the event of an international agreement for the further limitation of armament, to which the United States is signatory, the President is hereby authorized and empowered to suspend, in whole or in part, any such naval or military construction or mechanization and motorization of Army units: *Provided further,* That this title shall not be applicable to public works under the jurisdiction or control of the Architect of the Capitol or of any commission or committee for which such Architect is the contracting and/or executive officer.

SEC. 203. (a) With a view to increasing employment quickly (while reasonably securing any loans made by the United States) the President is authorized and empowered, through the Administrator or through such other agencies as he may designate or create, (1) to construct, finance, or aid in the construction or financing of any public-works project included in the program prepared pursuant to section 202; (2) upon such terms as the President shall prescribe, to make grants to States, municipalities, or other public bodies for the construction, repair, or improvement of any such project, but no such grant shall be in excess of 30 per centum of the cost of the labor and materials employed upon such project; (3) to acquire by purchase, or by exercise of the power of eminent domain, any real or personal property in connection with the construction of any such project, and to sell any security acquired or any property so constructed or acquired or to lease any such property with or without the privilege of purchase: *Provided,* That all moneys received from any such sale or lease or the repayment of any loan shall be used to retire obligations issued pursuant to section 209 of this Act, in addition to any other moneys required to be used for such purpose; (4) to aid in the financing of such railroad maintenance and equipment as may be approved by the Interstate Commerce Commission as desirable for the improvement of transportation facilities; and (5) to advance, upon request of the Commission having jurisdiction of the project, the unappropriated balance of the sum authorized for carrying out the provisions of the Act entitled "An Act to provide for the construction and equipment of an annex to the Library of Congress", approved June 13, 1930 (46 Stat. 583); such advance to be expended under the direction of such Commission and in accordance with such Act: *Provided,* That in deciding to extend any aid or grant hereunder to any State, county, or municipality the President may consider whether action is in process or in good faith assured therein reasonably designed to bring the ordinary current expenditures thereof within the prudently estimated revenues thereof. The provisions of this section and section 202 shall extend to public works in the several States, Hawaii, Alaska, the District of Columbia, Puerto Rico, the Canal Zone, and the Virgin Islands. . . .

APPROPRIATION

SEC. 220. For the purposes of this Act, there is hereby authorized to be appropriated, out of any money in the Treasury not otherwise appropriated, the sum of $3,300,000,000. The President is authorized to allocate so much of said sum, not in excess of $100,000,000, as he may determine to be necessary for expenditures in carrying out the Agricultural Adjustment Act and the purposes, powers, and functions heretofore and hereafter conferred upon the Farm Credit Administration. . . .

SHORT TITLE

SEC. 304. This Act may be cited as the "National Industrial Recovery Act."

Approved, June 16, 1933, 11:55 a.m.

Source: 48 Stat.195

Document 3.6   "Bombshell Message" to London Economic Conference, July 3, 1933

FDR was an internationalist and had raised some hope that the World Economic Conference that would meet in London in the summer of 1933 might take international action to restore trade and stimulate the world economy. But he concluded shortly before the conference that he wanted to be able to take independent action to stimulate the U.S. economy. This message, which he cabled via an intermediary to Secretary of State Cordell Hull, scuttled whatever chances the conference had for a meaningful agreement on international trade.

Franklin Roosevelt to William Phillips, Acting Secretary of State:

U.S.S. *Indianapolis,* July 2, 1933, 6 p.m.
[Radiogram] Please send following to Hull as soon as possible:

Herewith is a statement which I think you can use Monday morning as a message from me to you. If you think it best not to give it out in London let me know at once and in that event I will release it here as a White House statement.

I would regard it as a catastrophe amounting to a world tragedy if the great Conference of Nations, called to bring about a more real and permanent financial stability and a greater prosperity to the masses of all nations, should, in advance of any serious effort to consider these broader problems, allow itself to be diverted by the proposal of a purely artificial and temporary experiment affecting the monetary exchange of a few nations only. Such action, such diversion, shows a singular lack of proportion and a failure to remember the larger purposes for which the Economic Conference originally was called together.

I do not relish the thought that insistence on such action should be made an excuse for the continuance of the basic economic errors that underlie so much of the present world-wide depression.

The world will not long be lulled by the specious fallacy of achieving a temporary and probably an artificial stability in foreign exchange on the part of a few large countries only.

The sound internal economic system of a nation is a greater factor in its well being than the price of its currency in changing terms of the currencies of other nations.

It is for this reason that reduced cost of government, adequate government income, and ability to service government debts are all so important to ultimate stability. So too, old fetishes of so called International bankers are being replaced by efforts to plan national currencies with the objective of giving to those currencies a continuing purchasing power which does not greatly vary in terms of the commodities and need of modern civilization. Let me be frank in saying that the United States seeks the kind of a dollar which a generation hence will have the same purchasing and debt paying power as the dollar value we hope to attain in the near future. That objective means more to the good of other nations than a fixed ratio for a month or two in terms of the pound or franc.

Our broad purpose is the permanent stabilization of every nation's currency. Gold or gold and silver can well continue to be a metallic reserve behind currencies but this is not the time to dissipate gold reserves. When the world works out concerted policies in the majority of nations to produce balanced budgets and living within their means, then we can properly discuss a better distribution of the world's gold and silver supply to act as a reserve base of national currencies. Restoration of world trade is an important partner, both in the means and in the result. Here also temporary exchange fixing is not the true answer. We must rather mitigate existing embargoes to make easier the exchange of products which one nation has and the other nation has not.

The Conference was called to better and perhaps to cure fundamental economic ills. It must not be diverted from that effort.

ROOSEVELT

Source: Samuel I. Rosenman, ed., *The Public Papers and Addresses of Franklin D. Roosevelt* (1938; reprint, New York: Russell and Russell, 1969), 2:264–265.

Document 3.7   "Quarantine Speech"
Chicago, October 5, 1937

As Roosevelt watched Europe and Asia move closer to war in 1937, he wanted the United States to take a more forceful position. But Americans' isolationist sentiment was strong, and Roosevelt had to tread carefully. In this speech he suggested that aggressor nations should be treated as if they were the carriers of an infectious disease and "quarantined." To Roosevelt's cha-

grin, relatively few Americans were prepared to endorse a bolder foreign policy.

I am glad to come once again to Chicago and especially to have the opportunity of taking part in the dedication of this important project of civic betterment.

On my trip across the continent and back I have been shown many evidences of the result of common-sense cooperation between municipalities and the federal government, and I have been greeted by tens of thousands of Americans who have told me in every look and word that their material and spiritual well-being has made great strides forward in the past few years.

And yet, as I have seen with my own eyes the prosperous farms, the thriving factories, and the busy railroads, as I have seen the happiness and security and peace which covers our wide land, almost inevitably I have been compelled to contrast, our peace with very different scenes being enacted in other parts of the world.

It is because the people of the United States under modern conditions must, for the sake of their own future, give thought to the rest of the world, that I, as the responsible executive head of the nation, have chosen this great inland city and this gala occasion to speak to you on a subject of definite national importance.

The political situation in the world, which of late has been growing progressively worse, is such as to cause grave concern and anxiety to all the peoples and nations who wish to live in peace and amity with their neighbors.

Some fifteen years ago the hopes of mankind for a continuing era of international peace were raised to great heights when more than sixty nations solemnly pledged themselves not to resort to arms in furtherance of their national aims and policies. The high aspirations expressed in the Briand-Kellogg peace pact and the hopes for peace thus raised have of late given way to a haunting fear of calamity. The present reign of terror and international lawlessness began a few years ago.

It began through unjustified interference in the internal affairs of other nations or the invasion of alien territory in violation of treaties, and has now reached a stage where the very foundations of civilization are seriously threatened. The landmarks and traditions which have marked the progress of civilization toward a condition of law, order, and justice are being wiped away.

Without a declaration of war and without warning or justification of any kind, civilians, including vast numbers of women and children, are being ruthlessly murdered with bombs from the air. In times of so-called peace, ships are being attacked and sunk by submarines without cause or notice. Nations are fomenting and taking sides in civil warfare in nations that have never done them any harm. Nations claiming freedom for themselves deny it to others.

Innocent peoples, innocent nations, are being cruelly sacrificed to a greed for power and supremacy which is devoid of all sense of justice and humane considerations. . . .

The peace-loving nations must make a concerted effort in opposition to those violations of treaties and those ignorings of humane instincts which today are creating a state of international anarchy and instability from which there is no escape through mere isolation or neutrality.

Those who cherish their freedom, and recognize and respect the equal right of their neighbors to be free and live in peace, must work together for the triumph of law and moral principles in order that peace, justice, and confidence may prevail in the world. There must be a return to a belief in the pledged word, in the value of a signed treaty. There must be recognition of the fact that national morality is as vital as private morality. . . .

There is a solidarity and interdependence about the modern world, both technically and morally, which makes it impossible for any nation completely to isolate itself from economic and political upheavals in the rest of the world, especially when such upheavals appear to be spreading and not declining. There can be no stability or peace either within nations or between nations except under laws and moral standards adhered to by all. International anarchy destroys every foundation for peace. It jeopardizes either the immediate or the future security of every nation, large or small. It is, therefore, a matter of vital interest and concern to the people of the United States that the sanctity of international treaties and the maintenance of international morality be restored. . . .

In those nations of the world which seem to be piling armament on armament for purposes of aggression, and those other nations which fear acts of aggression against them and their security, a very high proportion of their national income is being spent directly for armaments. It runs from 30 to as high as 50 percent. We are fortunate. The proportion that we in the United States spend is far less—11 or 12 percent.

How happy we are that the circumstances of the moment permit us to put our money into bridges and boulevards, dams and reforestation, the conservation of our soil, and many other kinds of useful works rather than into huge standing armies and vast supplies of implements of war.

I am compelled and you are compelled, nevertheless, to look ahead. The peace, the freedom, and the security of 90 percent of the population of the world is being jeopardized by the remaining 10 percent who are threatening a breakdown of all international order and law. Surely the 90 percent who want to live in peace under law and in accordance with moral standards that have received almost universal acceptance through the centuries can and must find some way to make their will prevail. . . .

It seems to be unfortunately true that the epidemic of world lawlessness is spreading.

When an epidemic of physical disease starts to spread, the community approves and joins in a quarantine of the patients in order to protect the health of the community against the spread of the disease.

It is my determination to pursue a policy of peace. It is my determination to adopt every practicable measure to avoid involvement in war. It ought to be inconceivable that in this modern era, and in the face of experience, any nation could be so foolish and ruthless as to run the risk of plunging the whole world into war by invading and violating, in contravention of solemn treaties, the territory of other nations that have done them no real harm and are too weak to protect themselves adequately. Yet the peace of the world and the welfare and security of every nation, including our own, is today being threatened by that very thing.

No nation which refuses to exercise forbearance and to respect the freedom and rights of others can long remain strong and retain the confidence and respect of other nations. No nation ever loses its dignity or its good standing by conciliating its differences, and by exercising great patience with, and consideration for, the rights of other nations.

War is a contagion, whether it be declared or undeclared. It can engulf states and peoples remote from the original scene of hostilities. We are determined to keep out of war, yet we cannot insure ourselves against the disastrous effects of war and the dangers of involvement. We are adopting such measures as will minimize our risk of involvement, but we cannot have complete protection in a world of disorder in which confidence and security have broken down.

If civilization is to survive, the principles of the Prince of Peace must be restored. Trust between nations must be revived.

Most important of all, the will for peace on the part of peace-loving nations must express itself to the end that nations that may be tempted to violate their agreements and the rights of others will desist from such a course. There must be positive endeavors to preserve peace.

America hates war. America hopes for peace. Therefore, America actively engages in the search for peace.

Source: Samuel I. Rosenman, ed., *The Public Papers and Addresses of Franklin D. Roosevelt* (1941; reprint, New York: Russell and Russell, 1969), 6:406–411.

Document 3.8   Offer to Exchange American Destroyers for Leases on British Bases, August 13, 1940

In this message Roosevelt proposed an exchange of American naval vessels for ninety-nine–year leases on naval bases in British possessions in the Western Hemisphere. The deal, which was soon accepted by Churchill, was the first major direct aid the United States provided to the British in World War II. Churchill referred to himself in his correspondence with Roosevelt as "Former Naval Person" and Roosevelt addressed him that way.

Washington [via U.S. Embassy] Aug. 13, 1940, 6 P.M.

From the President to the Former Naval Person.

I have been studying very carefully the message transmitted to me through the British Ambassador in Washington on August 8, and I have also been considering the possibility of furnishing the assistance in the way of releases and priorities contained in the memorandum attached to your message.

It is my belief that it may be possible to furnish to the British Government as immediate assistance at least 50 destroyers, the motor torpedo boats heretofore referred to, and, insofar as airplanes are concerned, five planes of each of the categories mentioned, the latter to be furnished for war testing purposes. Such assistance, as I am sure you will understand, would only be furnished if the American people and the Congress frankly recognized that in return therefor the national defense and security of the United States would be enhanced. For that reason it would be necessary, in the event that it proves possible to release the material above mentioned, that the British Government find itself able and willing to take the two following steps:

1. Assurance on the part of the Prime Minister that in the event that the waters of Great Britain become untenable for British ships of war, the latter would not be turned over to the Germans or sunk, but would be sent to other parts of the Empire for continued defense of the Empire.

2. An agreement on the part of Great Britain that the British Government would authorize the use of Newfoundland, Bermuda, the Bahamas, Jamaica, St. Lucia, Trinidad and British Guiana as naval and air bases by the United States in the event of an attack on the American hemisphere by any non-American nation; and in the meantime the United States to have the right to establish such bases and to use them for training and exercise purposes with the understanding that the land necessary for the above could be acquired by the United States through purchase or through a 99-year lease.

With regard to the agreement suggested in point 2 above, I feel confident that specific details need not be considered at this time and that such questions as the exact locations of the land which the United States might desire to purchase or lease could be readily determined upon subsequently through friendly negotiation between the two Governments.

With regard to your reference to publicity concerning the contingent destination of the British fleet, I should make it clear that I have not had in mind any public statement by you but merely an assurance to me along the lines indicated, as for example, reiteration to me of your statement to Parliament on June 4.

I should welcome a reply as soon as may be possible.

Source: Warren F. Kimball, ed., *Churchill and Roosevelt: The Complete Correspondence* (Princeton: Princeton University Press, 1984), 1:58–59.

Document 3.9   Annual Message to Congress: "The Four Freedoms," January 6, 1941

In his annual message to Congress at the beginning of 1941, Roosevelt laid out what would be the basic war aims of his administration, although the nation would not enter the war for another eleven months. FDR's enunciation of the Four Freedoms proved to be one of his most memorable and important legacies.

Mr. President, Mr. Speaker, Members of the Seventy-seventh Congress: I address you, the members of the Seventy-seventh Congress, at a moment unprecedented in the history of the Union. I use the word unprecedented because at no previous time has American security been as seriously threatened from without as it is today.

Since the permanent formation of our government under the Constitution, in 1789, most of the periods of crisis in our history have related to our domestic affairs. Fortunately, only one of these—the four-year War Between the States—ever threatened our national unity. Today, thank God, 130 million Americans, in forty-eight states, have forgotten points of the compass in our national unity.

It is true that prior to 1914 the United States often had been disturbed by events in other continents. We had even engaged in two wars with European nations and in a number of undeclared wars in the West Indies, in the Mediterranean, and in the Pacific for the maintenance of American rights and for the principles of peaceful commerce. But in no case had a serious threat been raised against our national safety or our continued independence.

What I seek to convey is the historic truth that the United States as a nation has at all times maintained clear, definite opposition to any attempt to lock us in behind an ancient Chinese wall while the procession of civilization went past. Today, thinking of our children and of their children, we oppose enforced isolation for ourselves or for any other part of the Americas.

That determination of ours, extending over all these years, was proved, for example, during the quarter century of wars following the French Revolution.

While the Napoleonic struggles did threaten interests of the United States because of the French foothold in the West Indies and in Louisiana, and while we engaged in the War of 1812 to vindicate our right to peaceful trade, it is nevertheless clear that neither France nor Great Britain, nor any other nation, was aiming at domination of the whole world.

In like fashion, from 1815 to 1914—ninety-nine years—no single war in Europe or in Asia constituted a real threat against our future or against the future of any other American nation.

Except in the Maximilian interlude in Mexico, no foreign power sought to establish itself in this hemisphere; and the strength of the British fleet in the Atlantic has been a friendly strength. It is still a friendly strength.

Even when the World War broke out in 1914, it seemed to contain only small threat of danger to our own American future. But, as time went on, the American people began to visualize what the downfall of democratic nations might mean to our own democracy.

We need not overemphasize imperfections in the Peace of Versailles. We need not harp on failure of the democracies to deal with problems of world reconstruction. We should remember that the Peace of 1919 was far less unjust than the kind of "pacification" which began even before Munich, and which is being carried on under the new order of tyranny that seeks to spread over every continent today. The American people have unalterably set their faces against that tyranny.

Every realist knows that the democratic way of life is at this moment being directly assailed in every part of the world—assailed either by arms, or by secret spreading of poisonous propaganda by those who seek to destroy unity and promote discord in nations that are still at peace.

During sixteen long months this assault has blotted out the whole pattern of democratic life in an appalling number of independent nations, great and small. The assailants are still on the march, threatening other nations, great and small.

Therefore, as your president, performing my constitutional duty to "give to the Congress information of the state of the Union," I find it, unhappily, necessary to report that the future and the safety of our country and of our democracy are overwhelmingly involved in events far beyond our borders.

Armed defense of democratic existence is now being gallantly waged in four continents. If that defense fails, all the population and all the resources of Europe, Asia, Africa, and Australasia will be dominated by the conquerors. Let us remember that the total of those populations and their resources in those four continents greatly exceeds the sum total of the population and the resources of the whole of the Western Hemisphere—many times over.

In times like these it is immature—and incidentally, untrue—for anybody to brag that an unprepared America, singlehanded, and with one hand tied behind its back, can hold off the whole world.

No realistic American can expect from a dictator's peace international generosity, or return of true independence, or world disarmament, or freedom of expression, or freedom of religion—or even good business. . . .

I have recently pointed out how quickly the tempo of modern warfare could bring into our very midst the physical attack which we must eventually expect if the dictator nations win this war.

There is much loose talk of our immunity from immediate and direct invasion from across the seas. Obviously, as long as the British navy retains its power, no such danger exists. Even if there were no British navy, it is not probable that any enemy would be stupid enough to attack us by landing troops in the United States from across thousands of miles of ocean, until it had acquired strategic bases from which to operate.

But we learn much from the lessons of the past years in Europe—particularly the lesson of Norway, whose essential seaports were captured by treachery and surprise built up over a series of years.

The first phase of the invasion of this hemisphere would not be the landing of regular troops. The necessary strategic points would be occupied by secret agents and their dupes—and great numbers of them are already here, and in Latin America.

As long as the aggressor nations maintain the offensive, they—not we—will choose the time and the place and the method of their attack.

That is why the future of all the American republics is today in serious danger. . . .

Our national policy is this:

First, by an impressive expression of the public will and without regard to partisanship, we are committed to all-inclusive national defense.

Second, by an impressive expression of the public will and without regard to partisanship, we are committed to full support of all those resolute peoples, everywhere, who are resisting aggression and are thereby keeping war away from our hemisphere. By this support, we express our determination that the democratic cause shall prevail; and we strengthen the defense and the security of our own nation.

Third, by an impressive expression of the public will and without regard to partisanship, we are committed to the proposition that principles of morality and considerations for our own security will never permit us to acquiesce in a peace dictated by aggressors and sponsored by appeasers. We know that enduring peace cannot be bought at the cost of other people's freedom. . . .

Therefore, the immediate need is a swift and driving increase in our armament production. . . .

New circumstances are constantly begetting new needs for our safety. I shall ask this Congress for greatly increased new appropriations and authorizations to carry on what we have begun.

I also ask this Congress for authority and for funds sufficient to manufacture additional munitions and war supplies of many kinds, to be turned over to those nations which are now in actual war with aggressor nations.

Our most useful and immediate role is to act as an arsenal for them as well as for ourselves. They do not need manpower, but they do need billions of dollars worth of the weapons of defense.

The time is near when they will not be able to pay for them all in ready cash. We cannot, and we will not, tell them that they must surrender, merely because of present inability to pay for the weapons which we know they must have.

I do not recommend that we make them a loan of dollars with which to pay for these weapons—a loan to be repaid in dollars.

I recommend that we make it possible for those nations to continue to obtain war materials in the United States, fitting their orders into our own program. Nearly all their material would, if the time ever came, be useful for our own defense. . . .

For what we send abroad, we shall be repaid within a reasonable time following the close of hostilities, in similar materials, or, at our option, in other goods of many kinds, which they can produce and which we need.

Let us say to the democracies: "We Americans are vitally concerned in your defense of freedom. We are putting forth our energies, our resources, and our organizing powers to give you the strength to regain and maintain a free world. We shall send you, in ever-increasing numbers, ships, planes, tanks, guns. This is our purpose and our pledge." In fulfillment of this purpose we will not be intimidated by the threats of dictators that they will regard as a breach of international law or as an act of war our aid to the democracies which dare to resist their aggression. Such aid is not an act of war, even if a dictator should unilaterally proclaim it so to be.

When the dictators—if the dictators—are ready to make war upon us, they will not wait for an act of war on our part. They did not wait for Norway or Belgium or the Netherlands to commit an act of war. . . .

The nation takes great satisfaction and much strength from the things which have been done to make its people conscious of their individual stake in the preservation of democratic life in America. Those things have toughened the fiber of our people, have renewed their faith and strengthened their devotion to the institutions we make ready to protect.

Certainly this is no time for any of us to stop thinking about the social and economic problems which are the root cause of the social revolution which is today a supreme factor in the world.

For there is nothing mysterious about the foundations of a healthy and strong democracy.

The basic things expected by our people of their political and economic systems are simple.

They are:

Equality of opportunity for youth and for others.
Jobs for those who can work.
Security for those who need it.
The ending of special privilege for the few.
The preservation of civil liberties for all.
The enjoyment of the fruits of scientific progress in a wider and constantly rising standard of living.

These are the simple, basic things that must never be lost sight of in the turmoil and unbelievable complexity of our modern world. The inner and abiding strength of our economic and political systems is dependent upon the degree to which they fulfill these expectations.

Many subjects connected with our social economy call for immediate improvement.

As examples:

We should bring more citizens under the coverage of old-age pensions and unemployment insurance.

We should widen the opportunities for adequate medical care.

We should plan a better system by which persons deserving or needing gainful employment may obtain it.

I have called for personal sacrifice. I am assured of the willingness of almost all Americans to respond to that call. . . .

In the future days, which we seek to make secure, we look forward to a world founded upon four essential human freedoms.

The first is freedom of speech and expression—everywhere in the world.

The second is freedom of every person to worship God in his own way—everywhere in the world.

The third is freedom from want—which, translated into world terms, means economic understandings which will secure to every nation a healthy peacetime life for its inhabitants everywhere in the world.

The fourth is freedom from fear—which, translated into world terms, means a worldwide reduction of armaments to such a point and in such a thorough fashion that no nation will be in a position to commit an act of physical aggression against any neighbor—anywhere in the world.

That is no vision of a distant millennium. It is a definite basis for a kind of world attainable in our own time and generation. That kind of world is the very antithesis of the so-called new order of tyranny which the dictators seek to create with the crash of a bomb.

To that new order we oppose the greater conception—the moral order. A good society is able to face schemes of world domination and foreign revolutions alike without fear.

Since the beginning of our American history, we have been engaged in change—in a perpetual peaceful revolution, a revolution which goes on steadily, quietly adjusting itself to changing conditions—without the concentration camp or the quick-lime in the ditch. The world order which we seek is the cooperation of free countries, working together in a friendly, civilized society.

This nation has placed its destiny in the hands and heads and hearts of its millions of free men and women; and its faith in freedom under the guidance of God. Freedom means the supremacy of human rights everywhere. Our support goes to those who struggle to gain those rights or keep them. Our strength is our unity of purpose.

To that high concept there can be no end save victory.

Source: Samuel I. Rosenman, ed., *The Public Papers and Addresses of Franklin D. Roosevelt* (1941; reprint, New York: Russell and Russell, 1969), 9:663–672.

Document 3.10   The Atlantic Charter, August 1941

Although the United States was not yet a belligerent in the war, Roosevelt and British Prime Minister Winston Churchill agreed in August 1941 on a set of war aims based largely on the idealistic vision that Roosevelt had laid out in his "Four Freedoms" speech. Because Churchill was desperate for American assistance, he agreed to provisions that were not at all to his liking, such as "the right of all peoples to choose the form of government under which they will live," which had unpleasant implications for the future of the British Empire.

The president of the United States of America and the prime minister, Mr. Churchill, representing His Majesty's government in the United Kingdom, being met together, deem it right to make known certain common principles in the national policies of their respective countries on which they base their hopes for a better future for the world.

First, their countries seek no aggrandizement, territorial or other;

Second, they desire to see no territorial changes that do not accord with the freely expressed wishes of the peoples concerned;

Third, they respect the right of all peoples to choose the form of government under which they will live; and they wish to see sovereign rights and self-government restored to those who have been forcibly deprived of them;

Fourth, they will endeavor, with the respect of their existing obligations, to further the enjoyment by all states, great and small, victor or vanquished, of access, on equal terms, to the trade and to the raw materials of the world which are needed for their economic prosperity;

Fifth, they desire to bring about the fullest collaboration between all nations in the economic field with the object of securing, for all, improved labor standards, economic advancement, and social security;

Sixth, after the final destruction of the Nazi tyranny, they hope to see established a peace which will afford to all nations the means of dwelling in safety within their own boundaries, and which will afford assurance that all the men in all the lands may live out their lives in freedom from fear and want;

Seventh, such a peace should enable all men to traverse the high seas and oceans without hindrance;

Eighth, they believe that all of the nations of the world, for realistic as well as spiritual reasons must come to the abandonment of the use of force. Since no future peace can be maintained if land, sea, or air armaments continue to be employed by nations which threaten, or may threaten, aggression outside of their frontiers, they believe, pending the establishment of a wider and permanent system of general security, that the disarmament of such nations is essential. They will likewise aid and encourage all other practicable measures which will lighten for peace-loving peoples the crushing burden of armaments.

Source: Samuel I. Rosenman, ed., *The Public Papers and Addresses of Franklin D. Roosevelt* (1950; reprint, New York: Russell and Russell, 1969), 10:314–315.

Document 3.11   Address before Congress on the Yalta Conference, March 1, 1945

When Roosevelt returned from his meeting with Churchill and Stalin at Yalta, he reported to Congress and the American people on the outcome of the talks, putting a favorable spin on the agreements. He was, of course, unable to speak publicly about what he thought was the most important achievement of the conference: firm agreement for Soviet entry into the war against Japan after Germany's defeat.

I hope that you will pardon me for this unusual posture of sitting down during the presentation of what I want to say, but I know that you will realize that it makes it a lot easier for me not to have to carry about ten pounds of steel around on the bottom of my legs; and also because of the fact that I have just completed a fourteen-thousand-mile trip.

First of all, I want to say, it is good to be home.

It has been a long journey. I hope you will also agree that it has been, so far, a fruitful one.

Speaking in all frankness, the question of whether it is entirely fruitful or not lies to a great extent in your hands. For unless you here in the halls of the American Congress—with the support of the American people—concur in the general conclusions reached at Yalta, and give them your active support, the meeting will not have produced lasting results.

That is why I have come before you at the earliest hour I could after my return. I want to make a personal report to you—and, at the same time, to the people of the country. Many months of earnest work are ahead of us all, and I should like to feel that when the last stone is laid on the structure of international peace, it will be an achievement for which all of us in America have worked steadfastly and unselfishly—together. . . .

I come from the Crimea Conference with a firm belief that we have made a good start on the road to a world of peace.

There were two main purposes in this Crimea Conference.

The first was to bring defeat to Germany with the greatest possible speed, and the smallest possible loss of Allied men. That purpose is now being carried out in great force. The German army, and the German people, are feeling the ever increasing might of our fighting men and of the

Allied armies. Every hour gives us added pride in the heroic advance of our troops in Germany—on German soil—toward a meeting with the gallant Red Army.

The second purpose was to continue to build the foundation for an international accord that would bring order and security after the chaos of the war, that would give some assurance of lasting peace among the nations of the world.

Toward that goal also, a tremendous stride was made.

At Teheran, a little over a year ago, there were long-range military plans laid by the Chiefs of Staff of the three most powerful nations. Among the civilian leaders at Teheran, however, at that time, there were only exchanges of views and expressions of opinion. No political arrangements were made and none was attempted.

At the Crimea Conference, however, the time had come for getting down to specific cases in the political field.

There was on all sides at this conference an enthusiastic effort to reach an agreement. Since the time of Teheran, a year ago, there had developed among all of us a—what shall I call it?—a greater facility in negotiating with each other, that augurs well for the peace of the world. We know each other better.

I have never for an instant wavered in my belief that an agreement to insure world peace and security can be reached. . . .

When we met at Yalta, in addition to laying our strategic and tactical plans for the complete and final military victory over Germany, there were other problems of vital political consequence.

For instance, first, there were the problems of the occupation and control of Germany—after victory—the complete destruction of her military power, and the assurance that neither the Nazis nor Prussian militarism could again be revived to threaten the peace and the civilization of the world.

Second—again for example—there was the settlement of the few differences that remained among us with respect to the International Security Organization after the Dumbarton Oaks Conference. As you remember, at that time, I said that we had agreed 90 percent. Well, that's a pretty good percentage. I think the other 10 percent was ironed out at Yalta.

Third, there were the general political and economic problems common to all of the areas which had been or would be liberated from the Nazi yoke. This is a very special problem. We over here find it difficult to understand the ramifications of many of these problems in foreign lands, but we are trying to.

Fourth, there were the special problems created by a few instances such as Poland and Yugoslavia.

Days were spent in discussing these momentous matters and we argued freely and frankly across the table. But at the end, on every point, unanimous agreement was reached. And more important even than the agreement of words, I may say we achieved a unity of thought and a way of getting along together.

Of course, we know that it was Hitler's hope—and the German warlords'—that we would not agree, that some slight crack might appear in the solid wall of Allied unity, a crack that would give him and his fellow gangsters one last hope of escaping their just doom. That is the objective for which his propaganda machine has been working for many months.

But Hitler has failed.

Never before have the major Allies been more closely united—not only in their war aims but also in their peace aims. And they are determined to continue to be united with each other and with all peace-loving nations—so that the ideal of lasting peace will become a reality. . . .

We made it clear again at Yalta, and I now repeat, that unconditional surrender does not mean the destruction or enslavement of the German people. The Nazi leaders have deliberately withheld that part of the Yalta declaration from the German press and radio. They seek to convince the people of Germany that the Yalta declaration does mean slavery and destruction for them—they are working at it day and night for that is how the Nazis hope to save their own skins, and deceive their people into continued and useless resistance.

We did, however, make it clear at the conference just what unconditional surrender does mean for Germany.

It means the temporary control of Germany by Great Britain, Russia, France, and the United States. Each of these nations will occupy and control a separate zone of Germany—and the administration of the four zones will be coordinated in Berlin by a Control Council composed of representatives of the four nations.

Unconditional surrender means something else. It means the end of Nazism. It means the end of the Nazi party—and of all its barbaric laws and institutions.

It means the termination of all militaristic influence in the public, private, and cultural life of Germany.

It means for the Nazi war criminals a punishment that is speedy and just—and severe.

It means the complete disarmament of Germany; the destruction of its militarism and its military equipment; the end of its production of armament; the dispersal of all its armed forces; the permanent dismemberment of the German General Staff which has so often shattered the peace of the world.

It means that Germany will have to make reparations in kind for the damage which has been done to the innocent victims of its aggression. . . .

Of equal importance with the military arrangements at the Crimea Conference were the agreements reached with respect to a general international organization for lasting world peace.

The foundations were laid at Dumbarton Oaks. There was one point, however, on which agreement was not reached at Dumbarton Oaks. It involved the procedure of voting in the Security Council. I want to try to make it clear by making it simple. It took me hours and hours to get the thing straight in my own mind—and many conferences.

At the Crimea Conference, the Americans made a proposal on this subject which, after full discussion was, I am glad to say, unanimously adopted by the other two nations.

It is not yet possible to announce the terms of that agreement publicly, but it will be in a very short time.

When the conclusions reached with respect to voting in the Security Council are made known, I think and I hope that you will find them a fair solution of this complicated and difficult problem. They are founded in justice, and will go far to assure international cooperation in the maintenance of peace.

A conference of all the United Nations of the world will meet in San Francisco on April 25, 1945. There, we all hope, and confidently expect, to execute a definite charter of organization under which the peace of the world will be preserved and the forces of aggression permanently outlawed. . . .

As the Allied armies have marched to military victory, they have liberated people whose liberties had been crushed by the Nazis for four long years, whose economy has been reduced to ruin by Nazi despoilers.

There have been instances of political confusion and unrest in these liberated areas—that is not unexpected—as in Greece or in Poland or in Yugoslavia, and there may be more. Worse than that, there actually began to grow up in some of these places queer ideas of, for instance, "spheres of influence" that were incompatible with the basic principles of international collaboration. If allowed to go on unchecked, these developments might have had tragic results in time. . . .

We met in the Crimea, determined to settle this matter of liberated areas. Things that might happen that we cannot foresee at this moment might happen suddenly—unexpectedly—next week or next month. And I am happy to confirm to the Congress that we did arrive at a settlement—and, incidentally, a unanimous settlement.

The three most powerful nations have agreed that the political and economic problems of any area liberated from Nazi conquest, or of any former Axis satellite, are a joint responsibility of all three governments. They will join together, during the temporary period of instability—after hostilities—to help the people of any liberated area, or of any former satellite state, to solve their own problems through firmly established democratic processes.

They will endeavor to see to it that the people who carry on the interim government between occupation of Germany and true independence will be as representative as possible of all democratic elements in the population, and that free elections are held as soon as possible thereafter.

Responsibility for political conditions thousands of miles away can no longer be avoided by this great nation. Certainly, I do not want to live to see another war. As I have said, the world is smaller—smaller every year. The United States now exerts a tremendous influence in the cause of peace throughout all the world. What we people over here are thinking and talking about is in the interest of peace, because it is known all over the world. The slightest remark in either house of the Congress is known all over the world the following day. We will continue to exert that influence, only if we are willing to continue to share in the responsibility for keeping the peace. It will be our own tragic loss, I think, if we were to shirk that responsibility.

The final decisions in these areas are going to be made jointly; and therefore they will often be a result of give-and-take compromise. The United States will not always have its way 100 percent—nor will Russia nor Great Britain. We shall not always have ideal answers—solutions to complicated international problems, even though we are determined continuously to strive toward that ideal. But I am sure that under the agreements reached at Yalta, there will be a more stable political Europe than ever before. . . .

One outstanding example of joint action by the three major Allied powers in the liberated areas was the solution reached on Poland. The whole Polish question was a potential source of trouble in postwar Europe—as it has been sometimes before—and we came to the conference determined to find a common ground for its solution. And we did—even though everybody does not agree with us, obviously.

Our objective was to help to create a strong, independent, and prosperous nation. That is the thing we must always remember, those words, agreed to by Russia, by Britain, and by the United States: the objective of making Poland a strong, independent, and prosperous nation, with a government ultimately to be selected by the Polish people themselves. . . .

Throughout history, Poland has been the corridor through which attacks on Russia have been made. Twice in this generation, Germany has struck at Russia through this corridor. To insure European security and world peace, a strong and independent Poland is necessary to prevent that from happening again. . . .

I am convinced that the agreement on Poland, under the circumstances, is the most hopeful agreement possible for a free, independent, and prosperous Polish state.

The Crimea Conference was a meeting of the three major military powers on whose shoulders rested chief responsibility and burden of the war. Although, for this reason, France was not a participant in the conference, no one should detract from the recognition that was accorded there of her role in the future of Europe and the future of the world.

France has been invited to accept a zone of control in Germany, and to participate as a fourth member of the Allied Control Council of Germany.

She has been invited to join as a sponsor of the International Conference at San Francisco next month.

She will be a permanent member of the International Security Council together with the other four major powers.

And, finally, we have asked that France be associated with us in our joint responsibility over all the liberated areas of Europe. . . .

The Crimea Conference was a successful effort by the three leading nations to find a common ground for peace. It ought to spell the end of the system of unilateral action, the exclusive alliances, the spheres of influence, the balances of power, and all the other expedients that have been tried for centuries—and have always failed.

We propose to substitute for all these a universal organization in which all peace-loving nations will finally have a chance to join.

I am confident that the Congress and the American people will accept the results of this conference as the beginnings of a permanent structure of peace upon which we can begin to build, under God, that better world in which our children and grandchildren—yours and mine, the children and grandchildren of the whole world—must live, and can live.

And that, my friends, is the principal message I can give you. But I feel it very deeply, as I know that all of you are feeling it today, and are going to feel it in the future.

Source: Samuel I. Rosenman, ed., *The Public Papers and Addresses of Franklin D. Roosevelt* (1950; reprint, New York: Russell and Russell, 1969), 13:570–586.

Josef Stalin, FDR, and Winston Churchill at the Teheran conference, November 29, 1943.

CHAPTER FOUR

Crises and Flashpoints:

From the Banking Crisis to Yalta

H ow a president responds to crises is a major determinant of how posterity will judge his presidency. During FDR's twelve years in office he dealt with the two largest crises of the twentieth century (and the second and third largest crises, after the Civil War, in U.S. history). Americans overwhelmingly approved of FDR's approach to these crises, and he is now among the ranks of great presidents.

THE GREAT DEPRESSION AND THE FIRST NEW DEAL

By the eve of Franklin Roosevelt's inauguration the nation's banking system had collapsed. Deposits were not insured and, as more banks failed, depositors grew fearful and removed their money from accounts even in relatively stable banks. As a result, financial institutions were pulled under in increasing numbers. Although the government kept no official statistics on unemployment, at least a quarter and possibly a third of the U.S. workforce was unemployed.

On the other hand, these terrible times were an extraordinary opportunity for a new president. FDR presided over an economy that could only improve, and, at least initially, the American people would measure him against a predecessor they thought an abject failure. Any leadership that the new chief executive could show and any successes he could achieve would be magnified by a citizenry hungry for both. "Not for years," Arthur Krock wrote in the *New York Times,* the day before Roosevelt's inauguration, "has a new President been more likely to gain gratitude and praise beyond the merits of his accomplished program for the simple fact of being able to achieve any program at all," (*New York Times,* March 3, 1933)

"Action, and Action Now"

Roosevelt's first inaugural address is generally considered one of the four most memorable inaugural speeches ever made by a U.S. president (the others being Thomas Jefferson's first, Abraham Lincoln's second, and John F. Kennedy's). In addition to asserting that "the only thing we have to fear is fear itself," FDR denounced the "mad chase for evanescent profits" and the "generation of self-seekers" that had led to the depression. He called for cooperation and unselfishness to overcome the "evils of the old order," and pledged "action, and action now," guided by a newfound or renewed realization of "our interdependence on each other" (Rosenman 1969, 2:11–16; see Document 3.1).

It was a speech that hit exactly the right notes to boost morale. The new president delivered on his promise of quick action by calling Congress into session to deal with the banking crisis. He closed down the banking system for a few days while members of Hoover's Treasury Department worked with Roosevelt's advisers to draw up a distinctly unradical Emergency Banking Bill. At a time when public hostility toward bankers was such that a government seizure of the banking system might have been accepted, Roosevelt showed he had no such socialist goals. The bill simply lent government help to the same private bankers FDR had just denounced in his inaugural as "the money changers [who] have fled from their high seats in the temple of our civilization" (Rosenman 1969, 2:12). When Congress convened, it immediately passed the bill without any debate.

Roosevelt then went on the radio for the first of his "fireside chats" with the American people. FDR's skill at communicating in a seemingly personal way over this mass medium was key to his success as a leader. Speaking in a homey manner, he reassured people about the safety of their money in the banks and about the capabilities of their new leader. Roosevelt was able almost instantly to achieve what Hoover had persistently said was needed but had never been able to stimulate: a restoration of confidence, or at least of hope (see Document 4.1). The extraordinary feeling of personal connection that Roosevelt had made with the American public was demonstrated in an outpouring of letters—more than half a million people wrote to him during his first ten days in office. Letter writers sometimes referred to the president as their "personal friend" (McElvaine 1983, 223; see Document 4.2).

What Roosevelt had done with the Emergency Banking Act and his reassuring words was to gain public approval for a plan largely devised by Hoover's advisers. Moley exaggerated when he later asserted that "capitalism was saved in eight days" (Leuchtenburg 1963, 45), but there is no question that the first example of FDR's "action now" went in the direction of saving capitalism, not reforming it much, and certainly not replacing it.

Legislation in the First Hundred Days

With Congress assembled and the public ready to support his proposals, Roosevelt proceeded to address other economic and social issues in the opening months of his presidency by offering or agreeing to an unprecedented amount of major legislation in what came to be called the "hundred days" (a reference to Napoleon's time back in power in 1815 after his return from exile on the island of Elba). The military analogy was in keeping with Roosevelt's view that the struggle against the depression was analogous to war. He had said in his inaugural address that, if Congress failed to act promptly, he would ask it for "broad Executive power to wage a war against the emergency, as great as the power that would be given to me if we were in fact invaded by a foreign foe" (Rosenman 1969, 2:15).

To partially redeem a foolish campaign promise to cut federal spending, Roosevelt's next move was the Economy Act, which gave the president the power to cut the pay of federal employees and benefits to veterans. Had it not been for the enormity of the crisis and Roosevelt's great popularity, Democrats would probably have rebelled (as some, but not enough, did) against his leadership and defeated this ill-advised bill. But it passed only two days after the bank bill.

Then the president asked for the legalization of beer with 3.2 percent alcohol. That might have helped people forget their troubles, but hardly addressed their roots. (Congress had passed a repeal of Prohibition, and although a sufficient number of states had yet to ratify the bill,

Roosevelt took the popular step of permitting the sale of beer with the highest alcohol content allowed under the outgoing regulations.) Still, there was excitement. And now Roosevelt began to move in a different direction. His pet project for getting poor youth out of the cities and into jobs in the beneficial fresh air of parks and forests reached fruition in the Civilian Conservation Corps (CCC) before March was over.

Meanwhile, Roosevelt was pushing for what he believed was the key to recovery: legislation that would increase farm income and so, he hoped, create a market for industrial products and revive the whole economy. Agriculture had been in depression throughout most of the so-called prosperity decade of the 1920s. With this long background of crisis, many different proposals for aiding farmers were in circulation. Most of the plans focused on reducing overproduction, which was believed to be the main cause of the low farm prices. Roosevelt wanted a program that the farm leaders could agree on, so he insisted that they get together and come up with something. The resulting Agricultural Adjustment Act (AAA), which paid farmers to take land out of production, was not passed until mid-May 1933 (see Document 4.3). This was after planting was well underway in warmer sections of the country, and the production cutbacks were achieved by plowing under crops. The image of destroying food while many were hungry was one that stuck with the AAA, and the program was never successful. In 1936 the Supreme Court found the processing tax that financed the program to be unconstitutional.

On the same day that the AAA was enacted (May 12, 1933), Congress passed the Emergency Farm Mortgage Act to refinance farm mortgages and forestall foreclosures. Congress also approved an appropriation of $500 million for direct relief to be distributed through a new Federal Emergency Relief Administration (FERA). Under the leadership of Harry Hopkins, the FERA began with great speed to funnel money to the needy. (Hopkins had headed the Temporary Emergency Relief Administration, a New York state agency, before he and FDR had moved to Washington, D.C.) Hopkins set the tone by spending $5 million in his first two hours on the job. Although there was some criticism of such spending, the need for helping hungry people and the hope of stimulating the economy through spending both pointed toward this approach.

A week after the approval of the AAA and FERA, Congress agreed to Roosevelt's proposal to create the Tennessee Valley Authority (TVA), a vast regional planning program that would build dams to provide electricity for the depressed region and to control flooding and erosion. Private power interests fought it every step of the way.

Over the remaining month of the first hundred days, Congress enacted the Truth-in-Securities Act (which obliged companies issuing new securities to fully disclose their financial information), the Glass-Steagall Banking Act (which guaranteed bank deposits and separated investment banking from commercial banking), the Home Owners' Loan Act (which provided for federal refinancing of home mortgages), and the National Industrial Recovery Act (NIRA, which provided for industries to set up codes of acceptable practices and appropriated $3.3 billion for a vast public works program, the Public Works Administration). (See Chapter 3 for details on this legislation.)

Roosevelt may not have been entirely sure in what direction he was leading the nation, other than toward a sense of greater social responsibility, but the feeling of movement and excitement that he created in his first months in office was contagious. It was, indeed, "action now," and legions of people wanted a piece of it. Suddenly Washington was the place to be. Energetic and ambitious young (and not so young) people flocked to the capital in hope of becoming "New Dealers." Writer Edmund Wilson summed up the change in outlook: "The bright boys of the Eastern universities, instead of being obliged to choose, as they were twenty years ago, between business, the bond-selling game and the field of foreign missions, can come and get jobs in Washington" (Maney 1992, 55). By the fall of 1933 college students were asking for courses that "would point them toward the 'brain trust.'" (McElvaine 1984, 145). The whole attitude toward government, which had been overwhelmingly negative during the Hoover years (and, for that matter, throughout the 1920s), turned nearly 180 degrees.

For all the activity of the first hundred days, what had been accomplished beyond a lifting of spirits? The provision of direct relief to the unemployed through the FERA was significant. It did nothing to cure the depression, but it made living with its effects endurable for millions. The Home Owners' Loan Corporation (HOLC) and the Emergency Farm Mortgage Act protected lenders from losing their money when the buyers of homes or farms could not meet their mortgage payments, but it also helped a substantial number of middle-class families who had been hit by hard times to keep their homes and farms. The Tennessee Valley

Authority would prove, by almost any standard, to be a great success in regional planning and development. The CCC was a boon to the young men who joined it and to the families who received their paychecks. The Emergency Banking Act, though it did nothing to reform the financial system, restored enough confidence to make the banking system viable again, especially when combined with the June 1933 Glass-Steagall Act, which separated commercial and investment banking and created the Federal Deposit Insurance Corporation (an idea for which FDR had little more enthusiasm than most bankers did, but which he felt could not be blocked).

The AAA, on which FDR had pinned his primary hopes for recovery, was unsuccessful. It helped landowners, but also gave them an incentive to force sharecroppers and tenants off their land. The National Industrial Recovery Act (NIRA) stimulated the economy briefly in 1933, but failed to bring about recovery, industrial or otherwise. Its provision of some protection for labor unions resulted in an expansion of a few unions and helped to produce a series of major strikes in 1934. The NIRA's public works program, the Public Works Administration (PWA), ultimately constructed many worthwhile public projects, but under the cautious direction of Harold Ickes it moved and spent too slowly to significantly boost the economy.

Roosevelt said that the goals of the New Deal were to bring about relief, recovery, and reform. The activity of the first hundred days produced some relief but precious little recovery (mainly because Roosevelt, along with a majority of Congress and the public, was too fiscally conservative to accept the level of deficit spending needed to jolt the economy back to life) and no significant reform beyond the Truth-in-Securities Act and the precedent for greater government intervention. Judged by the standard that Roosevelt himself had set in his "forgotten man" radio address in 1932—"a real economic cure must go to the killing of the bacteria in the system rather than to the treatment of external symptoms"—the early New Deal must be found wanting (Rosenman 1969, 1:625). Its successes were almost entirely in relieving symptoms. The economic germs were still in command, beyond the reach of any of the treatments so far prescribed by "Dr. New Deal."

Yet it would be a mistake to conclude that the early New Deal was a failure. Herbert Hoover had been right all along in saying that what was most needed was a restoration of confidence, and Roosevelt had gone a long way toward achieving that elusive objective. He also had joined forces with Congress to transform the word *Washington* from the name of a revered Founding Father to that of a newfound fatherly government that provided paternalistic assistance in times of need. Hope, which had been dead a few months before, had been resurrected by the summer of 1933. Idealism displaced cynicism as a can-do, all-things-are-possible attitude spread widely. The early New Deal can be seen as a revival on the scale of the Great Awakenings of the eighteenth and nineteenth centuries.

The New Dealer in Chief

All of this can perhaps be best understood by realizing what Franklin Roosevelt was and what he was not. He was a politician, one of the best that the United States has ever seen. He was guided by a simple religious faith and a basic sense of morality (the Golden Rule). He was not a philosopher or an economist. He took the ideas of his academic advisers and refashioned them in ways that usually worked well politically, with little regard to whether they were logically inconsistent or even contradictory. Given these basic facts about the New Dealer in Chief, it is unsurprising that the early New Deal was much better politics than it was economics.

And what of FDR's heralded experimental approach? "Take a method and try it," he famously said in his 1932 commencement address at Oglethorpe University in Georgia, "if it fails, admit it frankly and try another"(Rosenman 1969, 1:646). As Patrick Maney has noted in his FDR biography, *The Roosevelt Presence,* one of the best examples of Roosevelt's failure to consistently apply this experimental approach was his attitude toward work relief. The combination of the failure of the National Recovery Administration (NRA) and AAA to bring about quick recovery with the slowness of Ickes in providing employment through PWA projects meant that as the winter of 1933–1934 approached, millions of jobless Americans were facing the prospect of hunger and homelessness. Harry Hopkins, who as head of the FERA had taken the opposite approach to that of Ickes and spent money rapidly to provide relief, persuaded the president that a work relief program must be instituted. The resulting Civil Works Administration (CWA) was a huge success. Moving with the alacrity that had been lacking in Ickes's PWA, Hopkins put 2.6 million people to work at government-created jobs in a month and 4 million by a month later. Wages, although well below the minimum for a decent living standard, were two-and-a-half times the average FERA relief payment. In a few months the CWA provided about a billion dollars of stimulus to the economy and restored the self-respect of vast numbers of the unemployed. The experiment worked—and FDR ordered it stopped. He feared the cost of a vast work relief program, the budget deficits that were likely to result, and the precedent that the government would serve as an employer of last resort for everyone who could not secure a job in the private sector. In contrast, the NRA was a dismal failure, but Roosevelt refused to "admit it frankly and try another" method. He kept the NRA going until the Supreme Court did him the favor of declaring it unconstitutional (see Chapter 3).

CONTINUING ECONOMIC CRISIS, "THUNDER ON THE LEFT," AND THE SECOND NEW DEAL

FDR had tried to achieve consensus during his first few years in the White House. Fear of the social and economic consequences of the depression remained high in the first months of his presidency, and Roosevelt generally could count on the acquiescence, if not the outright support, of all but the extreme elements on both his right and left. But as time went on and the New Deal proved itself in relief but not recovery, critics on both flanks were emboldened.

In some ways this was a continuation of the economic and political crisis that FDR inherited when he took office. But in other ways the rising opposition from conservative big business and the growing "thunder on the left" constituted a second major crisis of the Roosevelt presidency. The time was coming when he would have to abandon consensus and choose a side.

Abandoning Consensus and Turning Left

Conservative opponents of the New Deal, including FDR's erstwhile political ally Alfred E. Smith and many of Smith's business-oriented Democratic backers, came together in 1934 to launch the American Liberty League. Although its founders publicly asserted that the organization was not anti-Roosevelt, there was no doubt that its stated purpose of "combat[ing] radicalism, preserv[ing] property rights, [and] uphold[ing] and preserv[ing] the Constitution" meant protecting against the "threat" of the New Deal (*New York Times*, August 23, 1934).

If the right was beginning to defect from Roosevelt in 1934, indicators showed that the greater danger might come from the left. The voters endorsed the New Deal in the congressional elections of 1934, in which the Democrats gained seats on top of the large majorities that the party had gained in the anti-Hoover landslide two years before. But the 1934 elections also signaled that the nation's political center of gravity was shifting farther to the left, beyond Roosevelt's moderate progressivism. The success at the polls of the Minnesota Farmer-Labor Party—whose leader Governor Floyd B. Olson was openly denouncing capitalism, calling for a "cooperative commonwealth," and criticizing the New Deal for collaborating with such business interests as the NRA—and the Wisconsin Progressive Party, indicated that voters were ready for more radical change (Schlesinger 1960, 101). The same message was apparent in California, where socialist novelist Upton Sinclair switched to the Democratic Party, called for the establishment of a parallel socialist economy among the unemployed of the state, and won a big victory in the gubernatorial primary. Sinclair sought the president's endorsement and thought he had obtained it when he visited FDR at Hyde Park in early September. Wholeheartedly falling victim to the famous Roosevelt charm and manipulation, Sinclair said to reporters after his audience with FDR, "I talked with one of the kindest and most genial and frank and open-minded and loveable men I have ever met." (Davis 1986, 409). But Sinclair's attempt to get Roosevelt's endorsement turned into Sinclair endorsing Roosevelt. Sinclair lost in November, but the popularity of his radical program was evidence of the country's leftward drift.

So, too, were a series of bloody confrontations between workers and authorities in the summer of 1934. Strikes in Minneapolis, San Francisco, and elsewhere and a continuing struggle to organize textile workers in the South marked the beginning of a massive stirring of workers. Although many people from the upper classes feared a revolution, Roosevelt did not send in federal troops (as, for example, Grover Cleveland had in response to labor disputes), and the strikes ended with relatively little bloodshed.

And there were the movements led by Sen. Huey P. Long, D-La., who was calling for wealth sharing; Father Charles Coughlin, who used his weekly radio shows to demand what he termed "social justice"; and Dr. Francis Townsend, a retired California physician who proposed to pay every American over age sixty $200 a month. The following of these three men was growing into several million people each, and it looked like they might threaten Roosevelt's reelection in 1936 if they united in support of a third party candidate. Political necessity indicated a presidential turn to the left.

Roosevelt abandoned the quest for consensus with great reluctance. He seems sincerely to have wanted to cooperate with business as long as he could. In November 1934 he was still saying, "One of my principal tasks is to prevent bankers and businessmen from committing suicide" (McElvaine 1984, 252). A month later, however, Roosevelt made clear that the time for that role was running out. "All I can say," he told Secretary of Commerce Daniel Roper, "is that business will have only to January 3 [when he would submit his budget to Congress] to make up its mind whether it will cooperate or not" (Davis 1986, 436).

When the clock ran out on a rapprochement with business, Roosevelt realized that he would have to find ways to demonstrate his allegiance to the lower classes and, as he put it privately in the spring of 1935, to "steal [Huey] Long's thunder" (Moley 1971, 305). The result was the "second New Deal" of 1935.

While still giving hints that he would try to appease business, FDR took steps in the spring and summer of 1935 that included what would prove to be the most important and lasting reforms of his presidency. These included the Public Utilities Holding Company Act, a massive appropriation for public works that included the creation of the Works Progress Administration (WPA), the Social Security Act, and the National Labor Relations Act (also known as the Wagner Act; see Chapters 3 and 5).

Roosevelt had a knack not only for making a virtue of necessity, but also for taking up as his own positions those that had been forced upon him. Although one of the two most important reforms of the second New Deal, Social Security, may have been hastened by the growing strength of Dr. Townsend's movement, the basic idea was not alien to Roosevelt's outlook. He had long favored the creation of some sort of old-age pensions, unemployment insurance, and health insurance. The other major innovation of 1935, however, the Wagner Act, was not at all in keeping with Roosevelt's paternalistic outlook. He wanted to do things *for* workers, much as a nobleman might for the peasants on his estate, but before 1935 he had never been enamored of workers helping themselves through unionization. In fact, the president had asked the bill's sponsor, Sen. Robert F. Wagner, D-N.Y., not to push it the previous year. Now, though, as it became clear that the momentum behind the bill in Congress could not be stopped and that Roosevelt needed, for political reasons, to identify himself with workers, Roosevelt suddenly placed the labor measure on his "must list" of legislation and gladly took whatever credit for it he could get. A year later Roosevelt was proudly displaying a union membership card at campaign stops.

Roosevelt had no use for Senator Long or his demagogic calls for confiscating the fortunes of the rich. But Long was gaining in popularity, the rich were very unpopular, and many of the rich had turned on Roosevelt without, as he saw it, any good reason. This combination of circumstances provided a perfect setting for Roosevelt to stage a rhetorical attack on the rich. In June 1935 the president sent a tax message to Congress calling for more steeply graduated income taxes, a stiff corporate tax, and inheritance taxes to reduce what many people saw as swollen fortunes (see Document 4.4). It was a wonderful way to lash out at those who had turned against him and to appeal to the masses hearkening to Long's calls for redistribution. But it was essentially all talk. Roosevelt did almost nothing to push the legislation, which passed in a watered-down form.

As the legislation of the second New Deal was making its way through Congress, the Supreme Court in May destroyed the last possible bridge back to cooperation between the administration and business when it invalidated the National Recovery Administration in the case of *Schechter Poultry Corp. v. United States* (see Chapter 5). Although striking down the failed NRA has aptly been described as a mercy killing, the decision angered Roosevelt and turned him even more against the conservatives on the Court and in Congress and the business interests they represented.

In Roosevelt's 1936 reelection campaign he vocally identified with the workers, unemployed, and middle class against "the forces of selfishness and lust for power" (Rosenman 1969, 5:568). The result was one of the largest victories ever recorded in a contested presidential election (see Chapter 2).

A landslide victory in an election can be a mixed blessing if it leads the victor to believe that the people will support any move he makes. Such was the case following Roosevelt's trouncing of Alf Landon and the Republicans in 1936. Convinced that voters had given him a mandate and that the Supreme Court was blocking the will of the people by invalidating New Deal laws, Roosevelt decided to "reform" the Court (see Document 5.3). His motivation is understandable, but undoubtedly the decision to pursue what was immediately dubbed by his opponents as "Court packing" was heavily influenced by the landslide election.

In an age of dictators such as Adolf Hitler, Josef Stalin, and Benito Mussolini, anything that smacked of a power grab and possible subversion of the constitutional system of checks and balances was sure to make Americans uneasy. This was doubly true for those who were already suspicious of Roosevelt or who simply opposed his policies and resented his popularity. For many southern Democrats in Congress, who had become increasingly uncomfortable with some of Roosevelt's policies but had felt trapped into supporting them because of the president's popularity, the Court-packing issue provided the cover they needed to oppose him. The coalition that these southern Democrats formed (or, more accurately, revived) with Republicans for the Court fight would survive and be a major impediment to future Roosevelt proposals on domestic issues. Roosevelt eventually withdrew the Court-packing proposal, which had become unnecessary because the Court had begun to uphold the constitutionality of New Deal measures. (For details on FDR's relations with the Court, see Chapter 5).

A Year of Frustration

Because FDR had not embraced the idea that intentional government spending far in excess of revenues was not only acceptable but necessary to stimulate the economy, after his reelection was secured he ordered a sharp cutback in spending on Works Progress Administration work relief and other programs. The result was to plunge the economy, which had improved by 1936 but had remained in depression, into a new collapse in 1937. Never one to see himself at fault, Roosevelt concluded that his enemies among big business people and bankers had orchestrated the "recession" (as it was called to make it sound less severe or ominous than a renewed depression) to get back at him.

Roosevelt was frustrated by a number of things in 1937, a year he had expected to spend basking in the glory of his enormous victory the preceding November. There was, first, the hostile reaction to his Court proposal, which came not only from the usual suspects in business and the Republican Party but also from some of his supporters, who feared that tampering with the Court might set a precedent for future presidents they did not support. Then there was the spread of sit-down strikes by workers affiliated with the new Congress of Industrial Organizations (CIO). (In a sit-down strike the striking workers occupy the factory, thus making it impossible for the company to bring in strike-breakers.) Roosevelt had cast his lot with labor in 1936, but now the unions were going beyond what he—and much of the American middle class—felt comfortable with, because it seemed to be an attack on private property. During a strike in the spring of 1937 against the smaller steel companies, a frustrated Roosevelt, who probably felt that labor was being as ungrateful as big business had been earlier in his presidency, said to the CIO and the steel companies, "a plague on both your houses" (Bernstein 1969, 496). (For details on Roosevelt's relations with the CIO, see Chapter 5.)

By this time the recession was underway, and Roosevelt's talent for bringing together opposing sides looked less like an asset and more like a form of vacillation. At times during these difficult months, Roosevelt attempted to placate conservative businessmen by trying to balance the budget with further cuts in spending. In this mode FDR seemed to be endorsing the Hoover approach to economic crisis. Roosevelt found his legislative program, such as it was by this time, stalled in a Congress overwhelmingly of his own party, and he had few new ideas to offer. Under pressure from growing unemployment and a new stock market plunge in early 1938, the president finally acquiesced to Hopkins' demand for more spending. In April Roosevelt called for an additional $3 billion for public works projects.

A frustrated and somewhat shaken Roosevelt concluded that his lack of support from a heavily Democratic Congress was caused by an unclear ideological division between the parties. FDR also felt that he needed to regain the offensive. He decided to try to make the Democratic Party the liberal party by using presidential influence in congressional primaries in 1938 to deny nominations to certain conservative opponents of the New Deal. Part of the motivation for this action was the president's quest for revenge against those who had deserted him in the Court fight. Regardless, it was another ill-advised move; Roosevelt's popularity had slid considerably with the Court controversy and the recession, and most voters do not like national leaders to tell them how they should vote in state and local elections. The episode gave Roosevelt's political opponents another opening. Alluding to the terrible purges being carried out by Josef Stalin in the Soviet Communist Party, FDR's enemies labeled his attempt to remove uncooperative Democrats, "Roosevelt's purge."

On defense, Roosevelt's forces were very successful, with three incumbent liberal southern senators fending off challenges from conservative Democrats. Indeed, it was the resounding primary victory of Sen. Claude D. Pepper, D-Fla., in May that persuaded enough southern Democrats to allow the enactment of the Fair Labor Standards Act, which provided for a federal minimum wage and a maximum forty-hour work week and was the last major legislative achievement of the New Deal (see Document 4.5). On offense, however, the New Dealers were less successful. All five of the targeted Democratic senators won renomination in the 1938 primaries, including three against whom the president took a public stand. But Roosevelt did succeed in defeating a major Democratic opponent of the New Deal in the House, John J. O'Connor, D-N.Y. FDR then made the dubious claim that he was satisfied because "Harvard lost the schedule but won the Yale game" (Leuchtenburg 1963, 268). It is doubtful that he took much comfort from such an argument.

As the New Deal began to peter out in the late 1930s, both because of the revived conservative coalition after the Court fight and because the Roosevelt administration was running short of new ideas for solving the continuing domestic problem, the president started to focus more on foreign policy.

WORLD WAR II

The news that reached the White House from Honolulu on December 7, 1941, placed Roosevelt for a second time at the helm of a nation in extraordinary crisis. FDR's third term would test him as a wartime leader much as his first term had tested him as a political, economic, and societal leader. In Roosevelt's first inaugural address, at the beginning of the Great Depression, he said that he might ask Congress to grant him "broad Executive power to wage a war against the emergency, as great as the power that would be given to me if we were in fact invaded by a foreign foe" (Rosenman 1969, 2:15). Now a foreign foe had presented itself, and the war would not be metaphorical.

But the second huge crisis of FDR's presidency had actually begun long before the Japanese attack on Pearl Harbor. Roosevelt had concluded as early as 1938 that war with Adolf Hitler's Germany was inevitable. He felt that he could do little to prepare for such an eventuality, however, because of strong isolationist sentiment in the United States. Especially alarming was a warning that Alexander Sachs, an economist who sometimes advised the president, relayed to him in October 1939. It came from a group of physicists, including Albert Einstein, who had fled the Nazis in Europe. Einstein had tried to pass this warning directly to Roosevelt two months earlier in a letter, but the president did not grasp its significance then (see Document 4.6). The scientists said that recent developments in nuclear physics indicated that it might be possible to construct a bomb of unprecedented destructive power and that it was likely that Germany was pursuing research toward this end. "Alex, what you are after is to see that the Nazis don't blow us up," FDR said (Maney 1992, 121). Little was done for several months, but after the fall of France in June 1940, Roosevelt ordered an all-out American effort to develop an atomic bomb. The resulting Manhattan Project was close to testing the weapon when Roosevelt died. Although he was not around to see the dawn of the nuclear age, Roosevelt's decision to invest great resources in this effort was one of the most fateful of his presidency.

Isolationism Abates

Even before the fall of France, the German *blitzkrieg* (the "lightning war" whereby Hitler's armies overran the low countries, Denmark, Norway, and northern France) in the spring of 1940 had begun to soften Americans' opposition to getting involved in the war. Opinion polls now indicated that most Americans thought that helping the British should be a higher priority than keeping the United States out of war. Roosevelt took the opportunity to paint a stark picture for his constituents. He spoke of the "nightmare" existence that Americans would face if the Nazis won the war, called for a huge increase in military spending, and pledged material assistance to the opponents of Hitler's forces.

As the war worsened for the British, Roosevelt moved toward more open support for the beleaguered nation. The first major step was the destroyers-for-bases deal (see Chapter 3). At the beginning of 1941, British Prime Minister Winston Churchill outlined for Roosevelt Britain's desperate need for U.S. assistance (see Document 4.7). Roosevelt responded with the Lend-Lease program, which allowed the British to "borrow" American military supplies and equipment. The president used the homey image of lending a neighbor a garden hose when his house was on fire to make this decision seem like the only decent thing to do (see Document 4.8). Meanwhile, however, isolationist opposition persisted. Roosevelt attacked his isolationist critics with increasing vitriol, and they responded in kind. Isolationist senator Burton K. Wheeler, D-Mont., called the Lend-Lease bill "the New Deal's triple 'A' [referring to the Agricultural Adjustment Act] foreign policy—it will plow under every fourth American boy." (Freidel 1990, 362) Roosevelt angrily shot back at his next press conference, saying of Wheeler's comment, "I regard [it] as the most untruthful, as the most dastardly, unpatriotic thing that has ever been said. Quote me on that" (Freidel 1990, 362).

Through 1941 FDR slowly expanded the role of the United States in assisting British convoys in the Atlantic. When Hitler suddenly broke his nonaggression pact with the Soviet Union in June of that year, FDR made Lend-Lease aid available to the Soviets, and he seems for a time to have entertained the hope that a two-front war for Germany might make full U.S. participation unnecessary. As the year went on, though, the president did everything short of active belligerence to aid the anti-Nazi cause. By December 1941 the United States was engaged in an undeclared naval war with Germany in the Atlantic, but how this conflict would be converted into declared war was unclear.

Because Roosevelt seemed to desire full U.S. participation in the war that he believed, at least most of the time, was necessary to defeat Hitler, there have long been allegations that FDR knew in advance that the Japanese would attack Hawaii and did nothing to stop it. This is untrue, but not entirely off base. American cryptanalysts had broken the Japanese diplomatic code in August 1940. When they decoded messages in November 1941, they learned that the Japanese were likely to launch a military strike at American territory somewhere by early December 1941. There was no expectation, however, that the attack would be against Hawaii. The Philippines seemed a more likely target, partly because Americans did not believe the Japanese capable of a bold, long-distance attack. The truth of the matter, however, is that although the president did not know about the Pearl Harbor attack in advance, he and some of his top advisers knew that war was imminent and did nothing to stop it.

Whether this analysis is reason to condemn Roosevelt is another question. He was right about the need for U.S. participation in the war, and the Japanese attack served the purpose of bringing a unified American people into the struggle to save the world from fascism. The day after the attack on Pearl Harbor, the president appeared before Congress to seek a declaration of war against Japan (see Document 4.9). His brief message to Churchill later that day expressed both satisfaction that his country had joined the struggle and conviction that the cause would end in victory. "Today all of us are in the same boat with you and the people of the Empire," he wrote, "and it is a ship that will not and cannot be sunk" (Kimball 1984, 1:283; see Document 4.10).

Even before the United States entered the war, the conflict had been affecting U.S. social and economic conditions. Roosevelt's call in May 1940 for the building of at least 50,000 planes a year, followed in 1941 by the stimulus provided by construction for the Lend-Lease program, began finally to pull the nation's economy out of depression. And the prospect of increased job opportunities fueled plans for a march on Washington to demand an end to racial injustice. Roosevelt feared that the march, organized by A. Philip Randolph of the Brotherhood of Sleeping Car Porters, might touch off violence. FDR also feared the march would hold up American injustice for condemnation worldwide. So he issued an executive order setting up a Fair Employment Practices Committee to guard against racial discrimination in defense industries (see Chapter 3).

A Wartime Leader

Roosevelt's leadership in the war crisis paralleled his leadership in the economic crisis. His calm, confident approach was again contagious. The phrase, "nothing to fear but fear itself," was perhaps less true in 1942 than it had been a decade earlier (and it had not been all that accurate for many Americans even then), but it served a useful purpose during a dangerous crisis. When it came to building morale, Roosevelt was second to none. A fireside chat broadcast in February 1942 was particularly effective; Roosevelt explained a frightening situation in terms the public could understand. He preached courage and confidence (see Document 4.11), and the success of his message was evident in a one-sentence telegram a listener sent to FDR the next day: "AS FAR AS IM CONCERNED YOUR SPEECH HAS ALREADY WON THE WAR" (Levine and Levine 2002, 423). Once again, as in 1933, Roosevelt's extraordinary personal optimism, his sense of destiny, his almost congenital belief that things would turn out well no matter how bad they looked at the moment, made him the right man in the right place at the right time.

Two major strategic questions had to be decided soon after the United States entered the war. The first was whether to give top priority to defeating Japan, as much of the public wanted after Pearl Harbor, or to concentrate on the more formidable and dangerous German military. For Churchill and the British, of course, the answer was obvious. Roosevelt agreed at a meeting with Churchill in Washington, D.C., in late December 1941 that a "Europe first" strategy was essential, even if it was somewhat unpopular with the American people.

This conclusion raised the second strategic question: How soon and in what area could U.S. forces engage the German enemy? Convinced that the American people demanded "action now"—or at least as quickly as possible—Roosevelt was eager to prepare for a landing on the European continent at the earliest feasible time. But Churchill soon persuaded Roosevelt that it would be a long time before the Allies would have the military strength to ensure a successful invasion across the English Channel. Roosevelt accepted Churchill's alternative: an attack on German-held North Africa in the fall of 1942. For the next several months, however, Roosevelt wavered back and forth between the North African campaign and an early cross-channel attack, which Roosevelt's top military advisers favored and the beleaguered Soviets begged for. Finally, he went with Churchill. Gen. Dwight D. Eisenhower, who would command the operation, said, with more than a little hyperbole, that the day the decision to invade North Africa was made was "the blackest day in history" (Maney 1992, 153).

The war was not going at all well for the Allies, especially in the Pacific, in the first months of U.S. participation. Japan seized the Philippines from U.S. control and Singapore from the British, and made gains across the entire southwest Pacific area. About the only good news was a bombing raid on Tokyo in April 1942 led by army Lt. Col. James H. Doolittle. Although the damage was insignificant, the Doolittle raid boosted U.S. morale and showed the Japanese that their homeland was vulnerable to air assault. The United States checked the Japanese advance toward New Guinea in the Battle of the Coral Sea and then finally won a critical battle near Midway Island, west of Hawaii, in late May and early June 1942.

Three Tragic Decisions
As the war against Japan got underway, a dim chapter in U.S. history was unfolding at home. In the wake of Pearl Harbor, suspicion of and hos-

tility toward Americans of Japanese ancestry intensified. Discrimination against Japanese Americans and other people of Asiatic descent had long been endemic on the West Coast of the United States. Although the immediate reaction after Pearl Harbor was surprisingly mild, anti-Japanese sentiment exploded in the following weeks. In February, Gen. John L. DeWitt, chief of the army's Western Defense Command, who had said a month before, "An American citizen, after all, is an American citizen," declared: "A Jap's a Jap. . . . It makes no difference whether he is an American citizen or not. . . . I don't want any of them" (Kennedy 1999, 749). Asserting by baffling logic that "the very fact that no sabotage has taken place to date is a disturbing and confirming indication that such action will be taken," DeWitt asked for authority to remove all people of Japanese ancestry from the West Coast (tenBroek, Barnhart, and Matson 1954, 110). Roosevelt himself had proclaimed a week after Pearl Harbor, on the 150th anniversary of the ratification of the Bill of Rights, "We will not, under any threat, or in the face of any danger, surrender the guarantees of liberty our forefathers framed for us in the Bill of Rights" (Rosenman 1969, 10:556). But whatever his personal views on the matter, FDR was not one to go against public sentiment. On February 19, 1942, he signed an executive order allowing the War Department to "prescribe military areas . . . from which any and all persons may be excluded" (Daniels 1993, 129–130). Although the order made no specific reference to Japanese Americans, its intent was clear (see Document 4.12). As a result, some 112,000 people, two-thirds of them American citizens, were taken from their homes and forced to move to internment centers in the interior of the country. Roosevelt made clear his political motivation in this shameful episode when he declined to change the policy before the 1944 election, even though Attorney General Francis Biddle told him there was no longer any need or justification for it.

Acquiescence in the internment of Japanese Americans for no reason other than ethnicity was probably the worst thing that Roosevelt did on the home front during World War II. Overseas, two decisions had monstrous consequences. By the end of 1942 Roosevelt had been given irrefutable evidence that the Nazis had begun a program of exterminating all European Jews. Roosevelt raised no questions when military advisers, some of them apparently motivated by their own anti-Semitism, rejected a proposal to bomb the railroads leading to the death camps. Such a program, which was well within the capabilities of U.S. air power, might have saved hundreds of thousands of lives. Roosevelt did establish a War Refugee Board in 1944, which was instrumental in saving large numbers of Jewish people and others, but his failure to do more is a great stain on his reputation.

The other tragedy of American military policy under Roosevelt was the decision to target civilian populations, something that had horrified people in Britain and the United States when the fascists had done it during the Spanish Civil War in the 1930s and in the Nazi invasion of Poland. Before Roosevelt's death, this policy killed 35,000 people in a firebombing of Dresden, Germany, on February 13–14, 1945, and nearly 90,000 in a similar firebombing of Tokyo on March 9–10. Having crossed the Rubicon of mass targeting of civilians, the decision to use atomic bombs against Japanese cities, made by President Harry S. Truman and his advisers, was almost a foregone conclusion.

Developments in North Africa

If the war began to take a turn for the better for the Allies in the Pacific (although not without more serious losses) in the summer of 1942, it took a while longer to turn around in the European theater. The initial success was the landing of U.S. forces in North Africa. After some early reverses for the unseasoned troops under Eisenhower, the tide turned. Still, it was not until May 1943 that British and American forces achieved the dubious goal of driving remaining Axis troops out of North Africa. At about the same time the Allies achieved a much more important objective: they took control of the Atlantic shipping lanes from the German submarines that had been wreaking havoc on the transport of troops and supplies from the United States.

Early in the North African campaign, in January 1943, Roosevelt and Churchill met at Casablanca in French Morocco. Although the U.S. and British leaders said they understood that the Soviets were bearing the brunt of the war and pledged (as Roosevelt had done months before without result) to relieve the pressure on the Red Army by opening a second front in Europe, no date or place for such an attack was forthcoming. The most notable decision at Casablanca was one that Roosevelt made almost casually on his own. At a joint press conference with Churchill, Roosevelt declared that he and the prime minister were determined to accomplish "the total elimination of German and Japanese war power" (Rosenman 1969, 12:39). This objective could be achieved,

FDR said, only by the unconditional surrender of the Axis powers (see Document 4.13).

ENVISIONING A POSTWAR WORLD

Shortly after the Casablanca conference the war took a decisive turn. In February 1943 the Soviets emerged victorious at the end of the horrible two-and-a-half month Battle of Stalingrad. From this point onward the Russian front would move west, back toward Germany. But the question of opening a second front in Europe continued to be a leading issue among the three major Allies. Because Stalin distrusted the motives of the western Allies (he increasingly believed that Roosevelt and especially Churchill wanted the Soviets to suffer the bulk of the casualties and so be weakened in the quest for influence in the postwar world), it was imperative to agree on a second European front and on arrangements for the postwar world.

Always the optimist, FDR sometimes ignored reality and argued that bitter disputes could be overcome with ease. He blithely offered his view that Muslims and Hindus in India could resolve their differences, as could Arabs and Jews in Palestine and Communists and anti-Communists in China. A mixture of realism and idealism would guide Roosevelt's attempts to shape a satisfactory postwar world order. The mix was, for example, clearly evident in FDR's idea of combining a world organization for all nations with his "four policemen" concept of giving special responsibility for maintaining security to the major powers: the United States, Britain, the Soviet Union, and China.

Roosevelt had his first meeting with Stalin at Teheran, Iran, in November 1943. FDR had wanted to meet with Stalin alone, but Churchill insisted on being included. Roosevelt assumed that he could deal with the Soviet dictator much as he dealt with everyone else. As Harry Hopkins, who had become more powerful than ever during the war, put it, Roosevelt "had spent his life managing men, and Stalin at bottom could not be so very different from other people" (Kennedy 1999, 676). In this expectation FDR was disappointed. "I couldn't get any personal connection with Stalin," he later told Secretary of Labor Frances Perkins. "He was correct, stiff, solemn, not smiling, nothing human to get a hold of" (Perkins 1946, 83–84). It would be a tough sell to convince the paranoid Soviet leader that he did not have more to fear than fear itself. But being a political salesman was what Roosevelt knew.

Indeed, FDR was as wedded to his personal approach as Hoover was to his economic and social beliefs. If Roosevelt's personal charm failed to work on someone, as it seemed with Stalin, Roosevelt would not "admit it frankly and try another" approach. He would try again to make a personal connection—and was prone to believe that he had made such a connection even when he had not. If Hoover's background of business success had ill prepared him to empathize with depression victims, Roosevelt's time-tested use of charm to soften opposition left him poorly equipped for dealing with the likes of Josef Stalin. "I think the Russians are perfectly friendly," the president remarked a few months after his meeting with Stalin at Teheran. "They aren't trying to gobble up all the rest of Europe or the world. They didn't know us, that's really the fundamental difference. They are friendly people" (Rosenman 1969, 13:99).

The combination of FDR's willingness to take a realist view of political and military circumstances with his desire to make friends with Stalin led Roosevelt at Teheran to intimate to the Soviet dictator that he would take no action against Soviet designs on the Baltic states or Stalin's plan to move the borders of Poland westward. By telling Stalin that "it would be helpful for him [FDR] personally if some public declaration in regard to . . . future elections [in eastern Europe] could be made," Roosevelt seemed to be winking to Stalin that they were both politicians and practical men and sometimes they did not need to tell the public their true intentions (Kennedy 1999, 678). Understandably, Stalin left Teheran with the impression that he would be able to exercise a free hand in eastern Europe at the end of the war without fear of retaliation from the United States. What Stalin did not understand was that Roosevelt was less than forthcoming.

The Teheran conference did conclude with a clear and major decision on the second front in Europe. Despite Churchill's continuing talk of adventures in the Mediterranean and the Balkans, Roosevelt finally and unequivocally declared that an invasion across the English Channel would begin on May 1, 1944, and the "Big Three" approved the plan for Operation Overlord (see Document 4.14).

The success of the Allied forces after D day (see Document 4.15), which was postponed a little over a month from the date Roosevelt had set at Teheran, meant that the end of the European war was coming closer. Decisions on postwar issues would have to be made. Churchill and Stalin met without Roosevelt (who was represented by Hopkins) at Moscow in October 1944. They agreed to divide influence in the Balkans between the British and Soviets, with no hint of idealism or self-determination. Roosevelt endorsed this *Realpolitik*[1] agreement. But thornier issues had to await another meeting of the Big Three. This took place at the Black Sea resort of Yalta in February 1945. Roosevelt's principal interests were assuring Soviet participation in the United Nations and Soviet entry into the war with Japan soon after Germany was defeated. The immediate disposition of eastern Europe was not a high priority for Roosevelt at this point—not to mention the fact that the Red Army's occupation of Poland and other large chunks of the region made it almost impossible for the Western leaders to persuade Stalin on issues in a region so important to Russian security. An agreement on Poland was included in the Yalta Protocol, but it was, as Adm. William D. Leahy of the Joint Chiefs of Staff pointed out, "so elastic that the Russians can stretch it all the way from Yalta to Washington without ever technically breaking it" (Kennedy 1999, 802; see Document 4.16).

A secret agreement at Yalta called for the Soviet Union, in exchange for concessions in East Asia, to declare war on Japan three months after Germany's final defeat. At this point it was thought likely that the war against Japan would go on at length and that Soviet participation would hasten its end and save American lives. The unknown factor in this equation was the new super weapon that U.S. scientists had been secretly working on in Oak Ridge, Tennessee; Hanford, Washington; and Los Alamos, New Mexico, since early in the war. The outcome of the Manhattan Project was still uncertain at the time of Yalta, so Roosevelt's gaining a firm Soviet agreement to join the war against Japan was an important achievement.

Less than two months after his return from Yalta, FDR was dead. Although he did not live to see the fruits of his leadership in the second huge crisis of his presidency, he had unquestionably helped save the world from fascism.

NOTE

1. National policy based on the realities of power, with the advancement of national interest as its only principle.

BIBLIOGRAPHY

The volume of historical literature on the two huge crises of the Roosevelt years, the Great Depression and World War II, is immense. There is space here to discuss only a fraction of what is available. David M. Kennedy examines both crises in detail in *Freedom from Fear: The American People in Depression and War, 1929–1945* (New York: Oxford University Press, 1999).

On the causes of the Great Depression, see Robert S. McElvaine, *The Great Depression: America, 1929–1941* (New York: Times Books, 1984); John A. Garraty, *The Great Depression* (San Diego: Harcourt Brace Jovanovich, 1986); Michael Bernstein, *The Great Depression: Delayed Recovery and Economic Change in the American Economy, 1929–1939* (New York: Cambridge University Press, 1987); and Michael D. Bordo, Claudia Goldin, and Eugene N. White, eds., *The Defining Moment: The Great Depression and the American Economy in the Twentieth Century* (Chicago: University of Chicago Press, 1998).

The depression at the time of Roosevelt's election and when he took office is discussed in Jordan A. Schwarz, *The Interregnum of Despair: Hoover, Congress, and the Depression* (Urbana: University of Illinois Press, 1970). Frank Freidel, *FDR: Launching the New Deal* (Boston: Little, Brown, 1956) provides an excellent account of the deepening crisis in the period between Roosevelt's election and his inauguration.

The best source for beginning to understand the personal connection that Franklin Roosevelt established with the American people is the letters that these people wrote to him. A sampling can be found in Robert S. McElvaine, ed., *Down and Out in the Great Depression: Letters from the "Forgotten Man"* (Chapel Hill: University of North Carolina Press, 1983). Lawrence W. Levine and Cornelia R. Levine, *The People and the President: America's Conversation with FDR* (Boston: Beacon, 2002) presents a fascinating sampling of the public's letters responding to FDR's fireside chats. Feelings toward Roosevelt can also be seen in retrospect in Studs Terkel, *Hard Times: An Oral History of the Great Depression* (New York: Pantheon, 1970).

On the New Deal, William E. Leuchtenburg, *Franklin D. Roosevelt and the New Deal* (New York: Harper and Row, 1963) remains the indispensable starting point. Anthony J. Badger, *The New Deal: The Depression Years, 1933–1940* (New York: Farrar, Straus, and Giroux, 1989) is the best recent survey. Paul K. Conkin, *The New Deal*, 2d ed. (New York: Thomas Y. Crowell, 1975) takes a much more critical view than do many other accounts. At the opposite extreme is Arthur M. Schlesinger Jr.'s highly favorable analysis in *The Coming of the New Deal* (Boston: Houghton Mifflin, 1958).

On the crises of the mid-thirties, "thunder on the left" can be explored in Alan Brinkley, *Voices of Protest: Huey Long, Father Coughlin, and the Great Depression* (New York: Knopf, 1982); and Irving Bernstein, *Turbulent Years: A History of the American Worker, 1933–1941* (Boston: Houghton Mifflin, 1969).

The major programs of the second New Deal have received less book-length scholarly attention than one might expect. On Social Security, see Andrew Achenbaum, *Social Security: Visions and Revisions* (New York: Cambridge University Press, 1986). On the Wagner Act, James Gross, *The Reshaping of the National Labor Relations Board* (Albany: State University of New York Press, 1981). Mark H. Leff, *The Limits of Symbolic Reform: The New Deal and Taxation* (New York: Cambridge University Press, 1984) includes a discussion of Roosevelt's "wealth tax" proposal, as well as the tax effects of the Social Security payroll levy. Much attention has been paid to the various arts projects under the WPA, but less to the WPA as a whole.

World War II is second only to the Civil War in all subjects in American history when it comes to the amount written about it. Robert Dallek, *Franklin D. Roosevelt and American Foreign Policy, 1932–1945* (New York: Oxford University Press, 1979) is a good starting point for Roosevelt's overall dealings with foreign affairs. William L. Langer and S. Everett Gleason, *The Challenge to Isolation, 1937–1940* (New York: Harper and Row, 1952) and the same authors' *The Undeclared War, 1940–1941* (New York: Harper and Row, 1953) provide in-depth coverage of the years leading up to U.S. entry into the war.

Eric Labaree, *Commander in Chief: Franklin Delano Roosevelt, His Lieutenants, and Their War* (New York: Harper and Row, 1987) is excellent on U.S. strategy in the war. One of the best books on Pearl Harbor is Gordon W. Prange, *At Dawn We Slept: The Untold Story of Pearl Harbor* (New York: Penguin, 1982).

The home front (as well as the Roosevelt family's own home front) is examined in Doris Kearns Goodwin, *No Ordinary Time: Franklin and Eleanor Roosevelt: The Home Front in World War II* (New York: Simon and

Schuster, 1994). On the internment of Japanese Americans, see Jacobus tenBroek, Edward N. Barnhart, and Floyd W. Matson, *Prejudice, War, and the Constitution* (Berkeley: University of California Press, 1954); and Greg Robinson, *By Order of the President: FDR and the Internment of Japanese Americans* (Cambridge, Mass.: Harvard University Press, 2001). David Wyman, *The Abandonment of the Jews: America and the Holocaust, 1941–1945* (New York: Pantheon, 1984) explores the failings of the U.S. government under Roosevelt to do what it could have to lessen the horror of the Holocaust.

Warren F. Kimball, *The Juggler: Franklin Roosevelt as Wartime Statesman* (Princeton: Princeton University Press, 1991) argues that FDR pursued a clear vision of what he hoped to achieve in the postwar world. Diane Shaver Clements, *Yalta* (New York: Oxford University Press, 1970) explores the critical final Big Three meeting of Roosevelt's life. Richard Rhodes, *The Making of the Atomic Bomb* (New York: Simon and Schuster, 1986) is a solid account of the Manhattan Project.

Other works cited in this chapter are Roger Daniels, *Prisoners without Trial: Japanese Americans in World War II* (New York: Hill and Wang, 1993); Kenneth S. Davis, *FDR: The New Deal Years, 1933–1937* (New York: Random House, 1986); Frank Freidel, *Franklin D. Roosevelt: A Rendezvous with Destiny* (Boston: Little, Brown, 1990); Warren F. Kimball, ed., *Churchill and Roosevelt: The Complete Correspondence,* 3 vols. (Princeton: Princeton University Press, 1984); Patrick J. Maney, *The Roosevelt Presence: A Biography of Franklin D. Roosevelt* (New York: Twayne, 1992); Raymond Moley, *After Seven Years: A Political Analysis of the New Deal* (1939; reprint, Lincoln: University of Nebraska Press, 1971); Frances Perkins, *The Roosevelt I Knew* (New York: Viking, 1946); Samuel I. Rosenman, ed., *The Public Papers and Addresses of Franklin D. Roosevelt,* 13 vols. (1938–1950; reprint, New York: Russell and Russell, 1969); and Arthur M. Schlesinger Jr., *The Politics of Upheaval, 1935–1936* (Boston: Houghton Mifflin, 1960).

Document 4.1   First "Fireside Chat," March 12, 1933

In Roosevelt's first radio talk with the American people, he sought to explain the banking crisis in terms they could understand and to restore confidence in the banking system. It was a measure of how effective he was at "personal" communication with the masses that this talk achieved its goals.

I want to talk for a few minutes with the people of the United States about banking—with the comparatively few who understand the mechanics of banking but more particularly with the overwhelming majority who use banks for the making of deposits and the drawing of checks. I want to tell you what has been done in the last few days, why it was done, and what the next steps are going to be. I recognize that the many proclamations from State capitols and from Washington, the legislation, the Treasury regulations, etc., couched for the most part in banking and legal terms, should be explained for the benefit of the average citizen. I owe this in particular because of the fortitude and good temper with which everybody has accepted the inconvenience and hardships of the banking holiday. I know that when you understand what we in Washington have been about I shall continue to have your cooperation as fully as I have had your sympathy and help during the past week.

First of all, let me state the simple fact that when you deposit money in a bank the bank does not put the money into a safe deposit vault. It invests your money in many different forms of credit—bonds, commercial paper, mortgages and many other kinds of loans. In other words, the bank puts your money to work to keep the wheels of industry and of agriculture turning around. A comparatively small part of the money you put into the bank is kept in currency—an amount which in normal times is wholly sufficient to cover the cash needs of the average citizen. In other words, the total amount of all the currency in the country is only a small fraction of the total deposits in all of the banks.

What, then, happened during the last few days of February and the first few days of March? Because of undermined confidence on the part of the public, there was a general rush by a large portion of our population to turn bank deposits into currency or gold—a rush so great that the soundest banks could not get enough currency to meet the demand. The reason for this was that on the spur of the moment it was, of course, impossible to sell perfectly sound assets of a bank and convert them into cash except at panic prices far below their real value.

By the afternoon of March 3d scarcely a bank in the country was open to do business. Proclamations temporarily closing them in whole or in part had been issued by the Governors in almost all the States.

It was then that I issued the proclamation providing for the nationwide bank holiday, and this was the first step in the Government's reconstruction of our financial and economic fabric.

The second step was the legislation promptly and patriotically passed by the Congress confirming my proclamation and broadening my powers so that it became possible in view of the requirement of time to extend the holiday and lift the ban of that holiday gradually. This law also gave authority to develop a program of rehabilitation of our banking facilities. I want to tell our citizens in every part of the Nation that the national Congress—Republicans and Democrats alike—showed by this action a devotion to public welfare and a realization of the emergency and the necessity for speed that it is difficult to match in our history. . . .

A question you will ask is this: why are all the banks not to be reopened at the same time? The answer is simple. Your Government does not intend that the history of the past few years shall be repeated. We do not want and will not have another epidemic of bank failures. . . .

It is possible that when the banks resume a very few people who have not recovered from their fear may again begin withdrawals. Let me make it clear that the banks will take care of all needs—and it is my belief that hoarding during the past week has become an exceedingly unfashionable pastime. It needs no prophet to tell you that when the people find that they can get their money—that they can get it when they want it for all legitimate purposes—the phantom of fear will soon be laid. People will again be glad to have their money where it will be safely taken care of and where they can use it conveniently at any time. I can assure you that it is safer to keep your money in a reopened bank than under the mattress.

The success of our whole great national program depends, of course, upon the cooperation of the public—on its intelligent support and use of a reliable system. . . .

I hope you can see from this elemental recital of what your Government is doing that there is nothing complex, or radical, in the process.

We had a bad banking situation. Some of our bankers had shown themselves either incompetent or dishonest in their handling of the people's funds. They had used the money entrusted to them in speculations and unwise loans. This was, of course, not true in the vast majority of our banks, but it was true in enough of them to shock the people for a time into a sense of insecurity and to put them into a frame of mind where they did not differentiate, but seemed to assume that the acts of a comparative few had tainted them all. It was the Government's job to straighten out this situation and do it as quickly as possible. And the job is being performed.

I do not promise you that every bank will be reopened or that individual losses will not be suffered, but there will be no losses that possibly could be avoided; and there would have been more and greater losses had we continued to drift. I can even promise you salvation for some at least of the sorely pressed banks. We shall be engaged not merely in reopening sound banks but in the creation of sound banks through reorganization.

It has been wonderful to me to catch the note of confidence from all over the country. . . .

After all, there is an element in the readjustment of our financial system more important than currency, more important than gold, and that is the confidence of the people. Confidence and courage are the essentials of success in carrying out our plan. You people must have faith; you must not be stampeded by rumors or guesses. Let us unite in banishing fear. We have provided the machinery to restore our financial system; it is up to you to support and make it work.

It is your problem no less than it is mine. Together we cannot fail.

Source: Samuel I. Rosenman, ed., *The Public Papers and Addresses of Franklin D. Roosevelt* (1938; reprint, New York: Russell and Russell, 1969), 2:61–65.

Document 4.2   Letter to FDR from a Man in Columbus, Georgia, October 24, 1934

Roosevelt's success at achieving a sense of personal connection with huge numbers of Americans is evidenced in the unprecedented number of letters that people wrote to him. These communications often indicated that the writer saw Roosevelt as a personal friend.

[Dear President Roosevelt:]

I hope you can spare the time for a few words from a cotton mill family, out of work and almost out of heart and in just a short while out of a house in which to live. You know of course that the realators are putting the people out when they cannot pay the rent promptly. and how are we to pay the rent as long as the mills refuse us work, merely because we had the nerve to ask or "demand", better working conditions.

I realize and appreciate the aid and food which the government is giving to the poor people out of work. Thanks to you .

but is it even partly right for us to be thrown out of our homes, when we have no chance whatever of paying, so long as the big corporations refuse of work. I for one am very disheartened and disappointed. guess my notice to move will come next.

what are we to do. wont you try to help us wont you appeal, "for us all." to the real estate people and the factories hoping you'll excuse this, but I've always thought of F.D.R. as my personal friend.

C. L. F. [male]

Source: Robert S. McElvaine, ed., *Down and Out in the Great Depression: Letters from the "Forgotten Man"* (Chapel Hill: University of North Carolina Press, 1983), 223.

Document 4.3   The Agricultural Adjustment Act, May 12, 1933

The Agricultural Adjustment Act was the compromise that issued from Roosevelt's insistence that farm organization leaders agree on a program to raise the income, and so the purchasing power, of farmers. Initially, FDR thought that this was all that would be needed to bring about general recovery. The bill also included provisions giving the president power to manipulate the money supply through any of a variety of devices. It was hoped that an increase in the money supply would help farmers by increasing the prices they received for their products and by making it easier to repay debts.

AN ACT

To relieve the existing national economic emergency by increasing agricultural purchasing power, to raise revenue for extraordinary expenses incurred by reason of such emergency, to provide emergency relief with respect to agricultural indebtedness, to provide for the orderly liquidation of joint-stock land banks, and for other purposes.

Be it enacted by the Senate and the House of Representatives of the United States of America in congress assembled:

TITLE I—AGRICULTURAL ADJUSTMENT
DECLARATION OF EMERGENCY

That the present acute economic emergency being in part the consequence of a severe and increasing disparity between the prices of agricultural and other commodities, which disparity has largely destroyed the purchasing power of farmers for industrial products, has broken down the orderly exchange of commodities, and has seriously impaired the agricultural assets supporting the national credit structure, it is hereby declared that these conditions in the basic industry of agriculture have affected transactions in agricultural commodities with a national public interest, have burdened and obstructed the normal currents of commerce in such commodities, and render imperative the immediate enactment of title I of this Act.

DECLARATION OF POLICY

SEC. 2. It is hereby declared to be the policy of Congress—

(1) To establish and maintain such balance between the production and consumption of agricultural commodities, and such marketing conditions therefor, as will reestablish prices to farmers at a level that will give agricultural commodities a purchasing power with respect to articles that farmers buy, equivalent to the purchasing power of agricultural commodities in the base period. The base period in the case of all agricultural commodities except tobacco shall be the prewar period, August 1909–July 1914. In the case of tobacco, the base period shall be the postwar period, August 1919–July 1929.

(2) To approach such equality of purchasing power by gradual correction of the present inequalities therein at as rapid a rate as is deemed feasible in view of the current consumptive demand in domestic and foreign markets.

(3) To protect the consumers' interest by readjusting farm production at such level as will not increase the percentage of the consumers' retail expenditures for agricultural commodities, or products derived therefrom, which is returned to the farmer, above the percentage which was returned to the farmer in the prewar period, August 1909–July 1914. . . .

PART 2—COMMODITY BENEFITS

GENERAL POWERS

SEC. 8. In order to effectuate the declared policy, the Secretary of Agriculture shall have power—

(1) To provide for reduction in the acreage or reduction in the production for market, or both, of any basic agricultural commodity, through agreements with producers or by other voluntary methods, and to provide for rental or benefit payments in connection therewith or upon that part of the production of any basic agricultural commodity required for domestic consumption, in such amounts as the Secretary deems fair and reasonable, to be paid out of any moneys available for such payments. Under regulations of the Secretary of Agriculture requiring adequate facilities for the storage of any non-perishable agricultural commodity on the farm, inspection and measurement of any such commodity so stored, and the locking and sealing thereof, and such other regulations as may be prescribed by the Secretary of Agriculture for the protection of such commodity and for the marketing thereof, a reasonable percentage of any benefit payment may be advanced on any such commodity so stored. In any such case, such deduction may be made from the amount of the benefit payment as the Secretary of Agriculture determines will reasonably compensate for the cost of inspection and sealing, but no deduction may be made for interest. . . .

TITLE III—FINANCING—AND EXERCISING POWER CONFERRED BY SECTION 8 OF ARTICLE I OF THE CONSTITUTION: TO COIN MONEY AND TO REGULATE THE VALUE THEREOF

SEC. 43. Whenever the President finds, upon investigation, that (1) the foreign commerce of the United States is adversely affected by reason of the depreciation in the value of the currency of any other government or governments in relation to the present standard value of gold, or (2) action under this section is necessary in order to regulate and maintain the parity of currency issues of the United States, or (3) an economic emergency requires an expansion of credit, or (4) an expansion of credit is necessary to secure by international agreement a stabilization at proper levels of the currencies of various governments, the President is authorized, in his discretion—

(a) To direct the Secretary of the Treasury to enter into agreements with the several Federal Reserve banks and with the Federal Reserve Board whereby the Federal Reserve Board will, and it is hereby authorized to, notwithstanding any provisions of law or rules and regulations to the contrary, permit such reserve banks to agree that they will, (1) conduct, pursuant to existing law, throughout specified periods, open market operations in obligations of the United States Government or corporations in which the United States is the majority stockholder, and (2) purchase directly and hold in portfolio for an agreed period or periods of time Treasury bills or other obligations of the United States Government in an aggregate sum of $3,000,000,000 in addition to those they may then hold, unless prior to the termination of such period or periods the Secretary shall consent to their sale. No suspension of reserve requirements of the Federal Reserve banks, under the terms of section 11(c) of the Federal Reserve Act, necessitated by reason of operations under this section, shall require the imposition of the graduated tax upon any deficiency in reserves as provided in said section 11(c). Nor shall it require any automatic increase in the rates of interest or discount charged by any Federal Reserve bank, as otherwise specified in that section. The Federal Reserve Board, with the approval of the Secretary of the Treasury, may require the Federal Reserve banks to take such action as may be necessary, in the judgment of the Board and of the Secretary of the Treasury, to prevent undue credit expansion.

(b) If the Secretary, when directed by the President, is unable to secure the assent of the several Federal Reserve banks and the Federal Reserve Board to the agreements authorized in this section, or if operations under the above provisions prove to be inadequate to meet the purposes of this section, or if for any other reason additional measures are required in the judgment of the President to meet such purposes, then the President is authorized—

(1) To direct the Secretary of the Treasury to cause to be issued in such amount or amounts as he may from time to time order, United States notes, as provided in the Act entitled "An Act to authorize the issue of United States notes and for the redemption of funding thereof and for funding the floating debt of the United States", approved February 25, 1862, and Acts supplementary thereto and amendatory thereof, in the same size and of similar color to the Federal Reserve notes heretofore issued and in denominations of $1, $5, $10, $20, $50, $100, $500, $1,000, and $10,000; but notes issued under this subsection shall be issued only for the purpose of meeting maturing Federal obligations to repay sums borrowed by the United States and for purchasing United States bonds and other interest-bearing obligations of the United States: *Provided,* That when any such notes are used for such purpose the bond or other obligation so acquired or taken up shall be retired and canceled. Such notes shall be issued at such times and in such

amounts as the President may approve but the aggregate amount of such notes outstanding at any time shall not exceed $3,000,000,000. There is hereby appropriated, out of any money in the Treasury not otherwise appropriated, an amount sufficient to enable the Secretary of the Treasury to retire and cancel 4 per centum annually of such outstanding notes, and the Secretary of the Treasury is hereby directed to retire and cancel annually 4 per centum of such outstanding notes. Such notes and all other coins and currencies heretofore or hereafter coined or issued by or under the authority of the United States shall be legal tender for all debts public and private.

(2) By proclamation to fix the weight of the gold dollar in grains nine tenths fine and also to fix the weight of the silver dollar in grains nine tenths fine at a definite fixed ratio in relation to then gold dollar at such amounts as he finds necessary from his investigation to stabilize domestic prices or to protect the foreign commerce against the adverse effect of depreciated foreign currencies, and to provide for the unlimited coinage of such gold and silver at the ratio so fixed, or in case the Government of the United States enters into an agreement with any government or governments under the terms of which the ratio between the value of gold and other currency issued by the United States and by any such government or governments is established, the President may fix the weight of the gold dollar in accordance with the ratio so agreed upon, and such gold dollar, the weight of which is so fixed, shall be the standard unit of value, and all forms of money issued or coined by the United States shall be maintained at a parity with this standard and it shall be the duty of the Secretary of the Treasury to maintain such parity, but in no event shall the weight of the gold dollar be fixed so as to reduce its present weight by more than 50 per centum. . . .

SEC. 45.(a) The President is authorized, for a period of six months from the date of the passage of this Act, to accept silver in payment of the whole or any part of the principal or interest now due, or to become due within six months after such date, from any foreign government or governments on account of any indebtedness to the United States, such silver to be accepted at not to exceed the price of 50 cents an ounce in United States currency. The aggregate value of the silver accepted under this section shall not exceed $200,000,000.

(b) The silver bullion accepted and received under the provisions of this section shall be subject to the requirements of existing law and the regulations of the mint service governing the methods of determining the amount of pure silver contained, and the amount charges or deductions, if any, to be made; but such silver bullion shall not be counted as part of the silver bullion authorized or required to be purchased and coined under the provisions of existing law.

(c) The silver accepted and received under the provisions of this section shall be deposited in the Treasury of the United States, to be held, used, and disposed of as in this section provided.

(d) The Secretary of the Treasury shall cause silver certificates to be issued in such denominations as he deems advisable to the total number of dollars for which such silver was accepted in payment of debts. Such silver certificates shall be used by the Treasurer of the United States in payment of any obligations of the United States.

(e) The silver so accepted and received under this section shall be coined into standard silver dollars and subsidiary coins sufficient, in the opinion of the Secretary of the Treasury, to meet any demands for redemption of such silver certificates issued under the provisions of this section, and such coins shall be retained in the Treasury for the payment of such certificates on demand. The silver so accepted and received under this section, except so much thereof as is coined under the provisions of this section, shall be held in the Treasury for the sole purpose of aiding in maintaining the parity of such certificates as provided in existing law. Any such certificates or reissued certificates, when presented at the Treasury, shall be redeemed in standard silver dollars, or in subsidiary silver coin, at the option of the holder of the certificates: *Provided,* That, in the redemption of such silver certificates issued under this section, not to exceed one third of the coin required for such redemption may in the judgment of the Secretary of the Treasury be made in subsidiary coins, the balance to be made in standard silver dollars.

(f) When any silver certificates issued under the provisions of this section are redeemed or received into the Treasury from any source whatsoever, and belong to the United States, they shall not be retired, canceled, or destroyed, but shall be reissued and paid out again and kept in circulation; but nothing herein shall prevent the cancelation and destruction of mutilated certificates and the issue of other certificates of like denomination in their stead, as provided by law.

(g) The Secretary of the Treasury is authorized to make rules and regulations for carrying out the provisions of this section.

SEC. 46. Section 19 of the Federal Reserve Act, as amended, is amended by inserting immediately after paragraph (c) thereof the following new paragraph:

"Notwithstanding the foregoing provisions of this section, the Federal Reserve Board, upon the affirmative vote of not less than five of its members and with the approval of the President, may declare that an emergency exists by reason of credit expansion, and may by regulation during such emergency increase or decrease from time to time, in its discretion, the reserve balances required to be maintained against either demand or time deposits."

Approved, May 12, 1933.

Source: 48 Stat. 31 (May 12, 1933).

Document 4.4   Message to Congress on Tax Revision, June 19, 1935

Roosevelt's 1935 message to Congress calling for tax revision was a response to the growing "thunder on the left," particularly the popularity of Sen. Huey P. Long's, D-La., calls to "Share Our Wealth." Long took credit for getting the president to take a stance in favor of "soaking the rich," but the message was far more political than economic, and the president did little to promote passage of the steeply progressive levies he proposed.

To the Congress:

As the fiscal year draws to its close it becomes our duty to consider the broad question of tax methods and policies. I wish to acknowledge the timely efforts of the Congress to lay the basis, through its committees, for administrative improvements, by careful study of the revenue systems of our own and of other countries. These studies have made it very clear that we need to simplify and clarify our revenue laws.

The Joint Legislative Committee, established by the Revenue Act of 1926, has been particularly helpful to the Treasury Department. The members of that Committee have generously consulted with administrative officials, not only on broad questions of policy but on important and difficult tax cases.

On the basis of these studies and of other studies conducted by officials of the Treasury, I am able to make a number of suggestions of important changes in our policy of taxation. These are based on the broad principle that if a government is to be prudent its taxes must produce ample revenues without discouraging enterprise; and if it is to be just it must distribute the burden of taxes equitably. I do not believe that our present system of taxation completely meets this test. Our revenue laws have operated in many ways to the unfair advantage of the few, and they have done little to prevent an unjust concentration of wealth and economic power.

With the enactment of the Income Tax Law of 1913, the Federal Government began to apply effectively the widely accepted principle that taxes should be levied in proportion to ability to pay and in proportion to the benefits received. Income was wisely chosen as the measure of benefits and of ability to pay. This was, and still is, a wholesome guide for national policy. It should be retained as the governing principle of Federal taxation. The use of other forms of taxes is often justifiable, particularly for temporary periods; but taxation according to income is the most effective instrument yet devised to obtain just contribution from those best able to bear it and to avoid placing onerous burdens upon the mass of our people.

The movement toward progressive taxation of wealth and of income has accompanied the growing diversification and interrelation of effort which marks our industrial society. Wealth in the modern world does not come merely from individual effort; it results from a combination of individual effort and of the manifold uses to which the community puts that effort. The individual does not create the product of his industry with his own hands; he utilizes the many processes and forces of mass production to meet the demands of a national and international market.

Therefore, in spite of the great importance in our national life of the efforts and ingenuity of unusual individuals, the people in the mass have inevitably helped to make large fortunes possible. Without mass cooperation great accumulations of wealth would be impossible save by unhealthy speculation. As Andrew Carnegie put it, "Where wealth accrues honorably, the people are always silent partners." Whether it be wealth achieved through the cooperation of the entire community or riches gained by speculation in either case the ownership of such wealth or riches represents a great public interest and a great ability to pay.

I

My first proposal, in line with this broad policy, has to do with inheritances and gifts. The transmission from generation to generation of vast fortunes by will, inheritance, or gift is not consistent with the ideals and sentiments of the American people.

The desire to provide security for oneself and one's family is, natural and wholesome, but it is adequately served by a reasonable inheritance. Great accumulations of wealth cannot be justified on the basis of personal and family security. In the last analysis such accumulations amount to the perpetuation of great and undesirable concentration of control in a relatively few individuals over the employment and welfare of many, many others.

Such inherited economic power is as inconsistent with the ideals of this generation as inherited political power was inconsistent with the ideals of the generation which established our Government.

Creative enterprise is not stimulated by vast inheritances. They bless neither those who bequeath nor those who receive. As long ago as 1907, in a message to Congress, President Theodore Roosevelt urged this wise social policy:

> "A heavy progressive tax upon a very large fortune is in no way such a tax upon thrift or industry as a like tax would be on a small fortune. No advantage comes either to the country as a whole or to the individuals inheriting the money by permitting the transmission in their entirety the enormous fortunes which would be affected by such a tax; and as an incident to its function of revenue raising, such a tax would help to preserve a measurable equality of opportunity for the people of the generations growing to manhood."

A tax upon inherited economic power is a tax upon static wealth, not upon that dynamic wealth which makes for the healthy diffusion of economic good.

Those who argue for the benefits secured to society by great fortunes invested in great businesses should note that such a tax does not affect the essential benefits that remain after the death of the creator of such a business. The mechanism of production that he created remains. The benefits of corporate organization remain. The advantages of pooling many investments in one enterprise remain. Governmental privileges such as patents remain. All that are gone are the initiative, energy and genius of the creator—and death has taken these away.

I recommend, therefore, that in addition to the present estate taxes, there should be levied an inheritance, succession, and legacy tax in respect to all very large amounts received by any one legatee or beneficiary; and to prevent, so far as possible, evasions of this tax, I recommend further the imposition of gift taxes suited to this end.

Because of the basis on which this proposed tax is to be levied and also because of the very sound public policy of encouraging a wider distribution of wealth, I strongly urge that the proceeds of this tax should be specifically segregated and applied, as they accrue, to the reduction of the national debt. By so doing, we shall progressively lighten the tax burden of the average taxpayer, and, incidentally, assist in our approach to a balanced budget.

II

The disturbing effects upon our national life that come from great inheritances of wealth and power can in the future be reduced, not only, through the method I have just described, but through a definite increase in the taxes now levied upon very great individual net incomes.

To illustrate: The application of the principle of a graduated tax now stops at $1,000,000 of annual income. In other words, while the rate for a man with a $6,000 income is double the rate for one with a $4,000 income, a man having a $5,000,000 annual income pays at the same rate as one whose income is $1,000,000.

Social unrest and a deepening sense of unfairness are dangers to our national life which we must minimize by rigorous methods. People know that vast personal incomes come not only through the effort or ability or luck of those who receive them, but also because of the opportunities for advantage which Government itself contributes. Therefore, the duty rests upon the Government to restrict such incomes by very high taxes.

III

In the modern world scientific invention and mass production have brought many things within the reach of the average man which in an earlier age were available to few. With large-scale enterprise has come the great corporation drawing its resources from widely diversified activities and from a numerous group of investors. The community has profited in those cases in which large scale production has resulted in substantial economies and lower prices.

The advantages and the protections conferred upon corporations by Government increase in value as the size of the corporation increases. Some of these advantages are granted by the State which conferred a charter upon the corporation; others are granted by other States which, as a matter of grace, allow the corporation to do local business within their borders. But perhaps the most important advantages, such as the carrying on of business between two or more States, are derived through the Federal Government. Great corporations are protected in a considerable measure from the taxing power and regulatory power of the States by virtue of the interstate character of their businesses. As the profit to such a corporation increases, so the value of its advantages and protection increases.

Furthermore, the drain of a depression upon the reserves of business puts a disproportionate strain upon the modestly capitalized small enterprise. Without such small enterprises our competitive economic society would cease. Size begets monopoly. Moreover, in the aggregate these little businesses furnish the indispensable local basis for those nationwide markets which alone can ensure the success of our mass production industries. Today our smaller corporations are fighting not only for their own local well-being but for that fairly distributed national prosperity, which makes large-scale enterprise possible.

It seems only equitable, therefore, to adjust our tax system in accordance with economic capacity, advantage and fact. The smaller corporations should not carry burdens beyond their powers; the vast concentrations of capital should be ready to carry burdens commensurate with their powers and their advantages.

We have established the principle of graduated taxation in respect to personal incomes, gifts and estates. We should apply the same principle to corporations. Today the smallest corporation pays the same rate on its net profits as the corporation which is a thousand times its size.

I, therefore, recommend the substitution of a corporation income tax graduated according to the size of corporation income in place of the present uniform corporation income tax of 13 ¾ percent. The rate for smaller corporations might well be reduced to 10 ¾ percent, and the rates graduated upward to a rate of 16 ¾ percent on net income in the case of the largest corporations, with such classifications of business enterprises as the public interest may suggest to the Congress.

Provision should, of course, be made to prevent evasion of such graduated tax on corporate incomes through the device of numerous subsidiaries or affiliates, each of which might technically qualify as a small concern even though all were in fact operated as a single organization. The most effective method of preventing such evasions would be a tax on dividends received by corporations. Bona fide investment trusts that submit to public regulation and perform the function of permitting small investors to obtain the benefit of diversification of risk may well be exempted from this tax.

In addition to these three specific recommendations of changes in our national tax policies, I commend to your study and consideration a number of others. Ultimately, we should seek through taxation the simplification of our corporate structures through the elimination of unnecessary holding companies in all lines of business. We should likewise discourage unwieldy and unnecessary corporate surpluses. These complicated and difficult questions cannot adequately be debated in the time remaining in the present Session of this Congress. . . .

Source: Samuel I. Rosenman, ed., *The Public Papers and Addresses of Franklin D. Roosevelt* (1938; reprint, New York: Russell and Russell, 1969), 4:270–276.

Document 4.5   Fair Labor Standards Act

The final major piece of legislation of the New Deal, the Fair Labor Standards Act of 1938, achieved the long sought goal of setting a federal minimum wage and a limit on the length of the work week. A small portion of the law is excerpted here.

To provide for the establishment of fair labor standards in employments in and affecting interstate commerce, and for other purposes.

Be it enacted by the Senate and House of Representatives of the United States of America in Congress assembled, That this Act may be cited as the "Fair Labor Standards Act of 1938."

FINDING AND DECLARATION OF POLICY

SEC. 2. (a) The Congress hereby finds that the existence, in industries engaged in commerce or in the production of goods for commerce, of labor conditions detrimental to the maintenance of the minimum standard of living necessary for health, efficiency, and general well-being of workers (1) causes commerce and the channels and instrumentalities of commerce to be used to spread and perpetuate such labor conditions among the workers of the several States; (2) burdens commerce and the free flow of goods in commerce; (3) constitutes an unfair method of competition in commerce; (4) leads to labor disputes burdening and obstructing commerce and the free flow of goods in commerce; and (5) interferes with the orderly and fair marketing of goods in commerce. The Congress further finds that the employment of persons in domestic service in households affects commerce.

(b) It is hereby declared to be the policy of this Act, through the exercise by Congress of its power to regulate commerce among the several States and with foreign nations, to correct and as rapidly as practicable to eliminate the conditions above referred to in such industries without substantially curtailing employment or earning power. . . .

MINIMUM WAGES
SEC. 6. (a) Every employer shall pay to each of his employees who in any workweek is engaged in commerce or in the production of goods for commerce, or is employed in an enterprise engaged in commerce or in the production of goods for commerce, wages at the following rates:

(1) except as otherwise provided in this section, not less than $0.25 an hour. . . .

MAXIMUM HOURS
SEC. 7. (a) (1) Except as otherwise provided in this section, no employer shall employ any of his employees who in any workweek is engaged in commerce or in the production of goods for commerce, or is employed in an enterprise engaged in commerce or in the production of goods for commerce, for a workweek longer than forty hours unless such employee receives compensation for his employment in excess of the hours above specified at a rate not less than one and one-half times the regular rate at which he is employed. . . .

Source: 29 U.S.C. 201.

Document 4.6   Letter from Albert Einstein to FDR, August 2, 1939
Albert Einstein tried to alert Roosevelt to the grave danger that German work on nuclear physics posed to the world. FDR does not appear to have fully

appreciated the situation until two months later, when he revisited the subject
with adviser Alexander Sachs. The resulting Manhattan Project, a massive,
highly secret effort to develop the atomic bomb, and one of the most fateful
decisions of his presidency.

Sir:

Some recent work by E. Fermi and L. Szilard, which has been communicated to me in manuscript, leads me to expect that the element uranium may be turned into a new and important source of energy in the immediate future. Certain aspects of the situation which has arisen seem to call for watchfulness and, if necessary, quick action on the part of the Administration. I believe therefore that it is my duty to bring to your attention the following facts and recommendations:

In the course of the last four months it has been made probable—through the work of Joliot in France as well as Fermi and Szilard in America—that it may become possible to set up a nuclear chain reaction in a large mass of uranium, by which vast amounts of power and large quantities of new radium-like elements would be generated. Now it appears almost certain that this could be achieved in the immediate future.

This new phenomenon would also lead to the construction of bombs, and it is conceivable— though much less certain—that extremely powerful bombs of a new type may thus be constructed. A single bomb of this type, carried by boat and exploded in a port, might very well destroy the whole port together with some of the surrounding territory. However, such bombs might very well prove to be too heavy for transportation by air.

The United States has only very poor ores of uranium in moderate quantities. There is some good ore in Canada and the former Czechoslovakia, while the most important source of uranium is Belgian Congo.

In view of this situation you may think it desirable to have some permanent contact maintained between the Administration and the group of physicists working on chain reactions in America. One possible way of achieving this might be for you to entrust with this task a person who has your confidence and who could perhaps serve in an inofficial capacity. His task might comprise the following:

a.) to approach Government Departments, keep them informed of the further development, and put forward recommendations for Government action, giving particular attention to the problem of securing a supply of uranium ore for the United States;

b.) to speed up the experimental work, which is at present being carried on within the limits of the budgets of University laboratories, by providing funds, if such funds be required, through his contacts with private persons who are willing to make contributions for this cause, and perhaps also by obtaining the co-operation of industrial laboratories which have the necessary equipment.

I understand that Germany has actually stopped the sale of uranium from the Czechoslovakian mines which she has taken over. That she should have taken such early action might perhaps be understood on the ground that the son of the German Under-Secretary of State, von Weizsäcker, is attached to the Kaiser-Wilhelm-Institute in Berlin where some of the American work on uranium is now being repeated.

Yours very truly,
[signed] Albert Einstein

Source: Richard N. Current and John A. Garraty, *Words That Made American History,* 2d ed. (Boston: Little, Brown, 1965), 2:516–517.

Document 4.7   Telegram from Winston Churchill Outlining the Gravity of the War and Seeking American Assistance, December 7, 1940

In a long message to Roosevelt in December, 1940, British Prime Minister Winston Churchill argued that the British cause in the war was in the vital interests of the United States. His plea for more assistance from the United States was a major impetus to Roosevelt's proposal of the Lend-Lease program.

My Dear Mr. President,

As we reach the end of this year I feel that you will expect me to lay before you the prospects for 1941. I do so strongly and confidently because it seems to me that the vast majority of American citizens have recorded their conviction that the safety of the United States as well as the future of our two democracies and the kind of civilisation for which they stand are bound up with the survival and independence of the British Commonwealth of Nations. Only thus can those bastions of sea-power, upon which the control of the Atlantic and the Indian Oceans depends, be preserved in faithful and friendly hands. The control of the Pacific by the United States Navy and of the Atlantic by the British Navy is indispensable to the security of the trade routes of both our countries and the surest means to preventing the war from reaching the shores of the United States.

2. There is another aspect. It takes between three and four years to convert the industries of a modern state to war purposes. Saturation point is reached when the maximum industrial effort that can be spared from civilian needs has been applied to war production. Germany certainly reached this point by the end of 1939. We in the British Empire are now only about half-way through the second year. The United States, I should suppose, was by no means so far advanced as we. Moreover, I understand that immense programmes of naval, military and air defence are now on foot in the United States, to complete which certainly two years are needed. It is our British duty in the common interest as also for our own survival to hold the front and grapple with Nazi power until the preparations of the United States are complete. Victory may come before the two years are out; but we have no right to count upon it to the extent of relaxing any effort that is humanly possible. Therefore I submit with very great respect for your good and friendly consideration that there is a solid identity of interest between the British Empire and the United States while these conditions last. It is upon this footing that I venture to address you.

3. The form which this war has taken and seems likely to hold does not enable us to match the immense armies of Germany in any theatre where their main power can be brought to bear. We can however by the use of sea power and air power meet the German armies in the regions where only comparatively small forces can be brought into action. We must do our best to prevent German domination of Europe spreading into Africa and into Southern Asia. We have also to maintain in constant readiness in this Island armies strong enough to make the problem of an overseas invasion insoluble. For these purposes we are forming as fast as possible, as you are already aware, between fifty and sixty divisions. Even if the United States was our ally instead of our friend and indispensable partner we should not ask for a large American expeditionary army. Shipping, not men, is the limiting factor and the power to transport munitions and supplies claims priority over the movement by sea of large numbers of soldiers.

4. The first half of 1940 was a period of disaster for the Allies and for the Empire. The last five months have witnessed a strong and perhaps unexpected recovery by Great Britain; fighting alone but with invaluable aid in munitions and in destroyers placed at our disposal by the great Republic of which you are for the third time chosen Chief.

5. The danger of Great Britain being destroyed by a swift overwhelming blow has for the time being very greatly receded. In its place there is a long, gradually maturing danger, less sudden and less spectacular but equally deadly. This mortal danger is the steady and increasing diminution of sea tonnage. We can endure the shattering of our dwellings and the slaughter of our civilian population by indiscriminate air attacks and we hope to parry these increasingly as our science develops and to repay them upon military objectives in Germany as our Air Force more nearly approaches the strength of the enemy. The decision for 1941 lies upon the seas; unless we can establish our ability to feed this Island, to import munitions of all kinds which we need, unless we can move our armies to the various theatres where Hitler and his confederate Mussolini must be met, and maintain them there and do all this with the assurance of being able to carry it on till the spirit of the continental dictators is broken, we may fall by the way and the time needed by the United States to complete her defensive preparations may not be forthcoming. It is therefore in shipping and in the power to transport across the oceans, particularly the Atlantic Ocean, that in 1941 the crunch of the whole war will be found. If on the other hand we are able to move the necessary tonnage to and fro across the salt water indefinitely, it may well be that the application of superior air power to the German homeland and the rising anger of the German and other Nazi-gripped populations will bring the agony of civilization to a merciful and glorious end. But do not let us underrate the task.

6. Our shipping losses, the figures for which in recent months are appended, have been on a scale almost comparable to that of the worst years of the last war. . . . Were the diminution to continue at this rate it would be fatal, unless indeed immensely greater replenishment than anything at present in sight could be achieved in time. Although we are doing all we can to meet this situation by new methods, the difficulty of limiting the losses is obviously much greater than in the last war. We lack the assistance of the French Navy, the Italian Navy and the Japanese Navy and above all the United States Navy which was of such vital help to us during the culminating years. . . . We need ships both to hunt down and to

escort. Large as are our resources and preparations we do not possess enough. . . .

10. A third sphere of danger is in the Far East. Here it seems clear that the Japanese are thrusting Southward through Indo China to Saigon and other naval and air bases, thus bringing them within a comparatively short distance of Singapore and the Dutch East Indies. It is reported that the Japanese are preparing five good divisions for possible use as an overseas expeditionary force. We have to-day no forces in the Far East capable of dealing with this situation should it develop.

11. In the face of these dangers, we must try to use the year 1941 to build up such a supply of weapons, particularly aircraft, both by increased output at home in spite of bombardment, and through ocean-borne supplies, as will lay the foundation of victory. In view of the difficulty and magnitude of this task, as outlined by all the facts I have set forth to which many others could be added, I feel entitled, nay bound, to lay before you the various ways in which the United States could give supreme and decisive help to what is, in certain aspects, the common cause.

12. The prime need is to check or limit the loss of tonnage on the Atlantic approaches to our Islands. This may be achieved both by increasing the naval forces which cope with attacks, and by adding to the number of merchant ships on which we depend. For the first purpose there would seem to be the following alternatives:

(1) the reassertion by the United States of the doctrine of the freedom of the seas from illegal and barbarous warfare in accordance with the decisions reached after the late Great War, and as freely accepted and defined by Germany in 1935. From this, the United States ships should be free to trade with countries against which there is not an effective legal blockade.

(2) It would, I suggest, follow that protection should be given to this lawful trading by United States forces i.e. escorting battleships, cruisers, destroyers and air flotillas. Protection would be immediately more effective if you were able to obtain bases in Eire for the duration of the war. I think it is improbable that such protection would provoke a declaration of war by Germany upon the United States though probably sea incidents of a dangerous character would from time to time occur. Hitler has shown himself inclined to avoid the Kaiser's mistake. He does not wish to be drawn into war with the United States until he has gravely undermined the power of Great Britain. His maxim is "one at

a time". The policy I have ventured to outline, or something like it, would constitute a decisive act of constructive non-belligerency by the United States, and more than any other measure would make it certain that British resistance could be effectively prolonged for the desired period and victory gained.

(3) Failing the above, the gift, loan or supply of a large number of American vessels of war, above all destroyers already in the Atlantic is indispensable to the maintenance of the Atlantic route.

Further, could not United States naval forces extend their sea control over the American side of the Atlantic, so as to prevent molestation by enemy vessels of the approaches to the new line of naval and air bases which the United States is establishing in British islands in the Western Hemisphere. The strength of the United States naval forces is such that the assistance in the Atlantic that they could afford us, as described above, would not jeopardise control over the Pacific. . . .

14. Moreover we look to the industrial energy of the Republic for a reinforcement of our domestic capacity to manufacture combat aircraft. Without that reinforcement reaching us in a substantial measure, we shall not achieve the massive preponderance in the air on which we must rely to loosen and disintegrate the German grip on Europe. The development of the Air Forces of the Empire provides for a total of nearly 7000 combat aircraft in the fighting squadrons by the spring of 1942, backed by about an equal number in the training units. But it is abundantly clear that this programme will not suffice to give us the weighty superiority which will force open the doors of victory. In order to achieve such superiority it is plain that we shall need the greatest production of aircraft which United States of America are capable of sending us. It is our anxious hope that in the teeth of continuing bombardment we shall realize the greater part of production which we have planned in this country. But not even with the addition to our squadrons of all the aircraft which under present arrangements, we may derive from the planned output in the United States can we hope to achieve the necessary ascendancy. May I invite you then, Mr. President, to give earnest consideration to an immediate order on joint account for a further 2,000 combat aircraft a month? Of these aircraft I would submit that the highest possible proportion should be heavy bombers, the weapon on which above all others we depend to shatter the foundations of German military power. I am aware of the formidable task that this would impose upon the industrial organisation of the United

States. Yet, in our heavy need, we call with confidence to the most resourceful and ingenious technicians in the world. We ask for an unexampled effort believing that it can be made. . . .

16. I am arranging to present you with a complete programme of munitions of all kinds which we seek to obtain from you, the greater part of which is of course already agreed. An important economy of time and effort will be produced if the types selected for the United States Services should, whenever possible, conform to those which have proved their merit under actual conditions of war. In this way reserves of guns and ammunition and of aeroplanes become inter-changeable and are by that very fact augmented. This is however a sphere so highly technical that I do not enlarge upon it.

17. Last of all I come to the question of finance. The more rapid and abundant the flow of munitions and ships which you are able to send us, the sooner will our dollar credits be exhausted. They are already as you know very heavily drawn upon by payments we have made to date. Indeed as you know orders already placed or under negotiation, including expenditure settled or pending for creating munitions factories in the United States, many times exceed the total exchange resources remaining at the disposal of Great Britain. The moment approaches when we shall no longer be able to pay cash for shipping and other supplies. While we will do our utmost and shrink from no proper sacrifice to make payments across the exchange, I believe that you will agree that it would be wrong in principle and mutually disadvantageous in effect if, at the height of this struggle, Great Britain were to be divested of all saleable assets so that after victory was won with our blood, civilisation saved and time gained for the United States to be fully armed against all eventualities, we should stand stripped to the bone. Such a course would not be in the moral or economic interests of either of our countries. We here would be unable after the war to purchase the large balance of imports from the United States over and above the volume of our exports which is agreeable to your tariffs and domestic economy. Not only should we in Great Britain suffer cruel privations but widespread unemployment in the United States would follow the curtailment of American exporting power.

18. Moreover I do not believe the Government and people of the United States would find it in accordance with the principles which guide them, to confine the help which they have so generously promised only to such munitions of war and commodities as could be immediately paid for.

You may be assured that we shall prove ourselves ready to suffer and sacrifice to the utmost for the Cause, and that we glory in being its champion. The rest we leave with confidence to you and to your people, being sure that ways and means will be found which future generations on both sides of the Atlantic will approve and admire.

19. If, as I believe, you are convinced, Mr. President, that the defeat of the Nazi and Fascist tyranny is a matter of high consequence to the people of the United States and to the Western Hemisphere, you will regard this letter not as an appeal for aid, but as a statement of the minimum action necessary to the achievement of our common purpose.

I remain, Yours very sincerely, Winston S. Churchill.

Source: Warren F. Kimball, ed., *Churchill and Roosevelt: The Complete Correspondence* (Princeton: Princeton University Press, 1984), 1:102–109.

Document 4.8   Press Conference Calling for Lend-Lease Program, December 17, 1940

In this press conference, FDR made his case for the Lend-Lease program that he would formally propose the following month. Using the homey images at which he was so adept, he indicated that sending aid to the British was similar to lending one's garden hose to a neighbor whose house was on fire—it would be inappropriate to ask how the items would be paid for in the event they could not be returned.

THE PRESIDENT: . . . I don't think there is any particular news, except possibly one thing that I think is worth my talking about. In the present world situation of course there is absolutely no doubt in the mind of a very overwhelming number of Americans that the best immediate defense of the United States is the success of Great Britain in defending itself; and that, therefore, quite aside from our historic and current interest in the survival of democracy in the world as a whole, it is equally important from a selfish point of view of American defense, that we should do everything to help the British Empire to defend itself.

I have read a great deal of nonsense in the last few days by people who can only think in what we may call traditional terms about finances. Steve

[Early, Roosevelt's press secretary] was asking me about it this morning, and I thought it was better that I should talk to you than for Steve to talk to you; but I gave him one line which he would have used this morning if anybody had asked him, and that was this: In my memory, and your memory, and in all history, no major war has ever been won or lost through lack of money.

I remember 1914 very well. . . .

There was the best economic opinion in the world that the continuance of war was absolutely dependent on money in the bank. Well, you know what happened.

Now we have been getting stories, speeches, et cetera, in regard to this particular war that is going on, which go back a little bit to that attitude. It isn't merely a question of doing things the traditional way; there are lots of other ways of doing them. I am just talking background, informally; I haven't prepared any of this—I go back to the idea that the one thing necessary for American national defense is additional productive facilities; and the more we increase those facilities—factories, shipbuilding ways, munition plants, et cetera, and so on—the stronger American national defense is.

Orders from Great Britain are therefore a tremendous asset to American national defense; because they automatically create additional facilities. I am talking selfishly, from the American point of view—nothing else. Therefore, from the selfish point of view, that production must be encouraged by us. There are several ways of encouraging it—not just one, as the narrow-minded fellow I have been talking about might assume, and has assumed. He has assumed that the only way was to repeal certain existing statutes, like the Neutrality Act and the old Johnson Act and a few other things like that; and then to lend the money to Great Britain to be spent over here—either lend it through private banking circles, as was done in the earlier days of the previous war, or make it a loan from this Government to the British Government.

Well, that is one type of mind that can think only of that method somewhat banal.

There is another one which is also somewhat banal—we may come to it, I don't know—and that is a gift; in other words, for us to pay for all these munitions, ships, plants, guns, et cetera, and make a gift of them to Great Britain. I am not at all sure that that is a necessity, and I am not at all sure that Great Britain would care to have a gift from the taxpayers of the United States. I doubt it very much.

Well, there are other possible ways, and those ways are being explored. All I can do is to speak in very general terms, because we are in the middle of it. I have been at it now three or four weeks, exploring other methods of continuing the building up of our productive facilities and continuing automatically the flow of munitions to Great Britain. I will just put it this way, not as an exclusive alternative method, but as one of several other possible methods that might be devised toward that end.

It is possible—I will put it that way—for the United States to take over British orders, and, because they are essentially the same kind of munitions that we use ourselves, turn them into American orders. We have enough money to do it. And thereupon, as to such portion of them as the military events of the future determine to be right and proper for us to allow to go to the other side, either lease or sell the materials, subject to mortgage, to the people on the other side. That would be on the general theory that it may still prove true that the best defense of Great Britain is the best defense of the United States, and therefore that these materials would be more useful to the defense of the United States if they were used in Great Britain, than if they were kept in storage here.

Now, what I am trying to do is to eliminate the dollar sign. That is something brand new in the thoughts of practically everybody in this room, I think—get rid of the silly, foolish old dollar sign.

Well, let me give you an illustration: Suppose my neighbor's home catches fire, and I have a length of garden hose four or five hundred feet away. If he can take my garden hose and connect it up with his hydrant, I may help him to put out his fire. Now, what do I do? I don't say to him before that operation, "Neighbor, my garden hose cost me $15; you have to pay me $15 for it." What is the transaction that goes on? I don't want $15—I want my garden hose back after the fire is over. All right. If it goes through the fire all right, intact, without any damage to it, he gives it back to me and thanks me very much for the use of it. But suppose it gets smashed up — holes in it—during the fire; we don't have to have too much formality about it, but I say to him, "I was glad to lend you that hose; I see I can't use it any more, it's all smashed up." He says, "How many feet of it were there?" I tell him, "There were 150 feet of it." He says, " All right, I will replace it." Now, if I get a nice garden hose back, I am in pretty good shape.

In other words, if you lend certain munitions and get the munitions back at the end of the war, if they are intact haven't been hurt—you are all right; if they have been damaged or have deteriorated or have been lost completely, it seems to me you come out pretty well if you have them replaced by the fellow to whom you have lent them.

I can't go into details; and there is no use asking legal questions about how you would do it, because that is the thing that is now under study; but the thought is that we would take over not all, but a very large number of, future British orders; and when they came off the line, whether they were planes or guns or something else, we would enter into some kind of arrangement for their use by the British on the ground that it was the best thing for American defense, with the understanding that when the show was over, we would get repaid sometime in kind, thereby leaving out the dollar mark in the form of a dollar debt and substituting for it a gentleman's obligation to repay in kind. I think you all get it. . . .

Q. Let us leave out the legal phase of it entirely; the question I have is whether you think this takes us any more into the war than we are?
THE PRESIDENT: No, not a bit.
Q. Even though goods that we own are being used?
THE PRESIDENT: I don't think you go into a war for legalistic reasons; in other words, we are doing all we can at the present time. . . .

Source: Samuel I. Rosenman, ed., *The Public Papers and Addresses of Franklin D. Roosevelt* (1941; reprint, New York: Russell and Russell, 1969), 9:604–615.

Document 4.9   Message to Congress Asking for a Declaration of War, December 8, 1941

Roosevelt's message to Congress the day after the attack on Pearl Harbor is one of the most memorable speeches he ever made. It summarizes the nation's outrage and the reasons for Americans' unity in the coming conflict.

Yesterday, December 7, 1941—a date which will live in infamy—the United States of America was suddenly and deliberately attacked by naval and air forces of the Empire of Japan.

The United States was at peace with that Nation and, at the solicitation of Japan, was still in conversation with its Government and its Emperor looking toward the maintenance of peace in the Pacific. Indeed, one hour after Japanese air squadrons had commenced bombing in Oahu, the

Japanese Ambassador to the United States and his colleague delivered to the Secretary of State a formal reply to a recent American message. While this reply stated that it seemed useless to continue the existing diplomatic negotiations, it contained no threat or hint of war or armed attack.

It will be recorded that the distance of Hawaii from Japan makes it obvious that the attack was deliberately planned many days or even weeks ago. During the intervening time the Japanese Government has deliberately sought to deceive the United States by false statements and expressions of hope for continued peace.

The attack yesterday on the Hawaiian Islands has caused severe damage to American naval and military forces. Very many American lives have been lost. In addition American ships have been reported torpedoed on the high seas between San Francisco and Honolulu.

Yesterday the Japanese Government also launched an attack against Malaya.

Last night Japanese forces attacked Hong Kong.

Last night Japanese forces attacked Guam.

Last night Japanese forces attacked the Philippine Islands.

Last night the Japanese attacked Wake Island.

This morning the Japanese attacked Midway Island.

Japan has, therefore, undertaken a surprise offensive extending throughout the Pacific area. The facts of yesterday and today speak for themselves. The people of the United States have already formed their opinions and well understand the implications to the very life and safety of our nation.

As Commander-in-Chief of the Army and Navy, I have directed that all measures be taken for our defense.

But always will our whole Nation remember the character of the onslaught against us.

No matter how long it may take us to overcome this premeditated invasion, the American people in their righteous might will win through to absolute victory.

I believe I interpret the will of the Congress and of the people when I assert that we will not only defend ourselves to the uttermost but will make very certain that this form of treachery shall never again endanger us.

Hostilities exist. There is no blinking at the fact that our people, our territory and our interests are in grave danger.

With confidence in our armed forces—with the unbounding determination of our people—we will gain the inevitable triumph—so help us God.

I ask that the Congress declare that since the unprovoked and dastardly attack by Japan on Sunday, December seventh, a state of war has existed between the United States and the Japanese Empire.

Source: Samuel I. Rosenman, ed., *The Public Papers and Addresses of Franklin D. Roosevelt* (1950; reprint, New York: Russell and Russell, 1969), 10:514–515.

Document 4.10   Message to Winston Churchill, December 8, 1941

This message, sent by FDR to British Prime Minister Winston Churchill shortly after the United States's declaration of war, reveals Roosevelt's satisfaction that his country had finally joined the cause and his determination that the cause would be successful.

For the Former Naval Person:

The Senate passed the all-out declaration of war eighty-two to nothing, and the House has passed it three hundred eighty-eight to one. Today all of us are in the same boat with you and the people of the Empire and it is a ship that will not and cannot be sunk.

F.D.R.

Source: Warren F. Kimball, ed., *Churchill and Roosevelt: The Complete Correspondence* (Princeton: Princeton University Press, 1984), 1:283.

Document 4.11   Fireside Chat on the War, February 23, 1942

Roosevelt's fireside chat on the war in February 1942 is one of his most famous and effective. It is classic Roosevelt in its use of patriotic images and its uplifting spirit in the face of crisis.

My fellow Americans:

WASHINGTON'S BIRTHDAY is a most appropriate occasion for us to talk with each other about things as they are today and things as we know they shall be in the future.

For eight years, General Washington and his Continental Army were faced continually with formidable odds and recurring defeats. Supplies and equipment were lacking. In a sense, every winter was a Valley Forge. Throughout the thirteen states there existed fifth columnists—and selfish men, jealous men, fearful men, who proclaimed that Washington's cause was hopeless, and that he should ask for a negotiated peace.

Washington's conduct in those hard times has provided the model for all Americans ever since, a model of moral stamina. He held to his course, as it had been charted in the Declaration of Independence. He and the brave men who served with him knew that no man's life or fortune was secure, without freedom and free institutions.

The present great struggle has taught us increasingly that freedom of person and security of property anywhere in the world depend upon the security of the rights and obligations of liberty and justice everywhere in the world.

This war is a new kind of war. It is different from all other wars of the past, not only in its methods and weapons but also in its geography. It is warfare in terms of every continent, every island, every sea, every air lane in the world.

That is the reason why I have asked you to take out and spread before you a map of the whole earth, and to follow with me the references which I shall make to the world-encircling battle lines of this war. Many questions will, I fear, remain unanswered tonight; but I know you will realize that I cannot cover everything in any one short report to the people.

The broad oceans which have been heralded in the past as our protection from attack have become endless battlefields on which we are constantly being challenged by our enemies.

We must all understand and face the hard fact that our job now is to fight at distances which extend all the way around the globe.

We fight at these vast distances because that is where our enemies are. Until our flow of supplies gives us clear superiority we must keep on striking our enemies wherever and whenever, we can meet them, even if, for a while, we have to yield ground. Actually, though, we are taking a heavy toll of the enemy every day that goes by.

We must fight at these vast distances to protect our supply lines and our lines of communication with our allies—protect these lines from the enemies who are bending every ounce of their strength, striving against time, to cut them. The object of the Nazis and the Japanese is to separate the

United States, Britain, China, and Russia, and to isolate them one from another, so that each will be surrounded and cut off from sources of supplies and reinforcements. It is the old familiar Axis policy of "divide and conquer."

There are those who still think in terms of the days of sailing ships. They advise us to pull our warships and our planes and our merchant ships into our own home waters and concentrate solely on last-ditch defense. But let me illustrate what would happen if we followed such foolish advice.

Look at your map. Look at the vast area of China, with its millions of fighting men. Look at the vast area of Russia, with its powerful armies and proven military might. Look at the British Isles, Australia, New Zealand, the Dutch Indies, India, the Near East, and the continent of Africa, with their resources of raw materials, and of peoples determined to resist Axis domination. Look too at North America, Central America, and South America.

It is obvious what would happen if all of these great reservoirs of power were cut off from each other either by enemy action or by self-imposed isolation:

First, in such a case, we could no longer send aid of any kind to China— to the brave people who, for nearly five years, have withstood Japanese assault, destroyed hundreds of thousands of Japanese soldiers and vast quantities of Japanese war munitions. It is essential that we help China in her magnificent defense and in her inevitable counteroffensive—for that is one important element in the ultimate defeat of Japan.

Second, if we lost communication with the Southwest Pacific, all of that area, including Australia and New Zealand and the Dutch Indies, would fall under Japanese domination. Japan in such a case could release great numbers of ships and men to launch attacks on a large scale against the coasts of the Western Hemisphere—South America and Central America, and North America—including Alaska. At the same time, she could immediately extend her conquests in the other direction toward India, and through the Indian Ocean to Africa, to the Near East, and try to join forces with Germany and Italy.

Third, if we were to stop sending munitions to the British and the Russians in the Mediterranean, in the Persian Gulf, and the Red Sea, we would be helping the Nazis to overrun Turkey, Syria, Iraq, Persia, Egypt and the Suez Canal, the whole coast of North Africa itself, and with that inevitably the whole coast of West Africa—putting Germany within easy striking distance of South America- fifteen hundred miles away.

Fourth, if by such a fatuous policy we ceased to protect the North Atlantic supply line to Britain and to Russia, we would help to cripple the splendid counteroffensive by Russia against the Nazis, and we would help to deprive Britain of essential food supplies and munitions.

Those Americans who believed that we could live under the illusion of isolationism wanted the American eagle to imitate the tactics of the ostrich. Now, many of those same people, afraid that we may be sticking our necks out, want our national bird to be turned into a turtle. But we prefer to retain the eagle as it is—flying high and striking hard.

I know that I speak for the mass of the American people when I say that we reject the turtle policy and will continue increasingly the policy of carrying the war to the enemy in distant lands and distant waters—as far away as possible from our own home grounds. . . .

In spite of the length, and in spite of the difficulties of this transportation, I can tell you that in two and a half months we already have a large number of bombers and pursuit planes, manned by American pilots and crews, which are now in daily contact with the enemy in the Southwest Pacific. And thousands of American troops are today in that area engaged in operations not only in the air but on the ground as well.

In this battle area, Japan has had an obvious initial advantage. For she could fly even her short-range planes to the points of attack by using many stepping stones open to her bases in a multitude of Pacific islands and also bases on the China coast, Indo-China coast, and in Thailand and Malay coasts. Japanese troop transports could go south from Japan and from China through the narrow China Sea which can be protected by Japanese planes throughout its whole length. . . .

We knew that the war as a whole would have to be fought and won by a process of attrition against Japan itself. We knew all along that, with our greater resources, we could outbuild Japan and ultimately overwhelm her on sea, on land, and in the air. We knew that, to attain our objective, many varieties of operations would be necessary in areas other than the Philippines.

Now nothing that has occurred in the past two months has caused us to revise this basic strategy of necessity—except that the defense put up by General MacArthur has magnificently exceeded the previous estimates of endurance; and he and his men are gaining eternal glory therefore.

MacArthur's army of Filipinos and Americans, and the forces of the United Nations in China, in Burma, and the Netherlands East Indies, are all together fulfilling the same essential task. They are making Japan pay an increasingly terrible price for her ambitious attempts to seize control of the whole Asiatic world. Every Japanese transport sunk off Java is one less transport that they can use to carry reinforcements to their army opposing General MacArthur in Luzon.

It has been said that Japanese gains in the Philippines were made possible only by the success of their surprise attack on Pearl Harbor. I tell you that this is not so.

Even if the attack had not been made your map will show that it would have been a hopeless operation for us to send the fleet to the Philippines through thousands of miles of ocean, while all those island bases were under the sole control of the Japanese.

The consequences of the attack on Pearl Harbor—serious as they were—have been wildly exaggerated in other ways. And these exaggerations come originally from Axis propagandists; but they have been repeated, I regret to say, by Americans in and out of public life.

You and I have the utmost contempt for Americans who, since Pearl Harbor, have whispered or announced "off the record" that there was no longer any Pacific Fleet—that the fleet was all sunk or destroyed on December 7—that more than a thousand of our planes were destroyed on the ground. They have suggested slyly that the Government has with-held the truth about casualties—that eleven or twelve thousand men were killed at Pearl Harbor instead of the figures as officially announced. They have even served the enemy propagandists by spreading the incredible story that shiploads of bodies of our honored American dead were about to arrive in New York Harbor to be put into a common grave.

Almost every Axis broadcast—Berlin, Rome, Tokyo—directly quotes Americans who, by speech or in the press, make damnable misstatements such as these.

The American people realize that in many cases details of military operations cannot be disclosed until we are absolutely certain that the announcement will not give to the enemy military information which he does not already possess.

Your Government has unmistakable confidence in your ability to hear the worst, without flinching or losing heart. You must, in turn, have complete confidence that your Government is keeping nothing from you except information that will help the enemy in his attempt to destroy us. In a democracy there is always a solemn pact of truth between

Government and the people; but there must also always be a full use of discretion and that word "discretion" applies to the critics of Government as well.

This is war. The American people want to know, and will be told, the general trend of how the war is going. But they do not wish to help the enemy any more than our fighting forces do; and they will pay little attention to the rumor-mongers and the poison peddlers in our midst.

To pass from the realm of rumor and poison to the field of facts: The number of our officers and men killed in the attack on Pearl Harbor on December 7 was 2,340, and the number wounded was 946. Of all the combatant ships based at Pearl Harbor—battleships, heavy cruisers, light cruisers, aircraft carriers, destroyers and submarines—only three are permanently put out of commission.

Very many of the ships of the Pacific Fleet were not even in Pearl Harbor. Some of those that were there were hit very slightly; and others that were damaged have either rejoined the fleet by now or are still undergoing repairs. And when those repairs are completed, the ships will be more efficient fighting machines than they were before.

The report that we lost more than a thousand planes at Pearl Harbor is as baseless as the other weird rumors. The Japanese do not know just how many planes they destroyed that day, and I am not going to tell them. But I can say that to date—and including Pearl Harbor—we have destroyed considerably more Japanese planes than they have destroyed of ours.

We have most certainly suffered losses—from Hitler's U-boats in the Atlantic as well as from the Japanese in the Pacific—and we shall suffer more of them before the turn of the tide. But, speaking for the United States of America, let me say once and for all to the people of the world: We Americans have been compelled to yield ground, but we will regain it. We and the other United Nations are committed to the destruction of the militarism of Japan and Germany. We are daily increasing our strength. Soon, we and not our enemies will have the offensive; we, not they, will win the final battles; and we, not they, will make the final peace.

Conquered Nations in Europe know what the yoke of the Nazis is like. And the people of Korea and of Manchuria know in their flesh the harsh despotism of Japan. All of the people of Asia know that if there is to be an honorable and decent future for any of them or any of us, that future depends on victory by the United Nations over the forces of Axis enslavement.

If a just and durable peace is to be attained, or even if all of us are merely to save our own skins, there is one thought for us here at home to keep uppermost—the fulfillment of our special task of production.

Germany, Italy, and Japan are very close to their maximum output of planes, guns, tanks, and ships. The United Nations are not—especially the United States of America.

Our first job then is to build up production—uninterrupted production—so that the United Nations can maintain control of the seas and attain control of the air—not merely a slight superiority, but an overwhelming superiority.

On January 6 of this year, I set certain definite goals of production for airplanes, tanks, guns, and ships. The Axis propagandists called them fantastic. Tonight, nearly two months later, and after a careful survey of progress by Donald Nelson and others charged with responsibility for our production, I can tell you that those goals will be attained.

In every part of the country, experts in production and the men and women at work in the plants are giving loyal service. With few exceptions, labor, capital, and farming realize that this is no time either to make undue profits or to gain special advantages, one over the other.

We are calling for new plants and additions to old plants. We are calling for plant conversion to war needs. We are seeking more men and more women to run them. We are working longer hours. We are coming to realize that one extra plane or extra tank or extra gun or extra ship completed tomorrow may, in a few months, turn the tide on some distant battlefield; it may make the difference between life and death for some of our own fighting men. We know now that if we lose this war it will be generations or even centuries before our conception of democracy can live again. And we can lose this war only if we slow up our effort or if we waste our ammunition sniping at each other.

Here are three high purposes for every American:

1. We shall not stop work for a single day. If any dispute arises we shall keep on working while the dispute is solved by mediation, conciliation, or arbitration—until the war is won.
2. We shall not demand special gains or special privileges or special advantages for any one group or occupation.
3. We shall give up conveniences and modify the routine of our lives if our country asks us to do so. We will do it cheerfully, remembering

that the common enemy seeks to destroy every home and every freedom in every part of our land.

This generation of Americans has come to realize, with a present and
personal realization, that there is something larger and more important
than the life of any individual or of any individual group—something for
which a man will sacrifice, and gladly sacrifice, not only his pleasures, not
only his goods, not only his associations with those he loves, but his life
itself. In time of crisis when the future is in the balance, we come to understand, with full recognition and devotion, what this Nation is, and what
we owe to it. . . .

Ever since this Nation became the arsenal of democracy—ever since
enactment of lend-lease—there has been one persistent theme through all
Axis propaganda.

This theme has been that Americans are admittedly rich, that Americans
have considerable industrial power—but that Americans are soft and deca-
dent, that they cannot and will not unite and work and fight.

From Berlin, Rome, and Tokyo we have been described as a Nation of
weaklings—"playboys"—who would hire British soldiers, or Russian soldiers, or Chinese soldiers to do our fighting for us.

Let them repeat that now!

Let them tell that to General MacArthur and his men.

Let them tell that to the sailors who today are hitting hard in the far
waters of the Pacific.

Let them tell that to the boys in the Flying Fortresses.

Let them tell that to the Marines!

The United Nations constitute an association of independent peoples
of equal dignity and equal importance. The United Nations are dedicated
to a common cause. We share equally and with equal zeal the anguish and
the awful sacrifices of war. In the partnership of our common enterprise,
we must share in a unified plan in which all of us must play our several
parts, each of us being equally indispensable and dependent one on the
other.

We have unified command and cooperation and comradeship.

We Americans will contribute unified production and unified acceptance of sacrifice and of effort. That means a national unity that can know
no limitations of race or creed or selfish politics.

The American people expect that much from themselves. And the
American people will find ways and means of expressing their determina-

tion to their enemies, including the Japanese Admiral who has said that he will dictate the terms of peace here in the White House.

We of the United Nations are agreed on certain broad principles in the kind of peace we seek. The Atlantic Charter applies not only to the parts of the world that border the Atlantic but to the whole world; disarmament of aggressors, self-determination of Nations and peoples, and the four freedoms—freedom of speech, freedom of religion, freedom from want, and freedom from fear. . . .

The task that we Americans now face will test us to the uttermost. Never before have we been called upon for such a prodigious effort. Never before have we had so little time in which to do so much.

"These are the times that try men's souls." Tom Paine wrote those words on a drumhead, by the light of a campfire. That was when Washington's little army of ragged, rugged men was retreating across New Jersey, having tasted nothing but defeat.

And General Washington ordered that these great words written by Tom Paine be read to the men of every regiment in the Continental Army, and this was the assurance given to the first American armed forces:

"The summer soldier and the sunshine patriot will, in this crisis, shrink from the service of their country; but he that stands it now, deserves the love and thanks of man and woman. Tyranny, like hell, is not easily conquered; yet we have this consolation with us, that the harder the sacrifice, the more glorious the triumph."

So spoke Americans in the year 1776.

So speak Americans today!

Source: Samuel I. Rosenman, ed., *The Public Papers and Addresses of Franklin D. Roosevelt* (1950; reprint, New York: Russell and Russell, 1969), 11:105–116.

Document 4.12   Executive Order 9066, February 19, 1942

The fear of Japanese attack or sabotage, combined with racial prejudice, created a widespread clamor for the removal of all people of Japanese ancestry from the West Coast. Although no sabotage had occurred, Roosevelt gave in to this demand for political reasons. The following executive order, which does not mention Japanese Americans directly but is still clear in its intent, is among the worst blots on FDR's record.

EXECUTIVE ORDER NO. 9066
AUTHORIZING THE SECRETARY OF WAR
TO PRESCRIBE MILITARY AREAS

WHEREAS the successful prosecution of the war requires every possible protection against espionage and against sabotage to national-defense material, national-defense premises, and national-defense utilities as defined in section 4, Act of April 20, 1918, 40 Stat. 533, as amended by the act of November 30, 1940, 54 Stat. 1220, and the Act of August 21, 1941, 55 Stat. 655 (U. S. C., Title 50, Sec. 104):

NOW, THEREFORE, by virtue of the authority vested in me as President of the United States, and Commander in Chief of the Army and Navy, I hereby authorize and direct the Secretary of War, and the Military Commanders whom he may from time to time designate, whenever he or any designated Commander deems such actions necessary or desirable, to prescribe military areas in such places and of such extent as he or the appropriate Military Commanders may determine, from which any or all persons may be excluded, and with such respect to which, the right of any person to enter, remain in, or leave shall be subject to whatever restrictions the Secretary of War or the appropriate Military Commander may impose in his discretion. The Secretary of War is hereby authorized to provide for residents of any such area who are excluded therefrom, such transportation, food, shelter, and other accommodations as may be necessary, in the judgement *[sic]* of the Secretary of War or the said Military Commander, and until other arrangements are made, to accomplish the purpose of this order. The designation of military areas in any region or locality shall supersede designations of prohibited and restricted areas by the Attorney General under the Proclamations of December 7 and 8, 1941, and shall supersede the responsibility and authority of the Attorney General under the said Proclamations in respect of such prohibited and restricted areas.

I hereby further authorize and direct the Secretary of War and the said Military Commanders to take such other steps as he or the appropriate Military Commander may deem advisable to enforce compliance with the restrictions applicable to each Military area hereinabove authorized to be designated, including the use of Federal troops and other Federal Agencies, with authority to accept assistance of state and local agencies.

I hereby further authorize and direct all Executive Departments, independent establishments and other Federal Agencies, to assist the Secretary of War or the said Military Commanders in carrying out this Executive

Order, including the furnishing of medical aid, hospitalization, food, clothing, transportation, use of land, shelter, and other supplies, equipment, utilities, facilities and services.

This order shall not be construed as modifying or limiting in any way the authority heretofore granted under Executive Order No. 8972, dated December 12, 1941, nor shall it be construed as limiting or modifying the duty and responsibility of the Federal Bureau of Investigation, with respect to the investigation of alleged acts of sabotage or the duty and responsibility of the Attorney General and the Department of Justice under the Proclamations of December 7 and 8, 1941, prescribing regulations for the conduct and control of alien enemies, except as such duty and responsibility is superseded by the designation of military areas hereunder.

Source: Federal Register Doc. 42-1563, in Roger Daniels, *Prisoners without Trial: Japanese Americans in World War II* (New York: Hill and Wang, 1993), 129–130.

Document 4.13   FDR and Winston Churchill, Joint Press Conference at Casablanca, January 24, 1943

At the Casablanca Conference in January 1943, Roosevelt indicated that the Allies would accept nothing short of the unconditional surrender of Germany and Japan. This policy, intended to avoid the situation that had followed the armistice at the end of the first World War, which had made it possible for Hitler and others to argue that Germany had not really been defeated, had important ramifications for the ending of the war with Japan and the use of the atomic bomb.

THE PRESIDENT: This meeting goes back to the successful landing operations last November, which as you all know were initiated as far back as a year ago, and put into definite shape shortly after the Prime Minister's visit to Washington in June.

After the operations of last November, it became perfectly clear, with the successes, that the time had come for another review of the situation, and a planning for the next steps, especially steps to be taken in 1943. That is why we came here, and our respective staffs came with us, to discuss the practical steps to be taken by the United Nations for prosecution of the war. We have been here about a week.

I might add, too, that we began talking about this after the first of December, and at that time we invited Mr. Stalin to join us at a convenient meeting place. Mr. Stalin very greatly desired to come, but he was precluded from leaving Russia because he was conducting the new Russian offensive against the Germans along the whole line. We must remember that he is Commander in Chief, and that he is responsible for the very wonderful detailed plan which has been brought to such a successful conclusion since the beginning of the offensive.

In spite of the fact that Mr. Stalin was unable to come, the results of the staff meeting have been communicated to him, so that we will continue to keep in very close touch with each other.

I think it can be said that the studies during the past week or ten days are unprecedented in history. Both the Prime Minister and I think back to the days of the first World War when conferences between the French and British and ourselves very rarely lasted more than a few hours or a couple of days. The Chiefs of Staffs have been in intimate touch; they have lived in the same hotel. Each man has become a definite personal friend of his opposite number on the other side.

Furthermore, these conferences have discussed, I think for the first time in history, the whole global picture. It isn't just one front, just one ocean, or one continent—it is literally the whole world; and that is why the Prime Minister and I feel that the conference is unique in the fact that it has this global aspect.

The Combined Staffs, in these conferences and studies during the past week or ten days, have proceeded on the principle of pooling all of the resources of the United Nations. And I think the second point is that they have reaffirmed the determination to maintain the initiative against the Axis powers in every part of the world.

These plans covering the initiative and maintenance of the initiative during 1943 cover certain things, such as united operations conducted in different areas of the world. Second, the sending of all possible material aid to the Russian offensive, with the double object of cutting down the manpower of Germany and her satellites, and continuing the very great attrition of German munitions and materials of all kinds which are being destroyed every day in such large quantities by the Russian armies.

And, at the same time, the Staffs have agreed on giving all possible aid to the heroic struggle of China—remembering that China is in her sixth year of the war—with the objective, not only in China but in the whole of the Pacific area, of ending any Japanese attempt in the future to dominate the Far East.

Another point. I think we have all had it in our hearts and our heads before, but I don't think that it has ever been put down on paper by the Prime Minister and myself, and that is the determination that peace can come to the world only by the total elimination of German and Japanese war power.

Some of you Britishers know the old story—we had a General called U. S. Grant. His name was Ulysses Simpson Grant, but in my, and the Prime Minister's, early days he was called "Unconditional Surrender" Grant. "The elimination of German, Japanese, and Italian war power" means the unconditional surrender by Germany, Italy, and Japan. That means a reasonable assurance of future world peace. It does not mean the destruction of the population of Germany, Italy, or Japan, but it does mean the destruction of the philosophies in those countries which are based on conquest and the subjugation of other people. . . .

THE PRIME MINISTER: I agree with everything that the President has said, and I think it was a very happy decision to bring you gentlemen here to Casablanca to this agreeable spot, Anfa Camp, which has been the center—the scene—of much the most important and successful war conference which I have ever attended or witnessed. Nothing like it has occurred in my experience, which is a long while—the continuous work, hours and hours every day from morning until often after midnight, carried on by the staffs of both sides, by all the principal officers of the two Nations who are engaged in the direction of the war.

This work has proceeded with an intensity, and thoroughness, and comprehensiveness, the like of which I have never seen, and I firmly believe that you will find that results will come from this as this year unfolds. You will find results will come from it which will give our troops, and soldiers, and fliers the best possible chance to gather new victories from the enemy. Fortune turned a more or less somber face upon us at the close of last year, and we meet here today at this place— we have been meeting here—which in a way is the active center of the war direction. We wish indeed it was possible to have Premier Stalin, and the Generalissimo, and others of the United Nations here, but geography is a stubborn thing; and the difficulties and the preoccupations of the men engaged in fighting the enemy in other countries are also very clear obstacles to their free movement, and therefore we have had to meet here together.

Well, one thing I should like to say, and that is—I think I can say it with full confidence—nothing that may occur in this war will ever come between me and the President. He and I are in this as friends and partners, and we work together. We know that our easy, free conversation is one of the sinews of war—of the Allied powers. It makes many things easy that would otherwise be difficult, and solutions can be reached when an agreement has stopped, which would otherwise be impossible, even with the utmost good will, of the vast war machinery which the English-speaking people are operating. . . .

I hope you gentlemen will find this talk to be of assistance to you in your work, and will be able to build up a good and encouraging story to our people all over the world. Give them the picture of unity, thoroughness, and integrity of the political chiefs. Give them that picture, and make them feel that there is some reason behind all that is being done. Even when there is some delay there is design and purpose, and as the President has said, the unconquerable will to pursue this quality, until we have procured the unconditional surrender of the criminal forces who plunged the world into storm and ruin. . . .

Source: Samuel I. Rosenman, ed., *The Public Papers and Addresses of Franklin D. Roosevelt* (1950; reprint, New York: Russell and Russell, 1969), 12:37–45.

Document 4.14   Anglo-American-Russian Declaration of Teheran Conference, December 1, 1943

At the Teheran conference in November 1943, Roosevelt met with Soviet Marshal Josef Stalin for the first time. Little of substance was decided, as the joint declaration issued at the conference's conclusion suggests. Behind the scenes, however, FDR believed he had established a relationship with Stalin that could be useful in the future, and Stalin said that the Soviet Union would enter the war against Japan after Germany was defeated. It was also agreed that Operation Overlord, the invasion across the English Channel, would begin in May 1944. These matters were, of course, not included in the public declaration.

Declaration of the Three Powers:

We, The President of the United States, the Prime Minister of Great Britain, and the Premier of the Soviet Union, have met these four days past, in this, the Capital of our ally, Iran, and have shaped and confirmed our common policy.

We express our determination that our Nations shall work together in war and in the peace that will follow.

As to war—our military staffs have joined in our round-table discussions, and we have concerted our plans for the destruction of the German forces. We have reached complete agreement as to the scope and timing of the operations to be undertaken from the east, west, and south.

The common understanding which we have here reached guarantees that victory will be ours.

And as to peace— we are sure that our concord will win an enduring peace. We recognize fully the supreme responsibility resting upon us and all the United Nations to make a peace which will command the good will of the overwhelming mass of the peoples of the world and banish the scourge and terror of war for many generations.

With our diplomatic advisers we have surveyed the problems of the future. We shall seek the cooperation and active participation of all Nations, large and small, whose peoples in heart and mind are dedicated, as are our own peoples, to the elimination of tyranny and slavery, oppression and intolerance. We will welcome them, as they may choose to come, into a world family of democratic Nations.

No power on earth can prevent our destroying the German armies by land, their U-boats by sea, and their war plants from the air.

Our attack will be relentless and increasing.

Emerging from these cordial conferences we look with confidence to the day when all peoples of the world may live free lives, untouched by tyranny, and according to their varying desires and their own consciences.

We came here with hope and determination. We leave here, friends in fact, in spirit, and in purpose.

Signed: Roosevelt, Churchill, and Stalin

Signed at Teheran, December 1, 1943

Source: Samuel I. Rosenman, ed., *The Public Papers and Addresses of Franklin D. Roosevelt* (1950; reprint, New York: Russell and Russell, 1969), 12:532–533.

Document 4.15   D Day Prayer, June 6, 1944

When the long-awaited and oft-delayed cross-channel invasion of Nazi-occupied Europe, Operation Overlord, began on "D day," June 6, 1941, Roosevelt spoke to the nation by radio and offered a prayer.

My Fellow Americans: Last night, when I spoke with you about the fall of Rome, I knew at that moment that troops of the United States and our allies were crossing the Channel in another and greater operation. It has come to pass with success thus far.

And so, in this poignant hour, I ask you to join with me in prayer.

Almighty God: Our sons, pride of our nation, this day have set upon a mighty endeavor, a struggle to preserve our Republic, our religion, and our civilization, and to set free a suffering humanity.

Lead them straight and true; give strength to their arms, stoutness to their hearts, steadfastness in the faith.

They will need Thy blessings. Their road will be long and hard. For the enemy is strong. He may hurl back our forces. Success may not come with rushing speed, but we shall return again and again; and we know that by Thy grace, and by the righteousness of our cause, our sons will triumph.

They will be sore tried, by night and day, without rest—until the victory is won. The darkness will be rent by noise and flame. Men's souls will be shaken with the violences of war.

For these men are lately drawn from the ways of peace. They fight not for the lust of conquest. They fight to end conquest. They fight to liberate. They fight to let justice arise, and tolerance and goodwill among all Thy people. They yearn but for the end of battle, for their return to the haven of home.

Some will never return. Embrace these, Father, and receive them, Thy heroic servants, into Thy kingdom.

And for us at home—fathers, mothers, children, wives, sisters, and brothers of brave men overseas, whose thoughts and prayers are ever with them—help us, Almighty God, to rededicate ourselves in renewed faith in Thee in this hour of great sacrifice.

Many people have urged that I call the nation into a single day of special prayer. But because the road is long and the desire is great, I ask that our people devote themselves in a continuance of prayer. As we rise to each new day, and again when each day is spent, let words of prayer be on our lips, invoking Thy help to our efforts.

Give us strength, too—strength in our daily tasks, to redouble the contributions we make in the physical and the material support of our armed forces.

And let our hearts be stout, to wait out the long travail, to bear sorrows that may come, to impart our courage unto our sons wheresoever they may be.

And, O Lord, give us faith. Give us faith in Thee; faith in our sons; faith in each other; faith in our united crusade. Let not the keenness of our spirit ever be dulled. Let not the impacts of temporary events, of temporal matters of but fleeting moment—let not these deter us in our unconquerable purpose.

With Thy blessing, we shall prevail over the unholy forces of our enemy. Help us to conquer the apostles of greed and racial arrogancies. Lead us to the saving of our country, and with our sister nations into a world unity that will spell a sure peace—a peace invulnerable to the schemings of unworthy men. And a peace that will let all of men live in freedom, reaping the just rewards of their honest toil.

Thy will be done, Almighty God.

Amen.

Source: Samuel I. Rosenman, ed., *The Public Papers and Addresses of Franklin D. Roosevelt* (1950; reprint, New York: Russell and Russell, 1969), 13:152–153.

Document 4.16   Yalta Protocol, February 11, 1945

The last "Big Three" meeting that Roosevelt attended, held at Yalta on the Crimean Peninsula in the Soviet Union in February 1945, became the focus of much controversy in later years. Roosevelt's critics charged that he had "given" eastern Europe to the Soviets. In fact, the Red Army had occupied much of the territory by the time the conference occurred and the issue was much more one of what the Soviets could be persuaded to do in the region, rather than what the United States and Great Britain would give them. Most outstanding issues on the establishment of the United Nations were settled and included in this protocol. The agreement for Soviet entry into the war against Japan was considered to be of great importance in reducing likely

American casualties in that theater of the war. Some provisions of the Yalta Protocol, most notably those regarding Soviet entry into the war against Japan, were not made public at the time.

PROTOCOL OF PROCEEDINGS OF CRIMEA CONFERENCE

The Crimea Conference of the heads of the Governments of the United States of America, the United Kingdom, and the Union of Soviet Socialist Republics, which took place from Feb. 4 to 11, came to the following conclusions:

I. WORLD ORGANIZATION

It was decided:

1. That a United Nations conference on the proposed world organization should be summoned for Wednesday, 25 April, 1945, and should be held in the United States of America.

2. The nations to be invited to this conference should be:

(a) the United Nations as they existed on 8 Feb., 1945; and

(b) Such of the Associated Nations as have declared war on the common enemy by 1 March, 1945. (For this purpose, by the term "Associated Nations" was meant the eight Associated Nations and Turkey.) When the conference on world organization is held, the delegates of the United Kingdom and United States of America will support a proposal to admit to original membership two Soviet Socialist Republics, i.e., the Ukraine and White Russia.

3. That the United States Government, on behalf of the three powers, should consult the Government of China and the French Provisional Government in regard to decisions taken at the present conference concerning the proposed world organization.

4. That the text of the invitation to be issued to all the nations which would take part in the United Nations conference should be as follows:

"The Government of the United States of America, on behalf of itself and of the Governments of the United Kingdom, the Union of Soviet Socialistic Republics and the Republic of China and of the Provisional Government of the French Republic invite the Government of ———— to send representatives to a conference to be held on 25 April, 1945, or soon thereafter, at San Francisco, in the United States of America, to prepare a charter for a general international organization for the maintenance of international peace and security.

"The above-named Governments suggest that the conference consider as affording a basis for such a Charter the proposals for the establishment of a general international organization which were made public last October as a result of the Dumbarton Oaks conference and which have now been supplemented by the following provisions for Section C of Chapter VI:

C. Voting
"1. Each member of the Security Council should have one vote.

"2. Decisions of the Security Council on procedural matters should be made by an affirmative vote of seven members.

"3. Decisions of the Security Council on all matters should be made by an affirmative vote of seven members, including the concurring votes of the permanent members; provided that, in decisions under Chapter VIII, Section A and under the second sentence of Paragraph 1 of Chapter VIII, Section C, a party to a dispute should abstain from voting.

"Further information as to arrangements will be transmitted subsequently.

"In the event that the Government of ———— desires in advance of the conference to present views or comments concerning the proposals, the Government of the United States of America will be pleased to transmit such views and comments to the other participating Governments."

Territorial trusteeship:
It was agreed that the five nations which will have permanent seats on the Security Council should consult each other prior to the United Nations conference on the question of territorial trusteeship.

The acceptance of this recommendation is subject to its being made clear that territorial trusteeship will only apply to (a) existing mandates of the League of Nations; (b) territories detached from the enemy as a result of the present war; (c) any other territory which might voluntarily be placed under trusteeship; and (d) no discussion of actual territories is contemplated at the forthcoming United Nations conference or in the preliminary consultations, and it will be a matter for subsequent agreement which territories within the above categories will be placed under trusteeship.

II. DECLARATION OF LIBERATED EUROPE

The following declaration has been approved:

The Premier of the Union of Soviet Socialist Republics, the Prime Minister of the United Kingdom and the President of the United States of America have consulted with each other in the common interests of the people of their countries and those of liberated Europe. They jointly declare their mutual agreement to concert during the temporary period of instability in liberated Europe the policies of their three Governments in assisting the peoples liberated from the domination of Nazi Germany and the peoples of the former Axis satellite states of Europe to solve by democratic means their pressing political and economic problems.

The establishment of order in Europe and the rebuilding of national economic life must be achieved by processes which will enable the liberated peoples to destroy the last vestiges of nazism and fascism and to create democratic institutions of their own choice. This is a principle of the Atlantic Charter—the right of all people to choose the form of government under which they will live—the restoration of sovereign rights and self-government to those peoples who have been forcibly deprived to them by the aggressor nations.

To foster the conditions in which the liberated people may exercise these rights, the three governments will jointly assist the people in any European liberated state or former Axis state in Europe where, in their judgment conditions require, (a) to establish conditions of internal peace; (b) to carry out emergency relief measures for the relief of distressed peoples; (c) to form interim governmental authorities broadly representative of all democratic elements in the population and pledged to the earliest possible establishment through free elections of Governments responsive to the will of the people; and (d) to facilitate where necessary the holding of such elections.

The three Governments will consult the other United Nations and provisional authorities or other Governments in Europe when matters of direct interest to them are under consideration.

When, in the opinion of the three Governments, conditions in any European liberated state or former Axis satellite in Europe make such action necessary, they will immediately consult together on the measure necessary to discharge the joint responsibilities set forth in this declaration.

By this declaration we reaffirm our faith in the principles of the Atlantic Charter, our pledge in the Declaration by the United Nations and our determination to build in cooperation with other peace-loving nations world order, under law, dedicated to peace, security, freedom and general well-being of all mankind.

In issuing this declaration, the three powers express the hope that the Provisional Government of the French Republic may be associated with them in the procedure suggested.

III. DISMEMBERMENT OF GERMANY

It was agreed that Article 12 (a) of the Surrender terms for Germany should be amended to read as follows:

"The United Kingdom, the United States of America and the Union of Soviet Socialist Republics shall possess supreme authority with respect to Germany. In the exercise of such authority they will take such steps, including the complete dismemberment of Germany as they deem requisite for future peace and security."

The study of the procedure of the dismemberment of Germany was referred to a committee consisting of Mr. Anthony Eden, Mr. John Winant, and Mr. Fedor T. Gusev. This body would consider the desirability of associating with it a French representative.

IV. ZONE OF OCCUPATION FOR THE FRENCH AND CONTROL COUNCIL FOR GERMANY

It was agreed that a zone in Germany, to be occupied by the French forces, should be allocated France. This zone would be formed out of the British and American zones and its extent would be settled by the British and Americans in consultation with the French Provisional Government.

It was also agreed that the French Provisional Government should be invited to become a member of the Allied Control Council for Germany.

V. REPARATION

The following protocol has been approved:
Protocol

On the Talks Between the Heads of Three Governments at the Crimean Conference on the Question of the German Reparations in Kind

1. Germany must pay in kind for the losses caused by her to the Allied nations in the course of the war. Reparations are to be received in the first

instance by those countries which have borne the main burden of the war, have suffered the heaviest losses and have organized victory over the enemy.

2. Reparation in kind is to be exacted from Germany in three following forms:

(a) Removals within two years from the surrender of Germany or the cessation of organized resistance from the national wealth of Germany located on the territory of Germany herself as well as outside her territory (equipment, machine tools, ships, rolling stock, German investments abroad, shares of industrial, transport and other enterprises in Germany, etc.), these removals to be carried out chiefly for the purpose of destroying the war potential of Germany.

(b) Annual deliveries of goods from current production for a period to be fixed.

(c) Use of German labor.

3. For the working out on the above principles of a detailed plan for exaction of reparation from Germany an Allied reparation commission will be set up in Moscow. It will consist of three representatives—one from the Union of Soviet Socialist Republics, one from the United Kingdom and one from the United States of America.

4. With regard to the fixing of the total sum of the reparation as well as the distribution of it among the countries which suffered from the German aggression, the Soviet and American delegations agreed as follows:

"The Moscow reparation commission should take in its initial studies as a basis for discussion the suggestion of the Soviet Government that the total sum of the reparation in accordance with the points (a) and (b) of the Paragraph 2 should be 22 billion dollars and that 50 per cent should go to the Union of Soviet Socialist Republics."

The British delegation was of the opinion that, pending consideration of the reparation question by the Moscow reparation commission, no figures of reparation should be mentioned.

The above Soviet-American proposal has been passed to the Moscow reparation commission as one of the proposals to be considered by the commission.

VI. MAJOR WAR CRIMINALS

The conference agreed that the question of the major war criminals should be the subject of inquiry by the three Foreign Secretaries for report in due course after the close of the conference.

VII. POLAND

The following declaration on Poland was agreed by the conference:

"A new situation has been created in Poland as a result of her complete liberation by the Red Army. This calls for the establishment of a Polish Provisional Government which can be more broadly based than was possible before the recent liberation of the western part of Poland. The Provisional Government which is now functioning in Poland should therefore be reorganized on a broader democratic basis with the inclusion of democratic leaders from Poland itself and from Poles abroad. This new Government should then be called the Polish Provisional Government of National Unity.

"M. Molotov, Mr. Harriman and Sir A. Clark Kerr are authorized as a commission to consult in the first instance in Moscow with members of the present Provisional Government and with other Polish democratic leaders from within Poland and from abroad, with a view to the reorganization of the present Government along the above lines. This Polish Provisional Government of National Unity shall be pledged to the holding of free and unfettered elections as soon as possible on the basis of universal suffrage and secret ballot. In these elections all democratic and anti-Nazi parties shall have the right to take part and to put forward candidates.

"When a Polish Provisional of Government National Unity has been properly formed in conformity with the above, the Government of the U.S.S.R., which now maintains diplomatic relations with the present Provisional Government of Poland, and the Government of the United Kingdom and the Government of the United States of America will establish diplomatic relations with the new Polish Provisional Government National Unity, and will exchange Ambassadors by whose reports the respective Governments will be kept informed about the situation in Poland.

"The three heads of Government consider that the eastern frontier of Poland should follow the Curzon Line with digressions from it in some regions of five to eight kilometers in favor of Poland. They recognize that Poland must receive substantial accessions in territory in the north and west. They feel that the opinion of the new Polish Provisional Government of National Unity should be sought in due course of the extent of these accessions and that the final delimitation of the western frontier of Poland should thereafter await the peace conference."

VIII. YUGOSLAVIA

It was agreed to recommend to Marshal Tito and to Dr. Ivan Subasitch:

(a) That the Tito-Subasitch agreement should immediately be put into effect and a new government formed on the basis of the agreement.

(b) That as soon as the new Government has been formed it should declare:

(I) That the Anti-Fascist Assembly of the National Liberation (AVNOJ) will be extended to include members of the last Yugoslav Skupstina who have not compromised themselves by collaboration with the enemy, thus forming a body to be known as a temporary Parliament. . . .

AGREEMENT REGARDING JAPAN

The leaders of the three great powers—the Soviet Union, the United States of America and Great Britain—have agreed that in two or three months after Germany has surrendered and the war in Europe is terminated, the Soviet Union shall enter into war against Japan on the side of the Allies on condition that:

1. The status quo in Outer Mongolia (the Mongolian People's Republic) shall be preserved.

2. The former rights of Russia violated by the treacherous attack of Japan in 1904 shall be restored, viz.:

(a) The southern part of Sakhalin as well as the islands adjacent to it shall be returned to the Soviet Union;

(b) The commercial port of Dairen shall be internationalized, the pre-eminent interests of the Soviet Union in this port being safeguarded, and the lease of Port Arthur as a naval base of the U.S.S.R. restored;

(c) The Chinese-Eastern Railroad and the South Manchurian Railroad, which provide an outlet to Dairen, shall be jointly operated by the establishment of a joint Soviet-Chinese company, it being understood that the pre-eminent interests of the Soviet Union shall be safeguarded and that China shall retain sovereignty in Manchuria;

3. The Kurile Islands shall be handed over to the Soviet Union.

It is understood that the agreement concerning Outer Mongolia and the ports and railroads referred to above will require concurrence of Generalissimo Chiang Kai-shek. The President will take measures in order to maintain this concurrence on advice from Marshal Stalin.

The heads of the three great powers have agreed that these claims of the Soviet Union shall be unquestionably fulfilled after Japan has been defeated.

For its part, the Soviet Union expresses it readiness to conclude with the National Government of China a pact of friendship and alliance between the U.S.S.R. and China in order to render assistance to China with its armed forces for the purpose of liberating China from the Japanese yoke.

Joseph Stalin
Franklin D. Roosevelt
Winston S. Churchill

Source: Foreign Relations of the United States: Diplomatic Papers—The Conferences at Malta and Yalta 1945 (Washington, D.C.: U.S. Government Printing Office, 1955), 975–982.

Roosevelt holds a press conference in the Oval Office.

CHAPTER FIVE

Institutional Relations

Over the course of his twelve-year presidency, Franklin D. Roosevelt developed significant relationships with all the major institutions in the United States. He maintained a generally warm relationship with the media and the military despite some friction with such military leaders as Gen. Douglas MacArthur. Although FDR's relationship with business was largely hostile during the New Deal, it became somewhat friendlier during World War II. He was on good terms with Congress during his first administration, but that relationship deteriorated somewhat in his second administration. Roosevelt was at odds with the Supreme Court through 1937, but this began to change as the Court filled with his appointees. No previous president had had such a friendly relationship with organized labor, although a small segment of the union movement led by John L. Lewis turned bitterly against Roosevelt from the middle of his second term until his death.

CONGRESS

As president during the worst crisis the nation had experienced since the Civil War, Franklin Roosevelt enjoyed almost unlimited support from Congress during the early years of his administration. Roosevelt's immense popularity augmented this good relationship, as did the growing Democratic majorities in Congress. Although the party hold-ing the presidency almost always loses congressional seats in off-year elections, Democrats made substantial gains in both houses in 1934, winning 26 of 35 Senate races and 322 House races to 103 for the Republicans. Presidents with such long coattails are not likely to meet much opposition from legislators of their own party.

Yet the relationship between Roosevelt and Congress even in the early New Deal was not one of complete presidential dominance. Several of the key proposals of the first hundred days were initiated by Congress and endorsed by the president, rather than the other way around. Because Roosevelt had no clear idea of how to bring about recovery—that is, beyond his hope that restoring the purchasing power of farmers would lift the whole economy—he was willing to entertain proposals that originated on Capitol Hill. Nor was FDR one to get deeply involved in legislative details. He was, for the most part, content to present the larger picture—the vision—to the public and let Congress work out the details.

Several of the most important pieces of legislation passed during the Roosevelt administration—the Federal Emergency Relief Act (FERA), the Tennessee Valley Authority (TVA), the Federal Deposit Insurance Corporation (FDIC), and the National Labor Relations Act (Wagner Act)—were largely the work of Congress. Both the FDIC and the Wag-ner Act were measures that Roosevelt had not supported until he saw that their passage was inevitable. The National Industrial Recovery Act (NIRA) was a hastily cobbled-together measure offered to head off a congressional initiative to limit the work week to thirty hours.

Yet the public was largely unaware that legislative traffic on Pennsyl-vania Avenue was running in both directions. Roosevelt was the leader, the symbol, the spokesman—and he got almost all of the credit. In the early days, most members of Congress were probably content with this perception. Action was needed, and bills were becoming law in substan-tial part because of Roosevelt's popularity. But over time the imbalance in recognition was bound to grate on some legislators. The president has a built-in advantage in getting attention for his work, but the combina-tion of the two extraordinary crises of the Great Depression and World War II with Roosevelt's great communication skills made it even more difficult for members of Congress to win media attention.

Nor was it only a matter of who received credit and attention. Much of the legislation of the New Deal—and more during the war—gave powers that normally were legislative prerogatives to newly created executive departments. Some members of Congress also were upset by FDR's expansion of the federal government as a whole. Southern Democrats, who favored states' rights, had to bite their tongues so long as FDR maintained his overwhelming popularity. But when Roosevelt tried to use his sweeping victory in 1936 to restructure (or, as his critics put it, "pack") the Supreme Court, he gave discontented conservative Democrats a rationale for opposition. The conservative coalition of Republicans and southern Democrats, which had been silent since 1932, was reborn. Roosevelt attempted to strike back with a "purge" of conservative Democrats in the primaries of 1938 (see Document 5.1). This effort failed and further damaged FDR's relations with conservative representatives in his own party.

As the president turned his attention to foreign problems in the later part of his second term, the mix of congressional supporters and opponents changed, with some conservatives taking a more favorable view of his military policies. As a wartime president, Roosevelt could generally count on strong congressional support for war-related legislation, although Republicans began to see opportunities for ending the Democratic domination of U.S. politics in steadfastly opposing any social programs without a clear tie to the war. (The unanimous approval of the G.I. Bill of Rights in 1944 showed how powerful the war connection could be in silencing congressional opposition.)

During the war Roosevelt generally tried to take a nonpartisan stance toward Congress. Accordingly, he offered little or no support in elections to other Democrats. (In fact, except for the failed attempt to influence primaries in 1938, Roosevelt did little directly on behalf of congressional Democrats in elections at any time during his presidency.) Congressional members of his party, in turn, felt that they owed little to the president. Furthermore, Roosevelt tended to ignore congressional leaders and take action without consulting them; even congressional Democrats worried that the executive branch was becoming too powerful. Early in 1944, Roosevelt vetoed a tax bill with a harsh message that seemed to question the honesty of his party's leaders in Congress. In response, Senate Majority Leader Alben Barkley of Kentucky, usually a loyal backer of Roosevelt, resigned from the leadership. Congress, still with Democratic majorities in both houses, then struck back sharply at Roosevelt. They overrode his veto and Democratic senators reelected Barkley as their leader.

A masterly politician in dealing with the electorate and foreign leaders, Roosevelt was a much less effective legislative politician. It was his extraordinary ability to lead the voters, not his direct dealings with the legislators on Capitol Hill, that often carried Congress along with Roosevelt's programs.

THE SUPREME COURT

FDR inherited a staunchly conservative Supreme Court in 1933, and none of its members retired during his first term. He was, in fact, the first president to serve a full term without appointing a single justice to the Supreme Court. As the Court began invalidating New Deal measures, including portions of the National Industrial Recovery Act (NIRA) and the Agricultural Adjustment Act (AAA), its relationship with Roosevelt reached a level of hostility not seen since Andrew Jackson's presidency. FDR responded angrily to the stinging rebuke the high court gave him in its decision in *Schechter Poultry Corp. v. United States* in 1935, which invalidated the National Recovery Administration (see Document 5.2). In an extraordinary press conference, FDR said it was probably "more important than any decision since the *Dred Scott* case," a reference to the infamous 1857 decision that said blacks cannot be citizens of the United States and that slaveholders could not be prevented from taking their slave property with them into territories. Roosevelt defined the issue raised by the *Schechter* decision as: "Is the United States going to decide, are the people of this country going to decide that their Federal Government shall in the future have no right under any implied power or any court-approved power to enter into a solution of a national economic problem, but that that national economic problem must be decided by the states?" Roosevelt's anger was genuine. As he saw it, the Supreme Court was going to turn back the clock and disarm the only force the American people had to combat economic problems: the federal government. "We are the only nation in the world that has not solved this problem," Roosevelt declared. "We thought we were solving it, and now it has been thrown right straight in our faces. We have been relegated to the horse-and-buggy definition of interstate commerce" (Rosenman 1969, 4:215, 221).

Tensions between the president and the Court grew worse in 1937 when Roosevelt tried to "pack" the Court with New Deal supporters.

Convinced that the public had given him a mandate to use the federal government to address economic and social problems, Roosevelt proposed that Congress pass legislation allowing the president to appoint an additional member to the Supreme Court for every member over the age of seventy. No one could doubt the actual reason for the proposal, but Roosevelt dissembled, saying that the Court was falling behind in its work because elderly justices could not keep up with the work load (see Document 5.3).

As it happened, some members of the high court were beginning to accept the constitutionality of New Deal laws. Now Roosevelt's troubling proposal was also unnecessary, and he finally admitted defeat. But the shift in the Court's majority also led to the retirement of some of the conservative justices, beginning with Willis Van Devanter in 1937, and so gave FDR an opportunity to reshape the Court without changing its size. Roosevelt began striking back at the opponents who had blocked his Court-packing plan by appointing a liberal—Hugo Black of Alabama. With the conservative majority broken, other retirements followed and Roosevelt had within four years appointed another six justices: Stanley Reed, Felix Frankfurter, William O. Douglas, Frank Murphy, James F. Byrnes, and Robert Jackson. His relationship with the Court improved considerably from the later part of his second term through the rest of his life, as he dealt with what had rather suddenly been transformed into a "Roosevelt Court."

The year 1937, then, saw both a humiliating defeat for Roosevelt's proposal to reform the Court and the beginning of a rapid revolution in the Court's position on the powers of the federal government. Roosevelt had won the war while losing its most prominent battle, and his own prestige and aura of invincibility had been casualties in the conflict.

THE MILITARY

Roosevelt was committed to internationalism, but for much of his presidency the American public was committed to isolationism. When Roosevelt ran for president in 1932 he felt obligated to reverse his favorable position on the League of Nations, declaring that he opposed American entry under current conditions, which he left undefined. In the first two years of his presidency, Roosevelt continued to hope for world disarmament. Thereafter he believed that the world was sliding toward another war and that the United States needed to prepare itself.

During FDR's first term and well into his second term, military efforts focused more on the navy than the army. FDR loved the sea and had a background in the Navy Department—and he believed that naval power was most important to the nation's defense. Yet his persistent fear of large budget deficits combined with his practical need to take account of the nation's and Congress's isolationist sentiment kept military spending low. Indeed, early in Roosevelt's presidency he called for cutting an already paltry army budget, and army Chief of Staff Gen. Douglas MacArthur went to the White House to protest. MacArthur, who had trouble accepting the idea that he was subordinate to the president (or anyone else), "spoke recklessly," as he recalled the meeting. He told the commander in chief that "when we lost the next war, and an American boy, lying in the mud with an enemy bayonet through his belly and an enemy foot on his dying throat, spat out his last curse, [he] wanted the name not to be MacArthur, but Roosevelt." FDR, who the year before had privately classified MacArthur as "one of the . . . most dangerous men in the country," was outraged and shouted back, "You must not talk that way to the President!" (MacArthur 1964, 101). MacArthur apologized and offered his resignation. Roosevelt knew better than to accept it, because that would create a public incident and put MacArthur on the outside and probably in open political opposition.

Roosevelt allowed the U.S. Army to decline through the 1930s to the point where it ranked nineteenth in the world in 1940, trailing, among others, Belgium, the Netherlands, Portugal, and Switzerland. This was not a reflection of any antimilitary sentiment on Roosevelt's part, but rather his acceptance of political reality in a staunchly isolationist country and his belief in the need for a balanced budget.

The string of stunning German victories in the spring of 1940 led to a rapid reversal in U.S. military policy, with large-scale spending to build up U.S. armaments and to assist the British. After the United States entered World War II, FDR got along famously with many military leaders but not so well with others. There was little room, however, for complaint from the brass at a time when the U.S. military was expanding to its largest size in history. When Roosevelt called in 1940 for constructing 50,000 planes, many experts thought the number impossibly high. Yet in 1943 U.S. industry turned out more than 85,000 aircraft.

Roosevelt's relationship with MacArthur was significant throughout. The president greatly distrusted and disliked the egotistical general. MacArthur, moreover, had failed to take prudent action, such as moving airplanes to protected locations, in the hours after Pearl Harbor. As a result U.S. planes in the Philippines were left unprotected and easy targets for Japanese attack the following day, when a hundred were destroyed. Although Roosevelt had ample reason to dismiss MacArthur, who had made other serious mistakes in losing the Philippines, the president acted, as he usually did, with pragmatism. Roosevelt believed that the American people needed heroes, and MacArthur was eager to play that role. Accordingly, Roosevelt went along with the MacArthur myth. Early in 1942 he heaped lavish praise on the dubious actions of the military prima donna. "The defense put up by General MacArthur has magnificently exceeded the previous estimates of endurance; and he and his men are gaining eternal glory therefore," Roosevelt proclaimed to the American people in a radio address on the war (Rosenman 1969, 11:110; see Document 4.11).

In the summer of 1944, with the war going well for the Allies in both theaters (Europe and the Pacific), Roosevelt traveled to Hawaii to meet with his Pacific commanders. The trip had a transparent political purpose. Rather than campaign directly in his bid for a fourth term, Roosevelt would simply impress voters by acting as commander in chief. MacArthur complained about being obliged to travel all the way from Australia: "The humiliation of forcing me to leave my command . . . for a picture-taking junket!" (Freidel 1990, 540). The comment was not without merit. The president spent six hours one day touring in an open car, seated between MacArthur and Adm. Chester Nimitz. Having helped make a hero of MacArthur, FDR presumably felt justified in profiting from the general's popularity. But the meeting was also about serious business, specifically a debate on the strategy in the war against Japan. In these meetings Roosevelt impressed the assembled commanders with his skillful steering of the discussion, always narrowing the areas of difference among the competing military leaders. In fact, Roosevelt's skill at navigating amid the large egos of his commanders (none larger, to be sure, than MacArthur's), combined with his storied charm, produced a more cordial relationship with MacArthur in the last months of the president's life.

Roosevelt's relationships with other leading military commanders were generally good. Although Roosevelt and Gen. George C. Marshall (army chief of staff from 1939 to 1945) had very different personalities, and Roosevelt sometimes exasperated Marshall by paying heed to proposals from Winston Churchill that Marshall thought wrongheaded, the two men usually worked well together. Roosevelt would have loved to enter the field of tactical decision making, especially in naval matters, but he resisted the temptation and reserved himself for the major strategic and political issues. Throughout most of the war, Roosevelt left tactical decisions in the Pacific theater to Adm. Ernest King in the Navy Department and Adm. Chester Nimitz in Hawaii. Roosevelt got along well with Gen. Dwight Eisenhower, who became the supreme allied commander in Europe.

On the whole, Roosevelt's skills in bridging differences and getting along with anyone with whom he had reason to get along led to good wartime relationships with his top military leaders.

THE MEDIA

More than any of his predecessors, Franklin Roosevelt understood the benefits of a good relationship with the press. He cultivated reporters by holding press conferences twice a week, by joking with reporters and treating them as individuals—indeed, as friends—and by respecting their need for stories. From the start, he did away with the policy that the president would take only written questions (see Document 5.4). "By the brilliant but simple trick of making news and *being* news," as Arthur Schlesinger noted, "Roosevelt outwitted the open hostility of the publishers and converted the press into one of the most effective channels of his public leadership" (Schlesinger 1958, 566).

In a newspaper article on the first anniversary of Roosevelt's inauguration, Herbert Hoover's former secretary, Theodore G. Joslin, marveled at the camaraderie that had developed between FDR and the press. "Mr. Roosevelt will wisecrack any day," Joslin noted. "Mr. Roosevelt talks with amazing freedom. There have been times when he has said little of consequence, but he has talked—and remember, that is the one thing the press wants the President to do." The result, Joslin correctly said, was that Roosevelt "has been and is ace high with most of the [press] corps" (Rosenman 1969, 2:45).

BUSINESS

Most businesspeople were so frightened in 1933 (at the depths of the Great Depression) that they went along with Roosevelt's early measures to help the downtrodden and stimulate the economy—even though some of these measures were unfriendly to business. But as soon as the worst of the crisis appeared to have passed, many business and financial leaders turned on Roosevelt as if he were the devil incarnate, or at least the leader of world Bolshevism. With a few important exceptions, especially in some of the newer industries and in Hollywood, the business community despised FDR. They called him a "traitor to his class," an epithet based on a mistaken view of Roosevelt's heritage. He came from "old money," and saw himself in a very different class—the American approximation of an aristocracy—and with a very different attitude toward the poor than most businesspeople had. FDR felt that his duties were those of stewardship and *noblesse oblige*, whereas businesspeople strove to maximize profits without much regard to the living condition of their workers.

In addition to this fundamental difference in outlook, Roosevelt also believed that the economy had changed and that in the new era of mass production, workers' living standards had to be raised so that they would be able to consume the products business was producing. Under these new conditions, the old, almost completely unregulated competitive system would not work. The Great Depression, he maintained, was proof. If the capitalist system were not reformed, it would collapse or be overthrown. Roosevelt saw himself as the savior of business and a modified capitalism.

During his 1936 reelection campaign, Roosevelt employed humor to express this perception of his role and his resentment of the injustice of business's hostility:

> In the summer of 1933 a nice old gentleman wearing a silk hat fell off the end of a pier. He was unable to swim. A friend ran down the pier, dived overboard and pulled him out; but the silk hat floated off with the tide. After the old gentleman had been revived, he was effusive in his thanks. He praised his friend for saving his life. Today, three years later, the old gentleman is berating his friend because his silk hat was lost. (Freidel 1990, 205)

Most business leaders took a very different view of FDR's role, but a few saw the situation as he did. In an important 1934 article in the *Nation,* Boston department store owner Edward A. Filene endorsed the New Deal, saying that the question was "whether our big-community business can operate under the old, little community code, and it has been amply shown that it cannot." Filene pointed out the necessity of higher living standards to "absorb the products of machine industry." "I am for the New Deal because I believe in profits," he declared, "and the New Deal opens up tremendously greater opportunities for legitimate and continuous profits, and opens them up to an incomparably greater number of people" (Filene 1934, 707–709)

Earlier that year, anti–New Deal businesspeople and disgruntled conservative political figures, including Al Smith (who had run against Roosevelt for the 1932 Democratic presidential nomination) and his key backers, had formed the American Liberty League to "defend and uphold the Constitution of the United States" and protect the rights of the owners of private property against the government. The Liberty League became the leading anti–New Deal organization in the mid-1930s.

Roosevelt tried to maintain as much business support as he could for as long as he could, but as the 1936 election approached, he realized that most of the business community wanted no part of a New Deal consensus. The president then turned business hostility to his advantage during the campaign. He railed against "economic royalists" and closed his campaign by declaring that the "forces of selfishness and of lust for power" had "never before in all of our history . . . been so united against one candidate as they stand today. They are unanimous in their *hate* for *me— and I welcome their hatred*" (Rosenman 1969, 5:568; see Document 5.5).

But this was not the final word on Roosevelt's relationship with business. After World War II began, and particularly after the United States entered the war, Roosevelt improved his relations with business. Surprisingly, this happened even as government controls on business were tightening above and beyond the ambitions of the New Deal. Roosevelt gained the cooperation of most businesspeople during the war by appealing to their patriotism and to their desire for large profits. Defense contracts and huge government spending for military equipment guaranteed a market for production—and a profit. Most businesspeople still disliked

Roosevelt and voted against him in elections, but they were willing to go along with him for the duration of the highly profitable war.

LABOR

Franklin Roosevelt was not particularly friendly toward organized labor when he assumed the presidency, but he became an ardent prounion politician by the time of his 1936 reelection campaign. Roosevelt favored helping working people, but he initially preferred a paternalistic approach over empowering workers to use unions to help themselves. He had not originally favored the proposal authored by New York senator Robert Wagner that became the National Labor Relations Act in 1935, but when it became clear that the bill would pass, Roosevelt suddenly added it to his "must" list of bills and wound up with a good deal of the credit. The act enabled workers to organize without fear of retaliation from employers and so opened the way for unions to change the landscape of U.S. labor relations (see Document 5.6).

As the possibility of maintaining good relations with business declined, Roosevelt moved closer to labor in 1936. On the campaign trail he even displayed a union card. Labor's support added greatly to Roosevelt's juggernaut in 1936. The success of the new Congress of Industrial Organizations (CIO) in organizing workers in such mass production industries as automobiles, steel, and rubber, and in gaining union recognition by General Motors and U.S. Steel in 1937, added to labor's political power. Polls indicated that about three-quarters of Americans in early 1937 approved of unions. Yet the CIO's success came in part through the use of an unpopular tactic called the sit-down strike (in which workers occupied a workplace instead of picketing outside it). The president seems to have agreed with his constituents: like them, he favored unions but was troubled by sit-down strikes.

Beyond his personal convictions, Roosevelt had to navigate the labor disputes in a way that would identify him with the increasingly powerful union movement without alienating the middle-class or rural parts of his New Deal coalition. In June 1937 Roosevelt showed that he was steering a middle course by commenting, "The nation, as a whole, in regard to the recent strike episodes . . . are saying just one thing, 'A plague on both your houses' " (Bernstein 1969, 496). It is not surprising that this stance did not sit well with union leaders, who felt that they had done a great deal to support Roosevelt. In a Labor Day address that year, CIO President John L. Lewis responded memorably to Roosevelt's statement. "It ill behooves one who has supped at labor's table and has been sheltered in labor's house to curse with equal fervor and fine impartiality both labor and its adversaries when they become locked in deadly embrace" (Dubofsky and Van Tine 1977, 327).

Roosevelt and Lewis had found an alliance in 1936 to be mutually beneficial, but theirs had always been a tense and unstable relationship. The two men had very different personalities. Roosevelt was indirect, ingratiating, and almost constantly cheerful. Lewis was direct, blunt, and often angry. Both men were theatrical in their own ways and demanded center stage. Given the great difference in the power of the positions they held, the war that Lewis declared on Roosevelt was one the labor leader had little chance of winning. Lewis's actual objective was to take Roosevelt's place as president. For a time he hoped he would succeed Roosevelt as the Democratic nominee in 1940. When it became likely that Roosevelt would seek a third term, Lewis promoted himself as the president's running mate. To Roosevelt, who intensely disliked and distrusted Lewis, the idea was ludicrous.

When Lewis realized he could not succeed Roosevelt, he decided to try to destroy him. In 1940 Lewis opposed Roosevelt's policies on virtually everything and found himself in a strange alliance with isolationists, Republicans, and Communists (who, because this was during the period of the Nazi-Soviet Pact, were opposing U.S. aid to Britain). Lewis endorsed Republican presidential nominee Wendell Willkie and declared that if Roosevelt won, Lewis would take it as a vote of no confidence from the nation's working people and retire as president of the CIO. When FDR was reelected by a large margin, Lewis sought a way to remain in his post, but he was outmaneuvered by his opponents and replaced by his lieutenant, Philip Murray.

Lewis continued to be a thorn in Roosevelt's side during the war. In 1943 he took his United Mine Workers out on strike, defying the president, public opinion, and patriotism. Roosevelt responded by having the government seize the coal mines and threatening to draft strikers into the military (see Document 5.7). Although Lewis finally won the wage hike he sought, it was at a terrible price to his already low public stature. Opinion polls named him the most unpopular man in America.

In addition to continuing difficulties with Lewis, Roosevelt took some steps during the war that did not sit well with organized labor. In July

1942 the National War Labor Board (NWLB) imposed a settlement of a wage dispute between steelworkers and the smaller steel companies that permitted a wage increase equal to inflation since January of the previous year. Combined with a cap on prices imposed a few months earlier by the Office of Price Administration, this "Little Steel Formula" was intended to stabilize workers' standard of living during the war. This limitation was not to the liking of union leaders, who saw in the greatly increased demand for labor an opportunity to substantially improve their members' living standards. But the NWLB promulgated another measure that pleased labor leaders very much. In June 1942 the board issued a "maintenance-of-membership" rule, which provided that new employees in workplaces already covered by a union contract would automatically be made members of the union unless they specifically requested not to be within their first fifteen days of employment. This rule greatly increased union membership. The measure put the unions into partnership with the government, but the unions were clearly the junior partners and somewhat dependent on the government.

In mid-1943, with the public mood toward unions soured by Lewis's strike, Congress passed the restrictive Smith-Connally War Labor Disputes Act. Among other provisions, the bill forbade political contributions by unions during wartime, an obvious attempt to weaken labor's power to assist Roosevelt. The president vetoed the measure, but Congress promptly overrode his veto.

The CIO's political action committee, headed by Sidney Hillman of the Amalgamated Clothing Workers, provided the most important support for Roosevelt's 1944 campaign by registering and getting to the polls masses of union members and their families and friends. Hillman's position was so important that Roosevelt was reported to have told aides to check with Hillman on whether the nomination of Harry Truman for the vice presidency was acceptable to labor. "Clear it with Sidney," Roosevelt's alleged words in this exchange, became the rallying cry of Republicans who wanted to persuade voters that Roosevelt was a captive of the unions, the CIO and, by extension, the Communists (Burns 1970, 525).

BIBLIOGRAPHY

James T. Patterson, *Congressional Conservatism and the New Deal: The Growth of the Conservative Coalition in Congress, 1933–1939* (Lexington: University of Kentucky Press, 1967) remains the starting point for examining FDR's relationship with Congress. John Allswang, *The New Deal and American Politics* (New York: Wiley, 1978) also examines this subject. Clyde P. Weed, *The Nemesis of Reform: The Republican Party During the New Deal* (New York: Columbia University Press, 1994) addresses Republican efforts to block Roosevelt.

William E. Leuchtenburg, *The Supreme Court Reborn: The Constitutional Revolution in the Age of Roosevelt* (New York: Oxford University Press, 1995) is the best analysis of Roosevelt's relationship with the judiciary. Joseph Alsop and Turner Catledge, *The 168 Days* (Garden City, N.Y.: Doubleday, Doran, 1938) is a contemporary account of the Court-packing controversy.

On Roosevelt's relationship with the military, Eric Labaree, *Commander in Chief: Franklin Delano Roosevelt, His Lieutenants, and Their War* (New York: Harper and Row, 1987) provides a detailed account.

Graham J. White, *FDR and the Press* (Chicago: University of Chicago Press, 1979); and Betty Houchin Winfield, *FDR and the News Media* (Urbana: University of Illinois Press, 1990) examine Roosevelt's relationship with the news media. The ultimate primary source on FDR's dealings with the press is *The Complete Presidential Press Conferences of Franklin D. Roosevelt*, 25 vols. (New York: DaCapo, 1972).

Irving Bernstein, *Turbulent Years: A History of the American Worker, 1933–1941* (Boston: Houghton Mifflin, 1969) is the most important work on labor in the era. Steve Fraser, *Labor Will Rule: Sidney Hillman and the Rise of American Labor* (New York: Free Press, 1991) is a massive biography of the labor leader with whom FDR developed a close relationship during World War II. Melvyn Dubofsky and Warren Van Tine, *John L. Lewis* (New York: Quadrangle, 1977) examines the labor leader who came to be one of Roosevelt's staunchest opponents.

Other works cited in this chapter include James MacGregor Burns, *Roosevelt: The Soldier of Freedom, 1940–1945* (New York: Harcourt Brace Jovanovich, 1970); Edward Filene, "What Businessmen Think: See the New Deal Through," *The Nation*, December 9, 1934, 707–709; Frank Freidel, *Franklin D. Roosevelt: A Rendezvous With Destiny* (Boston: Little Brown, 1990); Douglas MacArthur, *Reminiscences* (New York: McGraw-Hill, 1964); Samuel I. Rosenman, ed., *The Public Papers and Addresses of Franklin D. Roosevelt*, 13 vols. (1938–1950; reprint, New York: Russell and Russell, 1969); and Arthur M. Schlesinger Jr., *The Coming of the New Deal* (Boston: Houghton Mifflin, 1958).

Document 5.1   Fireside Chat on Intervening in Democratic Congressional Primaries, June 24, 1938

One of FDR's more conspicuous political failures was his intervention in Democratic congressional primaries in 1938. It was an attempt to, as his opponents put it, "purge" the party of conservative opponents of the New Deal. In this radio address Roosevelt outlines to the public his rationale for intervening in congressional primaries.

OUR GOVERNMENT, happily, is a democracy. As part of the democratic process, your President is again taking an opportunity to report on the progress of national affairs to the real rulers of this country—the voting public.

. . . the [seventy-fifth] Congress, striving to carry out the Platform on which most of its members were elected achieved more for the future good of the country than any Congress between the end of the World War and the spring of 1933.

I mention tonight only the more important of these achievements. . . .

1. It improved still further our agricultural laws to give the farmer a fairer share of the national income, to preserve our soil, to provide an all-weather granary, to help the farm tenant toward independence, to find new uses for farm products, and to begin crop insurance.

2. After many requests on my part the Congress passed a Fair Labor Standards Act, commonly called the Wages and Hours Bill. That Act—applying to products in interstate commerce—ends child labor, sets a floor below wages and a ceiling over hours of labor. . . .

3. The Congress has provided a fact-finding Commission to find a path through the jungle of contradictory theories about wise business practices—to find the necessary facts for any intelligent legislation on monopoly, on price-fixing and on the relationship between big business and medium-sized business and little business. . . . we in America persist in our belief in individual enterprise and in the profit motive; but we realize we must continually seek improved practices to insure the continuance of reasonable profits, together with scientific progress, individual initiative, opportunities for the little fellow, fair prices, decent wages and continuing employment. . . .

5. The Congress set up the United States Housing Authority to help finance large-scale slum clearance and provide low rent housing for the low income groups in our cities. And by improving the Federal Housing Act, the Congress made it easier for private capital to build modest homes and low rental dwellings. . . .

All these things together I call our program for the national defense of our economic system. It is a program of balanced action—of moving on all fronts at once in intelligent recognition that all our economic problems, of every group, of every section, are essentially one. . . .

You will remember that on February 5, 1937, I sent a message to the Congress dealing with the real need of Federal Court reforms of several kinds. In one way or another, during the sessions of this Congress, the ends—the real objectives—sought in that message, have been substantially attained.

The attitude of the Supreme Court toward constitutional questions is entirely changed. Its recent decisions are eloquent testimony of a willingness to collaborate with the two other branches of Government to make democracy work. The Government has been granted the right to protect its interests in litigation between private parties involving the constitutionality of Federal statutes, and to appeal directly to the Supreme Court in all cases involving the constitutionality of Federal statutes; and no single judge is any longer empowered to suspend a Federal statute on his sole judgment as to its constitutionality. . . .

Another indirect accomplishment of this Congress has been its response to the devotion of the American people to a course of sane consistent liberalism. The Congress has understood that under modern conditions government has a continuing responsibility to meet continuing problems, and that Government cannot take a holiday. . . .

I am still convinced that the American people, since 1932, continue to insist on two requisites of private enterprise, and the relationship of Government to it. The first is complete honesty at the top in looking after the use of other people's money, and in apportioning and paying individual and Corporate taxes according to ability to pay. The second is sincere respect for the need of all at the bottom to get work—and through work to get a really fair share of the good things of life, and a chance to save and rise.

After the election of 1936 I was told, and the Congress was told, by an increasing number of politically—and worldly—wise people that I should coast along, enjoy an easy Presidency for four years, and not take the Democratic platform too seriously. They told me that people were getting weary of reform through political effort and would no longer oppose that small minority which, in spite of its own disastrous leadership in 1929, is always eager to resume its control over the Government of the United States.

Never in our lifetime has such a concerted campaign of defeatism been thrown at the heads of the President and Senators and Congressmen as in the case of this Seventy-fifth Congress. . . .

This Congress has ended on the side of the people. My faith in the American people—and their faith in themselves—have been justified. I congratulate the Congress and the leadership thereof and I congratulate the American people on their own staying power .

One word about our economic situation. It makes no difference to me whether you call it a recession or a depression. In 1932 the total national income of all the people in the country had reached the low point of thirty-eight billion dollars in that year. With each succeeding year it rose. Last year, 1937, it had risen to seventy billion dollars—despite definitely worse business and agricultural prices in the last four months of last year. This year, 1938, while it is too early to do more than give an estimate, we hope that the national income will not fall below sixty billion dollars. We remember also that banking and business and farming are not falling apart like the one-hoss shay, as they did in the terrible winter of 1932–1933. . . .

It is because you are not satisfied, and I am not satisfied, with the progress we have made in finally solving our business and agricultural and social problems that I believe the great majority of you want your own Government to keep on trying to solve them. In simple frankness and in simple honesty, I need all the help I can get—and I see signs of getting more help in the future from many who have fought against progress with tooth and nail.

And now, following out this line of thought, I want to say a few words about the coming political primaries. . . .

What I am going to say to you tonight does not relate to the primaries of any particular political party, but to matters of principle in all parties— Democratic, Republican, Farmer-Labor, Progressive, Socialist, or any other. Let that be clearly understood. It is my hope that everybody affiliated with any party will vote in the primaries, and that every such voter will consider the fundamental principles for which his party is on record. That makes for a healthy choice between the candidates of the opposing parties on Election Day in November.

An election cannot give a country a firm sense of direction if it has two or more national parties which merely have different names but are as alike in their principles and aims as peas in the same pod.

In the coming primaries in all parties, there will be many clashes between two schools of thought, generally classified as liberal and conservative. Roughly speaking, the liberal school of thought recognizes that the new conditions throughout the world call for new remedies.

Those of us in America who hold to this school of thought, insist that these new remedies can be adopted and successfully maintained in this country under our present form of government if we use government as an instrument of cooperation to provide these remedies. We believe that we can solve our problems through continuing effort, through democratic processes instead of Fascism or Communism. We are opposed to the kind of moratorium on reform which, in effect, is reaction itself.

Be it clearly understood, however, that when I use the word "liberal," I mean the believer in progressive principles of democratic, representative government and not the wild man who, in effect, leans in the direction of Communism, for that is just as dangerous as Fascism.

The opposing or conservative school of thought, as a general proposition, does not recognize the need for Government itself to step in and take action to meet these new problems. It believes that individual initiative and private philanthropy will solve them—that we ought to repeal many of the things we have done and go back, for instance, to the old gold standard, or stop all this business of old age pensions and unemployment insurance, or repeal the Securities and Exchange Act, or let monopolies thrive unchecked—return, in effect, to the kind of Government we had in the twenties.

Assuming the mental capacity of all the candidates, the important question which it seems to me the primary voter must ask is this: "To which of these general schools of thought does the candidate belong?"

As President of the United States, I am not asking the voters of the country to vote for Democrats next November as opposed to Republicans or members of any other party. Nor am I, as President, taking part in Democratic primaries.

As the head of the Democratic Party, however, charged with the responsibility of carrying out the definitely liberal declaration of principles set forth in the 1936 Democratic platform, I feel that I have every right to speak in those few instances where there may be a clear issue between candidates for a Democratic nomination involving these principles, or involving a clear misuse of my own name.

Do not misunderstand me. I certainly would not indicate a preference in a State primary merely because a candidate, otherwise liberal in outlook, had conscientiously differed with me on any single issue. I should be far more concerned about the general attitude of a candidate toward present day problems and his own inward desire to get practical needs attended to in a practical way. We all know that progress may be blocked by outspoken reactionaries and also by those who say "yes" to a progressive objective, but who always find some reason to oppose any specific proposal to gain that objective. I call that type of candidate a "yes, but" fellow.

And I am concerned about the attitude of a candidate or his sponsors with respect to the rights of American citizens to assemble peaceably and to express publicly their views and opinions on important social and economic issues. There can be no constitutional democracy in any community which denies to the individual his freedom to speak and worship as he wishes. The American people will not be deceived by anyone who attempts to suppress individual liberty under the pretense of patriotism.

This being a free country with freedom of expression—especially with freedom of the press—there will be a lot of mean blows struck between now and Election Day. By "blows" I mean misrepresentation, personal attack and appeals to prejudice. It would be a lot better, of course, if campaigns everywhere could be waged with arguments instead of blows.

I hope the liberal candidates will confine themselves to argument and not resort to blows. In nine cases out of ten the speaker or writer who, seeking to influence public opinion, descends from calm argument to unfair blows hurts himself more than his opponent. . . .

I know that neither in the summer primaries nor in the November elections will the American voters fail to spot the candidate whose ideas have given out.

Source: Samuel I. Rosenman, ed., *The Public Papers and Addresses of Franklin D. Roosevelt* (1941; reprint, New York: Russell and Russell, 1969), 7:391–400.

Document 5.2   *Schechter Poultry Corp. v. United States,*
May 27, 1935

Roosevelt did not have a good relationship with the conservative Supreme Court during his first term. The Court delivered several blows to the New Deal, and the most notable came on May 27, 1935, when the justices unanimously invalidated the National Recovery Administration. The following is an excerpt from the decision by Chief Justice Charles Evans Hughes.

. . . The Congress is not permitted to abdicate or to transfer to others the essential legislative functions with which it is thus vested. . . .

What is meant by "fair competition" as the term is used in the act? Does it refer to a category established in the law, and is the authority to make codes limited accordingly?

Or is it used as a convenient designation for whatever set of laws the formulators of a code for a particular trade or industry may propose and the President may himself prescribe, as being wise and beneficent provisions for the government of the trade or industry in order to accomplish the broad purposes of rehabilitation, correction and expansion [of the economy] which are stated in the first section of Title I?

The act does not define "fair competition." "Unfair competition" as known to common law is a limited concept. . . .

But it is evident that in its widest range "unfair competition," as it has been understood in the law, does not reach the objectives of the codes which are authorized by the National Industrial Recovery Act. The codes may, indeed, cover conduct which existing law condemns, but they are not limited to conduct of that sort. The government does not contend that the act contemplates such a limitation. It would be opposed both to the declared purposes of the act and to its administrative construction. . . .

The President is authorized to impose such conditions "for the protection of consumers, competitors, employees and others, and in furtherance of the public interest, and may provide such exemptions from the provisions of such codes as the President in his discretion deems necessary to effectuate the policy herein declared. . . ."

The government urges that the code will "consist of rules of competition deemed fair for each industry by representative members of that industry, by the persons most vitally concerned and most familiar with its problems.". . .

But would it be seriously contended that Congress could delegate its legislative authority to trade or industrial associations or groups so as to empower them to enact the laws they deem to be wise and beneficent for the rehabilitation and expansion of their trade or industries? . . .

And could an effort of that sort be made valid by such a preface of generalities as to the permissible aims as we find in Section 1 of Title I? The answer is obvious. Such a delegation of legislative power is unknown to our law and is utterly inconsistent with the constitutional prerogatives and duties of Congress.

The question, then turns upon the authority which Section 3 of the Recovery Act vests in the President to approve or prescribe. If the codes have standing as penal statutes, this must be due to the effect of the executive action. But Congress cannot delegate legislative power to the President to exercise an unfettered discretion to make whatever laws he thinks may be needed or advisable for the rehabilitation and expansion of trade or industry. . . .

Instead of prescribing rules of conduct, it [the act] authorizes the making of codes to prescribe them. For that legislative undertaking, Section 3 sets up no standards. . . .

We think that the code-making authority thus conferred is an unconstitutional delegation of legislative power. . . .

If the commerce clause were construed to reach all enterprises and transactions which could be said to have an indirect effect upon interstate commerce, the Federal authority would embrace practically all the activities of the people and the authority of the State over its domestic concerns would exist only by sufferance of the Federal Government. . . . and for all practical purposes we would have a completely centralized government. . . .

It is not the province of the court to consider the economic advantages of such a centralized system. It is sufficient to say that the Federal Constitution does not provide for it. . . .

Stress is laid upon the great importance of maintaining wage distributions which would provide the necessary stimulus in starting "the cumulative forces making for expanding economic activity." Without in any way disparaging this motive, it is enough to say that the recuperative efforts of the Federal Government must be made in a manner consistent with the authority granted by the Constitution. . . .

On both the grounds we have discussed, the attempted delegation of legislative power and the attempted regulation of intrastate transactions which affect interstate commerce only indirectly, we hold the code provisions here in question to be invalid and that the judgment of conviction must be reversed.

Source: 295 U.S. 495

Document 5.3   Fireside Chat on the Reorganization of the Judiciary, March 9, 1937

Roosevelt was irate over the Supreme Court's extremely narrow and, as he believed, antiquated view of the powers of the federal government. Following Roosevelt's huge victory in the 1936 election, he decided to take decisive action. On February 5, 1937, he introduced to Congress his judiciary reorganization plan, which his opponents called the Court-packing plan. Opposition was stronger than the president had anticipated, and he went to the public on March 9 to explain his motivations.

Tonight, sitting at my desk in the White House, I make my first radio report to the people in my second term of office. . . .

In 1933 you and I knew that we must never let our economic system get completely out of joint again—that we could not afford to take the risk of another great depression.

We also became convinced that the only way to avoid a repetition of those dark days was to have a government with power to prevent and to cure the abuses and the inequalities which had thrown that system out of joint.

We then began a program of remedying those abuses and inequalities—to give balance and stability to our economic system—to make it bombproof against the causes of 1929.

Today we are only part-way through that program—and recovery is speeding up to a point where the dangers of 1929 are again becoming possible, not this week or month perhaps, but within a year or two.

National laws are needed to complete that program. Individual or local or state effort alone cannot protect us in 1937 any better than ten years ago.

It will take time—and plenty of time—to work out our remedies administratively even after legislation is passed. . . .

The American people have learned from the depression. For in the last three national elections an overwhelming majority of them voted a mandate that the Congress and the President begin the task of providing that protection—not after long years of debate, but now.

The Courts, however, have cast doubts on the ability of the elected Congress to protect us against catastrophe by meeting squarely our modern social and economic conditions.

We are at a crisis in our ability to proceed with that protection. It is a quiet crisis. There are no lines of depositors outside closed banks. But to the far-sighted it is far-reaching in its possibilities of injury to America.

I want to talk with you very simply about the need for present action in this crisis—the need to meet the unanswered challenge of one-third of a Nation ill-nourished, ill-clad, ill-housed.

Last Thursday I described the American form of Government as a three horse team provided by the Constitution to the American people so that their field might be plowed. The three horses are, of course, the three branches of government—the Congress, the Executive and the Courts. Two of the horses are pulling in unison today; the third is not. Those who have intimated that the President of the United States is trying to drive that team, overlook the simple fact that the President, as Chief Executive, is himself one of the three horses. . . .

I hope that you have re-read the Constitution of the United States in these past few weeks. Like the Bible, it ought to be read again and again.

. . . In its Preamble, the Constitution states that it was intended to form a more perfect Union and promote the general welfare; and the powers given to the Congress to carry out those purposes can be best described by saying that they were all the powers needed to meet each and every problem which then had a national character and which could not be met by merely local action. . . .

But the framers went further. Having in mind that in succeeding generations many other problems then undreamed of would become national problems, they gave to the Congress the ample broad powers "to levy taxes . . . and provide for the common defense and general welfare of the United States."

In the last four years the sound rule of giving statutes the benefit of all reasonable doubt has been cast aside. The Court has been acting not as a judicial body, but as a policy-making body.

When the Congress has sought to stabilize national agriculture, to improve the conditions of labor, to safeguard business against unfair competition, to protect our national resources, and in many other ways, to serve our clearly national needs, the majority of the Court has been assuming the power to pass on the wisdom of these Acts of the Congress to perform the mandate given us? It was said in last year's Democratic platform, "If these problems cannot be effectively solved within the Constitution, we shall seek such clarifying amendment as will assure the power to enact those laws, adequately to regulate commerce, protect public health and safety, and safeguard economic security." In other words, we said we would seek an amendment only if every other possible means by legislation were to fail.

When I commenced to review the situation with the problem squarely before me, I came by a process of elimination to the conclusion that, short of amendments, the only method which was clearly constitutional, and would at the same time carry out other much needed reforms, was to infuse new blood into all our Courts. We must have men worthy and equipped to carry out impartial justice. But, at the same time, we must have Judges who will bring to the Courts a present-day sense of the Constitution—Judges who will retain in the Courts the judicial functions of a court, and reject the legislative powers which the courts have today assumed.

In forty-five out of the forty-eight States of the Union, Judges are chosen not for life but for a period of years. In many States Judges must retire at the age of seventy. Congress has provided financial security by offering life pensions at full pay for Federal Judges on all Courts who are willing to retire at seventy. In the case of Supreme Court Justices, that pension is $20,000 a year. But all Federal Judges, once appointed, can, if they choose, hold office for life, no matter how old they may get to be.

What is my proposal? It is simply this: whenever a Judge or Justice of any Federal Court has reached the age of seventy and does not avail himself of the opportunity to retire on a pension, a new member shall be appointed by the President then in office, with the approval, as required by the Constitution, of the Senate of the United States.

That plan has two chief purposes. By bringing into the judicial system a steady and continuing stream of new and younger blood, I hope, first, to make the administration of all Federal justice speedier and, therefore, less costly; secondly, to bring to the decision of social and economic problems younger men who have had personal experience and contact with modern facts and circumstances under which average men have to live and work. This plan will save our national Constitution from hardening of the judicial arteries. The number of Judges to be appointed would depend wholly on the decision of present Judges now over seventy, or those who would subsequently reach the age of seventy. . . .

There is nothing novel or radical about this idea. It seeks to maintain the Federal bench in full vigor. It has been discussed and approved by many persons of high authority ever since a similar proposal passed the House of Representatives in 1869.

Why was the age fixed at seventy? Because the laws of many States, the practice of the Civil Service, the regulations of the Army and Navy, and the rules of many of our Universities and of almost every great private business enterprise, commonly fix the retirement age at seventy years or less.

The statute would apply to all the courts in the Federal system. There is general approval so far as the lower Federal courts are concerned. The plan has met opposition only so far as the Supreme Court of the United States itself is concerned. If such a plan is good for the lower courts it certainly ought to be equally good for the highest Court from which there is no appeal.

Those opposing this plan have sought to arouse prejudice and fear by crying that I am seeking to "pack" the Supreme Court and that a baneful precedent will be established. . . .

If by that phrase "packing the Court" it is charged that I wish to place on the bench spineless puppets who would disregard the law and would decide specific cases as I wished them to be decided, I make this answer: that no President fit for his office would appoint, and no Senate of honorable men fit for their office would confirm, that kind of appointees to the Supreme Court.

But if by that phrase the charge is made that I would appoint and the Senate would confirm Justices worthy to sit beside present members of the Court who understand those modern conditions, that I will appoint Justices who will not undertake to override the judgment of the Congress on legislative policy, that I will appoint Justices who will act as Justices and not as legislators—if the appointment of such Justices can be called "packing the Courts," then I say that I and with me the vast majority of the American people favor doing just that thing—now.

Is it a dangerous precedent for the Congress to change the number of the Justices? The Congress has always had, and will have, that power. The number of justices has been changed several times before, in the

Administration of John Adams and Thomas Jefferson—both signers of the Declaration of Independence—Andrew Jackson, Abraham Lincoln and Ulysses S. Grant. . . .

Like all lawyers, like all Americans, I regret the necessity of this controversy. But the welfare of the United States, and indeed of the Constitution itself, is what we all must think about first. Our difficulty with the Court today rises not from the Court as an institution but from human beings within it. But we cannot yield our constitutional destiny to the personal judgment of a few men who, being fearful of the future, would deny us the necessary means of dealing with the present.

This plan of mine is no attack on the Court; it seeks to restore the Court to its rightful and historic place in our Constitutional Government and to have it resume its high task of building anew on the Constitution "a system of living law." The Court itself can best undo what the Court has done. . . .

The present attempt by those opposed to progress to play upon the fears of danger to personal liberty brings again to mind that crude and cruel strategy tried by the same opposition to frighten the workers of America in a pay-envelope propaganda against the Social Security Law. The workers were not fooled by that propaganda then. The people of America will not be fooled by such propaganda now. . . .

Source: Samuel I. Rosenman, ed., *The Public Papers and Addresses of Franklin D. Roosevelt* (1941; reprint, New York: Russell and Russell, 1969), 6:122–133.

Document 5.4   President Roosevelt's First Press Conference, March 8, 1933

Roosevelt enjoyed an extraordinarily good relationship with the press, although not with the leadership of much of the national media, which was largely conservative and anti–New Deal. His easy manner, sense of humor, regular press conferences, and willingness to make news won over most reporters. The approach that he used so successfully was apparent from his first press conference as president.

THE PRESIDENT: It is very good to see you all. My hope is that these conferences are going to be merely enlarged editions of the kind of very delightful family conferences I have been holding in Albany for the last four years. . . . There will be a great many questions, of course, that I won't answer, either because they are "if" questions—and I never answer them—and Brother Stephenson will tell you what an "if" question is—

MR. STEPHENSON (Reporter): I ask forty of them a day.

THE PRESIDENT: And the others, of course, are the questions which for various reasons I do not want to discuss, or I am not ready to discuss, or I do not know anything about. There will be a great many questions you will ask that I do not know enough about to answer.

Then, in regard to news announcements, Steve [Early, assistant secretary to the President] and I thought that it would be best that straight news for use from this office should always be without direct quotations. In other words, I do not want to be directly quoted, unless direct quotations are given out by Steve in writing. That makes that perfectly clear.

Then there are two other matters we will talk about: The first is "background information," which means material which can be used by all of you on your own authority and responsibility, not to be attributed to the White House . . . .

Then the second thing is the "off the record" information which means, of course, confidential information which is given only to those who attend the conference. Now there is one thing I want to say right now about which I think you will go along with me. I want to ask you not to repeat this "off the record" confidential information either to your own editors or to your associates who are not here; because there is always the danger that, while you people may not violate the rule, somebody may forget to say, "This is off the record and confidential," and the other party may use it in a story. That is to say, it is not to be used and not to be told to those fellows who happen not to come around to the conference. In other words, it is only for those present.

Now, as to news, I don't think there is any. (*Laughter*)

Steve reminds me that I have just signed the application for Associate Membership in the Press Club, which I am very happy to do.

Q. Will you go to Congress or send your message?

THE PRESIDENT: Send it.

Q. When will it be available here for us?

THE PRESIDENT: Judging by the fact that I haven't started to write it, I should say at the very last minute possible. I shall let you have it as soon as I can. Of course it will be for release when transmitted. I doubt very much if you will get it very much more than half an hour before it is taken to the Capitol.

Q. Will it be brief?

THE PRESIDENT: The situation demands brevity.

Q. On the Hill they say you only recommend emergency stuff, and that Congress will possibly adjourn next Monday or earlier and reconvene a short time after, and take up permanent stuff as well as your complete program. Is that your idea of it?

THE PRESIDENT: I think I can put it this way—and this comes under the second category, "background information " and "not off the record," because there is no reason why you should not use it in writing your stories. The general thought at the present time is that it is absolutely impossible by tomorrow to draft any complete or permanent legislation either on banking, or on budget balancing, or on anything else, because the situation, as you all know, is changing very much from day to day, so much so that if I were to ask for any specific and detailed legislation it might be that the details will have to be changed by a week from today. Therefore it is necessary—I think you can make a pretty good guess—that I shall have to ask for fairly broad powers in regard to banking—such powers as would make it possible to meet the changing situation from day to day in different parts of the country. We cannot write a permanent banking act for the Nation in three days. That is about the size of it. . . .

Q. Do I understand you are going to keep hold of this banking situation until permanent legislation is enacted?

THE PRESIDENT: Off the record answer, yes.

Q. Your idea is that after getting through the emergency you may get a breathing spell until the permanent program is in form.

THE PRESIDENT: Yes, I was coming to that. This is what might be called the "present thought" because everything is subject to change these days within twenty-four or even twelve hours. The general thought is that we would try to get through the two or three emergency matters as quickly as possible, and that then—and, mind you, I haven't even talked to the Congressional leaders about this, so there is no agreement on it—Congress should recess for I don't know how long a time but not for very long—for a matter of two or three weeks—to enable me to work out and draft more permanent legislation. . . .

Q. What is going to happen after Thursday night, Mr. President, when the holiday ends? Are you going to call another one?

THE PRESIDENT: That depends on how fast things move. . . .

Q. In your Inaugural Address, in which you only touched upon things, you said you are for sound and adequate. . .

THE PRESIDENT: I put it the other way around. I said "adequate but sound."

Q. Now that you have more time, can you define what that is?

THE PRESIDENT: No. (*Laughter.*) In other words—and I should call this "off the record" information—you cannot define the thing too closely one way or the other. On Friday afternoon last we undoubtedly did not have adequate currency. No question about that. There wasn't enough circulating money to go around.

Q. I believe that. (*Laughter.*)

THE PRESIDENT: We hope that when the banks reopen a great deal of the currency that was withdrawn for one purpose or another will find its way back. We have got to provide an adequate currency. Last Friday we would have had to provide it in the form of scrip, and probably some additional issues of Federal Bank notes. If things go along as we hope they will, the use of scrip can be very greatly curtailed, and the amounts of new Federal Bank issues, we hope, can be also limited to a very great extent. In other words, what you are coming to now really is a managed currency, the adequateness of which will depend on the conditions of the moment. It may expand one week and it may contract another week.

That part is all off the record.

Q. Can we use that part-managed?

THE PRESIDENT: No, I think not. . . .

Q. Now you came down to adequacy; but you haven't defined what you think is sound. Don't you want to define that now?

THE PRESIDENT: I don't want to define "sound" now. In other words, in its essence—this is entirely off the record—in its essence we must not put the Government any further in debt because of failed banks. Now, the real mark of delineation between sound and unsound is when the Government starts to pay its bills by starting printing presses. That is about the size of it. . . .

Q. Can you tell us anything about guaranteeing of bank deposits?

THE PRESIDENT: I can tell you as to guaranteeing bank deposits my own views, and I think those of the old Administration. The general underlying thought behind the use of the word "guarantee" with respect to bank deposits is that you guarantee bad banks as well as good banks. The minute the Government starts to do that the Government runs into a probable loss. . . . The objective in the plan that we are working on can be best stated this way: There are undoubtedly some banks that are not going to pay one hundred cents on the dollar. We all know it is better to have that loss taken than to jeopardize the credit of the United States Government or to put the United States Government further in debt. Therefore, the one objective is going to be to keep the loss in the individual banks down to a minimum, endeavoring to get 100 percent on them. We do not wish to make the United States Government liable for the mistakes and errors of individual banks, and put a premium on unsound banking in the future. . . .

Q. That is off the record?

THE PRESIDENT: Yes.

Q. Couldn't you make it background? There is a demand for the guarantee proposition.

THE PRESIDENT: As long as you don't write stories to give the average depositor the thought that his own particular bank isn't going to pay. That is what I want to avoid, because, when you come down to it, the great majority of banks are going to pay up. There will be many other banks which won't payout the whole thing immediately, but will payout 100 percent in time. There will be a very small number of banks that will probably have to go to the Examiner; but I don't want anybody to get the idea in reading the stories that the average bank isn't going to pay one hundred cents on the dollar, because the average bank is going to pay it. . . .

Source: Samuel I. Rosenman, ed., *The Public Papers and Addresses of Franklin D. Roosevelt* (1938; reprint, New York: Russell and Russell, 1969), 2:30–40.

Document 5.5   Campaign Speech, New York, October 31, 1936

Having earned the enmity of the business community, Roosevelt declared during his 1936 campaign that he welcomed its hatred. Casting his lot with the people against "the Interests," Roosevelt warned against the dangers of "Government by organized money." In the last major address of his campaign that year, Roosevelt set up the class division of the election in the clearest possible terms.

. . . For twelve years this Nation was afflicted with hear-nothing, see-nothing, do-nothing Government. The Nation looked to Government but the Government looked away. Nine mocking years with the golden calf and three long years of the scourger! Nine crazy years at the ticker and three long years in the breadlines! Nine mad years of mirage and three long years of despair! Powerful influences strive today to restore that kind of government with its doctrine that that Government is best which is most indifferent.

For nearly four years you have had an Administration which instead of twirling its thumbs has rolled up its sleeves. We will keep our sleeves rolled up.

We had to struggle with the old enemies of peace—business and financial monopoly, speculation, reckless banking, class antagonism, sectionalism, war profiteering.

They had begun to consider the Government of the United States as a mere appendage to their own affairs. We know now that Government by organized money is just as dangerous as Government by organized mob.

Never before in all our history have these forces been so united against one candidate as they stand today. They are unanimous in their hate for me—and I welcome their hatred.

I should like to have it said of my first Administration that in it the forces of selfishness and of lust for power met their match. I should like to have it said of my second Administration that in it these forces met their master.

The American people know from a four-year record that today there is only one entrance to the White House—by the front door. Since March 4, 1933, there has been only one pass-key to the White House. I have carried that key in my pocket. It is there tonight. So long as I am President, it will remain in my pocket.

Those who used to have pass-keys are not happy. Some of them are desperate. . . .

Of course we will provide useful work for the needy unemployed; we prefer useful work to the pauperism of a dole.

Here and now I want to make myself clear about those who disparage their fellow citizens on the relief rolls. They say that those on relief are not merely jobless—that they are worthless. Their solution for the relief problem is to end relief—to purge the rolls by starvation. To use the language of the stock broker, our needy unemployed would be cared for when, as, and if some fairy godmother should happen on the scene.

You and I will continue to refuse to accept that estimate of our unemployed fellow Americans. Your Government is still on the same side of the street with the Good Samaritan and not with those who pass by on the other side.

Again—what of our objectives?

Of course we will continue our efforts for young men and women so that they may obtain an education and an opportunity to put it to use. Of course we will continue our help for the crippled, for the blind, for the mothers, our insurance for the unemployed, our security for the aged. Of course we will continue to protect the consumer against unnecessary price spreads, against the costs that are added by monopoly and speculation. We will continue our successful efforts to increase his purchasing power and to keep it constant.

For these things, too, and for a multitude of others like them, we have only just begun to fight. . . .

Source: Samuel I. Rosenman, ed., *The Public Papers and Addresses of Franklin D. Roosevelt* (1938; reprint, New York: Russell and Russell, 1969), 5:566–572.

Document 5.6   The National Labor Relations Act, 1935

The National Labor Relations Act, usually called the Wagner Act after its principal author, Sen. Robert Wagner, D-N.Y., was one of the most important measures enacted in the New Deal. Roosevelt had not pushed the bill, but when he saw it was going to pass, he climbed on the bandwagon. FDR's endorsement helped to cement his alliance with labor, which would be an important source of strength in his remaining three presidential elections.

AN ACT

To diminish the causes of labor disputes burdening or obstructing interstate and foreign commerce, to create a National Labor Relations Board, and for other purposes. . . .

FINDINGS AND POLICY

SEC. 1. The denial by employers of the right of employees to organize and the refusal by employers to accept the procedure of collective bargaining lead to strikes and other forms of industrial strife or unrest, which have the intent or the necessary effect of burdening or obstructing commerce by (a) impairing the efficiency, safety, or operation of the instrumentalities of commerce; (b) occurring in the current of commerce; (c) materially affecting, restraining, or controlling the flow of raw materials or manufactured or processed goods from or into the channels of commerce; or the prices of such materials or goods in commerce; or (d) causing diminution of employment and wages in such volume as substantially to impair or disrupt the market for goods flowing from or into the channels of commerce.

The inequality of bargaining power between employees who do not possess full freedom of association or actual liberty of contract, and employers who are organized in the corporate or other forms of ownership association substantially burdens and affects the flow of commerce, and tends to aggravate recurrent business depressions, by depressing wage rates and the purchasing power of wage earners in industry and by preventing the stabilization of competitive wage rates and working conditions within and between industries.

Experience has proved that protection by law of the right of employees to organize and bargain collectively safeguards commerce from injury, impairment, or interruption, and promotes the flow of commerce by removing certain recognized sources of industrial strife and unrest, by encouraging practices fundamental to the friendly adjustment of industrial disputes arising out of differences as to wages, hours, or other working conditions, and by restoring equality of bargaining power between employers and employees. . . .

SEC. 7. Employees shall have the right to self-organization, to form, join, or assist labor organizations, to bargain collectively through representatives of their own choosing, and to engage in concerted activities, for the purpose of collective bargaining or other mutual aid or protection.

SEC. 8. IT SHALL BE AN UNFAIR LABOR PRACTICE FOR AN EMPLOYER—

(1) To interfere with, restrain, or coerce employees in the exercise of the rights guaranteed in Section 7.

(2) To dominate or interfere with the formation or administration of any labor organization or contribute financial or other support to it. . . .

(3) By discrimination in regard to hire or tenure of employment or any term or condition of employment to encourage or discourage membership in any labor organization: Provided, That nothing in this Act. . . . or in any other statute of the United States, shall preclude an employer from making an agreement with a labor organization (not established, maintained, or assisted by any action defined in this Act as an unfair labor practice) to require as a condition of employment membership therein, if such labor organization is the representative of the employees as provided in Section 9(a), in the appropriate collective bargaining unit covered by such agreement when made.

(4) To discharge or otherwise discriminate against an employee because he has filed charges or given testimony under this Act.

(5) To refuse to bargain collectively with the representatives of his employees, subject to the provisions of Section 9(a).

REPRESENTATIVES AND ELECTIONS

SEC. 9. (a) Representatives designated or selected for the purposes of collective bargaining by the majority of the employees in a unit appropriate for such purposes, shall be the exclusive representatives of all the employees in such unit for the purposes of collective bargaining in respect to rates of pay, wages, hours of employment, or other conditions of employment: Provided, That any individual employee or a group of employees shall have the right at any time to present grievances to their employer. . . .

LIMITATIONS

SEC. 13. Nothing in this Act shall be construed so as to interfere with or impede or diminish in any way the right to strike.

Source: 49 Stat. 449 (July 5, 1935).

Document 5.7   FDR's Statement and Executive Order 9340 on the Seizure of Coal Mines, May 1, 1943

Roosevelt and United Mine Workers president John L. Lewis (also the former president of the Congress of Industrial Organizations; CIO) had long had a hostile relationship. When Lewis defied Roosevelt by taking his mine

workers out on strike in the midst of World War II, Roosevelt responded by
seizing the coal mines.

ON THURSDAY, April 29, I sent a telegram to John L. Lewis, and Thomas Kennedy, President and Secretary-Treasurer of the United Mine Workers, pointing out that the coal strikes were a direct interference with the prosecution of the war, and challenged the governmental machinery set up for the orderly and peaceful settlement of labor disputes, and the power of the Government to carry on the war.

I said that the continuance and spread of the strikes would have the same effect on the course of the war as a crippling defeat in the war. I appealed to the miners to resume work immediately, and to submit their case to the National War Labor Board for final determination.

I stated that if work were not resumed by ten o'clock Saturday morning, I should use all the power vested in me as President and Commander in Chief to protect the national interest and to prevent further interference with the successful prosecution of the war.

Except in a few mines the production of coal has virtually ceased. The national interest is in grave peril.

I have today by appropriate Executive Order directed the Secretary of the Interior . . . to take possession of and operate the coal mines, for the United States Government. . . .

I now call upon all miners who may have abandoned their work to return immediately to the mines and work for their Government. Their country needs their services as much as those of the members of the armed forces. I am confident that they do not wish to retard the war effort; that they are as patriotic as any other Americans; and that they will promptly answer this call to perform this essential war service.

I repeat that an investigation of the cost of living is now being made in the mining areas, and that the Government will insist that the prices be held in accordance with the directions of my recent Executive Order, and violations of the law promptly prosecuted.

Whenever the miners submit their case to the War Labor Board, it will be determined promptly, fairly, and in accordance with the procedure and law applicable to all labor disputes. If any adjustment of wages is made, it will be made retroactive.

The production of coal must and shall continue.

Executive Order:

WHEREAS widespread stoppages have occurred in the coal industry and strikes are threatened which will obstruct the effective prosecution of the war by curtailing vitally needed production in the coal mines directly affecting the countless war industries and transportation systems dependent upon such mines; and

WHEREAS the officers of the United Mine Workers of America have refused to submit to the machinery established for the peaceful settlement of labor disputes in violation of the agreement on the part of labor and industry that there shall be no strikes or lockouts for the duration of the war; and

WHEREAS it has become necessary for the effective prosecution of the war that the coal mines in which stoppages or strikes have occurred, or are threatened, be taken over by the Government of the United States in order to protect the interests of the Nation at war and the rights of workers to continue at work:

Now, THEREFORE, by virtue of the authority vested in me by the Constitution and laws of the United States, as President of the United States and Commander in Chief of the Army and Navy, it is hereby ordered as follows:

The Secretary of the Interior is authorized and directed to take immediate possession, so far as may be necessary or desirable, of any and all mines producing coal in which a strike or stoppage has occurred or is threatened, together with any and all real and personal property, franchises, rights, facilities, funds, and other assets used in connection with the operation of such mines, and to operate or arrange for the operation of such mines in such manner as he deems necessary for the successful prosecution of the war, and to do all things necessary for or incidental to the production, sale, and distribution of coal.

In carrying out this Order, the Secretary of the Interior shall act through or with the aid of such public or private instrumentalities or persons as he may designate. He shall permit the management to continue its managerial functions to the maximum degree possible consistent with the aims of this Order.

The Secretary of the Interior shall make employment available and provide protection to all employees resuming work at such mines and to all persons seeking employment so far as they may be needed; and upon the request of the Secretary of the Interior, the Secretary of War shall take such action, if any, as he may deem necessary or desirable to provide protection to all such persons and mines.

The Secretary of the Interior is authorized and directed to maintain customary working conditions in the mines and customary procedure for the adjustment of workers' grievances. He shall recognize the right of the workers to continue their membership in any labor organization, to bargain collectively through representatives of their own choosing, and to engage in concerted activities for the purpose of collective bargaining or other mutual aid or protection, provided that such concerted activities do not interfere with the operations of the mines.

Possession and operation of any mine or mines hereunder shall be terminated by the Secretary of the Interior as soon as he determines that possession and operation hereunder are no longer required for the furtherance of the war program.

Source: Samuel I. Rosenman, ed., *The Public Papers and Addresses of Franklin D. Roosevelt* (1950; reprint, New York: Russell and Russell, 1969), 12:185–188.

Roosevelt speaks on World War II, Washington, D.C., November 19, 1944.

CHAPTER SIX

Roosevelt's Place in History
The Dominant Figure of the Twentieth Century

I t is beyond serious question that Franklin Delano Roosevelt was the most important U.S. president—and perhaps world figure— of the twentieth century. His influence after his presidency has been enormous; in death, perhaps as much as in life, Roosevelt has been a dominant presence in U.S. politics and society.

"Great men have two lives," ambassador and former Roosevelt brain trust member Adolf Berle said about Roosevelt after his death. "One which occurs while they work on this earth; a second which begins at the day of their death and continues as long as their ideas and conceptions remain powerful. In this second life, the conceptions earlier developed exert influence on men and events for an indefinite period of time." Berle said that Roosevelt's "second, and perhaps greater, life" was just beginning at that time (Leuchtenburg 1983, viii–ix). "The President," noted journalist and novelist John Gunther five years after Roosevelt's death, "though dead, is still alive. Millions of Americans will continue to vote for Roosevelt as long as *they* live" (Gunther 1950, 379; see Document 6.1)

Roosevelt's "second life" of influence beyond his death will continue well into the twenty-first century, if not longer. As historian William Leuchtenburg said, all presidents since 1945 have had to operate "in the shadow of FDR" (Leuchtenburg 1983; see Document 6.2). Before exploring the contours of that shadow, a few concluding comments on the man who cast it are in order.

A CHARACTER PROFILE

If Emerson was right in proclaiming consistency to be "the hobgoblin of little minds," we can say with confidence that Roosevelt's mind was large enough that this particular ghost rarely haunted him (Mumford 1968, 95). If *consistent* is not an appropriate characterization, several other words beginning with the letter C are: *complex, contradictory, charming, compassionate, courageous, competitive, commanding, confident,* and, on occasion, *cruel.*

One of the most frequently quoted assessments of Roosevelt comes from former Supreme Court justice Oliver Wendell Holmes Jr. in 1933. The synopsis almost perfectly captures FDR's essence: "A second-class intellect, but a first-class temperament!" (Maney 1992, 201). That temperament was well matched with what the American people in the era of the Great Depression and World War II needed in a leader.

Roosevelt was a progressive in the literal sense of the word: he believed in progress, in the upward path of human development. He was an optimist, certainly on a personal level, but in a larger sense as well. He was, in fact, such an optimist that those around him rarely gave him bad news. His doctors, for example, never told him that he wouldn't walk again. This optimism, supported by his straightforward and unexamined religious faith in a God who had a purpose for him, was critical not only in Roosevelt's ability to lead the nation through depression and war, but also in his vision for the nation and the world after his presidency ended. When FDR died, a congressman summed up this quality of Roosevelt and its importance in the years of his presidency: "He was the only person I ever knew—anywhere—who was never afraid. God, how he could take it for all of us" (Burns 1956, 478).

Roosevelt's basic beliefs were simple. In addition to his faith in progress and God, he believed that people have a responsibility to look out for their fellow humans, that people can get along if they agree to follow certain basic rules, that those who come from privilege have a duty to try to improve the lives of the less fortunate, and that government has an obligation to curb the excesses of the free market.

FDR was as unsure of the specific route to his desired ends as he was sure that he, the nation, and the world would get there—or at least would keep drawing closer. Where his detractors saw a lack of principle, his supporters saw an admirable flexibility. He would stray from morality in his means because he remained supremely confident of the rightness of the ends. Roosevelt was, in short, that wonderful American paradox: a practical idealist.

CREATING THE MODERN PRESIDENCY AND RETOOLING THE FEDERAL GOVERNMENT

The presidency, he said, is "pre-eminently a place of moral leadership" (Schlesinger 1957, 483). Although Roosevelt could certainly lie and mislead when it suited his purposes, he seems to have been sincere in that statement. "I want to be a preaching president—like my cousin," FDR declared (Schlesinger 1958, 558). He was, perhaps above all else, an inspirational leader. His capacity in this regard was due largely to his extraordinary ability to communicate with masses of people via radio, but also to his perseverance in the face of serious disability.

The Roosevelt presidency did much more than offer new answers—it asked new questions. Only four years into the New Deal, the *Economist* argued that whereas Roosevelt might often have given the wrong answers, unlike his predecessors he had begun to ask the right questions. Since the Roosevelt era, those questions have been modified, but many of them remain fundamental to U.S. politics and policy. "All contemporary national politics descend from Franklin Roosevelt," Theodore H. White correctly stated in the early 1980s (Leuchtenburg 1983; see Document 6.2).

Building on a foundation laid by Abraham Lincoln, Theodore Roosevelt, and Woodrow Wilson, Franklin Roosevelt created the modern presidency. Since his time, all presidents have been expected to have a legislative program to present to Congress—to act almost as a prime minister. Presidents since FDR have been measured by their accomplishments in the first hundred days they are in office. Even first ladies since the Roosevelt years have been compared with Eleanor Roosevelt, who set a new standard for presidential spouses to at least as great an extent as her husband did for presidents.

Roosevelt attracted to government service brilliant, ambitious, and idealistic men and women. Ever since the New Deal, many intellectuals have identified themselves with the Democratic party and the Roosevelt legacy.

Roosevelt also substantially changed the role of the federal government and its relationship with the people and the states. "Washington" came to mean something quite different after FDR. Since his presidency, Washington, D.C., has been the place to which most Americans look whenever there is a serious problem. The role of the federal government grew during the Great Depression and again in World War II. Though Roosevelt never fully got over his qualms about Keynesian economics, it was the Roosevelt administration that showed Keynesianism to be effective. By the time FDR died in 1945, Keynes's theories were almost certain to be the basis of future economic policy in the United States.

Not only did FDR expand the role of the federal government, he eventually obtained widespread agreement that this larger role was necessary and proper. The Supreme Court initially rejected the Rooseveltian view that the new economy had created the need for an expanded federal role in regulating the nation's businesses, then changed its mind. Hence a different view of the U.S. constitutional framework prevailed at the end of Roosevelt's presidency than had held sway at its outset.

Roosevelt's administration teemed with significant and lasting changes. The following are some of the most notable.

- *The Social Security Act and the partial welfare state.* Although much was left out of the Social Security Act to forestall opposition, the basic old-age pensions and unemployment insurance quickly became accepted as permanent and desirable features of the American system.
- *The income tax.* The income tax hit the middle class for the first time during World War II. The practice of withholding estimated taxes from Americans' paychecks also began in that era.
- *Income redistribution.* Paradoxically, when the administration in the 1930s was trying to achieve this goal (or at least talking as if it were, as in Roosevelt's "Wealth Tax" message of 1935), it accomplished little. Yet when the administration's wartime policy was to maintain the status quo, there was considerable redistribution. This outcome resulted from full employment combined with very high wartime taxes on the highest incomes.

- *Growth of the middle class.* Large numbers of industrial workers were able to rise into the middle class as a result of the Wagner Act, which provided some government protections for unions. To this was added the G.I. Bill, which enabled veterans to become better educated, obtain jobs with good wages, and purchase homes. The Rural Electrification Administration transformed the lives of millions of Americans who lived on isolated farms and greatly expanded the market for electrical appliances, bringing another important segment of U.S. society into a middle-class lifestyle.

Many of these positive social and economic developments were achieved by enhancing the power of interest groups, such as labor unions. Although a socioeconomic system that disperses power across a variety of groups is clearly an improvement over a system in which only the wealthy have influence, the downside is that the new system leaves out people who are not represented by any interest group.

Civil Rights and the Women's Movement

On the surface, Roosevelt accomplished little in civil rights. But the ban on discrimination in New Deal agencies was a significant advance, even when followed only sporadically. African Americans benefited from the creation of an informal "Black Cabinet," the enthusiastic advocacy of Eleanor Roosevelt and Interior Secretary Harold Ickes, and Roosevelt's issuance of Executive Order 8802, which created the Fair Employment Practices Committee. A majority of blacks switched their allegiance from the party of Lincoln (Republican) to the party of Roosevelt (Democratic). African Americans became valued members of the New Deal coalition, and their migration into the Democratic Party reshaped American politics from that time to the present.

World War II spurred the other monumental social change of the second half of the twentieth century, the movement for women's equality. FDR had little hand in this, but he did appoint the first woman to the cabinet (Frances Perkins as secretary of labor), and he placed more women in important positions in his administration than had any of his predecessors. In addition, he was married to a woman who became an inspiration to a couple generations of ambitious women and who pushed as hard for policies helpful to women as she did for those helpful to blacks.

WAR AND THE WORLD STAGE

The United States in 1933 was potentially the greatest power in the world, but its people were not eager to play that role. The longstanding American tradition of isolationism, which had been briefly interrupted by participation in World War I, was again prevalent. Twelve years later, when Roosevelt died, internationalism held sway and the United States was the dominant world power. Plans for the United Nations, the World Bank, and the International Monetary Fund had been laid and Roosevelt was a principal advocate of all three.

The frightful reality that has hung over the world since 1945 is another child of the Roosevelt years. Though it would be inaccurate to say that Roosevelt was the father of the atomic bomb, it would be appropriate to call him the sire of the Manhattan Project that produced the first nuclear weapons. It is quite likely that these weapons of unprecedented destructive power would eventually have been built by someone later on. It is clearly the case, however, that had Roosevelt not authorized the huge, highly expensive secret project that developed fission bombs that would be used against Japan in 1945, the nuclear age would have been delayed.

Another of Roosevelt's dubious legacies is what President Dwight D. Eisenhower would later name the "military-industrial complex." Roosevelt's improved relations with business during the war were largely a consequence of his willingness to let industrialists develop close ties with military procurement officials in the War (later Defense) Department, assuring both an extraordinary level of production of war material and secure, high profits for military contractors. This cozy relationship, born in Roosevelt's third term, lived on in the ensuing cold war.

Roosevelt's term marked the beginning of what would later be called "the imperial presidency." Whereas his enhancement of the powers of the executive branch allowed modernization and a more effective means of fighting the economic depression, Roosevelt's presidency also pointed toward a future in which chief executives would increasingly try to take action on their own, especially in foreign policy and military affairs.

The final question is to what extent the momentous alterations that took place from 1933 to 1945 should be attributed directly to Roosevelt. "Throughout his career," historian and biographer Patrick Maney has noted, "Roosevelt had always reflected, more than he had shaped, the dominant tendencies of his time" (Maney 1992, 174). To this might be added: Yes, but therein lies much of his greatness as a leader. Roosevelt understood that effective leadership in a democracy means mobilizing people so they can achieve their goals. Few politicians have ever been more adept in this style of leadership than Franklin Delano Roosevelt.

The final, most direct way to summarize Roosevelt's impact is to point out that he changed the position of the presidency within the federal government, of the federal government within the United States, and of the United States within the world. He oversaw a renovation of the capitalist system that helped it survive, and he became a key leader in a world war that preserved democracy. That record, surely, marks him as one of the most important figures of the twentieth century and one of the most important presidents in the history of the United States. One need not be an adherent of the "great man" theory of history to realize that the world today would be quite different had Franklin Delano Roosevelt not been president.

BIBLIOGRAPHY

Two books by William E. Leuchtenburg, *In the Shadow of FDR: From Harry Truman to George W. Bush*, 3d ed. (Ithaca: Cornell University Press, 2001); and *The FDR Years: On Roosevelt and His Legacy* (New York: Columbia University Press, 1995), a collection of essays that collectively review and respond to a variety of criticisms of Roosevelt, are the best places to begin a more detailed examination of FDR's legacy and his place in history.

Steve Fraser and Gary Gerstle, eds., *The Rise and Fall of the New Deal Order, 1930–1980* (Princeton: Princeton University Press, 1989) contains excellent essays on the impact of New Deal policies and programs in the decades that followed Roosevelt's death.

Alan Brinkley, *The End of Reform: New Deal Liberalism in Depression and War* (New York: Knopf, 1995) deals with the often-neglected period of the late 1930s and how New Deal reform measures fared during, and, to a lesser extent, after, World War II. James T. Patterson, *America's*

Struggle against Poverty, 1900–1980 (Cambridge: Harvard University Press, 1981) contains excellent chapters on how the partial welfare state worked in the post-Roosevelt years. Ronald C. Tooby, *Technology as Freedom: The New Deal and the Electrical Modernization of the American Home* (Berkeley: University of California Press, 1996) demonstrates the impact of New Deal electrification programs on modernization and consumerism over the ensuing years.

Harvard Sitkoff, ed., *Fifty Years Later: The New Deal Evaluated* (Philadelphia: Temple University Press, 1985) demonstrates changing perspectives on the New Deal over a half century.

Other works cited in this chapter include James MacGregor Burns, *Roosevelt: The Lion and the Fox* (New York: Harcourt Brace and World, 1956); John Gunther, *Roosevelt in Retrospect: A Profile in History* (New York: Harper, 1950); William E. Leuchtenburg, *In the Shadow of FDR: From Harry Truman to Ronald Reagan* (Ithaca: Cornell University Press, 1983); Patrick J. Maney, *The Roosevelt Presence: A Biography of Franklin D. Roosevelt* (New York: Twayne, 1992); Lewis Mumford, ed., *Ralph Waldo Emerson: Essays and Journals* (Garden City, N.Y.: International Collectors Library, 1968); and Arthur M. Schlesinger Jr., *The Crisis of the Old Order, 1919–1933* (Boston: Houghton Mifflin, 1957); and *The Coming of the New Deal* (Boston: Houghton Mifflin, 1958).

Document 6.1   Roosevelt in Retrospect, 1950

Journalist and novelist John Gunther's assessment five years after Roosevelt's death reveals some of the president's serious faults, but on balance sees him as a truly great leader.

I once heard it said that Roosevelt's most effective quality was receptivity. But also he transmitted. He was like a kind of universal joint, or rather a switchboard, a transformer. The whole energy of the country; the whole power of one hundred and forty million people, flowed into him and through him; he not only felt this power, but he utilized it, he retransmitted it. Why does a country, if lucky, produce a great man when he is most needed? Because it really believes in something and focuses the entire energy of its national desires into a single human being; the supreme forces of the time converge into a single vessel. Roosevelt could manipulate this power, shooting it out at almost any angle, to provoke response, to irradiate ideas and men, to search out enormous issues. He was like a needle, always quivering, oscillating, responding to new impulses, throbbing at the slightest variation in current—a magnetic instrument measuring ceaselessly the tone and intensity of public impact. But no matter how much the needle quivered and oscillated, it seldom varied far from its own true north.

But this analysis, however suggestive, is too artificial for my taste, because the essence of F.D.R. was not mechanistic, but sublimely (and sometimes ridiculously) human. Of all his multifarious qualities the dominant was probably his extreme humanity. Later we shall try to break this term down; suffice it to say now that, being a man, he believed in men. The term "humanity" covers a wide arc—from amiability to compassion, from fertility in ideas to subtlety in personal relationships, from the happy expression of animal vitality to the deepest cognizance of suffering and primitive despair. The President was inveterately personal, and people were inveterately personal about him. A lady I know, by no means a sentimentalist, said two or three years after his death, "He made me glad I am a woman. I miss him actively, personally, every day." At least a dozen people all over the country told me early in 1945—the remark became almost trite—"I never met him, but I feel as if I had lost my greatest friend." . . .

His radiant, energetic smile—even with the touch of glucose in it, even when it seemed contrived—stirred people with confidence and hope. His lustrous voice, so soothing, so resonant, so alive, said, "My friends . . ."—and the people were. They were not merely his followers, but partners. He led by following, which was one of the most distinctive sources of his power. He lifted people above themselves—he gave them a goal—and hence no one was ever able to take the masses away from him. He gave citizens the sense that they, we, the country, were going forward, that life was still the kind of adventure it had been in pioneer days, that the pace was fast and that substantial rewards were attainable.

Yet, more than any modern president, he split the country—which is one of the more obvious Roosevelt paradoxes. Why was he hated so, defamed and calumniated so? Because he took from the rich and gave to the poor. But that is only one explanation. Why, five years after his death, is he still hated so? Because what he did lives after him. But that too is only part of the story.

Roosevelt stood for the "common man" (though this ambiguous phrase is a cliché earnestly to be avoided) but he was certainly not common himself. In fact he was a storybook Prince Charming, a fairy tale hero to the millions; he ruled with a wand—even if it was an ivory cigarette holder. Out in the rain, men and women strove—literally—to touch the hem of his cape as he passed, this man who could not walk. The "common" people chose him, a prince, to lead them, and he did things for them, as a good prince should. What was the New Deal except a vast exercise in *noblesse oblige?*

To a supreme degree Roosevelt had five qualifications for statesmanship: (a) courage; (b) patience, and an infinitely subtle sense of timing; (c) the capacity to see the very great in the very small, to relate the infinitesimal particular to the all-embracing general; (d) idealism, and a sense of fixed objectives; (e) ability to give resolution to the minds of men. Also he had plenty of bad qualities—dilatoriness, two-sidedness (some critics would say plain dishonesty), pettiness in some personal relationships, a cardinal lack of frankness (for which, however, there was often good reason), inability to say No, love of improvisation, garrulousness, amateurism, and what has been called "cheerful vindictiveness." Amateurism?—in a peculiar way, yes. But do not forget that he was the most masterfully expert practical politician ever to function in this republic. . . .

Probably what it all boils down to is the matter of contribution. He did not create a country, as did Masaryk, nor a continent of the imagination, like Beethoven, nor a new world of science, like Freud. He may not have been as stupendous a human being as, say, Michelangelo or Tolstoi, but if you measure a man practically by the work he leaves, FDR ranks very high. A Roosevelt advocate might say: (I) Almost singlehanded he saved democracy in the United States; (2) he brought the United States to world leadership for the first time. Certainly he belongs in the category of Washington and Lincoln as one of the three greatest presidents in American history, whether you like all he did or not. And think how he is missed!

Roosevelt was a man of his times, and what times they were!—chaotic, catastrophic, revolutionary, epochal—he was President during the greatest emergency in the history of mankind, and he never let history—or mankind—down. His very defects reflected the unprecedented strains and stresses of the decades he lived in. But he took history in his stride; he had vision and gallantry enough, oomph and zip and debonair benevolence enough, to foresee the supreme crises of our era, overcome them, and lead the nation out of the worst dangers it has ever faced.

Roosevelt was the greatest political campaigner and the greatest vote getter in American history. Thirty-one out of forty-eight states voted for him each of the four times he ran. His influence, far from having diminished since his death, has probably increased. When Mr. Truman won his surprising victory in 1948, which was made possible in part by the political influence left behind by FDR, it was altogether fitting that a London newspaper should head its story, "Roosevelt's Fifth Term."

Roosevelt believed in social justice—and fought for it—he gave hope and faith to the masses, and knew that the masses are the foundation of American democracy. He turned the cornucopia of American resource upside down and made it serve almost everybody. Mrs. Roosevelt has said that in the whole course of his career there was never any deviation from his original objective—"to make life better for the average man, woman, and child." I have heard men of the utmost sober conservatism say that they think FDR saved the country from overt revolution in 1932. He created the pattern of the modern democratic state, and made it function. To be a reformer alone is not enough. A reformer must make reform effective. This certainly Roosevelt did. Yet, as we have pointed out, he was a conservative as well as a liberal; he believed in free enterprise and the profit system. It is not beyond the bounds of possibility that thirty or forty years from now the country will have swung so much further left that what FDR stood for will be thought of as almost reactionary.

He was a rich man and an aristocrat; but he did more for the under-possessed than any American who ever lived. Moreover, as we know, FDR always operated within the framework of full democracy and civil liberties. He believed devoutly in the American political tradition. Much of the world outside the United States during his prodigious administrations had political liberty without economic security; some had security but no liberty. He gave both.

Mr. Roosevelt was the greatest war president in American history; it was he, almost singlehanded, who created the climate of the nation whereby we were able to fight at all. Beyond this he brought the United States to full citizenship in the world as a partner in the peace. He set up the frame in which a durable peace might have been written and a new world order established; if he had lived to fill in the picture contemporary history might be very different.

Above all FDR was an educator. He expanded and enlarged the role of the Presidency as no president before him ever did. He established what amounted to a new relationship between president and people; he turned the White House into a teacher's desk, a pulpit; he taught the people of the United States how the operations of government might be applied to their own good; he made government a much abler process, on the whole, than it has ever been before; he gave citizens intimate acquaintanceship with the realities of political power, and made politics the close inalienable possession of the man in every street.

One result of all this is that the President, though dead, is still alive. Millions of Americans will continue to vote for Roosevelt as long as *they* live.

Source: John Gunther, *Roosevelt in Retrospect: A Profile in History* (New York: Harper, 1950), 3–6, 378–379.

Document 6.2   In the Shadow of FDR, 1983

One of the leading scholars of the Roosevelt era, William E. Leuchtenburg of the University of North Carolina at Chapel Hill, makes a strong case that all presidents since FDR have lived in his shadow—that their achievements and expectations for their presidencies have been measured against Roosevelt's.

Roosevelt left his mark on his successors in a great many ways. Three of the first four presidents who came after him—Truman, Eisenhower, and Johnson—were men whose careers he had advanced, and the other, Kennedy, had first gained familiarity with Washington when Roosevelt named his father to high office. No one before Roosevelt had so dominated the political culture of his day, if for no better reason than that no one before him had been in the White House for so long, and in the process he created the expectation that the chief executive would be a primary shaper of his times—an expectation with which each of his successors has had to deal. He bequeathed them not only the legacy of the New Deal but that of a global foreign policy, as well as all those instrumentalities that emerged during the years when he was Dr. Win the War. The age of Roosevelt set the agenda for much of the postwar era, whose debates centered on such questions as whether price controls should be maintained, how far social security was to be extended, to what level the minimum wage ought to be raised, and how large the domain of public power should be. Long after FDR was gone, New Deal agencies such as the TVA and the SEC continued to administer statutes drafted in his first term, and the Fair Deal, the New Frontier, and the Great Society all drew heavily on the Roosevelt experiments.

Roosevelt's success as the architect of a new political era encouraged subsequent Democratic presidents, and even some Republicans, to identify with FDR. They fought off usurpers who claimed that they were the true heirs to the Roosevelt legacy, campaigned in the image of FDR, and year in, year out recited Roosevelt's sayings. They appointed to posts in their administrations men and women who had served under FDR, and made use of Roosevelt's approaches in coping with the problems of their own day. . . .

To be sure, much that American presidents did in the ensuing decades owed little or nothing to FDR. A Kennedy or a Johnson often responded to a pressing problem with no thought of Roosevelt. Each relied upon his own instincts or was driven by forces that emerged well after Roosevelt's death. Nor was FDR the only predecessor who was recalled. We need not take literally Lyndon Johnson's claim that he "walked with Lincoln every night" to recognize that there were other chief executives whose influence was pertinent. Not even direct citations of Roosevelt offer incontrovertible proof of his influence, for his successors sometimes cited him only ritualistically and used him selectively for their own purposes.

Moreover, the postwar presidents had to bear in mind that the public was deeply divided about Franklin Roosevelt. If there was a large cult of FDR-worshipers, millions of other Americans loathed him—for upsetting class relations, for showing disrespect toward venerated institutions such as the Supreme Court, for creating the leviathan state, and for leading the nation into a war that cost the lives of thousands of young men. Many others were not quite sure what they thought about him—he seemed to have brought both good and ill—and hence he was an uncertain model for his successors to emulate. A commission set up in 1946 to approve a memorial to Roosevelt encountered so many difficulties that by the summer of 1981 it had become the longest-running single-purpose commission in U.S. history.

Still, no one doubted that FDR was a protean figure. From 1945 to the present, historians have unfailingly ranked him with Washington and Lincoln, and the men who succeeded him found one question inescapable: How did they measure up to FDR? They were expected to tread in the rows that he had furrowed, even, like those who sought a sign of grace from a Chinese emperor, to exhibit the quality of *hsiao,* of filial piety. Little wonder that they sometimes felt much like the Athenian who voted to exile Aristides because he had wearied of hearing him called "the Just."

Source: William E. Leuchtenburg, *In the Shadow of FDR: From Harry Truman to Ronald Reagan* (Ithaca: Cornell University Press, 1983), vii–xi.

Appendix A
Notable Figures
of the Roosevelt Presidency

Arnold, Thurmond (1891–1969 b. Laramie, Wyoming)
Assistant attorney general, Antitrust Division, 1938–1943;
judge, U.S. Court of Appeals, District of Columbia, 1943–1945
Arnold had served as the mayor of Laramie, Wyoming, as a member of the Progressive Party before joining the faculty at Yale Law School in 1930. Jerome Frank, general counsel of the Agricultural Adjustment Administration (AAA), asked Arnold to assist in the development of the AAA, and Arnold had several informal assignments before being appointed assistant attorney general. While in the Antitrust Division he oversaw a robust antitrust campaign against monopolies. Arnold believed that only vigorous price competition in the marketplace could restore the economy and that the existing antitrust laws could be used to attack companies that dominated the market. During World War II he thought that monopolistic businesses had too much power in the mobilization effort. Arnold left the Justice Department after he was appointed to the federal court of appeals in 1943.

Bankhead, William B. (1874–1940 b. Moscow, Alabama)
U.S. House of Representatives, Alabama, 1917–1940; Speaker of the House, 1936–1940
Bankhead was elected to the U.S. House of Representatives in 1916. A Democrat, by 1934 he was chairman of the Rules Committee, and in 1936 he was elected Speaker of the House. Bankhead supported most New Deal legislation. He was the sponsor of the Bankhead-Jones Farm Tenant Bill, finally passed in 1937, designed to help tenant farmers own their own small farms; the Farm Security Administration (FSA) was set up to administer the law's provisions. Considered a possible contender for the 1940 Democratic presidential nomination, Bankhead had the support of many Democrats for the vice presidential nomination after Roosevelt decided to seek a third term. Bankhead died in 1940 before the election.

Barkley, Alben W. (1877–1956 b. Wheel, Graves County, Kentucky)
U.S. Senate, Kentucky, 1927–1949
Barkley, a Democrat, served in the U.S. House of Representatives for fourteen years before being elected to the Senate. Generally conservative, he had been influenced

by Woodrow Wilson's New Freedom as a congressman and generally supported New Deal legislation in Roosevelt's first term. Barkley became the Senate majority leader in 1937 and supported Roosevelt's Court-packing plan in Congress. Although Roosevelt and Barkley broke over Roosevelt's veto of the 1944 tax bill and Congress's subsequent override, Barkley was considered for the vice presidential nomination in 1944, but the party decided he was too old. Barkley later became Harry Truman's vice president in 1949.

Baruch, Bernard M. (1870–1965 b. Camden, South Carolina)
Chairman, presidential committee investigating rubber shortage, 1942; adviser to James Byrnes, Office of War Mobilization, 1943–1945
Baruch had served under Woodrow Wilson as the chairman of the War Industries Board during World War I. Later, he advised Herbert Hoover on the establishment of the Reconstruction Finance Corporation. During World War II Baruch worked on the initiative to develop artificial rubber, and in 1943 Roosevelt appointed him to lead a division in the War Mobilization Office to plan for the conversion to a peacetime economy. Though Baruch seldom had a formal position in government, he offered important financial support to the Democratic Party and, in part because of his ties to the business world, was influential in the Democratic Party and in Roosevelt's administrations.

Berle, Adolf A. Jr. (1895–1971 b. Boston, Massachusetts)
Special adviser, Reconstruction Finance Corporation, 1933–1935; assistant secretary of state, 1940–1944; ambassador to Brazil, 1945–1946
Berle was a law professor at Columbia University who became a member of Roosevelt's brain trust during the 1932 presidential campaign and then a special adviser to the Reconstruction Finance Corporation. Like Raymond Moley and Rexford Tugwell, Berle believed that large corporations were inevitable, and he advocated government-business cooperation in national economic planning. But Berle also believed that the ultimate goal of business should be providing goods and services to consumers, not earning profits, and he thought that the business community could develop a new ethic. Berle left the administration by 1935, but in 1940 he was appointed assistant secretary of state for Latin America. In 1945 Berle became the U.S. ambassador to Brazil.

Bethune, Mary Mcleod (1875–1955 b. Mayesville, South Carolina)
Director, Division of Negro Affairs, National Youth Administration, 1936–1944; special assistant to secretary of war, 1942
Bethune was an influential African American educator who founded what is now Bethune-Cookman College. When Roosevelt appointed her director of the Division of Negro Affairs of the National Youth Administration, she became the first

black woman appointed to head a federal office. During World War II she became a special assistant to the secretary of war to help select women to attend the Women's Army Corps officer's school. As a friend of Eleanor Roosevelt, Bethune had access to the administration and provided valuable insight into the state of race relations.

Biddle, Francis (1886–1968 b. Paris, France)

Member, National Labor Relations Board, 1934–1935; chief counsel to congressional committee investigating the Tennessee Valley Authority, 1938; director and deputy chairman, Federal Reserve Bank, 1938–1939; judge, Third Circuit Court of Appeals, 1939–1940; U.S. solicitor general, 1940–1941; U.S. attorney general, 1941–1945

Biddle was originally a Republican but was concerned about his party's failure to address social issues, especially working conditions. Biddle supported Roosevelt in 1932 and was appointed to the National Labor Relations Board in 1934. After several government appointments, Biddle became solicitor general in 1940 and defended New Deal legislation against constitutional challenges. In 1941 he succeeded Robert Jackson as attorney general and remained in that position until June 1945. During World War II Biddle implemented wartime directives, including the Japanese internment, which he opposed. After resigning as attorney general he served on the international tribunal at Nuremberg.

Black, Hugo L. (1886–1971 b. Harlan, Alabama)

U.S. Senate, Alabama, 1927–1937; associate justice, U.S. Supreme Court, 1937–1971

Black was a Democratic senator from Alabama during the New Deal years. A strong supporter of Roosevelt and most New Deal legislation, he led the congressional committee that investigated lobbyists for utility holding companies in 1935. Some members of Congress opposed Black's nomination to the Supreme Court in 1937 because of his membership in the Ku Klux Klan in the early 1920s. While on the Supreme Court, Black voted to uphold New Deal legislation.

Bohlen, Charles E. (1904–1974 b. Clayton, New York)

Adviser to the president, Soviet affairs, 1942–1943; chief, Division of Eastern European Affairs, State Department, 1943–1946

Bohlen was a foreign service professional who specialized in the Soviet Union. He went to Tokyo in 1940 and was briefly interned in Japan after the bombing of Pearl Harbor. Upon Bohlen's return Roosevelt appointed him as his special adviser on Soviet matters, and he served as a translator at both the Teheran and Yalta conferences. As chief of the Division of Eastern Economic Affairs, Bohlen enjoyed increased access to the administration.

Brandeis, Louis D. (1856–1941 b. Louisville, Kentucky)
Associate justice, U.S. Supreme Court, 1916–1939
Brandeis was an influential lawyer and jurist. An antimonopolist, Brandeis believed that the United States needed to return to more vigorous competition and glorified small business units. And both his legal and economic views influenced many New Dealers. Woodrow Wilson appointed Brandeis to the Supreme Court in 1916. He generally supported New Deal legislation on the bench, but joined in the unanimous decision in the *Schechter Poultry Corp. v. United States* case striking down the National Recovery Administration. Brandeis retired from the bench in 1939.

Byrnes, James F. (1879–1972 b. Charleston, South Carolina)
U.S. senator, South Carolina, 1931–1941; associate justice, U.S. Supreme Court, 1941; director, Office of Economic Stabilization, 1941–1943; director, Office of War Mobilization, 1943–1945
Byrnes, a South Carolina Democrat, served in the U.S. Senate from 1931 until 1941. Although he opposed many New Deal programs while in Congress, Roosevelt appointed him to the Supreme Court in 1941. The same year, however, he resigned to become the director of the Office of Economic Stabilization, an agency designed to control wartime inflation. In 1943 Byrnes headed up the new Office of War Mobilization, an agency that coordinated the allocation of materials for production and civilian workers. Byrnes was a close adviser to Roosevelt during the war and sought the Democratic vice presidential nomination in 1944, but Democratic political leaders believed that his segregationist views would hurt the ticket.

Cardozo, Benjamin N. (1870–1938 b. New York City)
Chief justice, New York Court of Appeals, 1927–1932; associate justice, U.S. Supreme Court, 1932–1938
Herbert Hoover appointed Cardozo to the Supreme Court in 1932. Cardozo became the intellectual leader of the liberal faction of the Court. He wrote the decision upholding the Social Security Act in 1937 and the lone dissent in the "hot oil case" striking down certain provisions of the National Industrial Recovery Administration (*Panama Refining Co. v. Ryan*) in 1934. However, he concurred with the majority in *United States v. Schecter Poultry Co.* that struck down the National Industrial Recovery Act based on its broad delegation of powers with few or no standards.

Cohen, Benjamin V. (1894–1983 b. Muncie, Indiana)
Associate general counsel, Public Works Administration, 1933–1934; counsel, National Power Policy Committee, Public Works Administration, 1934–1941; special assistant to the attorney general, 1936–1938; counsel to the U.S. ambassa-

dor to the Court of St. James, 1941; assistant to the director and general counsel, Office of Economic Stabilization, 1942; general counsel, Office of War Mobilization, 1943–1945

Cohen joined the Roosevelt administration in 1933 to work with Thomas Corcoran on the Securities Act of 1933. Although his official positions before 1941 were in the Interior Department, he drafted many pieces of New Deal legislation. Cohen also served as a special assistant to the attorney general in connection with the public utility holding company legislation. In 1940 Cohen advised Roosevelt on the "destroyers-for-bases" deal with Great Britain and was one of the drafters of the 1941 Lend-Lease Act. In 1941 Cohen became counsel to the U.S. ambassador to Great Britain. Later he served as general counsel for both the Office of Economic Stabilization and the Office of War Mobilization and helped draft the Dumbarton Oaks agreements, which provided the template for the United Nations charter.

Collier, John (1884–1968 b. Atlanta, Georgia)
Commissioner of Indian Affairs, 1933–1945

As commissioner of Indian Affairs, Collier was instrumental in the passage of the Indian Reorganization Act (1934), sometimes called the "Indian New Deal," which restored some lands to the Indian tribes, prohibited the future sale of reservation lands, and encouraged tribal self-government. With the passage of the act, the United States effectively reversed its previous policy of Native American assimilation.

Corcoran, Thomas G. (1900–1981 b. Pawtucket, Rhode Island)
Legal staff, Reconstruction Finance Corporation, 1932–1940; special assistant to the attorney general, 1933–1935

Corcoran was one the most talented drafters of New Deal legislation. He joined the staff of the Reconstruction Finance Corporation (RFC) in the final year of Herbert Hoover's administration. Corcoran had a close working relationship with Benjamin Cohen. Although officially employed with the RFC, Corcoran's work within the administration belied his official title, and examples of legislation written by Corcoran include the Securities Act of 1933, the Securities and Exchange Act of 1934, the Tennessee Valley Authority Act, the Public Utilities Holding Company Act, and the Fair Labor Standards Act. Corcoran resigned from government in 1940.

Coughlin, Charles E. (1891–1979 b. Hamilton, Ontario, Canada)
Popular radio host, 1926–1940

Coughlin, a Catholic priest, started radio broadcasts in 1926, and by 1930 his messages had become political and extremely popular. His Radio League of the Little

Flower attacked Herbert Hoover, the gold standard, internationalism, and communism. Although he initially supported the New Deal, Coughlin soon changed his mind, railing against the inequities of capitalism and bankers in particular. In 1934 he formed the National Union for Social Justice, and membership numbered in the millions. He temporarily joined with Francis Townsend and Gerald L. K. Smith to form the Union Party in 1936. Coughlin briefly stopped broadcasting in 1936 because of the extremely poor showing of the Union Party in the election, but when he returned to the airwaves in 1937 his attacks on Roosevelt were more virulent and his programs more anti-Semitic. He stopped broadcasting in 1940 at the request of the Catholic Church.

Cummings, Homer S. (1870–1956 b. Chicago, Illinois)
U.S. attorney general, 1933–1939
Cummings had been active in Democratic politics for many years and had served as the national chairman of the Democratic Party from 1914 until 1920. He supported Roosevelt's candidacy in 1932 and gave the seconding speech at the 1932 Democratic National Convention. As attorney general he expanded the role of the federal government in criminal prosecutions. Cummings also worked to bring more able lawyers, such as Robert Jackson, into the Justice Department. Nonetheless, many New Deal statutes were found to be unconstitutional during Cummings's tenure as attorney general, and he presented Roosevelt with the ill-fated Court-packing scheme as early as 1935.

Currie, Lauchlin (1902–1993 b. Nova Scotia, Canada)
Investigator, Federal Reserve Board, 1934–1939; assistant for economic affairs, 1939–1941; director of aid to China, 1941–1943; acting director, Foreign Economic Administration, 1943–1944
Currie was a Keynesian economist who held several positions in the Roosevelt administrations. In 1935 Currie, together with Marriner Eccles, prepared a memorandum that became the basis for the Banking Act of 1935. In 1934 Currie published the popular and influential book, *The Supply and Control of Money in the United States,* in which he advocated government spending as a means of recovery. While serving in the Foreign Economic Administration in China, Currie worked on the Lend-Lease program. He later was investigated by the House of Representatives' Un-American Activities Committee and in 1958 renounced his adopted U.S. citizenship (which he had gained in 1934).

Davis, Chester C. (1887–1975 b. Linden, Iowa)
Director of Productions Division, Agricultural Adjustment Administration, 1933; director, Agricultural Adjustment Administration, 1933–1935; Board of Governors, Federal Reserve System, 1936–1941; president, Federal Reserve Bank,

St. Louis, 1941–1951; member, National Defense Advisery Committee, 1940; war food administrator, 1943; adviser, Office of War Mobilization and Reconversion, 1943–1945

Davis had served as Montana's commissioner of agriculture before Roosevelt appointed him director of the production division of the Agricultural Adjustment Administration in 1933. With George Peek's resignation in late 1933, Davis became the agency's director until 1935, when the Supreme Court found the Agricultural Adjustment Act unconstitutional. Roosevelt appointed Davis to the Board of Governors of the Federal Reserve System in 1936. In 1941 he became the president of the Federal Reserve Bank of St. Louis, a position he held until 1951. Davis served on the National Defense Advisory Committee in 1940. He became the war food administrator in 1943, only to resign after two months because of differences with Roosevelt's wartime economic policies, but later served as an adviser to the Office of War.

Dewey, Thomas E. (1902–1971 b. Owosso, Michigan)
District attorney, New York County, 1937–1941; governor of New York, 1943–1955

Dewey was a New York governor and the Republican candidate for president in both 1944 and 1948. In 1935 Herbert H. Lehman, the Democratic governor of New York, appointed Dewey as a special prosecutor to investigate racketeering, and while he was district attorney for New York County his successful prosecution of a criminal syndicate brought him national attention. In Dewey's 1944 campaign against Roosevelt, Dewey claimed that Roosevelt and his administration had grown old and tired in office, and he attacked the dangers of one-person rule. He also charged that the Roosevelt administration had sold out to the communists, and he emphasized growing communist influence in the world. Dewey received 99 electoral votes to Roosevelt's 432.

Dewson, Molly (Mary Williams) (1874–1962 b. Quincy, Massachusetts)
Director, Women's Division, Democratic National Committee, 1933–1937; member, Committee on Economic Security, 1934; member, Social Security Board, 1937–1938

At the request of Eleanor Roosevelt, Dewson joined Al Smith's 1928 campaign, and in 1932 she organized women voters for Franklin Roosevelt. A friend of both of the Roosevelts, she encouraged the president to appoint Frances Perkins as the first woman cabinet member in 1933. Dewson ran the Women's Division of the National Democratic Committee from 1933 to 1937, and by 1936 the women's division, which designed special campaign literature directed to women, had more than 80,000 active supporters. As a member of the Committee on Economic Security in 1934, Dewson contributed to the report that became the basis for the Social

Security Act of 1935, and she served on the Social Security Board from 1937 until 1938.

Douglas, William O. (1898–1980 b. Maine, Minnesota)
Member, Securities and Exchange Commission, 1936–1939 (chairman, 1937–1939); associate justice, U.S. Supreme Court, 1939–1975
Douglas first became involved in Roosevelt's administration when James Landis of the Securities and Exchange Commission (SEC) asked Douglas to head an SEC study of bankruptcy and business reorganization in 1934. Roosevelt appointed him as a commissioner of the SEC in 1936, and Douglas became the chairman of the SEC in 1937. In 1939 Roosevelt appointed Douglas to the Supreme Court, where he served for thirty-seven years. Roosevelt considered Douglas as a vice presidential candidate in both 1940 and 1944. While on the Supreme Court, Douglas was known for his unflagging defense of civil liberties and his support of liberal causes.

Early, Stephen T. (1889–1951 b. Crozet, Virginia)
Press secretary to FDR, 1932–1945
A reporter for the United Press Wire Services, Early was covering the Democratic Convention in Baltimore when he met Roosevelt in 1912. Later, as a reporter for the Associated Press, Early covered Roosevelt as assistant secretary of the navy. In the 1920 campaign Early served as Roosevelt's advance man. He returned to the news business after the election, but in 1932 Roosevelt asked Early to become press secretary, a new position in the world of politics. Early had a good relationship with the press corps. He established regular press conferences for the president, and ended the practice of requiring written questions. Even after the onset of World War II, Early encouraged Roosevelt to continue to hold press conferences.

Eccles, Marriner C. (1890–1977 b. Logan, Utah)
Assistant secretary of the Treasury, 1934; chairman, Board of Governors, Federal Reserve System, 1935–1948
Eccles was a Utah banker who attracted national attention after he successfully stopped a run on one of his banks in the early days of the Great Depression. He contributed to the Emergency Banking Act of 1933 and other legislation. In 1934 Roosevelt appointed Eccles as assistant secretary of the Treasury, and later that year appointed him to the Federal Reserve Board. The Banking Act of 1935, which reorganized the Federal Reserve, was based in part on a memorandum that Eccles wrote for Roosevelt in late 1934. Eccles became chairman of the Board of Governors of the reorganized Federal Reserve System in 1935. Eccles was convinced that underconsumption was a major cause of the depression and advocated public works programs and more government spending, especially during the economic slump of 1937 and 1938.

Eisenhower, Dwight D. (1890–1969 b. Dennison, Texas)
Special assistant to Gen. Douglas MacArthur, army chief of staff, 1933–1935; assistant military adviser, Philippine Commonwealth, 1935–1939; general staff, Washington, D.C., 1941–1942; chief, War Plans Division, Office of the Army Chief of Staff, 1942; commanding general, U.S. forces in Great Britain, June 1942; commander in chief, Allied forces, 1942; supreme commander, Allied Expeditionary Force in Western Europe, 1943–1945
Eisenhower served under Gen. Douglas MacArthur during most of the 1930s, first while MacArthur was army chief of staff and later in the Philippines. Gen. George Marshall recognized Eisenhower's talent and appointed him as chief of the War Plans Division in 1942. Eisenhower commanded the invasions of North Africa, Italy, and Sicily, and he was promoted to brigadier general and major general in 1943. As supreme commander of the Allied Expeditionary Force he commanded the D Day invasion of France in June 1944. He was awarded the rank of general of the army in 1944 and accepted the German surrender in 1945.

Ezekiel, Mordecai (1899–1974 b. Richmond, Virginia)
Economic adviser to the secretary of agriculture, 1933–1941; assistant to vice chairman of the War Production Board, 1942–1943
Ezekiel first joined the Department of Agriculture in 1922. He helped draft the Agricultural Adjustment Act in 1933 and served as an economic adviser to Secretary of Agriculture Henry Wallace until 1941. An economic theorist, Ezekiel believed that national economic planning was essential, and his vision for it incorporated a procedure whereby representatives of labor, business, government, and consumers would develop an expansion plan for a particular industry. Any such plan would be approved by an interindustry agency and central planning board. Ezekiel's plan also provided that the government would purchase unsold production, much as the government purchased excess agricultural products. The Industrial Expansion Bill, introduced in Congress in 1937, never received much support.

Farley, James A. (1888–1976 b. Rockland County, New York)
Chairman, New York Democratic Committee, 1930–1944; chairman, National Democratic Committee, 1932–1940; postmaster general, 1933–1940
Farley was the gregarious leader of the New York Democratic Party and an instrumental force in engineering Franklin Roosevelt's gubernatorial victory in 1928 and his presidential nomination and election in 1932. As a member of the Roosevelt cabinet and as the leader of the Democratic Party, Farley was a liaison for Democrats seeking political patronage and for the New Dealers, many of whom were new to government. Educated in the traditional world of organized party politics, Farley was slow to recognize the importance of coalition politics and dismissed the impact of groups such as women and organized labor. Farley ran Roosevelt's reelec-

tion campaign in 1936 but opposed a third term for Roosevelt and actively sought the Democratic nomination himself in 1940.

Flynn, Edward J. (1891–1953 b. New York City)
New York secretary of state, 1929–1933; regional administrator, National Recovery Administration, 1933–1935; chairman, National Democratic Committee, 1940–1942

Flynn was a New York Democrat and an early supporter of Roosevelt. Appointed chairman of the Bronx County Democratic Executive Committee in 1922, Flynn skillfully used the political machine in local and national elections. After serving as secretary of state of New York while Roosevelt was governor, Flynn became a regional administrator of the National Recovery Administration and served as a liaison between the Roosevelt administration and the political machines of New York and Chicago. When James Farley opposed Roosevelt's bid for a third term in 1940, Flynn took over as chairman of the National Democratic Committee. Flynn pushed for Truman's nomination as vice president in 1944.

Frankfurter, Felix (1882–1965 b. Vienna, Austria)
Associate justice, U.S. Supreme Court, 1939–1962

Frankfurter was an adviser to FDR during his governorship of New York and his presidency, both directly and through the intelligent young lawyers—sometimes called the "Little Hot Dogs"—whom he sent to Washington from Harvard Law School. Frankfurter encouraged FDR to use the government to combat big business, reverse the trend toward economic concentration, and encourage competition. He was distrustful of economic and social planning, and thus was critical of the NRA and much of the legislation passed in the first two years of the New Deal. The Securities Act of 1933, which required complete disclosure of material information by public companies, and the Public Utilities Holding Company Act, which curtailed the power of utility holding companies, are examples of legislation crafted by Frankfurter or his protégés. Roosevelt appointed Frankfurter to the Supreme Court in 1939.

Garner, John Nance (1868–1967 b. Red River County, Texas)
U.S. House of Representatives, Texas, 1903–1933; vice president, 1933–1941

Garner generally disapproved of big government, but he also opposed big business interests. In 1932 he joined with Sen. Robert Wagner, D-N.Y., to pass a public works program that President Hoover vetoed. Garner became Speaker of the House in 1931 and was a serious contender for the Democratic presidential nomination in 1932. After he threw his support to Roosevelt, he was awarded the vice presidential nomination. Garner was not a typical New Dealer, and believed that the depression was caused, in part, by the government's failure to maintain its traditional functions. Although his experience in Congress helped FDR get many early New Deal programs through the legislative process, by 1938 he opposed most of the president's legislation. Garner was not chosen as Roosevelt's running mate in 1940 and he retired from politics in 1941.

Gellhorn, Martha (1908–1998 b. St. Louis, Missouri)
Reporter and novelist; field investigator, Federal Emergency Relief Administration, 1934–1935
Gellhorn was an accomplished reporter and novelist and one of the first female war reporters. She worked as a correspondent for United Press International from France, and in 1934 returned to the United States to become an investigator for the Federal Emergency Relief Administration, at which time she became a close friend of Eleanor Roosevelt. By 1937 Gellhorn was reporting on the Spanish Civil War for *Collier's Weekly*. She wrote reports of Hitler's rising power in Germany and covered World War II in Finland and China. Lacking press credentials on D Day, she went ashore at Normandy as a stretcher bearer after smuggling aboard a hospital ship. Despite promises to cover the remainder of the war from behind the lines, she traveled through Europe and wrote about what she saw, often reporting on the misery created by war.

Glass, Carter (1858–1946 b. Lynchburg, Virginia)
U.S. Senate, Virginia, 1920–1946
Glass was elected to the U.S. House of Representatives as a Democrat from Virginia in 1902 and served there until he became Woodrow Wilson's secretary of the Treasury in 1919. While in the House he coauthored the Federal Reserve Act of 1913. He entered the Senate in 1920 and remained there until his death in 1946. He declined an offer to become Roosevelt's Treasury secretary in 1933, but sponsored the Glass-Steagall Act of 1933 that separated commercial and investment banking and provided for federal deposit insurance. Glass was distrustful of the growing power of the federal government during the New Deal years, however, and he spoke out for states' rights and a balanced budget during Roosevelt's second term.

Harriman, William Averill (1891–1986 b. New York City)
Administrator, Division II, National Recovery Administration, 1934; administrator, National Recovery Administration, 1934–1935; member, Business Advisery Council of the Dept. of Commerce, 1933–1940 (chair, 1937–1940); chief, Raw Materials Branch, Office of Production Management, 1941; ambassador to the Soviet Union, 1943–1946
Harriman was the chairman of the Board of Union Pacific when he became an administrator of the National Recovery Administration (NRA). After the demise

of the NRA, Harriman served as a member and chairman of the Business Advisory Council of the Department of Commerce, which was designed to promote cooperation between government and business. He later served in the Office of Production Management, and in 1941 Roosevelt sent Harriman as a personal representative to Great Britain to coordinate the Lend-Lease program. In 1943, during World War II, he was appointed ambassador to the Soviet Union and attended the conferences at Teheran and Yalta.

Hearst, William Randolph (1863–1951 b. San Francisco, California)
Newspaper publisher
One of the most influential newspaper publishers of the twentieth century, Hearst first took over the *San Francisco Examiner* in 1887 and filled its pages with idealism and sensationalism. Hearst moved to New York after acquiring the *New York Journal* and served New York as a Democrat in the U.S. House of Representatives from 1903 to 1907. When he failed to win election as governor of New York or as mayor of New York City, his career as a candidate ended. He remained active in politics, however, and apparently delivered votes to Roosevelt at the 1932 Democratic convention when John Nance Garner's delegates were released. During the 1930s Hearst turned against the New Deal, and his newspapers vehemently criticized Roosevelt. In 1936 Hearst and his newspapers threw their full support behind Alf Landon. As war loomed in Europe, Hearst was a leading isolationist.

Hickok, Lorena (1893–1968 b. East Troy, Wisconsin)
Field reporter, Federal Emergency Relief Administration and Works Progress Administration, 1933–1936; executive director, Women's Division, National Democratic Party, 1941–1945
Hickok was a reporter for the Associated Press in New York and by 1932 was the best-known female reporter in the United States. She covered Eleanor Roosevelt during the 1932 campaign, and they became close friends. Hickok became enamored with Mrs. Roosevelt and in 1933 Hickok resigned from the Associated Press in the interest of objectivity. She then took a job writing field reports for Harry Hopkins of the Federal Emergency Relief Administration from 1933 to 1936, and produced a valuable record of Works Progress Administration projects. In early 1941 she became executive director of the Women's Division of the Democratic Party and lived at the White House from 1941 until 1945.

Hillman, Sidney (1887–1946 b. Zagare, Lithuania)
President, Amalgamated Clothing Workers of America, 1915–1946; member, Labor Advisory Board, National Recovery Administration, 1933–1935; member, National Industrial Recovery Board, National Recovery Administration,

1934–1935; member, Advisory Board, National Youth Administration, 1935–1943; member, National Defense Advisory Committee, 1940; associate director, Office of Production Management, 1940–1942; director, Labor Division, War Production Board, 1942–1943

After immigrating to the United States in 1907, Hillman became a garment worker in Chicago and was the first president of the Amalgamated Clothing Workers of America. Originally a supporter of the Socialist Party, he supported Roosevelt in 1933. Hillman believed that unfettered competition hurt labor, and he strongly supported some sort of cooperative national economic planning; he served on the Labor Advisory Board to the National Recovery Administration beginning in 1933. Hillman, along with John L. Lewis, formed Labor's Non-Partisan League in 1936, which worked for Roosevelt's reelection. Unlike Lewis, however, Hillman supported FDR in 1940, and continued his work within the administration as a member of the National Defense Advisory Committee, Office of Production Management, and War Production Board. In 1944 he organized the Congress of Industrial Organizations Political Action Committee, which provided important support for Roosevelt in 1944.

Hopkins, Harry L. (1890–1946 b. Sioux City, Iowa)

Chief, New York Temporary Emergency Relief Administration, 1931–1933; chief, Federal Emergency Relief Administration, 1933–1938; director, Civil Works Administration, 1933–1934; director, Works Progress Administration, 1935–1938; secretary of commerce, 1938–1940; administrator, Lend-Lease Program, 1941; special assistant to the president, 1941–1945

Hopkins was a New York social worker before Roosevelt appointed him to run the Temporary Emergency Relief Administration in New York. As administrator of the Federal Emergency Relief Administration, Hopkins became perhaps the leading proponent of public relief works in the Roosevelt Administration during the New Deal years. Both the short-lived Civil Works Administration and the Works Progress Administration were public works projects designed to inject money into the economy quickly and to provide jobs for the unemployed. Hopkins believed that unemployment would be a continuing problem and that government should provide a permanent public works program, unemployment insurance, health insurance, and affordable housing. He served as secretary of commerce from 1938 to 1941, when he resigned to be a special assistant to the president. Although he had been involved almost exclusively in domestic affairs, Hopkins was one of Roosevelt's closest advisers on international matters before and after the United States' entry into World War II. Hopkins made missions on Roosevelt's behalf to London and Moscow, forging relationships with both Churchill and Stalin, and accompanied the president to Teheran and Yalta.

Howe, Louis M. (1871–1936 b. Indianapolis, Indiana)
Secretary to the president, 1933–1936
Roosevelt asked Howe to run his successful state senatorial reelection campaign in 1912, after which Howe became Roosevelt's closest political adviser and confidant. Howe had recognized FDR's presidential potential at their first meeting and worked tirelessly to secure his political success. In addition to his skills as a shrewd political operative, Howe, along with Eleanor Roosevelt, encouraged FDR to return to politics after he contracted polio. Howe also became a close friend of Eleanor Roosevelt and pushed her to become active in Democratic politics in the 1920s. Howe was one of the first campaigners to use large newspaper advertisements, and he developed an impressive form letter procedure that enabled Roosevelt to send "personal" letters to his supporters. Never healthy, Howe died in 1936 before Roosevelt was elected to his second term.

Hughes, Charles Evans (1862–1948 b. Glens Falls, New York)
Chief justice, U.S. Supreme Court, 1930–1941
Hughes served as governor of New York from 1907 to 1910, when he was appointed as an associate justice of the Supreme Court. He left the bench to pursue the presidency on the Republican ticket in 1916, and later served as secretary of state under Warren Harding and Calvin Coolidge. Hughes returned to the Supreme Court as chief justice in 1930. During the New Deal years, he wrote the *Schecter Poultry Co. v. United States* decision striking down the National Recovery Administration and joined with the majority in the *Butler* decision invalidating the Agricultural Adjustment Act. Although he opposed Roosevelt's attempt to pack the Court in 1937, he generally supported New Deal legislation after 1938.

Hull, Cordell (1871–1955 b. Overton [now Pickett] County, Tennessee)
Secretary of state, 1933–1944
Hull served as a representative and senator for Tennessee before his appointment as secretary of state in 1933. He had been an advocate of Woodrow Wilson and was a champion of internationalism in an age of U.S. isolationism. Hull had long believed that reducing tariffs would encourage world peace, and he pushed for passage of the Trade Agreements Act in 1934, which gave the executive the power to adjust tariffs reciprocally. He also helped Roosevelt develop the Good Neighbor policy for Latin America. Hull urged intervention in the European war after 1939 and supported U.S. aid to the Allies. During World War II he encouraged the establishment of a world organization and was a delegate for the United States at the United Nations conference in San Francisco in 1945. He retired from his cabinet post in 1944 because of failing health. Hull received the Nobel Peace Prize in 1945.

Ickes, Harold L. (1874–1952 b. Blair County, Pennsylvania)

Secretary of the interior, 1933–1946; director, Public Works Administration, 1933–1939

Ickes, a Chicago newspaperman and lawyer, was a strong supporter of Theodore Roosevelt and the Progressive Party in 1912. Although he was a Republican, he supported Franklin Roosevelt in 1932 and was named secretary of the interior in 1933, a position he held for thirteen years. An early proponent of public spending, Ickes believed that it was important that public works projects be useful, and the PWA contracted with private builders to create large-scale public works such as roads, dams, government buildings, and power plants. Although Ickes distrusted business and believed that comprehensive national planning was required to bring about a better economic system, he criticized the National Recovery Administration as promoting monopoly. Ickes also worked to make the Interior Department a defender of public lands, and he attempted to bring more conservation programs under his control. During World War II Ickes was responsible for managing the nation's fuel resources. Ickes had a reputation as an outspoken man, and his *Secret Diary* provides historians with a detailed, albeit opinionated, view of the Roosevelt administrations.

Jackson, Robert H. (1892–1954 b. Spring Creek, Pennsylvania)

General counsel, Bureau of Internal Revenue, 1934; special counsel, Securities and Exchange Commission, 1935; assistant attorney general, Tax Division, 1936; assistant attorney general, Antitrust Division, 1937; U.S. solicitor general, 1938–1940; U.S. attorney general, 1940–1941; associate justice, U.S. Supreme Court, 1941–1954

Jackson was a member of the commission on the New York judicial system when Roosevelt was governor of New York. After participating in the 1932 campaign, Jackson served in several government legal positions. He led the investigation against former secretary of the Treasury Andrew Mellon for income tax evasion, and while in the Antitrust Division he instigated widely publicized antitrust actions. As solicitor general, Jackson handled many cases dealing with the constitutionality of New Deal legislation, and as attorney general he worked on the destroyers-for-bases deal with Great Britain. Appointed to the Supreme Court in 1941, he left temporarily in 1946 to become the chief prosecutor at the Nuremberg trials.

Johnson, Hugh S. (1882–1942 b. Fort Scott, Kansas)

Director, National Recovery Administration (NRA), 1933–1934

General Johnson, a West Point graduate, served in the U.S. Army until 1919. Because of his experience with the War Industries Board during World War I, in 1933 Raymond Moley asked Johnson to work on the proposed legislation that became the National Industrial Recovery Act (NIRA). Roosevelt appointed

Johnson as the head of the new National Recovery Administration (NRA). Generally sympathetic to business interests but distrustful of unfettered competition, Johnson spearheaded the campaign to obtain voluntary agreements from businesses to abide by the policies of the NIRA. He also created the highly visible Blue Eagle campaign to support and publicize the NRA. By 1934 his influence in the administration was waning, partly because of criticism by other New Dealers of his tight control over all aspects of the NRA and the perception that the NRA codes encouraged monopoly.

Jones, Jesse H. (1874–1956 b. Robertson County, Tennessee)
Member, Reconstruction Finance Corporation, 1928–1939 (chairman, 1933–1939); federal loan administrator, 1939–1945; secretary of commerce, 1940–1945
Jones was a Texas banker and businessman who personally paid off the Democratic Party's debt after the 1924 election. Herbert Hoover named Jones to the Reconstruction Finance Corporation (RFC) in 1929. After Roosevelt became president, Jones was named chairman of the RFC and the agency became more active, expanding credit availability and stabilizing the banking industry. In 1939 Jones became federal loan administrator, a position that controlled not only the RFC but also other federal credit sources. When he became secretary of commerce in 1940, Jones retained the title of federal loan administrator by special act of Congress. During the war, he created entities to facilitate the supply and distribution of needed materials. Jones resigned from all positions in 1945.

Kennedy, Joseph P. (1888–1969 b. Boston, Massachusetts)
Chairman, Securities and Exchange Commission, 1934–1935; chairman, U.S. Maritime Commission, 1935–1938; ambassador to the Court of St. James, 1938–1940
Kennedy was a wealthy businessman and a major contributor to the Democratic Party. In 1934 Roosevelt appointed Kennedy chairman of the newly formed Securities and Exchange Commission (SEC). He left the SEC in 1935 and became the chairman of the U.S. Maritime Commission. In 1938 Kennedy became ambassador to Great Britain, a post he held until late 1940. While Kennedy was in Great Britain, Roosevelt recognized the ambassador's pessimism about the ability of Great Britain to withstand the German onslaught and his perceived acceptance of Hitler's Germany. Kennedy opposed Roosevelt's decision to run for a third term.

Keyserling, Leon (1908–1987 b. Charleston, South Carolina)
Attorney, Department of Agriculture, 1933; assistant to Sen. Robert Wagner, D-N.Y., 1933–1937; general counsel, deputy administrator and acting administrator, United States Housing Authority, 1938–1942; general counsel, National Housing Agency, 1942–1946

Keyserling joined the legal staff of the Agricultural Adjustment Administration in 1933. The same year Sen. Robert Wagner of New York asked Keyserling to be his legislative assistant. In this position Keyserling drafted Section 7a of the National Industrial Recovery Act (later Section 7a of the National Labor Relations Act). Keyserling also worked on the development and drafting of the Social Security Act, the U.S. Housing Act, and the National Labor Relations Act (Wagner Act), and he drafted much of the Democratic platforms of 1936, 1940, and 1944. During World War II Keyserling administered the program to provide government housing for war workers.

Knox, Frank R. (1874–1944 b. Boston, Massachusetts)
Republican candidate for vice president, 1936; secretary of the navy, 1940–1944
Knox, a Republican businessman, had ridden with the Rough Riders in the Spanish-American War and had supported Theodore Roosevelt's campaign in 1912. Knox was the general manager of several of William Randolph Hearst's newspapers by 1927. As the publisher of the *Chicago Daily News,* he vehemently criticized Franklin Roosevelt's New Deal policies. An important fundraiser for the Republican Party, Knox was chosen as the vice presidential candidate to run with Alfred Landon in 1936. Openly interventionist in the late 1930s, Knox had advocated the development of a two-ocean navy before he entered government service. Roosevelt appointed Knox secretary of the navy in 1940 at the same time he appointed Republican Henry Stimson secretary of war, thus creating a bipartisan cabinet. Knox oversaw an unprecedented naval development during World War II. He died in office in 1944.

LaFollette, Philip F. *(1897–1965 b. Madison, Wisconsin)*
Governor of Wisconsin, 1931–1939
LaFollette was the son of Robert M. LaFollette of Wisconsin and the brother of Robert M. LaFollette Jr. LaFollette managed his brother's successful congressional campaign in 1925 and in 1930 was elected governor of Wisconsin as a progressive Republican. LaFollette campaigned against monopolies and political corruption, and legislation passed during his terms as governor included a collective bargaining code for labor, an old-age pension, and regulation of public utilities. In 1934 LaFollette formed the Wisconsin Progressive Party with his brother Robert and won reelection. Roosevelt allowed LaFollette to administer the WPA federal relief program in Wisconsin. The National Progressives of America, organized in 1938, were not successful, and LaFollette lost the 1938 gubernatorial election. An ardent noninterventionist, LaFollette did not support Roosevelt in 1940.

LaFollette, Robert M. Jr. (1895–1953 b. Madison, Wisconsin)
U.S. Senate, Wisconsin, 1925–1947

LaFollette was elected to the Senate in 1925 as a Republican and was reelected in 1934 and 1940 as a member of the Wisconsin Progressive Party. While in Congress he worked to pass legislation dealing with labor, farm relief, and unemployment compensation. LaFollette worked with senators Robert Wagner and Edward Costigan to draft the Federal Emergency Relief Act in 1933. In 1936 LaFollette served as the chairman of the Senate Civil Liberties Committee that investigated antiunion activities, wages, and working conditions. A supporter of New Deal legislation, he opposed U.S. membership in the World Court (a nearly powerless institution associated with the League of Nations), the amendment of the Neutrality Acts, and the establishment of the Lend-Lease program.

LaGuardia, Fiorella H. (1882–1947 b. New York City)

Mayor, New York City, 1935–1945; director, Office of Civilian Defense, 1941–1942; coordinator, U.S.–Canadian Joint Defense Committee, 1940–1946
LaGuardia was the colorful and popular mayor of New York from 1935 to 1945. Although a Republican, he was elected to office on a Fusion ticket and supported most New Deal programs. While serving in the U.S. House of Representatives (1923–1933), he supported old-age pensions and unemployment insurance, and, with George Norris, sponsored the Norris-LaGuardia Anti-Injunction Act in 1932. As mayor, he supported labor and established public works programs. In 1941 Roosevelt appointed LaGuardia as director of the Office of Civilian Defense, which was designed to involve civilians in the war effort.

Landon, Alfred M. (1887–1987 b. West Middlesex, Pennsylvania)

Governor, Kansas, 1933–1937; Republican candidate for president, 1936; vice chairman, U.S. Delegation to Inter-American Conference, Lima, Peru, 1938
Landon was a moderate Kansas Republican best known for his run against Roosevelt in the 1936 presidential election. When Landon won election as Kansas governor in 1932, he was seen as a politician who could work with members of both parties. He believed in economy and efficiency in government, and although he opposed many New Deal measures, he thought that some businesses, such as insurance companies and utilities, should be subject to some government regulation. The Republicans nominated Landon as their presidential candidate in 1936, but faced with Roosevelt's immense popularity, Landon received only eight electoral votes. After the election Landon was the titular head of the Republican Party and continued to speak out against Roosevelt, but he did support the president in some foreign policy matters. By 1941, however, Landon believed that Roosevelt was maneuvering to get the United States into the European war.

Leahy, William D. (1875–1959 b. Hampton, Iowa)

Chief, Bureau of Navigation, U.S. Navy, 1933–1937; chief of naval operations, 1937–1939; governor, Puerto Rico, 1939–1940; ambassador to Vichy France, 1941–1942; chairman, Joint Chiefs of Staff, 1942–1949

Admiral Leahy had served as an aide to Secretary of the Navy Josephus Daniels when Roosevelt was assistant secretary of the navy. As chief of naval operations in the late 1930s, Leahy worked to get higher congressional appropriations for the navy. When he reached the mandatory retirement age of sixty-five in 1939, he became governor of Puerto Rico and later was sent to Vichy France; however, Leahy was recalled to the United States in protest over the increasing power of the pro-Nazi faction in the Vichy government. In 1942 Roosevelt appointed him chairman of the newly created Joint Chiefs of Staff and also as Roosevelt's personal chief of staff. Later Leahy served on the British-American Combined Chiefs of Staff and was the first naval officer to be awarded the rank of fleet admiral.

LeHand, Marguerite ("Missy") (1898–1944 b. Potsdam, New York)
Private secretary to FDR, 1921–1941
Originally hired by Roosevelt to organize his correspondence after the unsuccessful Democratic presidential campaign of 1920, LeHand's duties expanded after he contracted polio. LeHand was Roosevelt's close companion and was regarded as a "second wife" by his friends and associates, acting as FDR's hostess when Eleanor was away. She often arranged dinner parties and other social gatherings for the president, picking the guest list and thereby influencing Roosevelt's contact with people and ideas. In addition, LeHand's attentiveness to FDR allowed Eleanor Roosevelt to maintain her independent lifestyle.

Lehman, Herbert H. (1878–1963 b. New York City)
Lieutenant governor, New York, 1929–1933; governor, New York, 1933–1942; head, Office of Foreign Relief and Rehabilitation Operations, 1942–1943; director general, U.N. Relief and Rehabilitation Administration, 1943–1946
Lehman was active in social work before he became involved in Democratic politics in New York. Lehman served as Roosevelt's lieutenant governor and became governor in 1933. Although not as charismatic as Roosevelt, Lehman was committed to social reform and designed the "Little New Deal" in New York. Lehman resigned as governor in 1942 to accept a position with the Office of Foreign Relief and Rehabilitation Operations, which provided food, clothing, and other supplies to northern Africa and the Middle East. In 1943 he took the position of director general of the Relief and Rehabilitation Agency, an organization providing aid to countries after the Axis powers were defeated. Lehman later served as U.S. senator from New York.

Lewis, John L. (1880–1969 b. Lucas County, Iowa)
President, United Mine Workers, 1920–1960; president, Congress of Industrial Organizations, 1938–1940
Lewis was an influential labor leader during the 1930s and 1940s and was instrumental in the organization of the mass production sector of laborers. Lewis and other labor leaders formed the Committee for Industrial Organizations (CIO)

within the American Federation of Labor (AFL) in 1935, and, along with Sidney Hillman, created Labor's Nonpartisan League in 1936. In 1938 the CIO formally split with the AFL and became the Congress of Industrial Organizations. Lewis broke with Roosevelt in 1937 during a steel strike and worked against FDR in the 1940 election. Lewis and Roosevelt continued to clash during World War II, when Lewis ordered coal miners to strike three times and each time Roosevelt ordered the strikers back to work. Nonetheless, Lewis did obtain some monetary concessions for miners during the war.

Lilienthal, David E. (1899–1981 b. Morton, Illinois)
Director, Tennessee Valley Authority, 1933–1941; chairman of the board, Tennessee Valley Authority, 1941–1946
Roosevelt appointed Lilienthal, along with Arthur E. Morgan and Harcourt A. Morgan, to the board of directors of the newly formed Tennessee Valley Authority (TVA) in 1933. Lilienthal saw the TVA as a business to be managed and owned by the people of the region it served, and he thought that power produced by the TVA should be distributed locally and directly at a low price. After World War II he became chairman of the U.S. Atomic Energy Commission.

Long, Huey P. (1893–1935 b. Winn Parish, Louisiana)
Governor, Louisiana, 1929–1932; U.S. Senate, Louisiana, 1931–1935
Long was a flamboyant Louisiana politician who dominated his state's politics in the early 1930s. Long promoted himself as the champion of the common man. After his election as governor in 1928, Long spent public money on roads, bridges, hospitals, and schools, as well as the state university in Baton Rouge, but supported few other political reforms. Known as the "Kingfish," he created a powerful political machine and had enormous power in the state. A critic of Herbert Hoover, Long advocated redistribution of wealth and supported Roosevelt in 1932, but he found New Deal programs too cautious and soon began to criticize the new president and his advisers. Elected to the Senate in 1930—although he did not give up his position as governor until 1932—Long had presidential aspirations. He publicized his Share Our Wealth Plan, characterized by high income and estate taxes and minimum guaranteed incomes. In September 1935 Long was shot to death in the Louisiana capitol by the son of one his political opponents.

MacArthur, Douglas (1880–1964 b. Little Rock, Arkansas)
Army chief of staff, 1930–1935; military adviser to the Philippines, 1935–1937; commander of U.S. Army forces in the Far East, 1941; commander of Allied forces in the Southwest Pacific, 1942–1944; commander, army forces in the Pacific, 1945
MacArthur was appointed army chief of staff by Herbert Hoover in 1930 and was criticized for his use of force in handling the Bonus Army (unemployed World War I veterans who had come to Washington seeking early payment of a bonus) in

1932. Although he retired from the army in 1937 after serving in the Philippines, he was recalled to active duty in 1941. Roosevelt gave MacArthur command of army forces in the Far East in 1941, and after the surrender of the Philippines to Japan he directed U.S. and Australian forces in the South Pacific. MacArthur returned to the Philippines in 1944, and was promoted to the rank of general of the army (five star general) in 1945. MacArthur accepted the Japanese surrender in 1945 and became the supreme commander of the Allied occupation forces in Japan.

Marshall, George C. (1880–1959 b. Uniontown, Pennsylvania)
Chief of staff, U.S. Army, 1939–1945
Marshall was a career military officer who had served as chief of operations of the First Army in World War I. During the early years of the New Deal, Marshall organized some Civilian Conservation Corps (CCC) camps in his position as an army officer, but had little contact with the Roosevelt administration. In 1939 Roosevelt asked Marshall to be chief of staff of the army. Marshall was responsible for the reorganization and mobilization of the army in the years before and during World War II. In addition, he took an active role in selecting the officer corps, often bypassing more senior officers for those he thought would be more effective, and was Roosevelt's most important strategic military adviser in fighting the global war. Later, Marshall served Truman as both secretary of state and secretary of defense, and is best known for his development of the Marshall Plan to aid in the postwar reconstruction of Europe.

Maverick, Maury (1895–1954 b. San Antonio, Texas)
U.S. House of Representatives, Texas, 1935–1939; mayor, San Antonio, Texas, 1940–1942; member, Office of Price Administration, 1941–1942; member, Office of Production Management (later War Management Board), 1942–1944; head, Smaller War Plants Corporation, 1944–1946
Maverick was elected to the U.S. House of Representatives as a Texas Democrat in 1934 and supported most New Deal programs. The organizer of a group of House liberals known as the "mavericks," he supported civil rights and antilynching legislation. He lost his seat in the 1938 election, but in 1939 he was elected mayor of San Antonio with support from Mexican Americans. After he failed to win reelection as mayor in 1941, Roosevelt appointed Maverick to the Office of Price Administration, and then to the Office of Production Management. In the later days of World War II Maverick was head of the Smaller War Plants Corporation, an agency of the Reconstruction Finance Corporation that promoted the use of smaller companies for war materials.

McIntyre, Marvin (1878–1943 b. LaGrange, Kentucky)
Assistant secretary to the president, 1933–1936; secretary to the president, 1936–1943

McIntyre was a press liaison for the Navy Department when Roosevelt was assistant secretary of the navy during the Woodrow Wilson administration. In 1920 McIntyre handled publicity for Roosevelt when he was the vice presidential candidate. McIntyre returned to the Roosevelt campaign in 1932. He became an assistant secretary to the president in charge of appointments after Roosevelt became president, and after the death of Louis Howe he was named secretary to the president; however, McIntyre never became as important a political adviser to Roosevelt as Howe had been.

Moley, Raymond B. (1886–1975 b. Berea, Ohio)
Assistant secretary of state, 1933
Moley was a leading member of FDR's brain trust. A Columbia professor specializing in criminal justice, he was a dominant force in the 1932 presidential campaign and in the weeks between the election and Roosevelt's inauguration. Moley was an impresario of political and intellectual talent and was instrumental in attracting other scholars to FDR's campaign and first administration. He also had a talent for brokering competing ideas, and he drafted some of Roosevelt's speeches. Moley believed that economic recovery required cooperation between government and business, and he advocated trade associations and self-governance by business groups. An economic nationalist, Moley clashed with Secretary of State Cordell Hull and resigned from the State Department in 1933. He continued to give informal advice to Roosevelt until 1936. More conservative than many of the original New Dealers, he criticized FDR and the New Deal in his later writings, notably his scathing 1939 assessment, *After Seven Years*.

Morgenthau, Henry Jr. (1891–1967 b. New York City)
Chairman, New York Agricultural Advisery Committee, 1929; conservation commissioner, New York State, 1930–1933; chairman, Federal Farm Board, 1933; governor, Farm Credit Administration, 1933; acting and undersecretary of Treasury, 1933–1934; secretary of Treasury, 1934–1945
After becoming governor of New York, Roosevelt appointed Morgenthau, an owner and editor of an eastern farm journal, as chairman of the state's Agricultural Advisory Committee and as conservation commissioner. When Roosevelt became president, Morgenthau ran the Farm Credit Administration but became acting secretary of Treasury in late 1933. Fiscally conservative, Morgenthau favored a balanced budget and controlled federal spending, but recognized the need for federal spending and relief programs. During World War II Morgenthau set up a system for the sale of war bonds that raised money for the war effort. In 1944 he served as chairman of the Bretton Woods conference that set up the International Monetary Fund and the World Bank. Morgenthau resigned from the cabinet after Roosevelt's death.

Murphy, Frank (1890–1949 b. Harbor Beach, Michigan)

Mayor, Detroit, 1931–1933; governor general, Philippines, 1933–1935; U.S. high commissioner to the Philippines, 1935–1936; governor, Michigan, 1936–1938; U.S. attorney general, 1939–1940; associate justice, U.S. Supreme Court, 1940–1949

Murphy, a strong supporter of Al Smith in the 1928 election, became mayor of Detroit in 1931, where he established city relief programs. He supported Roosevelt in 1932 and in 1933 resigned to take an appointment in the Philippines. Murphy was elected governor of Michigan in 1936 and while governor worked to facilitate an agreement between General Motors and the United Auto Workers to end a 1937 strike. As attorney general, Murphy created a civil liberties division in the Justice Department and led the investigation that culminated in the conviction of Thomas "Boss" Pendergast of Missouri. Roosevelt appointed Murphy to the Supreme Court in 1940.

Nelson, Donald M. (1888–1959 b. Hannibal, Missouri)

Head, National Defense Advisery Committee, 1940–1941; head, Division of Purchases, Office of Production Management, 1941–1942; head, Supply, Priorities, and Allocation Board, 1941; head, War Production Board, 1942–1944

Nelson, an executive vice president of Sears, Roebuck & Co., had been generally supportive of New Deal policies. In 1940 Roosevelt asked him to head the newly created National Defense Advisery Committee (NDAC). By 1941 the NDAC was replaced by the Office of Production Management, and Nelson was the head of its Division of Supply Priorities and Allocation Board. In January 1942 Nelson was appointed head of the War Production Board, which oversaw economic mobilization, the economic conversion to wartime production, and the allocation of materials. In 1944 he clashed with the military over the need to shift to consumer production and was forced out of office.

Norris, George (1896–1988 b. Windham, Connecticut)

U.S. Senate, Nebraska, 1913–1943

Norris was elected to the Senate in 1912 as a Republican. Norris's interests included labor, agriculture, and public utilities. He supported Al Smith's candidacy in 1928 and endorsed Roosevelt in 1932. Norris was reelected to the Senate in 1936 as an Independent Progressive. He supported most New Deal legislation and he worked with Roosevelt to develop the Tennessee Valley Authority (TVA). Norris also sponsored the Rural Electrification Act, which, like the TVA, reflected Norris's belief that utility production and distribution should be publicly owned. Although Norris was identified as an isolationist after World War I, he supported Roosevelt's request to enlarge the navy in 1938 and supported Lend-Lease legislation. Norris was defeated in the 1942 election.

Olson, Floyd B. (1891–1936 b. Minneapolis, Minnesota)
Governor of Minnesota, 1931–1936
Olson won the Minnesota gubernatorial election in 1930 on the Farmer-Labor Association ticket. He had been active in Minnesota politics before he became governor, and as the county attorney for Hennepin County he had investigated the Ku Klux Klan and prosecuted companies accused of price fixing. As governor his agenda included expansion of public works, securities regulation, and public relief programs. Despite his sympathy for labor and his background as a member of the International Workers of the World, when truckers called a strike in 1934 Olson declared martial law to force the strikers to mediate. Nonetheless, in the same year Olson was promoting the abolition of capitalism and common ownership of the means of production.

Pecora, Ferdinand (1882–1971 b. Nicosia, Sicily, Italy)
Counsel to Senate Banking and Currency Committee, 1933–1934; member, Securities and Exchange Commission, 1934–1935; New York Supreme Court, 1935–1965
Pecora immigrated to New York as a child in 1887. He served as assistant district attorney for New York from 1918 until 1930, and was known for his investigation and prosecution of "bucket shops"—cut-rate securities brokers that made it easy for people to buy stocks on very small margin—and stock fraud. In 1933 he was appointed chief counsel to the Senate Banking and Currency Committee's investigation of Wall Street practices. Known as the Pecora Committee, it was a high profile investigation into questionable practices by Wall Street firms and influenced the formulation of legislation such as the Glass-Steagall Banking Act of 1933, the Securities Act of 1933, and the Public Utility Holding Act of 1935. Pecora was appointed to a one-year term on the Securities and Exchange Commission in 1934 but resigned when New York governor Lehman appointed him to the state's supreme court.

Perkins, Frances C. (1880–1965 b. Boston, Massachusetts)
Executive secretary, New York Consumer's League, 1910–1912; executive secretary, New York Committee on Safety, 1912–1917; member and chairman, New York State Industrial Board, 1923–1929; industrial commissioner of New York, 1929–1933; secretary of labor, 1933–1945
Perkins was the first woman appointed to a cabinet position in the United States. She worked at Hull House in Chicago before becoming the executive secretary of the New York Consumers League. She served as a lobbyist in Albany and educated New York politicians, including Al Smith and Robert Wagner, about industrial working conditions for the poor. While governor of New York, Roosevelt appointed her industrial commissioner. As secretary of labor, Perkins was more

interested in working conditions than in labor organization. In addition to legislation that improved the lives of workers, such as minimum wage and maximum hours laws, Perkins supported federal old-age and unemployment insurance and worked to pass the Social Security Act in 1935. Perkins also worked for passage of the Fair Labor Standards Act, which finally became law in 1938.

Randolph, A. Philip (1889–1979 b. Crescent City, Florida)
Labor and civil rights leader; president, National Negro Congress, 1935–1940
Randolph was an influential civil rights leader who sought to link organized labor to the fight for racial equality. An African American, Randolph founded the Brotherhood of Sleeping Car Porters (BSCP) in 1925. By 1935 the BSCP was chartered by the American Federation of Labor; in 1937 it was awarded the first contract to a predominantly black union. In his magazine, *Black Worker*, Randolph exhorted black Americans to own homes, send their children to college, and support civil rights. In 1941 he planned a march on Washington, D.C., to protest racial discrimination in defense jobs, and by summer 1941 his March on Washington Movement had organized rallies in several cities. He agreed to call off the march when Roosevelt issued Executive Order 8802, which created a temporary wartime Fair Employment Practices Administration. After the war Randolph continued his efforts to integrate the military.

Reuther, Walter B. (1907–1970 b. Wheeling, West Virginia)
Executive board, United Auto Workers, 1936–1970
Labor leader Reuther was active in labor education and Socialist Party politics in Michigan beginning in the 1920s. In 1936 he was one of the organizers of the United Auto Workers (UAW), and in 1937 he conducted a successful sit-down strike at General Motors. Reuther broke with the Socialist Party in 1938 and supported Roosevelt in both 1940 and 1944. He also was a close friend of Eleanor Roosevelt, and she admired his idea to convert the War Production Board into a "peace production board" to oversee the economy's conversion from wartime production. In 1940 Reuther proposed a plan whereby leaders of government, industry, and labor would administer an aircraft production board, which would have effectively given the federal government control over production during World War II.

Richberg, Donald R. (1881–1960 b. Knoxville, Tennessee)
General counsel, National Recovery Administration, 1933–1935
Richberg was general counsel for the Railway Labor Executives Association from 1926 until 1933. Richberg worked on the draft of the Norris-LaGuardia Act in 1932, and supported Roosevelt's bid for the presidency. Richberg believed that labor and business should be free to settle disputes without government interfer-

ence, and that labor could be adequately protected by access to the courts and collective bargaining. As general counsel of the National Recovery Administration (NRA), he ruled that Section 7(a) of the National Industrial Recovery Act, ensuring the right to bargain with employers, applied not only to labor organizations but also to individuals, thus permitting open shops and company unions under the NRA. Richberg effectively became director of the NRA after Gen. Hugh Johnson resigned in 1934 and stayed in that position until the agency's demise in 1935. After returning to private practice he wrote books attacking the increased power of organized labor.

Robinson, Joseph T. (1872–1937 b. Lonoke, Arkansas)
U.S. Senate, Arkansas, 1913–1937
Robinson was a member of the U.S. House of Representatives when he was elected governor in 1912; however, in January 1913 Robinson sought and won election to the Senate, and had the distinction of being a congressman, a senator, and a governor for ten days in 1913. A Wilsonian Democrat, Robinson was Al Smith's running mate in 1928. He became the Senate majority leader in 1932 and, although he was more conservative than Roosevelt, he became one of the president's most loyal allies in Congress. While in the Senate he joined with Wright Patman of Texas to sponsor the Robinson-Patman Act of 1936, which eliminated price discrimination by suppliers to large and small businesses. Robinson spearheaded Roosevelt's attempt to modify the Supreme Court in 1937, and was the dominant force behind a compromise measure.

Roosevelt, (Anna) Eleanor (1884–1962 b. New York City)
First lady, 1933–1945; assistant director of the Office of Civil Defense 1941–1942
Eleanor Roosevelt became a first lady unlike any other, writing a weekly syndicated newspaper column called "My Day," holding press conferences for women reporters, and traveling throughout the country. She was both loved and hated by the American people. Eleanor was more committed to social reform than her politically astute husband, and often pressed him to do what she believed was right; she championed rights for women and minorities and was committed to many of the early New Deal projects. After the United States entered World War II, Eleanor was particularly interested in the advances made by women in the workplace and pressed for more equitable treatment for African American servicemen.

She was an important component of Roosevelt's presidency and he clearly valued her opinion. She was named assistant director of the Office of Civil Defense in 1941, marking the first time a first lady had an official government appointment. She had to resign this post because of public and congressional criticism.

Rosenman, Samuel I. (1896–1973 b. San Antonio, Texas)
Counsel to the governor, 1929–1932; justice, New York supreme court, 1932–1943; special counsel to the president, 1943–1946

Rosenman began writing speeches for Roosevelt when Rosenman served Roosevelt as counsel to the governor. Roosevelt appointed Rosenman to New York's supreme court in 1932, but Rosenman still worked on the 1932 campaign and was instrumental in establishing Roosevelt's brain trust. In 1936 Roosevelt asked Rosenman to work as his primary speechwriter. Rosenman continued to work with Roosevelt after the 1936 election but held no formal position with the administration until Roosevelt appointed him as special counsel to the president in 1943. At the time of Roosevelt's death, Rosenman was trying to get relief to Europe and was laying the groundwork for an international tribunal to try war criminals after the war.

Rutherfurd, Lucy Mercer (1891[?]–1948 b. Washington, D.C.)
Social secretary to Eleanor Roosevelt, 1913–1918
Mercer was Eleanor Roosevelt's social secretary while FDR was assistant secretary of the navy. In 1918 Eleanor discovered that her husband was having an affair with Lucy. The Roosevelts did not divorce and the affair apparently ended, although FDR continued to see Mercer at times in later years. She later married Winthrop Rutherfurd, who died in 1944. After her husband's death, Roosevelt asked his daughter Anna to arrange for Lucy to meet with him again. They had several visits before the final one in April 1945, when he died at Warm Springs, Georgia.

Smith, Alfred E. (1873–1944 b. New York City)
Governor, New York, 1919–1921, 1923–1929
Smith, a leader in New York Democratic politics, is best known as the first Roman Catholic presidential candidate for a major political party. A Tammany Hall politician, Smith served in the New York legislature before becoming governor in 1919. Smith believed that government could be used to promote social change, and created a commission to study the reconstruction and reorganization of state government. While governor, Smith supported legislation for better housing, child welfare, and improved industrial working conditions, and his constituency included ethnic groups and women. Smith was a favorite for the Democratic presidential nomination in 1924, but after a bitter struggle between Smith and William McAdoo, John Davis was nominated as a compromise. Finally nominated by the Democrats in 1928, Smith faced serious opposition as an urban, anti-Prohibition Roman Catholic, and was defeated by Herbert Hoover. Smith had encouraged Roosevelt to reenter active politics and run for governor in 1928. However, Roosevelt's independence as governor created a rift between the men. Although Smith supported Roosevelt in 1932, he was critical of the New Deal and endorsed Alfred Landon, the Republican candidate, in 1936.

Stettinius, Edward R. Jr. (1900–1949 b. Chicago, Illinois)
Member, National Defense Advisory Committee, 1940–1941; priorities director, Office of Production Management, 1941–1942; Lend-Lease administra-

tor, 1941–1943; under secretary of state, 1943–1944; secretary of state, 1944–1945

Stettinius first worked with the Roosevelt administration as a member of the Industrial Advisory Council of the National Recovery Administration and as a member of the Business Advisory Council of the Department of Commerce in the 1930s. Stettinius was chairman of the board of U.S. Steel in 1940 when he resigned to become a member of the National Defense Advisory Commission (NDAC). He later served as priorities director of the Office of Production Management, which replaced the NDAC. As undersecretary of state, he attended the Dumbarton Oaks conference, where the three Allied powers discussed the framework of a postwar international organization. After replacing Cordell Hull as secretary of state in 1944, Stettinius was a participant in the Yalta conference. Stettinius resigned from the cabinet in June 1945. He also served as chairman of the U.S. delegation to the San Francisco conference of the United Nations.

Stimson, Henry L. (1867–1950 b. New York City)
Secretary of war, 1940–1945

Stimson had a long political career and served both Republican and Democratic presidents. He unsuccessfully ran for governor of New York in 1910, the same year Roosevelt was first elected to the New York legislature. He served as secretary of war in the Taft administration and as secretary of state for Herbert Hoover. He met with Roosevelt several times after the 1932 election to discuss ongoing international affairs and served as a liaison between Hoover and Roosevelt. Stimson advocated support for the Allied cause after 1939, and Roosevelt appointed him secretary of war before the 1940 election, in part to gain bipartisan support. Stimson worked to organize the war effort, and after the United States entered the war he advocated a direct invasion of Germany through France. In addition, Stimson became Roosevelt's primary adviser on the development of the atomic bomb. He resigned in 1945.

Thomas, Norman M. (1884–1968 b. Marion, Ohio)
Leader, American Socialist Party, 1926–1968

Thomas joined the American Socialist Party in 1918 and was the party's presidential candidate in every election from 1928 to 1948. A supporter of child labor laws, wages and hours legislation, public works programs, and economic planning, as well as public ownership of the economy, Thomas also was concerned about the effects of racism in U.S. society. Distrustful of most New Deal measures, Thomas probably underestimated Roosevelt's skill at taking ideas that appealed to Thomas's constituency and incorporating them into a mainstream agenda. A pacifist, Thomas founded the Keep America Out of War Committee, but gave limited support to the war effort after the bombing of Pearl Harbor. During the war Thomas spoke out against Japanese internment and called for racial equality. Critical of Stalin and the Soviet Union, he also warned that it was important that the United States defeat both fascism and communism.

Townsend, Francis E. (1867–1960 b. Fairbury, Illinois)
Creator of the "Townsend Plan"

Townsend was a California physician who created the popular "Townsend Plan." In 1933 Dr. Townsend, a man in his sixties who had lost his medical practice, wrote a letter to a newspaper and proposed a federal pension of $200 a month for every citizen over sixty on the condition that the recipient spend the money within sixty days. The program was to be funded by a "turnover tax" on each business trans-action. By January 1934 more than 3,000 local "Townsend Clubs" existed, and by mid-1935 Townsend Clubs had over two million members nationwide. The basic concept of an old age pension was not unique, as many New Dealers had pushed for the creation of government retirement benefits, but the rapid rise of the Townsend Clubs demonstrated the popularity of the idea. The Social Security Act of 1935, although very different from the Townsend Plan, effectively stifled the growth of Townsend's movement.

Truman, Harry S. (1884–1972 b. Lamar, Missouri)
U.S. Senate, Missouri, 1935–1945; vice president, 1945; president, 1945–1953

Truman was a supporter of most New Deal programs but had little connection with the White House. During his first term he served on the Interstate Commerce Committee and investigated railroad financing, which led to the passage of the Transportation Act of 1940. Interested in foreign policy and military preparedness, he supported Roosevelt's efforts to aid the Allied forces. Truman was reelected to the Senate in 1940 with support from a diverse coalition of black voters, railroad unions, and a broad network of personal connections. During his second term he chaired the "Truman Committee" that investigated waste in military projects, con-tractor fraud, and other matters related to defense production. In 1944 James Far-ley and other Democratic Party leaders presented Truman as a viable vice presi-dential candidate to replace Henry Wallace, as Truman was popular with both liberal and conservative Democrats. Roosevelt agreed to his nomination, although he had had few dealings with Truman. After Truman became vice president he rarely saw Roosevelt and was not privy to administration policies or initiatives. Tru-man became president upon Roosevelt's death in April 1945.

Tugwell, Rexford G. (1891–1979 b. Sinclairville, New York)
Assistant secretary of agriculture, 1933–1934; undersecretary of agriculture, 1934–1936; director of resettlement administration, 1935–1936; governor, Puerto Rico, 1942–1946

Tugwell was an original member of Roosevelt's brain trust. Tugwell, whose ideas greatly influenced legislation in the early days of the New Deal, thought that big business was inevitable and that economic recovery and reform could be achieved only if business, labor, and government worked together to create a national economic plan. He also believed that business alone could not be trusted with self regulation and that government must play an active role in directing and regulating industry for the common good. Originally chosen to provide expertise on agricultural issues, he was interested in the effect of agricultural policy on the economy. Tugwell also was a leading proponent of conservation, especially in connection with farmlands, and believed that depleted land had to be taken out of production and that farmers should be resettled and retrained. Tugwell resigned from the administration in 1936. In 1942 he was appointed governor of Puerto Rico.

Tully, Grace G. (1900–1984 b. Bayonne, New Jersey)
Personal assistant to Marguerite LeHand, 1929–1941; personal secretary to Franklin Roosevelt, 1941–1945
In 1928 Tully took a job with the Manhattan office of the Democratic National Committee. Roosevelt was the Democratic candidate for governor, and Tully was assigned to work for Malvina Thompson, Eleanor Roosevelt's personal secretary. By the time Roosevelt became governor in 1929, Tully was the personal assistant to Marguerite LeHand, FDR's personal secretary. When LeHand became ill in 1941, Tully became the president's personal secretary. Although Tully was an integral part of Roosevelt's personal circle for many years, and after 1941 was a visible member of the president's staff, she did not have the close personal relationship with Roosevelt that LeHand had enjoyed.

Tydings, Millard E. (1890–1961 b. Havre de Grace, Maryland)
U.S. Senate, Maryland, 1927–1951
First elected to the U.S. Senate in 1926, Maryland Democrat Tydings initially supported Roosevelt's New Deal legislation but worried about the increase in government spending and supposedly coined the phrase "alphabetical monstrosities" to describe the CCC, AAA, NRA, TVA, and other New Deal agencies. In 1937 he led the fight against Roosevelt's Court-packing proposal, and although Roosevelt targeted him in his 1938 attempt to "purge" the Democratic Party, Tydings won reelection. Tydings served as the unofficial leader of the "irreconcilables," mostly southern Democrats who opposed the second New Deal and supported states' rights and economy in government. Tydings opposed Roosevelt's domestic policies throughout World War II.

Wagner, Robert F. (1877–1953 b. Hesse-Nassau, Germany)
New York legislator, 1911–1918; justice, New York Court of Appeals, 1919–1926; U.S. Senator, New York, 1927–1949

Wagner grew up in New York City after his family immigrated from Germany. He was involved in Tammany Hall politics early in his political career and became interested in labor and working conditions. Wagner served in the New York Senate and also as a justice on New York's supreme court. He was elected to the U.S. Senate in 1927 and introduced legislation to provide public relief as early as 1928. Wagner was keenly interested in developing a national policy for labor and in 1935 fought for passage of the National Labor Relations Act, also known as the Wagner Act. Wagner also was one of the drafters of the National Industrial Recovery Act and the Social Security Act. In 1937 Wagner was instrumental in the creation of the U.S. Housing Authority. Wagner unsuccessfully promoted antilynching legislation and a bill that would have allowed refugee children from Germany to enter the United States in 1939 and 1940.

Wallace, Henry A. (1888–1965 b. Adair County, Iowa)
Secretary of agriculture, 1933–1941; vice president, 1941–1945; head, Board of Economic Warfare, 1942–1943; secretary of commerce, 1945–1946
Wallace was the son of Henry C. Wallace, who had served as secretary of agriculture in the Harding administration. Although a Republican until 1928, Wallace supported Roosevelt's candidacy in 1932 and was appointed secretary of agriculture in 1933. Wallace, the editor of a popular farming journal, was extremely knowledgeable about agriculture and was concerned about the economic condition of farmers. Wallace believed that agricultural recovery was dependant on higher, more stable prices and lower production, and as secretary of agriculture he was in charge of the development and operation of the Agricultural Adjustment Administration. Roosevelt chose Wallace as his vice presidential candidate in 1940, although many Democrats viewed him as too liberal. Party leaders convinced Roosevelt to drop Wallace from the 1944 Democratic ticket. He served as secretary of commerce beginning in 1945 but publicly criticized Truman's foreign policy and was removed from the cabinet in 1946.

Weaver, Robert C. (1907–1997 b. Washington, D.C.)
Adviser on Negro affairs, Department of the Interior, 1933–1937; consultant, Housing Division, Public Works Administration, 1934–1937; special assistant, U.S. Housing Authority, 1937–1940; administrative assistant to Sidney Hillman, National Defense Advisory Committee, 1940; chief, Negro Employment and Training, Office of Price Management (later the War Production Board), 1940–1943; director, Negro Manpower Service, War Manpower Commission, 1943–1944
Weaver joined Roosevelt's administration in 1933 and had a variety of assignments, most involving the employment and housing of African Americans before and during World War II. While working for the Department of the Interior, he conducted a survey of African American skilled and white collar workers, and he also prepared

a study for the Tennessee Valley Authority documenting the participation of minorities in that agency's program. Part of the so-called "black cabinet," Weaver worked to ensure that minorities reaped some of the benefits of New Deal programs.

Welles, Sumner (1892–1961 b. New York City)
Assistant secretary of state, 1933–1937; undersecretary of state, 1937–1943
Welles' family was socially connected with the Roosevelts, and he chose a career in diplomacy at FDR's suggestion. Roosevelt appointed Welles as special adviser on Latin American affairs and as assistant secretary of state in 1933, and later Welles was in charge of Western Hemispheric policies. One of the architects of Roosevelt's Good Neighbor policy, Welles encouraged Roosevelt to organize a special inter-American peace conference in Buenos Aires in 1936 to end hostilities between Bolivia and Paraguay. In 1939 Welles attended an inter-American conference in Panama that set up a neutrality zone in the western hemisphere, and in early 1940 Roosevelt sent Welles to Rome, Berlin, Paris, and London to explore the possibility of a negotiated peace in Europe. In 1942 he chaired a State Department committee to plan for postwar international cooperation.

Wheeler, Burton K. (1882–1975 b. Hudson, Massachusetts)
U.S. Senate, Montana, 1923–1947
Wheeler had a western progressive constituency of farmers, workers, and small businessmen, and he opposed big business, big finance, and big government. As early as 1930 Wheeler was the first major Democrat to publicly support FDR for the presidency. After Roosevelt's election, Wheeler voted for most New Deal programs and was one of the leading congressional supporters of the Public Utility Holding Act of 1935. Often critical of Roosevelt, Wheeler broke with the president over the Court-packing plan in 1937. Wheeler opposed Roosevelt's efforts to aid the Allies, and by 1940 spoke out against what he saw as Roosevelt's movement toward war. He became a frequent speaker at America First rallies.

White, Walter F. (1893–1955 b. Atlanta, Georgia)
Executive secretary, National Association for the Advancement of Colored People (NAACP), 1931–1955
White investigated lynchings and race riots and used tools such as press releases, press conferences, and public rallies to publicize the conditions facing black Amer-

icans. White helped to establish the NAACP Legal Defense and Educational Fund, Inc., which crafted legislation against discrimination and supported litigation to challenge existing laws. White went to England, North Africa, and Italy as a war correspondent and wrote about the discriminatory treatment of black troops.

Williams, Aubrey W. (1890–1965 b. Springville, Alabama)

Field consultant, Reconstruction Finance Corporation, 1933; field representative, Federal Emergency Relief Administration, 1933–1935; deputy director, Works Progress Administration, 1935–1938; administrator, National Youth Administration, 1935–1943

After Roosevelt's election, Williams went to work for Harry Hopkins in the Federal Emergency Relief Administration. Later he became deputy director of the Works Progress Administration (WPA), and while holding that position was also in charge of the National Youth Administration (NYA). As head of the NYA he encouraged state organizations to hire African Americans, and he also brought Mary McLeod Bethune into the agency. Because he was seen as too liberal—possibly even a communist—by many congressmen, Williams did not become head of the WPA when Hopkins resigned in 1938, but the NYA separated from the WPA and Williams remained in charge of the program. His reputation also figured in Congress's decision to terminate the NYA in 1943, and Congress refused to confirm Williams as a director of the Rural Electrification Administration in 1945.

Willkie, Wendell L. (1892–1944 b. Elwood, Indiana)

Republican candidate for president, 1940

Willkie came to public attention for his active opposition to New Deal programs such as the Tennessee Valley Authority while serving as counsel to the Commonwealth & Southern Company. Although originally a Democrat, Willkie joined the Republican Party in 1939, and the GOP nominated him as its presidential candidate in 1940. A personable campaigner, Willkie was seen by some Republicans as having failed to emphasize his differences with the popular president. After 1940 Willkie supported Roosevelt's attempts to help the Allies and rounded up Republican support for the Lend-Lease Act. In 1942 he traveled around the world, meeting heads of state and ordinary people, and his 1943 book *One World* stressed the importance of international cooperation. Willkie also became involved with civil rights issues and spoke out in favor of federal action to ensure voting rights.

Appendix B

Key Events in Roosevelt's Life

1882

January 30 Roosevelt is born in Hyde Park, New York, the second son of James Roosevelt and the only child of his second wife, Sara Delano Roosevelt.

1896–1900

Roosevelt attends the Groton School in Massachusetts.

1900

December 8 James Roosevelt, FDR's father, dies.

1900–1904

Roosevelt attends Harvard University. In his final year, he edits the Harvard *Crimson*.

1904–1907

Roosevelt attends Columbia University Law School.

1905

March 17 Roosevelt marries Anna Eleanor Roosevelt, niece of Theodore Roosevelt and FDR's own fifth cousin once removed.

1906

May 3 Anna Eleanor, the first child of Franklin and Eleanor Roosevelt, is born.

1907

Roosevelt passes the New York bar exam in the spring, drops out of Columbia Law School, and in September takes a clerk's position with New York law firm Carter, Ledyard, and Milburn.

December 23 James, the second child of Franklin and Eleanor Roosevelt, is born.

1909

March 19 Franklin Delano Jr., the third child of Franklin and Eleanor Roosevelt, is born.

November 8 Infant Franklin Delano dies.

1910

September 23 Elliot Roosevelt, the fourth (third surviving) child of Franklin and Eleanor Roosevelt, is born.

November 8 Roosevelt is elected to the New York State Senate.

1912

Roosevelt supports Woodrow Wilson for the presidency

September Roosevelt falls ill and asks Louis McHenry Howe to take over his campaign for reelection to the state senate.

November 5 Roosevelt is reelected to the New York State Senate by a large margin; Woodrow Wilson is elected president.

1913

March 17 Roosevelt becomes assistant secretary of the navy.

1914

August 1 World War I begins.

August 17 The second Franklin Delano Jr., the fifth (fourth surviving) child of Franklin and Eleanor Roosevelt, is born.

September 28 Roosevelt is badly beaten in the Democratic primary for a U.S. Senate seat from New York by James Gerard, a candidate backed by the New York political machine known as Tammany Hall.

1916

Roosevelt begins a love affair with Lucy Mercer, his wife's social secretary.

March 13 John Aspinwall, the sixth (fifth surviving) child of Franklin and Eleanor Roosevelt, is born.

1917

April 6 The United States enters World War I.

1918

July–September Roosevelt tours Europe, including spots on the western front of the war; contracts Spanish influenza; Eleanor Roosevelt discovers evidence of her husband's affair with Lucy Mercer.

November 11 Armistice ends fighting in World War I.

1920

July Roosevelt is nominated for vice president on the Democratic ticket headed by James Cox.

November 2 Republican ticket of Warren Harding and Calvin Coolidge wins landslide victory over the Cox-Roosevelt ticket.

1921

August Roosevelt contracts infantile paralysis while at his vacation home on Campobello Island, New Brunswick, Canada.

1924

June 26 Roosevelt makes a triumphant return to the national political stage at the Democratic National Convention in New York by giving a nominating speech for Alfred Smith, whom he dubs "the Happy Warrior."

1927

Roosevelt establishes the Georgia Warm Springs Foundation to treat people afflicted by polio.

1928

November 6 Roosevelt wins election as governor of New York by a narrow margin while Herbert Hoover wins a landslide victory in the presidential election.

1929

October The stock market crashes, heralding the onset of the Great Depression.

1930

November 4 Roosevelt is reelected governor of New York by a huge margin.

1932

July 1–2 Roosevelt wins the Democratic nomination for the presidency, flies from Albany to Chicago to accept in person, and calls for a "new deal."

November 8 Roosevelt easily defeats incumbent Republican Herbert Hoover to win the presidency.

1933

February–March The banking crisis deepens; many states declare "bank holidays," preventing depositors from withdrawing their money.

February 15 An assassination attempt on Roosevelt fails in Miami.

March 4 Roosevelt is inaugurated as the thirty-second president of the United States.

March 9 Roosevelt signs the Emergency Banking Act.

March 12 Roosevelt gives his first "fireside chat" radio address to the American peop e.

M₁ rch 31 The Civilian Conservation Corps is established.

May 12 Roosevelt signs the Federal Emergency Relief Act and the Agricultural Adjustment Act.

May 18 Roosevelt signs the Tennessee Valley Authority Act.

June 16 Roosevelt signs the National Industrial Recovery Act.

June 12–July 28 London Economic Conference is held; Roosevelt blocks any chance of international agreement by deciding on a "go it alone" recovery policy for the United States.

November 15 The Civil Works Administration is created.

1934

Rising discontent—"Thunder on the Left"—reveals itself in labor strikes, widespread support for demagogues, and large votes for candidates calling for more radical measures than Roosevelt had proposed.

1935

April 8 The Emergency Relief Appropriation Act provides $4.8 billion for work relief and creates the Works Progress Administration.

May 27 In *Schechter Poultry Corp. v. United States*, the Supreme Court unanimously invalidates the National Industrial Recovery Act.

June 19 Roosevelt sends "wealth tax" proposal to Congress.

July 5 Roosevelt signs the Wagner Act (National Labor Relations Act).

August 15 Roosevelt signs the Social Security Act.

August 31 Roosevelt signs the Neutrality Act of 1935.

1936

November 3 Roosevelt is reelected president in a landslide over Alfred Landon.

1937

February 5 Roosevelt asks Congress for legislation to reform the Supreme Court, beginning the "Court-packing" controversy.

May 1 Congress agrees by joint resolution to the Neutrality Act of 1937.

September Economy turns downward in the "Roosevelt Recession," which lasts until June 1938.

1938

October 5 Roosevelt delivers the "Quarantine Speech" in Chicago.

1938

Roosevelt tries, unsuccessfully, to realign the parties by "purging" the Democratic party of conservative opponents of the New Deal.

June 25 Roosevelt signs the Fair Labor Standards Act.

1939

September 1 Germany invades Poland; France and Great Britain declare war on Germany two days later, and World War II begins.

November 4 The Neutrality Act is altered to allow belligerent nations to buy U.S. arms on a cash-and-carry basis.

1940

April–June Germany's blitzkrieg overruns Denmark, Norway, the low countries, and France.

July 18 Roosevelt is nominated for an unprecedented third term as president.

September 3 Roosevelt announces "destroyers-for-bases" deal with Great Britain.

September 16 Roosevelt signs the Selective Service Act of 1940.

November 5 Roosevelt easily defeats Republican Wendell Willkie to win a third term.

1941

March 11 Roosevelt signs the Lend-Lease Act.

June 22 Germany attacks the Soviet Union, after which the United States extends Lend-Lease aid to the Soviets.

June 25 Roosevelt issues Executive Order 8802, creating the Committee on Fair Employment Practice.

July 26 Roosevelt freezes Japanese assets in the United States.

August 9–12 Roosevelt and British Prime Minister Winston Churchill meet at Placentia Bay, Newfoundland, and agree to the Atlantic Charter.

September 7 Sara Delano Roosevelt, FDR's mother, dies.

December 7 Japan attacks Pearl Harbor.

December 8 Congress declares war against Japan.

December 11 Germany declares war on the United States.

December 22 Churchill arrives in Washington to discuss war strategy with Roosevelt.

1942

February 19 Roosevelt issues Executive Order 9066 authorizing removal of Japanese Americans from the West Coast.

November 7 American forces land in North Africa, beginning Operation Torch.

1943

January 14–24 Roosevelt and Churchill meet at the Casablanca conference and declare that they will accept nothing short of the unconditional surrender of the Axis powers.

November 28–December 1 Roosevelt, Churchill, and Soviet dictator Josef Stalin meet at the Teheran conference.

1944

June 6 D day: British and U.S. forces launch invasion of Europe across the English Channel into Normandy.

June 22 Roosevelt signs the G.I. Bill of Rights.

July 1–21 International conference at Bretton Woods, New Hampshire, sets up the International Monetary Fund and the International Bank for Reconstruction and Development.

September At the Dumbarton Oaks meetings in Washington, D.C., representatives of the United States, Great Britain, the Soviet Union, and China lay the groundwork for a postwar world security organization (the United Nations).

November 7 Roosevelt is elected to a fourth term, defeating Republican Thomas Dewey.

1945

February 4–12 Roosevelt meets with Churchill and Stalin at the Yalta conference.

April 12 Roosevelt dies at Warm Springs, Georgia.

Index

Text Credits